Quest for Freedom

Quest For Freedom

The United States and India's Independence

Kenton J. Clymer

Columbia University Press
New York

Columbia University Press
New York   Chichester, West Sussex

Copyright © 1995 Columbia University Press
Library of Congress Cataloging-in-Publication Data

Clymer, Kenton J.
    Quest for freedom : the United States and India's independence /
Kenton J. Clymer.
        p.   cm.
    Includes bibliographical references and index.
    ISBN 0–231–10044–2. — ISBN 0–231–10045–0 (pbk.)
    1. India—Politics and government—1917–1947.   2. India—Foreign
relations—United States.   3. United States—Foreign Policy–
DS480.45.C58   1995
327.73054—dc20   94-22120
                                                               CIP

Casebound editions of Columbia University Press books are printed on
permanent and durable acid-free paper.

Printed in the United States of America
c 10 9 8 7 6 5 4 3 2 1
p 10 9 8 7 6 5 4 3 2 1

For my children,

ARON KENTON CLYMER *and*

MEGAN ARROWSMITH CLYMER

Contents

List of abbreviations used in notes   ix

Preface   xi

Prologue — The United States and India to the 1930s   1

1 | The United States, Great Britain, and India
at the Beginning of World War II   11

2 | From Pearl Harbor to the The Cripps Mission
(December 1941–April 1942)   37

3 | The Johnson Mission (March–May 1942)   55

4 | From the Cripps Mission to the "Quit India" Crisis
(April–August 1942)   73

5 | "Quit India" Arrests to the Appointment of William
Phillips (August 1942–January 1943)   95

6 | The William Phillips Mission to India
(January–June 1943)   128

7 | American Disillusionment Grows
(June 1943–September 1944)   167

8 | Renewed American Interest in India
(September 1944–1945)   203

9 | To Independence (1946–August 1947)   238

    Conclusion   285

    Notes   295

    Bibliography   367

    Index   379

Abbreviations Used in Notes

CWMG *Collected Works of Mahatma Gandhi.* 90 vols. New Delhi: Publication Division, Ministry of Information and Broadcasting, Government of India, 1958–1984.

FOR Foreign Office Records, Public Record Office, Kew, England.

FRUS U.S. Department of State, *Foreign Relations of the United States.* Washington: Government Printing Office.

IOR Oriental and India Office Collections of the British Library (India Office Records), London.

NAI National Archives of India, New Delhi, India.

NRC National Records Center, Suitland, Maryland.

OF Official File

PPF President's Personal File

PSF President's Secretary's File

SWJN Gopal, Sarvepalli, ed. *Selected Works of Jawaharlal Nehru.* 15 vols. New Delhi: Jawaharlal Nehru Memorial Fund, 1972–82.

SWJN: Second Series Gopal, Sarvepalli, ed. *Selected Works of Jawaharlal Nehru: Second Series.* 14 vols. New Delhi: Jawaharlal Nehru Memorial Fund, 1984–1992.

Preface

This book developed from a desire to understand the American response to Asian nationalism. I chose to approach this topic with an in depth examination of the American response to the Indian independence struggle in its climactic final stages during and immediately after World War II. India's quest for freedom was one of the most important events of the twentieth century. The successful Indian independence struggle began a process of decolonization that redrew the maps of Asia, Africa, and the Pacific. The Vietnam war had its roots there, and the consequences and ramifications of the drive for national independence have still to work themselves out.

A number of interrelated questions arise. How much interest did the United States and Presidents Franklin D. Roosevelt and Harry S. Truman take in the Indian independence movement? What were the bases of that interest? I was particularly interested, as others have been, to learn how the United States balanced its traditional support for self-determination, on the one hand, with its wartime alliance with imperialist powers like Britain which sought to retain or regain their colonial possessions, on the other. How did the British, Government of India officials, and Indian nationalists attempt to influence American policy, and how did they react to American initiatives? In the later stages, did the developing Cold War with the Soviet Union affect American policy toward India in significant ways? How much influence did the United States have on the course of developments in India?

During World War II the United States found India of increasing importance to its own military, ideological, and strategic interests and for the first time formulated a policy toward India. I argue that American policy was the result of several often interrelated factors. Initially the war provided the crucial context. As early as 1938 officials in the American government realized that India could play a significant role should the United States be drawn into the war. It had important resources, an industrial base, and a large reserve of human resources. It would be the major base from which to supply China, which the United States desired at all costs to keep in the war. It therefore became American policy to keep India out of enemy hands and maximize its potential contribution to the war. Until Japanese forces in Burma were defeated in 1945 and it became clear that the road to victory would be through the Pacific rather than the Asian mainland, India's ability to contribute to the war was a major determinant of American policy.

Because antagonism between British rulers and Indian nationalists threatened to limit India's war contribution, perhaps even to make it vulnerable to a Japanese takeover, the United States encouraged a political settlement that would satisfy the Indians. The Indians would then presumably be more inclined to fight wholeheartedly for the Allied cause. A sullen populace, or worse a country racked with civil unrest or even civil war, would hardly provide the Allies with a secure base and source of personnel and supplies. Because the Americans determined that generally speaking it was the British who stood in the way of a settlement, they applied pressure from time to time on them to make concessions to the nationalists.

In the beginning, India's potential contribution to the war stood very nearly alone as the determinant of American policy. But increasingly other factors entered into American policy-making. One was an ideological devotion to anticolonialism. The United States had traditionally championed independence, self-determination, and democracy, and although there were contrary strains in the history of American foreign relations, particularly in the twentieth century, the anticolonial tradition was still important. By the late 1930s important Americans outside of the government, and some in the government, wanted India to be independent, not only because they thought an independent India would be a more reliable ally in the war but because it was ideologically and morally right that the country be free of foreign rule.

This work contends that President Roosevelt was very much a part of the anticolonial tradition. This is not to argue that his views were as advanced as those of some in the antiimperialist movement, that he was entirely consistent, or that he viewed the end of colonialism as the most important goal of the war. His intriguing views of race, for one thing, militated against championing immediate independence in some situations.[1] There was also a paternalistic cast to the postwar trusteeship system that the President hoped to institute.

Nevertheless, as historian William Roger Louis writes, "Roosevelt should be regarded as one of the fathers of the post-war world of politically independent nations."[2] He was genuinely incensed about the ill treatment of colonial people and insisted that, at the very least, their economic and social conditions be improved. But Roosevelt wanted far more than the bettering of conditions in the colonies. He wanted to see colonialism ended and insisted that the Atlantic Charter, with its support for self-determination, applied universally and not merely, as Prime Minister Winston Churchill contended, to Axis colonies and conquered territories. If the trusteeship system he envisaged did not provide for immediate independence, independence was nevertheless the goal. In the meantime the system's very existence would provide a platform to criticize continuing colonial rule. Historian M. S. Venkataramani is incorrect, I think, when he contends that Roosevelt knew little and cared less "about colonial peoples" and that his approach to their problems was "marked by astonishing naivete and shallowness," with the result that "at no time did he actually make even the slightest move in the direction of supporting the nationalist position."[3]

Roosevelt and many of those sympathetic to the anticolonialist position also felt that their perspective was realistic. Roosevelt was convinced that World War II had come about partly because of conflicting colonial ambitions.[4] Thus the elimination of colonialism would help ensure future peace. In addition, far more than Churchill and many Americans, Roosevelt had some grasp of how important Asian nationalism would be after the war. In the long run, Roosevelt knew that, whatever one thought of it, colonial rule was doomed. Better for the United States to be identified with those who would ultimately triumph. In 1945 the President expressed it this way: the American goal must be to help Asians "achieve independence" because "1,100,000,000 potential enemies are dangerous."[5] Consequently, the President was willing to challenge Churchill over the continuation of British rule in India. In sum, then, this book contends that during World War II American policy was driven first by military considerations but that anticolonialism became increasingly important as well, for both ideological and realistic reasons.

Because Roosevelt did not succeed in driving the British from India, and at times even seemed to acquiesce in British repression, he has been criticized even by those who generally acknowledge his commitment to anticolonialism. Gary R. Hess, for example, argues compellingly that Roosevelt was too timid. Britain's increasing dependence on the United States, he contends, gave it the leverage to force an early transfer of power to the Indians. Had the President done so, the postwar colonial struggles in Asia might have been averted.[6]

Undoubtedly Roosevelt should have pressed the Prime Minister more forcefully. On the other hand it is doubtful if even under the pressure of war Roosevelt could have forced Churchill to give up India. It is true that Britain was increasingly dependent on the United States and that Churchill desperately wanted close Anglo-American ties to continue into the postwar world (the only way, he reasoned, that Britain could continue to be a major world power). He wanted the wartime merger of the two countries' military commands, the Combined Chiefs of Staff, to continue indefinitely and hoped a similar integration of the foreign policy establishments could be brought about. He even urged common citizenship.[7] But on India he was immovable. In 1944 Clement Attlee, who would replace him as Prime Minister in the summer of 1945, described Churchill's feelings about India as "passionate."[8] India and other colonial issues he considered purely domestic and thus not within the scope of the joint foreign policy he sought, and he fully agreed with the secretary of state for India who told him that the Americans "must keep off the grass."[9] Had Roosevelt insisted that the British leave India, at the very least the Prime Minister would have resigned, with unknown consequences for the war. Roosevelt was not willing to run that risk. He probably should have, but his determination that there were larger considerations at stake was understandable. India was important, but it was not the only factor the President had to consider. Roosevelt's refusal to pressure Churchill to the point of resignation lends support to those historians who describe the President as a realistic idealist.[10]

By the time Harry S. Truman took office in April 1945, India had lost most of its military significance. President Truman was less clearly in the American anticolonial tradition than Roosevelt. Nevertheless under Truman the United States, for both idealistic and self-interested reasons, continued to press for Indian freedom. The Cold War and an expansive pattern of American strategic thinking, spelled out so cogently by historian Melvyn Leffler, affected American policy toward India.[11] But I argue that the Cold War and the new strategic thinking were of only middling significance in understanding American policy toward India between 1945 and 1947. Most aspects of American policy that had developed prior to the Cold War continued in place. The Cold War was an added consideration, but it seldom determined policy toward India.[12]

The subject of American interest in India's independence has not received extensive scholarly attention, but this work builds on a solid foundation laid by others. The first serious book about American interest in India's independence was A. Guy Hope's *America and Swaraj: The U.S. Role in Indian Independence*, published in 1968. Noting that up to that point British and American scholars interested in the Indian independence struggle had slighted the American role, Hope set out to correct the balance. Gary R. Hess's more thoroughly researched study, *America Encounters India, 1941–1947*, appeared three years later. Hess confirmed that there was a significant American interest in Indian developments, but he was more critical of American policy than Hope, concluding that in its first test with Asian nationalism "the United States substantially failed." M. S.

Venkataramani's and B. K. Shrivastava's works, *Quit India: The American Response to the 1942 Struggle* and *Roosevelt, Gandhi, Churchill: America and the Last Phase of India's Freedom Struggle*, were published in 1979 and 1983, respectively. Their volumes provide the most detailed account of American involvement from 1942–1945. While praising those Americans who spoke out for Indian freedom, Venkataramani and Shrivastava are strongly critical of Roosevelt and the American government for deferring to the British. My intellectual debt to all of these authors is evident in the numerous citations to them.[13]

While drawing on the earlier works, this study exhibits some significant differences and, as suggested above, questions some of their conclusions. It begins earlier, in 1939 when World War II in Europe broke out, and extends to the transfer of power in 1947. Aside from Hess's work, there are few scholarly explorations of the American role in the important period from 1945 to 1947.[14] This book is also based on a much wider range of archival sources, some of which were not available to previous authors. Records of the British Foreign Office and the India Office, which provide a wealth of information on Indo-British-American relations, were consulted extensively. So too were the unpublished records of the Government of India, the Jawaharlal Nehru Papers, the All-India Congress Committee Papers, and related collections in New Delhi. Some American sources, including the Louis Johnson Papers and some State Department and Office of Strategic Studies records, have only been available to researchers in recent years.[15]

The availability of these sources is in itself ample justification for a new look at American interest in India's independence, for they allow a more in depth account of virtually all aspects of American policy. British and Indian sources, of course, permit a more complete understanding of how the British, the Government of India, and Indian nationalists interacted with the United States, responded to American initiatives, and attempted to influence the United States. They also provide insight into the serious disagreements and divisions that existed within government circles over how to deal with the Americans. But in addition these records often include information about American decision-making and attitudes that is not in the American records. British and Government of India officials also kept close watch on American public opinion, and their reports supplement other measures of American opinion about Indian developments. Their intelligence reports provide considerable information about the activities of pro-nationalist groups in the United States.

I have also benefited from the excellent historical writing in recent years on the Cold War and especially on Anglo-American relations. Christopher Thorne's *Allies of a Kind: The United States, Britain, and the War Against Japan, 1941–1945*, is magisterial in scope and skillfully integrates the strategic, military, and political aspects of Anglo-American relations during the war years. William Roger Louis's equally impressive *Imperialism at Bay: The United States and the Decolonization of the British Empire, 1941–1945* is the most thorough discussion of the conflicting British and American attitudes about colonialism and focuses particularly close attention on the issue of trusteeship. Three excellent studies carry the story further by examining Anglo-American relations into the early postwar period: Robert M. Hathaway, *Ambiguous Partnership: Britain and America, 1944–1947*; Terry H. Anderson, *The United States, Great Britain, and the Cold War 1944–1947*; and Henry Butterfield Ryan, *The Vision of Anglo-America: The US-UK Alliance and the Emerging Cold War, 1943–1946*. Of these, only Thorne's book devotes extended attention to the Indian question as it affected Anglo-American relations, but all helped me to place the debates over India in the larger contexts of World War II, Anglo-American relations, and the developing Cold War.

Several important themes emerge from the new studies of Anglo-American relations. One is the relatively high level of tension, suspicion, and serious disagreements that existed between the two countries, in spite of the remarkable accomplishments of the alliance in general terms. Suspicions and disagreements, accentuated because of Britain's growing weakness and dependence on the United States, increased as the war drew to a close and continued into the postwar period. A particularly important insight is that many dimensions of Anglo-American relations in the postwar period had relatively little to do with the emerging Cold War. Recent American historiography has focused so exclusively on the Cold War's origins and development that other factors have often been ignored or obscured. I

found these themes and insights very helpful in attempting to understand American policy toward India during and after the war.

Finally, the book benefited from recent studies of the Indian independence struggle and the developments after the war that lead
eventually to India's division. R. C. Majumdar's *Struggle for Freedom*,
Sarvepalli Gopal's *Jawaharlal Nehru*, and Anita Inder Singh's *The Origins of the Partition of India, 1936–1947*, were particularly helpful.

Acknowledgments

Numerous individuals and institutions have assisted with this study. As with most of my writing, the idea of investigating American relations with India during the independence struggle originated in discussions in seminars with graduate students at the University of Texas at El Paso. The university provided funds for research through the University Research Institute and its Minigrant and Faculty Development programs. The three deans of liberal arts during the time I was researching and writing—Diana S. Natalicio, Jim Devine, and Carl T. Jackson—were all supportive.

Without the assistance of outside funding agencies, I could not have done the necessary research on three continents. The American Philosophical Society provided the first research grant, the National Endowment for the Humanities provided a Summer Stipend and a grant from the endowment's Travel To Collections program to defray costs of travel to British archives, and the Indo-U.S. Subcommission on Education and Culture funded a six-months research trip to India in 1987. Dr. Margaret Chatterjee, director of the Indian Institute of Advanced Studies in Simla, invited me to study at the institute for a month.

The staffs and administrators at all of the libraries and archives I consulted, as well as the staffs of the various funding agencies, were invariably helpful. I want to single out for special appreciation Dr. P. R. Mehendiratta, director of the American Institute of Indian Studies in New Delhi, and his able staff. Without their help, research in India would have been much more difficult. Professor B. K. Shrivastava welcomed me to Jawaharlal Nehru University in New Delhi and always found time for conversations about Indo-American relations. Mr. Lakshman Dewani of the Jawaharlal Nehru Memorial Fund in New Delhi helped with innumerable details while I was working at the adjoining Nehru Library and has continued his advice in future years. The Reverend and Mrs. Ronald Gibbins allowed me to live in their home in Kingston-Upon-Thames near London during the summers of 1983 and 1985. The University of London made me an Honorary Research Fellow during the summers as well and provided office space. Mr. Donald Johnson, curator of the University of Minnesota's Ames Library of South Asia, permitted me to use the library's excellent collections on several occasions.

My good friend Brigadier Irwin Kullar, retired, now living in Chandigarh, introduced me to Mrs. Vidya Stokes, then speaker of the house of the legislative assembly of Himachal Pradesh. Mrs. Stokes kindly gave me access to the papers of her late husband's father, Samuel Evans Stokes. I also want to express my deep appreciation to American embassy officials in New Delhi in 1987, especially David and San Harr, Donna McGovern, Susan Jacobs, and Bruce Roberts.

The manuscript was finished while I was teaching at the University of Göttingen in Germany. Professor Dr. Hermann Wellenreuther, among many other kindnesses, arranged for an assistant to help in the final stages of research and writing. I am indebted to Volker Depkat for his extraordinarily thorough job of checking footnotes and making suggestions for modifications.

The readers for Columbia University Press offered suggestions that greatly improved the manuscript. Bradford Perkins, under whose direction I began my graduate study, read portions of the manuscript and, as always, offered prompt and cogent comments. My father, Wayne K. Clymer, proposed the book's title, *Quest for Freedom*. Portions of chapters 3, 5, and 6 appeared previously as articles in *Diplomatic History* and the *Pacific Historical Review* and are incorporated with permission.

Quotations from Crown-copyright documents in the Oriental and India Office Collections of the British Library appear by permission of the Controller of Her Majesty's Stationery Office. Quotations from manuscript materials in the Nehru Memorial Museum and Library in New Delhi appear with permission. Quotations from the Louis Johnson Papers appear with permission of the University of Virginia Library. Quotations from the letters and diaries of William Phillips appear by permission of the Houghton Library, Harvard University, while permission to quote from the William Phillips interview comes from the Columbia University Oral History Research Office.

Finally, my wife, Marlee, deserves a very special note of appreciation. She has lived patiently with this project for many years and contributed to its completion in innumerable ways. In particular, she explored ways by which I could spend an extended period of time in India doing research.

Kenton J. Clymer
June 1994

Quest for Freedom

Prologue

Nationalist challenges to European rule in India and elsewhere in Asia began well before World War II. The Indian National Congress, the most important of the modern nationalist organizations in India, was founded in 1885. Ho Chi Minh emerged in 1919 to struggle against the French in Vietnam, while in the Dutch East Indies (Indonesia) nationalist resistance reached back to the first decade of the century. In the Philippines the United States defeated one of Asia's first nationalist movements in the Philippine-American War (1899–1902), yet nationalism survived and was an important reason the United States eventually decided to free the islands.

But outside of the Philippines World War II brought the independence struggles to fruition and permitted them to succeed more quickly than they otherwise would have. In most areas of Southeast Asia, the Japanese conquest and occupation seldom met with serious resistance from local people. Often the Japanese were welcomed. Though their brutality would eventually bring deep resentment, the conquest removed European (and American) rulers from the Philippines to Burma, demonstrated that the colonial rulers were not invincible and could not even protect their subjects, and allowed Southeast Asians (including in some cases the very nationalist leaders the colonial governments had suppressed) to administer their own countries for a period of years. While glad to be rid of Japanese rule after the war, the people were not likely to look with favor on a return to the status quo ante. Often there would be violent resistance to European efforts to restore their empires.

Although India was not occupied by the Japanese, the war advanced independence. The British had to deal with a reinvigorated nationalist challenge, and the Government of India put enormous time and resources into keeping control of the country. Although the British eventually won the war without having made many concessions to the nationalists, the war exhausted them. Despite Winston Churchill's rhetoric about holding what he had, in the end the British could not hold their own against a determined nationalist drive to oust them. As early as 1945 vicious riots engulfed Indian cities, and in 1947 the British transferred power to two successor states, India and Pakistan.

The end of empire in India could have come more gracefully. By and large Indian nationalists were not attracted to Nazism, fascism, or Japanese imperialism and under certain conditions were willing to make common cause with the British. Had the British discussed war aims with the nationalists, allowed them real power in running the government, and agreed to a timetable for independence, there is every reason to think an accommodation could have been reached. Had it been, India's contribution to the war might have been greater, the treacherous question of Pakistan might have been dealt with more rationally, riots might have been fewer, and the bitterness that nationalists came to feel about the British might have been avoided. There would also have been less tension between Britain and the United States.

But the British did none of these things: they brought India into the war without consulting Indian opinion; they insisted that any significant changes in constitutional arrangements would have to await the end of the war, and they refused to say specifically how and when changes might occur. When nationalists protested, they were jailed and sometimes whipped.

The Americans watched these developments with deep concern and often with an ambivalence that reflected diverse strains in their history. Born out of the first anticolonial revolution in modern times, disavowing the monarchy, and establishing a liberal democratic system, the United States traditionally sympathized with those who struggled to free themselves from foreign or despotic control. In the nineteenth century, England had been a particular villain in American eyes, and as late as 1896 William McKinley's supporters had thought it wise to publish a campaign pamphlet entitled, "How McKinley is Hated in England."[1]

But by the turn of the century the United States had itself become a colonial power with an overseas empire of its own, most notably in the Philippine Islands, which it annexed in the wake of the Spanish American War. Many Americans took pride in their new role and relished the opportunity to educate and uplift people thought incapable of taking care of themselves. To them, England was no longer a country to be despised but a model to be imitated. The British empire, they thought, provided a stabilizing hand in the underdeveloped areas of the world.

Still, the anticolonial tradition, though in retreat, had not disappeared, and if the new empire was a source of pride, even exhilaration, there was much discomfort about being a colonial ruler. As George F. Kennan once expressed it, "we are not set up to govern, even temporarily, great numbers of people in other parts of the world."[2] With Woodrow Wilson's election as President in 1912, the older tradition was again in the ascendant. Wilson turned administration of the Philippines over to Filipinos, signed legislation declaring for the first time that independence was the goal of American policy, and shortly before he left office declared that the Philippines ought to be freed.[3] Nor were his anticolonial instincts limited to the Pacific. Several of his famous Fourteen Points, designed to bring peace to a war torn Europe, had a distinctly anticolonial ring to them. In the 1930s the United States made good on Wilson's promises to the Philippines and became the first power in modern times that voluntarily set a date for independence of a colonial possession.

In addition to the competing American traditions about imperialism, Americans had over the years developed conflicting attitudes toward India and Indians that affected their view of the struggle for freedom in India. For centuries, Europeans and later Americans had been attracted to the mysterious Orient for its exotic culture and products. In fact, it is only a slight exaggeration to say that European America owes its very existence to India, in search of which Christopher Columbus had sailed west. Instead, he found a new continent, whose inhabitants he misnamed "los Indios." Other explorers followed in Columbus's wake, seeking a Northwest Passage to the fabled Orient. They never found it, and the European settlements in the New World were soon concerned mostly with their immediate survival needs. But the lure of Asia was never entirely absent, even in the earliest days of colonial settlement.

With American independence, American merchants sought world wide markets. Although the trade with China is better known to Americans, there was probably more trade with India in the first thirty-five years of the nation's existence. Some New England communities owed their prosperity to the India trade. Thus the seal of the town of Salem, Massachusetts, reads, "*Divitis Indiae usqua ad ultimum sinum*"—To the farthest gulf for the wealth of India.[4]

Intellectual contacts also produced positive images of India. In the seventeenth century, the third generation Puritan divine, Cotton Mather, whose catholic mind explored the entire world, corresponded with Danish missionaries in southern India. They sent him a Tamil translation of the New Testament, perhaps the first Asian publication to reach British America.[5] Interest in Indian thought also surfaced in the eighteenth century among some American Enlightenment thinkers but blossomed in the middle of the next when Ralph Waldo Emerson, Henry David Thoreau, and other Transcendentalists contrasted favorably the spirituality of Indian religions with western materialism.[6]

In the later nineteenth century the first serious American scholarship about India emerged, and like the Transcendentalists the scholars presented positive images of India. The Parliament of Religions, which met in Chicago in 1893 in conjunction with the World's Fair, offered favorable portrayals of Indian religions. Of the several Indian delegates, the most sensational was Swami Vivekananda. His fluency in English, combined with an impressive stage presence and gift of expression, brought him immediate and usually favorable attention.[7]

In the early twentieth century the several appearances in the United States of Rabindranath Tagore, the Indian philosopher and poet who won the Nobel prize for literature in 1913, added to the growing admiration for Indian ideas. Between 1912 and 1930, Tagore visited the United States five times and attracted great publicity. As historian R. S. Gupta writes, he was "the first Indian writer to attract serious interest in the United States."[8]

There was, however, a competing, negative perception of India that emerged in the nineteenth century, primarily from American missionaries who first went to the subcontinent in 1812. If the Transcendentalists admired philosophical Hinduism from the comfort of their New England libraries, the missionaries encountered popular Hinduism first hand, and they were not pleased with what they found. To them, practices such as self-mutilation and torture, even death for some worshipers of the god Jagannath, *sati* (or suttee), female infanticide, and similar mores seemed not only unreasonable but also to epitomize the degraded nature of Hinduism. Especially in the earlier years, "a relentless hostility" to Indian religions and religious practices characterized their often detailed accounts.[9] The missionary view of India, then, competed with, and perhaps had greater influence among the general populace, than the more gentle accounts of the literary gurus and the scholars. As late as the 1950s, Harold Isaacs, in his pathbreaking book, *Scratches on Our Minds*, found that missionary-inspired negative images of India predominated among Americans.[10]

By the twentieth century, there were many missionaries who took a much more sympathetic view of Indian religion and culture, but the older view was by no means entirely displaced. Traveler's accounts, novels, stories, and films often portrayed India in stereotypical ways. Helen Bannerman's book, *Little Black Sambo*, with its crudely racist caricatures was immensely popular.[11] By all accounts, however, the most influential of the negative portrayals in the early twentieth century was Katherine Mayo's book, *Mother India*. First published in 1927, the book publicized the most sensational aspects of Hindu Indian society, notably child marriage, sexual eccentricities, and the plight of the untouchables. Jawaharlal Nehru, who termed the book "a gross libel on Indians and an outrageous misrepresentation of Indian women," recalled being nauseated when he first read it.[12] But neither Nehru's repudiation of the book nor Mohandas K. Gandhi's famous dismissal of it as a "drain inspector's report" prevented it from being a best seller, far and away the most popular American book on India ever written. It went through twenty-seven editions and sold 256,697 copies.[13] Thirty years after the book's publication A. M. Rosenthal observed that "few books, if any, contributed more violent coloring to the American mental image of India than 'Mother India.' "[14]

Indians believed that *Mother India* had been written to discredit the nationalist movement, which by the 1920s was becoming increasingly militant. By emphasizing practices that often seemed barbaric, while at the same time praising the British rulers, Mayo seemed to be saying that India would not be ready for self-government in the foreseeable future. Indeed, they suspected, correctly as it developed, that Mayo had the active encouragement of British officials as she prepared her book.[15]

Those Americans brought up on *Little Black Sambo* and *Mother India* might be expected to support continued British rule in India. But those who identified with the American anticolonial tradition or who looked sympathetically on Indian culture were increasingly critical of the British. As early as 1906 William Jennings Bryan, after a visit to India, condemned British rule. Bryan, who had been the Democrat's presidential nominee in 1896 and 1900, and would be again in 1908, eventually became Wilson's first Secretary of State. British imperial rule demonstrated clearly, he wrote, "man's inability to exercise, with wisdom and justice, irresponsible power over the helpless people."[16] A little later several prominent American Progressives and religious figures joined the India Home Rule League, founded in 1914 by the important Indian nationalist Lala Lajpat Rai. The Reverend John Haynes Holmes, pastor of New York's Community Church, emerged as the leading American publicist for Gandhi, who in the aftermath of World War I was fast becoming the leading figure in the resistance to the British. In 1925 Holmes traveled to India where he addressed the Indian National Congress.[17] From 1926 to 1929, the Unitarian publication that Holmes edited, *Unity*, devoted itself to Gandhi and serialized the mahatma's autobiography, *The Story of My Experiments with Truth*.[18]

One of the most important of the early American supporters of Indian nationalism was Roger Baldwin, founder of the American Civil Liberties Union. Baldwin had endorsed Indian freedom at least since 1919 when, as a prisoner in New York's Tombs prison (he had refused to be drafted into the army), he met Sailendra Nath Ghose and Agnes Smedley, who had been incarcerated for running guns to India. After they were released, they joined Baldwin in organizing an American group to promote the cause of Indian independence.[19] Baldwin soon became a close associate of Jawaharlal Nehru and played a major role in educating the Indian leader about the nature of American foreign policy. It was probably because of Baldwin's influence that Nehru embarked upon an ill-fated decision in 1929 to accredit an American branch of the Indian National Congress, partly to counter the notoriety of *Mother India*. The American branch, headed by none other than Sailendra Nath Ghose (the former gunrunner) and Ramlal Bajpai, did little to further the nationalist cause. Ghose and Bajpai were incompetent and possibly dishonest and even took positions at odds with the Congress itself. In 1930 Nehru had to disaffiliate the branch. The incident had the unfortunate effect of souring Nehru on establishing any foreign branches in the future.[20]

The American who was most active in the movement in India itself was Samuel Evans Stokes, who moved to the subcontinent in 1904 after learning about India's poverty and disease from a medical doctor who had treated lepers in the Simla Hills region. Stokes was attracted to nationalism after World War I, when the British passed the infamous Rowlatt bills that allowed the summary arrest and trial of those involved in political agitation, without the usual procedural safeguards. The Amritsar massacre in 1919, which resulted in the deaths of hundreds of Indians who were peacefully protesting British rule, furthered Stokes's determination to become involved. He became friends with Gandhi and Nehru, wrote articles, delivered speeches, and castigated the government for its policy of forced labor in the hill country. By 1921 Stokes found himself on the All India Congress Committee, the only American ever to serve on the powerful directorate of the Indian National Congress. In November the government outlawed the Congress, and in December 1921 Stokes was arrested and soon sentenced to six months in jail.[21]

In sum, different Americans viewed the events in India quite differently. England always had its supporters, and even some state department officials were convinced that England's paternalistic hand should not be withdrawn for many years. This was, however, increasingly the minority view. As World War II continued, more Americans came to favor Indian independence.

As for official relations between the two countries, the United States appointed its first consul to India in 1792. In that year Benjamin Joy, a Boston merchant who had lived for many years in India, took up his post in Calcutta. Subsequently the United States appointed consuls to other cities in India. But in the early years the British East India Company refused to recognize them; they achieved little and made few reports. The pay was so inadequate that few consuls remained in the service very long. In sum, as historian Goberdhan Bhagat writes, "the impact of American consuls before 1856 was negligible."[22]

The first serious official American interest in India occurred with the struggle against the British that developed at the end of World War I. American consuls reported about Indian anger at the Rowlatt legislation, the Amritsar massacre, and Muslim rage at British interference with the Khilafat in Turkey (which led Gandhi to call for noncooperation with the government).[23] According to one scholar, American reporting during this period "showed a pronouncedly pro-British bias," with Consul General James Smith justifying the Rowlatt bills and arguing that the massacre at Amritsar only demonstrated the inability of Indians to govern themselves. After Smith left India in 1921, however, the reports were more balanced.[24]

In 1930 Gandhi organized a massive civil disobedience campaign and marched to Dandi on the seacoast to make salt in violation of British law. The immediate impulse for this action was the inability of Lord Irwin, "that most sensitive of Tory Viceroys,"[25] to give assurances that the British government was fully committed to granting dominion status to India. As the crisis developed, which ultimately resulted in the arrest of Gandhi, Nehru, and other Indian leaders, the Americans reported developments fully and objectively. Often they assessed the situation very differently than the British. The American consul general Robert Frazer predicted that the movement would advance the day when India would become an independent dominion.[26]

American consular officials reported carefully on the various events of significance in the 1930s: the Round Table Conferences of 1930 and 1931 (the latter in London attended by Gandhi); the new civil disobedience movement following the conferences' failure; the mahatma's "fast unto death" in 1932 to protest British plans to have separate communal electorates in India; the emergence, as a major figure in the Indian independence movement, of Nehru, a man who revered Gandhi and yet was so unlike him; the arrest of the Congress leaders again in 1934; Gandhi's temporary resignation that same year from the Indian National Congress; and, perhaps most important of all, the new Government of India Act of 1935 that provided considerably more provincial autonomy but which also gave the governors and the governor-general so many exceptional powers that the nationalists considered it a fraudulent reform. Nehru referred to it melodramatically as "a Charter of Slavery."[27] In 1937, however, the Congress did contest elections in the eleven provinces, winning outright majorities in five of them and strong enough pluralities in three others to be in control. It was a striking show of political strength.[28]

Throughout all of these events American officials in India found Gandhi fascinating. They had difficulty comprehending his mysterious ways, but they admired his abilities to stir the masses and to control the nationalist movement. Nehru they could understand for the most part, although they were worried about his socialist, perhaps even communist, ideas.

By the 1930s there was also considerably more public interest about India. Several groups of Americans and Indians living in the United States publicized the nationalist movement, and the press carried lengthy stories about Indian developments and took divergent positions about nationalist efforts to drive the British out. Resolutions were even introduced in the Senate condemning British repression in India. On the other side, Katherine Mayo entered the fray again in 1930 and 1931 to attack Gandhi publicly as nothing more than a front man for "the Hindu oligarch, the Hindu plutocrat, the Hindu slavemaster."[29]

But if interest had grown, Americans were too preoccupied with the Great Depression to give much sustained attention to foreign affairs, particularly to India, a country in which there seemed to be so few American interests. Furthermore, the country was in a deeply isolationist phase, epitomized by the passage of the Neutrality laws in 1935, which were strengthened and extended in 1936 and 1937. There was little pressure to define a policy. As the best student of official American attitudes toward India in the 1930s writes, "the United States could be described as reserved and cautious."[30] And so it remained until the outbreak of World War II forced the United States to pay more attention to developments in India.

1 | The United States, Great Britain, and India at the Beginning of World War II

By its own admission the United States had no policy toward India prior to the outbreak of World War II in Europe in September 1939.[1] However, in the late 1930s American interest in India's political situation grew substantially, the result of two different but often related factors. For one thing, the Indian nationalist movement was receiving greater publicity than at any time since Gandhi's march to the sea in 1930. Appealing to the American tradition of self-determination, the movement evoked a sympathetic response among Americans. By the time the United States entered World War II, the publicity had grown to the point that the British were taking steps to counter it. A few State Department officials were already sympathetic to the nationalist program, but the major impetus for official concern about Indian developments was the disturbing international situation in the late 1930s. As the Japanese advanced into China in 1937 and then threatened to move into Southeast Asia, India became increasingly important. The subcontinent could provide military bases and serve as a source of materials and manpower for the war. Indian industry could also make a major contribution to the war effort, if it could be harnessed successfully. There was serious discussion about making India the major industrial base for the war's prosecution.[2]

The nationalist challenge to British rule raised doubts about whether any of these American objectives could be achieved. Put simply, would the people cooperate with the British to resist possible Japanese advances? Might they not be tempted to side with an Asian country that promised to liberate them from their European overlords? American policy, increasingly active and insistent, encouraged the British and Indians to overcome their differences and join forces against a common enemy. This resulted in tension, sometimes with the nationalists, but more often with the British whom the Americans viewed as pursuing unimaginative, reactionary, and ultimately self-defeating policies.

Since at least the Open Door notes of 1899 and 1900, the United States had opposed domination of China by any outside power and therefore had long been at odds with Japan over the latter's often brutal expansionist policies, which challenged not only America's cherished missionary-inspired sentimental attachment to China but also its status as a potential market for American goods. In addition, Japan posed a threat to the defenseless Philippine Islands, then an American colony.

When the Japanese army attacked Manchuria in 1931, Herbert Hoover's administration vigorously condemned Japan but took no concrete action to stop the aggression. Tensions increased dramatically in 1937 when Japan renewed its war against China, steadily expanded its control over the country's northern provinces, and drove southward along the coast. While few Americans favored direct military intervention in the conflict, the feeling grew that something must be done to curb Japanese aggression.

Fears that Japan intended to move even further south, into Southeast Asia, increased American concern. Although the United States had always dreamed of the China market, by the mid 1930s there was actually more American trade with Southeast Asia. The region also contained vast amounts of raw materials on which the United States and its friends were dependent. Rubber was particularly important, for a synthetic substitute had not yet been invented. In the 1930s, 90 percent of American rubber came from Southeast Asia. Similarly, the United States obtained 75 percent of its tin from the region. American oil companies also had significant investments in the Netherlands East Indies. By 1939 American oil companies were producing 27 percent of the oil in the Indies. After the German occupation of the Netherlands in May 1940, the American stake in the Indies increased to the point that only days before the Japanese attack on Pearl Harbor a State Department report portrayed the Indies the "arsenal of strategic raw materials for the democracies."[3] Japanese control of the region would threaten American access to these resources, strengthen the Japanese military machine, and make the Philippines even more vulnerable to Japanese attack than it already was. At a time when Franklin D. Roosevelt's administration was moving toward military preparedness and would need still more of the region's vital resources, the importance of the Southeast Asia was clear.

In this context, the United States was forced to pay more attention to the colonial world than it ever had before. Would Vietnamese, Malayans, and Indonesians resist energetically Japanese efforts to exert control over them? Or would they view the Japanese as liberators? India took on major significance. If the Japanese gained control of Southeast Asia, they would be at the gates of Calcutta. If they moved into India, they would control most of Asia. This was not something American officials could contemplate without deep anxiety.

How well India was prepared to resist possible attack from Japan was therefore of considerable, if not yet urgent, importance. India's defenses could not rest on British might alone. Although Britain had impressive and high quality armed forces, they were stretched thin from England to Africa, the Middle East, India, and Southeast Asia. In 1939 England was in the process of forming twenty-six divisions, whereas Germany had ninety-eight. The British had fewer than half as many bombers as the Germans. As for the Pacific, as late as December 1941 Britain had only two capital ships in the Pacific and no aircraft carriers. Japan had ten capital ships and an equal number of carriers. Furthermore, it had more than 2,300 aircraft, while the British in the Pacific had 158, most of them obsolete.[4] If Germany and Japan should declare war, the British would be hard pressed to save India for the Allied cause. Much would depend, therefore, on the willingness of the Indians to align themselves enthusiastically with the British.

But gaining the support of Indians was problematic at best. During World War I the nationalists had supported the British but later felt betrayed. Even the pacifist Gandhi had supported the war effort, while Samuel Evans Stokes had served as a British recruiter. Once the war was over, the British took strong actions against the nationalists and jailed many of them, including Gandhi and Stokes. Relations between the British authorities and Indian nationalists deteriorated further in subsequent years, and it was an open question whether nationalists would again join with their British rulers in a common cause.

That the United States viewed this situation with alarm was evident as early as October 1938, when American diplomats reported that the loyalty of Indian troops was doubtful.[5] There were also increasing fears that nationalist movements might be susceptible to Nazi or Japanese propaganda. One American businessman with long-time experience in Asia reported to the American Military Intelligence Division that during a recent trip to India he was shocked to hear "an intelligent Indian friend" say that he "was in complete agreement with the Japanese."[6] American consular officials thought that the prominent nationalist Subhas Chanda Bose had, perhaps, taken German money but reported sensibly that most nationalists were "not pro-Japanese or pro-German;" rather, they were "anti-imperialist." When in October 1938, Rabindranath Tagore strongly condemned Japanese aggression in China, American officials were impressed.[7] If the British played their hand right, it seemed, Indians just might lend their support to the war. There would, however, be a price to pay for Indian loyalty. Because much Indian opinion was "distrustful if not hostile to the British," the Indians would expect "generous rewards for such assistance and cooperation as may be forthcoming," reported American representative Edward M. Groth.[8]

Groth had grasped the major issue that would confront British rulers and Indian nationalists in the months ahead: what price would the nationalists demand for cooperation, and would the British respond constructively? The United States hoped a resolution could be reached.

When Adolf Hitler's armies invaded Poland in September 1939, and Britain and France responded with declarations of war, the American government felt that a settlement of the Indian political problem was even more pressing, primarily for military reasons. "The Indian attitude towards the war is of great importance," wrote G. P. Merriam, an official in the State Department's Division of Near Eastern Affairs, which had responsibility for India. Wallace Murray, Merriam's superior, agreed. There were "large American interests in India," he wrote to Assistant Secretary of State Adolf A. Berle, Jr.[9] Chief of the Division of Near Eastern Affairs since 1937, Murray was attracted to the Indian cause and also understood how important India could be in winning the war.

The initial response of Indian nationalists to German aggression heartened the Americans. As American officials had reported, Nazism had no attraction for most nationalists, and many in India, including Gandhi and Nehru, had quickly indicated their support for the Allies. But the viceroy's subsequent decision to bring India into the war without consulting nationalist opinion soon reversed much of the early support, and on September 15, 1939, the Working Committee of the Indian National Congress, while insisting that India was "entirely on the side of democracy and freedom," refused to associate itself with the war effort until there was a clear statement of British war objectives that aimed at "the elimination of imperialism" in India. A negative response to the Congress demand by Lord Zetland, Secretary of State for India, angered the nationalists and was probably a factor in the decision of the All India Congress Committee's decision on October 10, 1939, to demand that India "must be declared an independent nation."[10]

The Americans, who felt that Gandhi and the Congress ought to be courted because at heart they sympathized with the anti-Nazi and anti-Japanese causes, regretted that the British remained unwilling to state more explicitly their intentions about the future status of India. From India, American officials reported sympathetically that the Congress's insistence on a statement of war aims was "not difficult to understand." They also believed that Britain was pursuing a divide and conquer policy, deliberately offending the predominantly Hindu Congress while courting the Muslims, in part because of British military interests in the Islamic Middle East.[11]

In Washington, Murray needed little convincing about the nature of British rule in India. The British response to nationalist demands had "given intense dissatisfaction to the Hindus," he observed. Like American officials in India, he believed that the British were pursuing a divide and conquer policy in India. He compared British policy in India to their "previous decision to conciliate the Palestinian Arabs at the expense of the Jews. In both instances," he explained, "it was decided to favor a fighting people having religious ties with other peoples strategically located on the Empire's 'life-line' as against an unwarlike group lacking such ties."[12] Such a policy, Murray would argue, was not likely to further the American objective of seeking a reasonable settlement of the Indian political problem. Keeping the waters roiled did not bode well for an India united against a common enemy.

For the remainder of 1939 the political situation in India deteriorated as all Congress governments in the provinces resigned in protest, and in December the Indian National Congress offered Gandhi the leadership role. The hopes of the viceroy, Lord Linlithgow, to defuse the situation by creating an advisory body floundered. On January 10, 1940, the viceroy attempted to end the political deadlock by reemphasizing Britain's commitment to full dominion status after the war, and the government sought to expand the viceroy's Executive Council by including Indian political leaders. Indian Liberals welcomed the speech, but the predominant nationalist opinion was negative. Rajendra Prasad, then president of the Indian National Congress, reminded the viceroy that the Congress wanted complete independence, and that a constituent assembly (something the viceroy had not mentioned) was necessary to resolve the claims of the various Indian groups. Other nationalist leaders were even less charitable. Bose, for example, saw "nothing new in it," while Nehru considered it "insufficient and unsatisfactory."[13]

John C. White, the American consul general in Calcutta, hoped that the viceroy's speech would lead to further discussions, but there was little progress. Strikes plagued certain sections of the country (whether they had a political dimension was much debated), and the Congress remained out of the government.

In March relations deteriorated further with the arrest of Jaya

Prakash Narayan, a Congress Socialist and former member of the Working Committee, whom Nehru described at the time as "one of the dearest and most valued of our comrades"; the arrest, he was certain, indicated "the determination of the government to declare war on the Congress." So angry were nationalists over Narayan's arrest that violence seemed likely to break out. Only Gandhi's resumption of control over the Indian National Congress prevented a violent response, or so an American consul reported. But relations with the government did not improve, and the viceroy himself told an American diplomat that there might be trouble in India if the Allies suffered more defeats in the war. There was, the American reported, a "spirit of pessimism" in the land.[14]

In June 1940, the Working Committee of Congress decided to sanction the use of force if necessary to deter external aggression. This was something of an olive branch to the British and a blow to Gandhi's pacifist position. But this concession did not result in a change of government policy. Gandhi was summoned to Simla, the summer capital in the Himalayan foothills, to meet with the viceroy, but little new seems to have been offered. The government, Gandhi was apparently informed, would grant dominion status after the war, and the viceroy's Executive Council would be increased with four additional Indian members, one of whom would come from the Indian National Congress. But the Congress quickly rejected the proposal, the Working Committee arguing that it was "more than ever convinced" that independence was required and that in the meantime a provisional national government, and not an expanded viceregal council, was essential.[15]

This impasse set the stage for the viceroy's famous offer of August 8, 1940, which, however, differed little from previously expressed governmental positions. For this Churchill and to a lesser extent the viceroy were responsible. The viceroy again proposed to enlarge his Executive Council and to create a War Advisory Council. Once the war was over, he would establish a body to devise a new constitution. India would remain in the Commonwealth, and the rights of Indian minorities would be protected.[16]

Congress was so infuriated at the viceroy's proposals that it authorized Gandhi to lead a mass civil disobedience campaign. "Britain cannot claim to stand for justice," Gandhi said, "if she fails to be just to India." But he determined that the time was not ripe for mass protest and urged instead that persons speak out individually against India's involvement in the war. In urging this action Gandhi was challenging the government to uphold the right of free speech, including pacifist speech and speech opposed to recruitment efforts. If the government allowed freedom of speech, he implied, there would be no organized effort to disrupt the actual recruitment of men for the army.[17]

American diplomatic reporting astutely predicted that the British would not agree to Gandhi's terms. By mid-September the Americans had picked up rumors that the government might soon begin to arrest nationalists.[18] American diplomats thought the government shortsighted. Although the Congress had rejected the viceroy's terms, its members were still reportedly "frightened" at the prospect of a Nazi victory and had offered "both moral and material assistance" to the government, over the objections of the pacifist Gandhi. But the government refused to pay Congress's price—creation of a representative government in New Delhi—and Congress, not knowing what else to do, had turned back to Gandhi to "do something." Ironically, the viceroy's offer had had the effect of bringing Gandhi and the Congress back together after a momentary estrangement. With the government intransigent, Gandhi and the Congress asked selected nationalists to deliver well publicized speeches opposing conscription.[19]

The government crackdown began on October 21, and a few days later Nehru himself was arrested, the first member of the Working Committee to be incarcerated since the war broke out. Nehru was subsequently given an usually harsh sentence of four years which, according to an American diplomat, "astonished even the Europeans" and perhaps the viceroy himself.[20] All in all 23,000 persons were convicted over the course of the next year of violating the Defence of India Act.

American reporting from India during these months was thorough and competent, but the State Department was sufficiently alarmed at the deteriorating situation that it demanded more timely reporting. Mailed dispatches, used to save money, took weeks to arrive. "We ought to poke up Calcutta to send some telegrams," urged one official. Soon the State Department was demanding telegraphic dispatches.[21] Indian events, then, were even more important to United States officials in Washington than American diplomats in India understood. The State Department feared that British intransigence would make India an unreliable base and source of supply in the coming struggle against Japan.

Indicative of increasing American concern, in 1940 the United States appointed Thomas M. Wilson to be the consul general in Calcutta. More assertive and outspoken than his predecessor, Wilson was strongly critical of the Government of India, the viceroy, and the home government in London.[22] In the immediate situation he thought that the government had probably "lost an opportunity to make its peace with the Congress . . . on conditions which . . . would have offended no other group in India." It would have been more intelligent, he thought, to have let the pacifists speak freely. Wilson clearly thought the government had mismanaged the whole affair.[23]

By May 1941 Wilson had concluded that conditions in India were "very serious indeed" and that the viceroy, whom he considered dull and lacking in imagination, was not the person to handle the matter. He was "aloof and dependent on his advisers" and gave "every indication of being a harassed, disillusioned, unhappy man" with a "small vision." Nor was the American any more sanguine about the home government, "whose Secretary of State for India continues unimaginatively to repeat himself."[24]

Reports such as these led to the first high-level discussion in the State Department about India. India, the Americans concluded, was a place of great importance. India had "a vast reservoir of manpower" and was the dominant supplier of "certain strategic war materials." Properly developed, India could provide supplies that might be crucial to the successful prosecution of the war. All in all, the United States wanted India made "an active, rather than a passive, partner." Its cooperative participation with the democracies "might well become of first importance." In order to bring this about, Berle asserted, there had to be a provisional settlement with the nationalists. Unfortunately, "the British seem to be doing nothing about it."[25]

This discussion took place in the context of a British request to add an official of the Government of India to their Washington embassy. Berle suggested that the United States, in return for agreeing to the British request, ask that India's status be upgraded by making it an equal partner in the British Commonwealth. The British refused, and Washington dropped the matter for the time being. But some kind of American intervention seemed to be a logical outcome of American policy toward India.

Throughout the summer Wilson continued to send reports detailing the increasingly serious political situation and the ineffective governmental responses. By mid-June he thought the situation "serious" and "in no sense improving." Regrettably, Wilson felt, the government failed to comprehend the serious state of affairs. "Statesmanship of anything approaching a high order is conspicuous by its absence. . . . Sterility seems to be the order of the day." If only the viceroy would take some dramatic action, such as freeing all political prisoners, it would "electrify public opinion," and Gandhi might well call off *satyagraha* (nonviolent resistance). But there was little likelihood that the government would do anything.[26]

As Wilson feared, the viceroy did nothing dramatic and instead in July simply offered the already discredited proposal of expanding the Executive Council and establishing a purely advisory National Defence Council, to which Indians would be named. It was, of course, rejected by all major political parties, including the Muslim League. A week later Wilson turned his critical analysis toward London. He observed that Leopold S. Amery, who had become Secretary of State for India in May 1940, could not "inspire confidence in his motives or to succeed in his appeals to political India by his speeches." Few Indians, he stated, felt any confidence in the secretary.[27]

Meanwhile the military situation was deteriorating, as the Japanese continued their southward drive into Indochina. Australian and New Zealand officials wanted better security agreements with England, and a settlement of the Indian matter would make such agreements more likely and enhance the security of the entire region. In London American Ambassador John Winant, aware of New Zealand and Australian fears and perhaps unaware that the State Department had made a tentative diplomatic intervention into Indian affairs the previous May, suggested that the United States pressure the British to settle their political differences with the Indians. "Among other considerations I believe this action would have a sobering effect upon the Japanese," he wrote. Berle supported the ambassador, but Undersecretary Sumner Welles would not go along.[28]

Nevertheless, as long as the British remained unwilling to make concessions acceptable to the Indian nationalists, the logic of American objectives pointed toward eventual intervention. Without American intervention, hopes for a settlement that would make India a safe base from which to fight a war in the Pacific, if that became necessary, appeared doomed. All the while, Japan advanced further to the South, and the war in Europe became more desperate.

Meanwhile, the nationalist movement was gaining increased publicity and favorable press comment in the United States. The nationalist struggle had long been featured in such liberal journals as *The Nation* and *The New Republic*. Even more consistent in its coverage was *The Christian Century* whose pacifist editor, Charles Clayton Morrison, greatly admired Gandhi. Of the approximately seventy articles about Gandhi that appeared in popular magazines from 1932 to 1935, *The Christian Century* accounted for nearly half. These journals reached an important, intellectual audience. But in the last half of the decade the nationalist movement received additional attention in the mass circulation press. In December 1938, for example, John Gunther's favorable portrait, "The Incredible Mr. Gandhi," appeared in *Reader's Digest*. Gandhi was also featured in such popular news outlets as *Time*, *Newsweek*, and the *Christian Science Monitor*.[29]

When the war broke out in Europe in 1939, the press gave extensive coverage to the Indian dimension. When the Indian National Congress insisted that the British clarify their war aims, for example, the *New York Times* carried approximately thirty stories about the issue in a two month period. *Time* magazine was openly skeptical of the British position. The Congress was "hot as chutney" over Linlithgow's response, chortled the magazine. Correctly predicting that Congress provincial governments would resign, *Time* concluded that the nationalists "might do as much to dislocate Britain's Empire as Herr Hitler's war machine." *The New Republic* put it even more strongly. Britain's response to the Congress was "a blunder of the magnitude of a crime," it felt.[30] The publicity in the United States was so extensive that Rajendra Prasad noted it approvingly in a speech he delivered before the All India Congress Committee. B. Shiva Rao, a prominent Indian correspondent, predicted that the kind of publicity which the nationalists were now enjoying in the American press would produce an impact "of a kind which Britain would not like to see in the United States of America just on the eve of the spring offensive by Germany."[31]

The kind of reporting Rao observed (his own dispatches and articles also appeared with some frequency in American newspapers and magazines, including a portrait of Gandhi in the *New York Times*)[32] only increased as the war in Europe continued into 1940. Both the viceroy's offer of August 1940, and the subsequent arrest of Indian nationalists met with growing criticism even in such conservative newspapers as the *Los Angeles Times* and the *Christian Science Monitor.* The *New York Times*, which was pro-British and from time to time criticized nationalist refusal to cooperate with Britain, found serious shortcomings in the viceroy's offer.[33]

Some of the credit for the new publicity and the often favorable editorial comment that the nationalists received was due to the efforts of nationalist Indians in the United States and their American friends. Until 1938 those efforts were not very effective. One such organization, the American League for India's Freedom, founded in 1932 to generate support for India's independence through nonviolent means, was exclusively American in membership. It obtained some prominence in the early 1930s, then went into decline. Indian publicists like Haridas T. Muzumdar, Anup Singh, and Krishnalal Shridharani wrote several books, journal articles, and pamphlets designed to keep interest in Indian nationalism alive. But their efforts were uncoordinated. "They did not have any means of focussing the attention of the American people towards the Indian fight for freedom," recalled Jagjit "J. J." Singh, an Indian businessman who moved to the United States in 1926.[34]

At the end of 1937 businessman N. R. Checker founded the India League of America to "serve as a clearing house for the problems confronting our people" and to "endeavour to supply authentic information about India" to Americans.[35] The new organization brought into one fold several nationalist leaders and publicized the cause by organizing meetings about India. But the league was not well run. When the Indian nationalist Kamaladevi Chattopadhyaya visited the United States in 1939 she criticized it severely. Partly as a result of Chattopadhyaya's criticisms, the league was thoroughly reorganized under the leadership of J. J. Singh. First attracted to the nationalist movement as a result of the infamous Jallianwala Bagh massacre in 1919, Singh became the most prominent of the nationalist spokespersons in the country.

Under Singh's direction the India League of America became the foremost Indian nationalist organization in the United States. Singh endeavored with considerable success to make himself the leading point of contact between the nationalist movement in India and the United States. He assiduously courted Americans in and out of government who were interested in Indian developments or who had official responsibilities for India. He testified before Congress on occasion. He wrote numerous articles, called many meetings, and in other ways used the league as a vehicle for getting the nationalist perspectives across much more effectively than any other organization had previously done. The league's publication, *India Today*, reached sympathetic people and those in a position to influence events. As journalist Robert Shaplen summed it up, before long Singh "was getting more newspaper space for the League and for himself than any other Indian organization had ever enjoyed here."[36]

The league was not a perfect organization. Nehru himself, while he corresponded with Singh, privately held him in low regard. "Unfortunately, the Indians in America are a very unsatisfactory lot," he confided in 1940 to Abul Kalam Azad, the president of the Congress. "They shout a lot and do no good work. Often they do injury to our cause." Nehru's point was well taken but not entirely fair to Singh, who devoted himself and his financial resources to the nationalist cause. Without the league, the nationalists in the United States would not have accomplished as much as they did. As Shaplen wrote, "Singh has been largely responsible for the most significant period of Indian activity in the United States."[37]

Nehru may not have had great respect for Singh, but Singh's hero was Nehru. By the late 1930s, Nehru had assumed a role almost equal to that of the revered mahatma in the nationalist cause. Few could match his eloquence. Consequently, J. J. Singh and numerous other Indians and Americans urged him to visit the United States and present the nationalist case in person.[38] Nehru was sorely tempted. He recognized the importance of the United States and knew that good publicity could be very useful to the cause of Indian freedom. "I agree with you that it is very desirable for Indian news and views to be properly represented in America," he told a friend in March 1940. "There are not too many people who can do this job well. Possibly I am one of the number."[39]

Although Nehru would not come to the United States until after India was independent, between 1938 and 1941 he became widely known in the country. His writings and speeches had occasionally appeared in American publications as early as 1931, but his first major contribution to an American journal was in January 1938, when the influential *Foreign Affairs* published his article, "The Unity of India." In the article Nehru provided a philosophical groundwork to justify ouster of the British. He introduced Americans to the underlying cultural unity that he claimed had long existed in India and blamed the British for encouraging divisions and for stifling India's cultural and economic development. If Nehru was sharply critical of Britain, Americans could take heart that he was no supporter of Britain's enemies. "In the world wide conflict of ideas and politics," he concluded, "India stands for democracy and against Fascism and the totalitarian state."[40]

Two years later, as the war raged in Europe and the Pacific, Nehru reached a wider audience with an important article in the *Atlantic*, in which he explained why Indians resented British decisions to involve India in the war without consulting the people and their refusal to issue a meaningful statement of war aims. As he had in the *Foreign Affairs* article, Nehru emphasized the British effort to encourage "disruptive and reactionary tendencies in India in order to preserve her imperial interests. She will not preserve them for they are destined to go," he wrote movingly, "but they will go in hostility and conflict if no better way is found."[41]

After Congress rejected the viceroy's offer of August 1940, Nehru defended the decision in an American publication, *Asia*. The British government still lived "in the ruts, and not all the shock of war and danger had taken them out," he concluded.[42]

Nehru's autobiography was published in an American edition early in 1941. When Pearl Buck's husband Richard Walsh, who had arranged for the volume's publication by John Day Co. informed Nehru, then imprisoned, that the book had received "magnificent notices," Nehru admitted to feeling "greatly bucked-up."[43] Actually, Walsh had written before most reviews had appeared, but he was not far wide of the mark. The autobiography was reviewed in at least twenty-five major magazines, journals, and newspapers, with virtually all of them being very positive. The reviewer for the *New York Times* fairly gushed over the book. "This is a dramatic story of a great man, greatly and dramatically told," he wrote. Particularly likely to irritate the British were the reviewer's comments about how effectively Nehru drew the inconsistency of the British championing democracy in Europe while keeping India under a dictatorship.[44]

Aside from Nehru's own writings, the Indian leader gained a substantial American audience through the generally favorable stories about him that were now appearing regularly in important books, newspapers, magazines, and journals.[45] The American writer John Gunther, author of the famous "inside" books, and his equally famous wife Frances, had much to do with the increased publicity for Nehru. The Gunthers had long been interested in Asian affairs, and in fact in the 1920s John had joined with Roger Baldwin, founder of the American Civil Liberties Union, to support Indian independence.[46] The Gunthers first met Nehru in 1936, and their relationship blossomed two year later. In 1939 *Life* magazine approached John Gunther with an idea for a story about Nehru and India, an idea Frances said was accepted "more or less over the head of Harry Luce," *Life*'s publisher, who protested that "nobody had ever heard of Nehru." The piece appeared in December to good reviews, though Frances contended to Nehru that "it took hours of practically blood-curdling argument to get John to go as far as he does. He, like everybody else over here, is a passionate, instinctive British agent."[47]

In keeping with *Life*'s popular style, much of the Gunthers' piece was devoted to Nehru's personal life. They thought him "an extraordinarily handsome and magnetic figure" with a "towering intellect."

But they also analyzed Nehru's opposition to British rule in a sympathetic way and asked Americans how they would feel if the Japanese, for example, ruled them, flew their flag over Washington, established clubs that excluded Americans, and milked American resources. Two months later *Reader's Digest* published a condensed version of the piece, thus giving Nehru and Indian nationalism an even wider American audience.[48]

Nehru and the cause of Indian nationalism also found publicity and support from influential American religious leaders. These included such well known figures as the missionary statesman Sherwood Eddy, John R. Mott, the famous leader of the Young Men's Christian Association's international work, and Frank Laubach, an American Board missionary whose experience in Asia went back to 1915 when he served in the Philippines. Laubach was best known for his method of increasing literacy. These men publicized Nehru's views and lobbied American officials, including the President, for a forceful American policy toward India.[49]

In sum, in the last half of the 1930s Americans had the nationalist case before them more fully than ever before. Japanese advances in Asia and the outbreak of war in Europe provided the crucial context, for India suddenly assumed an importance it had not previously had. Unimaginative British policies—involving India in the war without consultation, concentrating power in the viceroy, postponing any consideration of India's future for the duration of the war, refusing to make a reasonable statement of war aims, and arresting nationalists—also made it easier for Americans to consider supporting nationalist objectives. The United States, too, had been a colony and had traditionally supported self-determination.

But the case was also made because Indian nationalists in the United States and India and their American supporters made a concerted effort to influence American opinion. J. J. Singh arranged for much favorable publicity, Nehru wrote important articles for the American audience, and American writers found the nationalist leader good copy.

Whether all of this would cause the United States government to support the nationalists was not yet certain. Deeply worried about the prospects of a Nazi victory in Europe, Roosevelt was doing everything he could to bolster the British. In 1939 he had managed to have Congress repeal the arms embargo sections of the neutrality laws so that Britain could purchase armaments. In June 1940, he told a University of Virginia audience that he would aid Britain and France in whatever way he could. Later in 1940 he arranged to give the British fifty destroyers. Early in 1941 he established the Lend Lease program to move supplies as quickly as possible to beleaguered Britain. Soon, American ships were patrolling the Atlantic Ocean, convoying British and American merchant ships, and even shooting German submarines on sight. By 1941 he had in effect made the United States a nonbelligerent ally. And he did this at a time when the odds favored a British defeat. Any action against the British in India, therefore, seemed unlikely.

Nevertheless, the possibility for some American pressure on the India question existed. The State Department already feared that British actions tended to make India a less than secure base from which to prosecute the war, a point nationalists drove home at every opportunity. And the department was not unaware that the self-determination argument resonated powerfully in the domestic political context.

Certainly the British feared the effects of the new and favorable publicity that Indian nationalism was now receiving in the United States. To meet the increasing interest of the United States in Indian affairs, the British upgraded their publicity and intelligence activities and sought to neutralize the impact of pro-nationalist publicity. Intelligence authorities scrutinized applications for passports and often denied them on the slightest pretext. Once abroad, Indian students and travelers were likely to have their activities monitored, and if they made nationalist speeches or in other ways supported the cause of independence, they were subject to interrogation, arrest, and imprisonment upon return to India.

Although watching Indians abroad had been a longstanding practice, growing nationalist agitation and the pressures of World War II made the government even more alert than usual. By the end of the decade all Indians living abroad who were politically active had their files reviewed every six months. No roadblocks were put in the way of their return to India, however. As one official put it, once an "undesirable" Indian had returned, "it is easy enough to find an excuse for dealing with him in any way we think necessary."[50]

Two cases from the period 1939–1941 illustrate British responses to politically active Indians in the United States. Kamaladevi Chattopadhyaya was a leading figure in the nationalist movement. Born into a wealthy family in south India, she defied tradition when she married a man of her own choice after being widowed at an early age. She was a great admirer of Gandhi and Nehru and was jailed several times for her part in the freedom struggle. On July 31, 1938, Chattopadhyaya was granted a passport valid for travel in the British empire, most of Europe, the Middle East, East Asia, and the United States. In June 1939, she and her son left for London. For two years they traveled across the continent, the United States, Japan, and China. The largest portion of the time (nineteen months) was spent in the United States.

The sentiments Chattopadhyaya expressed were "consistently anti-British." She reportedly told an audience that there was little to choose between Nazism and British imperialism. India would take part in the war only if it became independent, she said. At the University of Hawaii she gave such a "virulently anti-British lecture" that the British consul in Honolulu considered ways to discredit her. However, she was said to have "created a profound impression on a certain section of the American public." Several organizations honored her, and Eleanor Roosevelt invited her to tea.

On her return Chattopadhyaya was not allowed to disembark at either Singapore or Sri Lanka (then Ceylon). Her reentry at Bombay went smoothly, but officials considered taking action against her, as the title of her government file indicates: "Anti-British activities of Mrs. Kamaladevi Chattopadhyaya in the U.S.A. and Japan. Question of action to be taken against her on her return to India."[51]

Though Chattopadhyaya avoided jail, incarceration was not unusual for those who dared to speak against the British while abroad. Such was certainly the case with Rajnikant ("Rajni") M. Patel.[52] Patel did not enjoy the same stature as Chattopadhyaya in the nationalist fold, but he was acquainted with Nehru and promoted independence while a student at Cambridge University. Because of his nationalist activities the British would not allow him to sit for the prestigious Indian Civil Service examination in 1937. He was, in fact, "pushed out of the examination room," according to Nehru. Denied a career in the civil service Patel took up law and successfully passed all parts of the bar examination in 1939.[53]

After becoming a barrister, Patel planned to return to India via the United States. He sailed to New York with Chattopadhyaya.[54] Sponsored by the American Youth Congress, he spoke at Harvard, Yale, Dartmouth, and numerous other colleges, universities, and at high schools, as well as to civic groups, including conventions of the YMCA and YWCA. He gave several radio talks and interviews to newspapers. By all accounts he was a charming and effective speaker, although the British naturally considered him ill-informed and demagogic. He met twice with Eleanor Roosevelt and took a special interest in black Americans because in London he had become good friends with the athlete and singer Paul Robeson and his wife, Eslanda, who provided introductions.[55]

Like Chattopadhyaya, Patel blamed India's ills on British imperial rule and refused to support the war. "Let God save the King," was his constant refrain. He predicted a massive civil disobedience campaign in India, with open revolt to follow. The overall impression, concluded one intelligence source after attending Patel's talk to the Seattle Chamber of Commerce, was "to arouse anti-British contempt and hatred, rather than any genuine interest in India's problems." But Patel found his trip exciting. "I have enjoyed the American trip immensely," he wrote to Nehru.[56]

The British were less exhilarated about Patel's activities. Patel intended to spend three weeks in China, but when he disembarked at Hong Kong British authorities ordered him to return to his ship immediately. At Singapore the authorities refused to allow him off the ship at all. On September 17, 1940, he arrived back in Bombay. His arrival time had been kept secret, and none of his friends was on hand to greet him. The police arrested and incarcerated him without informing him of the charges against him. Customs officials, meanwhile, searched his belongings meticulously and found that of the eighty-seven titles that he had brought back to India, thirty-five were wholly proscribed, including his own booklet, "Brother India" (of which he had 108 copies). All were confiscated.

When Nehru learned of Patel's detention, he wrote a newspaper column condemning the police action which he correctly assumed had resulted from Patel's speeches in America. Having been away from India for several years, Patel was now home. "But what a strange home-coming it was!" wrote Nehru. "Or perhaps it was not so strange after all. For in India the way to home for those who are straight and true leads often to the gates of prison."[57]

The Chattopadhyaya and Patel cases were unusual only in that they were more sensational and generated more publicity than others. But as the British became more concerned about American opinion, the government increased its efforts to monitor and, if possible, counter nationalist publicity abroad. For example, they compiled several files on the activities of V. K. Krishna Menon, the director of the India League in London. They intercepted his mail, withholding some letters altogether and allowing others to pass. In the winter of 1939 and 1940 Government of India authorities were interested in Menon's attempts to influence American journalists—"the only ones 'who count nowadays' "—through his periodic news conferences for American reporters at the St. James restaurant. They also investigated Menon's contacts with D. J. Vaidya, a journalist employed in the London office of *Time* and *Life*. Menon worked with Vaidya to get articles by Nehru into American publications, and Vaidya also offered to seek American publishers for Nehru's larger works, *The Unity of India* and *Glimpses of World History*.[58]

The government also attempted to prevent viewpoints from abroad that were sympathetic to the nationalists from reaching India. As the Patel case indicated, the Government of India banned large numbers of publications. One list from 1941, for example, proscribed twenty-six American journals and pamphlets, including the *American Civil Liberties Union News, Amerasia,* and *Scribner's Commentary,* along with a variety of Marxist publications.[59] The government was also worried about American religious groups operating in India, one official noting that "in view of the general suspicion attaching to American Missionaries," their mail should continue to be intercepted. In 1940 four American missionaries were expelled.[60]

The Government of India also kept close track of organizations that operated in the United States to further the cause of Indian independence. With the beginning of World War II in 1939 officials were especially concerned with the American League for India's Freedom and the India League of America. These and similar organizations were the subject of detailed intelligence reports.[61]

Concern at the apparent success of nationalist agitation in the United States, combined with a poor military situation in 1940 and a fear of serious civil disobedience in India, led some in the British government to consider opening up the constitutional question with Indians. It was not a course that Winston Churchill favored. As Labourite Stafford Cripps understated it in a letter to Nehru shortly after Churchill entered the government at the outbreak of the European war, "the addition of Winston Churchill has not added to the friends of Indian Freedom." However Labour representatives, notably Cripps, urged a new initiative. And even some Conservatives thought something ought to be done. The first results were Amery's proposals in June 1940 for a series of constitutional reforms, including a guarantee of dominion status within a year after the end of the war. Churchill was sufficiently powerful to water them down to such an extent that when they were announced on August 8 the concessions were so innocuous that all Indian parties rejected them out of hand.[62]

The failure of the British to make meaningful concessions and the subsequent repressions produced a sufficiently negative response in the United States to make British policymakers take notice. Thus in October 1940, Amery urged the British ambassador in Washington, Lord Lothian, who was then in England, to "come over one day and have a talk about the general American reactions to the Indian situation."[63]

Another indication of the growing concern with American opinion was Linlithgow's decision to go ahead with the establishment of an advisory National Defence Council. This long-promised body, something contained in the August offer, did not have the support of Churchill (or for that matter the nationalists), but Linlithgow and Amery went ahead anyway and received cabinet approval in June 1941. American opinion was a significant factor in their thinking. As Minister of Labour and National Service Ernest Bevin wrote to Amery, the move would create a favorable response in America, and "you are concerned about the effect on the United States of this step."[64]

Most significantly of all, the British decided to counter Indian nationalist gains in the United States by creating a new position in Washington to which they would appoint an Indian who would present their view of developments on the subcontinent. Rather ironically, as it turned out, the first suggestion that relations between the United States and India should be upgraded in this way came from Sir Girja Shankar Bajpai, a member of the viceroy's Executive Council. Born in 1891, Bajpai attended Oxford University and joined the elite Indian Civil Service. He served in various government posts in India and abroad, including that of India's representative to the League of Nations in 1929–30. He was appointed to the viceroy's council in April 1940.

In late August or early September 1940, Bajpai proposed that the head of the already existing Indian Trade Commission in New York be given the title of high commissioner to represent India in Washington. This would put the Indian representative on a par with representatives of the British dominions. Bajpai urged the action to counter Congress propaganda in the United States, arguing for "the importance of getting the right view of the Indian position before American eyes." The idea intrigued Linlithgow, who was convinced that Americans needed ample education about the Indian question.[65] Amery was "all in favour of the idea," and sounded out Lord Halifax, a former viceroy then in the Foreign Office. "It would afford opportunity for an intelligent representative Indian, both privately and on public occasions, to present a picture of Indian government very different" from the Congress view, he wrote to Halifax, who quickly concurred.[66]

Amery was now prepared to approach the Prime Minister. The propaganda advantages, he indicated, were his paramount concerns. In the short run the new representative would counteract misleading Congress propaganda. But Amery was already thinking of the postwar period, when the Americans might press "us hard over the Peace Settlement, to concede something quite impractical in India." If the representative did his job well, the United States might take a more reasonable position. Churchill did not need to be convinced and responded immediately that it was "a very good idea," one that he would take up soon with Lothian.[67]

Thus, by the end of October 1940, the Government of India and all important sectors of the British government—the Foreign Office, the India Office, the Prime Minister—were solidly behind the idea of appointing an Indian representative to the United States. The only questions remaining concerned such details as the appropriate title for the new representative, a complicated matter in view of India's confused international legal status, which would have to be discussed with the State Department. Lothian's death on December 12, 1940, delayed the matter for a time, but in February 1941, his successor, Halifax, was in contact with American authorities. He quickly discerned that the title "High Commissioner" would not be acceptable, since it was used by representatives of independent dominions within the British empire. Consequently he suggested "Agent General for India," a title used previously by Indian representatives in South Africa. Although the title of agent general was both "unusual and nondiplomatic," Halifax thought the United States would grant the representative diplomatic status, particularly if he were attached to the British embassy, something the India Office had heretofore opposed. Halifax also offered a final bit of advice: "It should in any case be remembered that Indians are practically unknown in Washington and that if possible [the] representative's appearance should therefore be such as to ensure that he would be readily recognised as Indian and not mistaken for an ordinary coloured man."[68]

Linlithgow preferred the title of minister, arguing that anything less would not provide sufficient status for carrying out effectively the important public relations activities he had in mind. At the same time he was, as always, opposed to anything resembling diplomatic contacts between the United States and India and insisted, therefore, that the representative not be allowed to "exercise diplomatic functions."[69]

In April the United States agreed to Halifax's suggestion of agent general with the understanding that the appointee would have the rank of a minister.[70] But while the United States was prepared to receive an Indian representative, State Department officials used the occasion to press certain related demands of their own. They had long chafed over the Government of India's refusal to allow consular representation in the capital of New Delhi. The American consul general, located in Calcutta more than a thousand miles from the Indian government, complained of constant obstruction and delays as long as six months in getting replies to inquiries. John C. White, reputed to be "a tried friend of Great Britain," had repeatedly complained about such conditions. Though the Government of India pointed out that only neighboring countries were allowed consular representatives in New Delhi, the United States responded that it was a more important country than Afghanistan, especially given the current world situation, and in any event the British were requesting special privileges for India in Washington. It was therefore logical to grant similar privileges to the United States.[71]

Shortly thereafter the United states increased its requirements. Instead of a consular officer in New Delhi, the Americans now wanted a foreign service officer with the rank of minister. Halifax hoped his government would meet the American request.[72] Amery and then Linlithgow agreed, though the viceroy asked that the American representative in New Delhi not be allowed to perform consular functions.[73]

By mid July 1941, everything was in order to open "quasi-diplomatic relations," as Amery himself put it, between the United States and a not yet independent India. The United States had agreed to accept Sir Girja, who had originally suggested the arrangement, as India's first agent general in the United States, and India had agreed to the appointment of a United States "commissioner" in New Delhi, a post that would be held by career diplomat Thomas M. Wilson. American consular headquarters would remain in Calcutta, though at least one Government of India official believed that if the United States had pressed the issue New Delhi would have agreed to have consular functions in the capital as well.[74]

Upgrading the Indo-American relationship did not improve Anglo-American relations. Wilson continued to criticize Amery's lack of political astuteness and had little sympathy with the viceroy.[75] Making the situation palpably worse was Prime Minister Churchill's speech to the House of Commons on September 9, 1941, in which he made it clear that the self-determination portion of the Atlantic

Charter did not apply to India. The Atlantic Charter, a press release issued jointly by Roosevelt and Churchill the previous month, resulted from informal talks the two leaders had held off Newfoundland on a number of issues related to the war. In Article III they agreed to "respect the right of all peoples to choose the form of government under which they will live; and they wish to see sovereign rights and self-government restored to those who have been forcibly deprived of them."

Contrary to some accounts, it is doubtful if either leader had given much thought to the precise meaning of the article. Historian William Roger Louis, in one of the most thorough accounts of the colonial issue during the war, states that Article III was not the subject of much discussion because it "appeared to be innocuous." It quickly became the most discussed portion of the Charter, and there was considerable public and private debate about its meaning. British Labour Party spokesman and Deputy Prime Minister Clement Attlee immediately stated that the Charter had universal applicability, for example, a position that Roosevelt too would soon take.[76] But the Colonial Office, the India Office, and the Prime Minister had very different ideas. To them the Charter applied only to territories then under Nazi control. This is what Churchill told the House of Commons.

The Prime Minister's speech created a furor in India. It was, as Wilson reported at the end of October, "a most unfortunate pronouncement" which "went far toward banishing perhaps forever most of the good feeling towards him." As for the Government of India, there was "no leadership worthy of the name anywhere to be found."[77]

Five weeks later Japan attacked Pearl Harbor, and the United States entered the war. By that time, the political situation in India had become an important concern for the United States. India was thought to be potentially very significant as a military and industrial base for the war in the Pacific. This was the foremost concern of American diplomats. They were interested in the Indian political situation primarily because they feared that an unstable India would interfere with the military objective. The United States, therefore, hoped that the British would make honest efforts to conciliate the

Indians and arrive at solutions that would end the hostility and allow for a smooth prosecution of the war. As the British took actions that alienated the populace instead of conciliating it, the Americans moved tentatively toward intervention. In May 1941, they momentarily pressed the British to make changes as the price for allowing the British to add an Indian agent general to their Washington embassy. When the British proved adamant, the Americans backed off. They were not, after all, in the war yet, and they were getting other significant concessions from the British. Nevertheless, intervention was the logical outcome of American policy if there were no changes in India.

If the government was concerned mostly about the military aspects of the Indian situation, the public debate was much broader. Here, ideological, idealistic, and sentimental concerns were much more in evidence. These concerns had not yet had much direct impact on American policy, although in May 1941, Berle had written that "considerations of principle as well as of policy" dictated that an effort be made to settle the Indian problem.[78] But more and more there would be pressure from the advocates of Indian independence, for whom ideological reasons were as important as military ones, for a more forceful American policy. They were fortunate that the President of the United States shared many of their views. Increasingly, American policy toward India would blend idealistic and realistic considerations.

2 | From Pearl Harbor to the Cripps Mission
(December 1941–April 1942)

Two weeks after the Japanese attack on Pearl Harbor Winston Churchill came to Washington to discuss American involvement in World War II. He stayed for three weeks. At one point President Roosevelt raised the sensitive question of India's status and urged that the British grant independence to the subcontinent. It was not a happy moment for the Prime Minister, who had no intention of changing imperial arrangements. But he felt his impassioned response had convinced the President not to interfere. "I do not think you will have any trouble with American opinion," he telegraphed Clement Attlee from Washington. Later, he remembered the confrontation even more dramatically. "I reacted so strongly and at such length," Churchill recalled, "that he never raised it verbally again." Yet less than two months after the Prime Minister returned to London the War Cabinet seriously debated altering British policy toward India to such an extent that the viceroy sent in his resignation.[1] In the end the government deferred a new declaration of policy and the viceroy remained at his post; but the cabinet did send Sir Stafford Cripps, an austere Labourite who was proud of his long-time friendship with Indian nationalists, to the subcontinent to discuss possible policy changes with Indian nationalist leaders.

Did this potentially far-reaching move in the British approach to

India have an American connection? The evidence suggests that American opinion, official and unofficial, had a great deal to do with the British debate over Indian policy. Churchill had incorrectly assessed his earlier discussion with the President.

Churchill's meeting with Roosevelt came as British forces were being humiliated in Asia. The story of the first months of the war was "one of scarcely relieved gloom."[2] Even while the Prime Minister was in Washington, British and Australian forces were being pushed out of Malaya and into Singapore. Of the 138,700 British and Commonwealth troops in the Malayan campaign, 130,000 were taken prisoner. The Japanese, by contrast, suffered 9,824 casualties. Singapore fell on February 15. It was, as Churchill admitted to Roosevelt, "the greatest disaster in our history."[3] Ten days later the Allied command in the Dutch East Indies withdrew, and its head, General Archibald Wavell, flew back to India. India was now to take on great importance, for after Singapore's fall it was, as the official British history of the war puts it, "the only base from which the war in the Far East could be prosecuted and a counter-offensive launched."[4]

The Japanese advance was relentless and quick. After a day of minimal resistance Thailand surrendered, and the Japanese were soon attacking Burma. On March 8 Rangoon was in Japanese hands, as was Java. As *Time* put it, "the whole Far East was atremble" as waves of refugees fled to India. By early April the Japanese had attacked Akyab on the west coast of Burma and were within 100 miles of the Indian border. Their warplanes destroyed two British cruisers in the Bay of Bengal, the *Dorsetshire* and the *Cornwall,* and attacked a nearly defenseless Ceylon. India itself appeared seriously threatened. The *New York Times* reflected the common view: "the attempted invasion of India by Japan is only a matter of days or hours distant."[5] As the Germans advanced in North Africa and the Soviet Union, there was a widespread belief that they planned to link up with the Japanese in India and the Middle East.

The British defeats in Southeast Asia affected Anglo-American relations in fundamental ways. As historian Christopher Thorne writes, "the manner and consequences of these defeats were to burden British Far Eastern diplomacy and Anglo-American relations for the remainder of the war."[6] Furthermore, they brought India square-ly into the American consciousness and at the end of March led to the most significant American intervention in Indian affairs. The major American concern remained, as before, India's potential con-tribution to the war. The country could provide a base for Allied troops, vast amounts of manpower, large quantities of important resources, and potentially a sizable industrial capacity. India also remained one of the few places available from which to transship goods to China. Now that the Japanese were on the verge of actually conquering all of Southeast Asia, India's several potential contribu-tions were no longer viewed as merely important; many saw them as crucial to victory in Asia. Early in March the influential newscaster Raymond Gram Swing told his radio audience that it would probably be from India that the Allies would make their stand against Japan.[7] Because India was potentially so important in the war, many Ameri-cans believed that the British could no longer claim the exclusive right to determine India's internal arrangements. Other Allies, such as the United States and China, they insisted, had the right to influ-ence events.

If military considerations were still predominant in American thinking about India in the months after the attack on Pearl Harbor, more and more attention was being given to the larger questions of the future of imperial rule in Asia. Arguments about colonialism ranged from the highly idealistic to the coldly realistic. On the ideal-istic side, support for colonial rule contradicted the idea of self deter-mination to which many Americans professed allegiance, in spite of their country's inconsistent record. President Roosevelt shared this view, telling a press conference in March 1941, that no people should be the master of another and that all people had a right to determine their own "nationhood."[8] On the realistic side, it was observed that most colonial people in Southeast Asia had not rushed to defend their countries from the Japanese. Imperialism had not created loyal citizens. Roosevelt himself felt that European imperialism made the fight against Japan more difficult.[9] Furthermore, many believed, whatever one might think about it, that the age of imperialism was passing and would not long survive the war. Nationalist movements existed in all colonial regions of Asia. Followers of Ho Chi Minh had been struggling against the French in Vietnam for many years, while in Indonesia the Dutch had had to exile the nationalist leader Sukarno to the small island of Banda. Japanese occupation would only strengthen anti-European sentiment, and even if the European colonial powers triumphed in the end they would be severely weakened and unable to return to the status quo ante in their colonies. Undersecretary of State Sumner Welles stated this theme succinctly in an address on Memorial Day, 1942. "The age of imperialism is ended," he said, adding that the principles of the Atlantic Charter had universal applicability.[10]

Though American postwar interests were not yet formulated with great precision, the United States was well aware of the importance of South and East Asia. The area had important material resources, included vital lanes of sea trade (such as the straits of Malacca), and was important to prevent future military threats that might emerge in the Pacific. Some American diplomats emphasized American economic interests, notably the need to insist on an open door in Asia for imports, exports, and investment.[11] Secure, satisfied, friendly democratic societies in Asia would clearly be to the future advantage of the United States. Aligning the United States with the new order would serve American interests. On the other hand, should the region prove to be unfriendly to the United States, its interests would be imperiled.

Whether for reasons of military necessity, idealism, or realistic accommodation to the forces of change, British imperial rule in India was subjected to growing and impassioned American attack in these months. One study of American public opinion concludes that stories and editorials about India reached "mammoth proportions" in 1942.[12]

To be sure, early in January 1942 Churchill wrote to Clement Attlee that American press comments had been "singularly restrained, especially since they entered the war," and he felt that there would be no trouble from the United States about India.[13] Criticism does in fact appear to have dropped off in the immediate aftermath of Pearl Harbor, and the British always had their defenders, both within the government and in the public debate, who argued that the middle of a war was no time to enact far reaching changes in a terribly divided India. But within a few weeks antiimperialist ideas were again gaining ground. The terrifying Japanese advance into Burma was at the heart of much of the immediate popular concern. If Japan was going to be stopped, it had to be in India, many felt. Chiang Kai-shek's visit to India in February gave rise to exaggerated hopes that there could be united Indian-Chinese action to stop the Japanese, and Chiang was outspoken in his views that nationalist demands must be met if India was to contribute to victory. By mid-February even the *New York Times* acknowledged that India and China were "no longer suppliants at the white man's door. Not all the faded trappings of imperialism, not all the pomp of viceroys, not all the arrogance of the 'old China hands,' has much meaning for them now."[14]

That same month columnists Walter Lippmann and John Thompson and editorials in such newspapers as the *New York Journal and American*, the *Los Angeles Examiner*, and the *San Francisco News* all argued that British imperial policy would have to change. In March more comment critical of British rule came from popular newsmagazines and journals of opinion, with some of them supporting the Indian National Congress' demand for independence and others urging Roosevelt to intervene. In the *New Republic* publicist John Bates sketched a desperate military situation. Noting British defeats in North Africa, the failure of the Soviet Union in the Crimea, and the Japanese drive toward the Indian Ocean, Bates speculated that the Axis powers planned to converge on India and gain control of "all the vitalizing wealth of Asia." "Nothing since the outbreak of the war has been so startling," he wrote. The answer was to give India immediate independence. It was, Bates wrote in a thoughtful conclusion, "the necessary act which unites realism with idealism."[15]

Perhaps more indicative of general public opinion was *Newsweek*, which usually supported the British position. Now, however, the magazine acknowledged that the situation had changed. With the United States taking the military lead against the Japanese, it had the right (so the magazine implied) to exert pressure on the British to grant concessions in India.[16]

Organizations and influential private citizens also attacked British imperialism in India and called for American pressure on the British.

J. J. Singh's India League of America and the revived American League for India's Freedom issued statements supporting the nationalist demand for independence. Officers of the latter organization, while acknowledging the military importance of India, argued for India's freedom primarily on idealistic grounds, noting that Britain's continuing imperialism caused a "sense of uneasiness" and "embarrassment" among allies engaged in a war for democracy.[17] The Congregational Ministers Association of St. Louis wrote to the State Department urging Roosevelt to use his influence to bring about a settlement between the British and Indian nationalists. The George W. Vroman American Legion Post No. 2 of Casper, Wyoming, petitioned the government to obtain the "immediate freedom for India under any terms necessary to secure their cooperation at this time." The petition was a good example of how frightening the military situation in Asia appeared.[18]

Several prominent persons wrote to the President's advisers urging him to take strong action. Frank Laubach, for example, demanded, on grounds of political principle, that Britain extend dominion status to India immediately. Frances Gunther urged the President to support India's independence. Like Laubach, Gunther used idealistic arguments but combined them with appeals to the military advantages the United States would have by supporting Asian nationalism. "Nothing less. . .," she wrote, "can win the confidence of vast peoples of India and Asia and swing them to our support in this war."[19]

Of the unofficial letters, the one that had the most impact came from author Pearl Buck, who wrote to Eleanor Roosevelt on March 7. Writing as "an American citizen who has lived most of her life in the Pacific war area," Buck's letter included idealistic points. But her main arguments centered on military realities. Rank and file Indians were "appallingly bitter" about the British. Under these conditions, Indians would not make an effective defense of their country, she contended. Buck even predicted "revengeful massacres against all white people on a scale much greater than have taken place in Malaya and Burma." Buck had no policy recommendations, except to warn any American troops sent to India of the dangers. But the implication that things could only improve if the British left was clear. Eleanor Roosevelt showed the letter to her husband, who read it with "real interest" and kept it on file, in spite of the author's request that it be destroyed.[20] It is likely that Buck's letter fortified the President in his determination to intervene in the Indian fray three days later.

Public sentiment caused reaction in Congress. In 1941 there was only one reference to India in the *Congressional Record*. By contrast, in February 1942 the Senate Foreign Relations Committee held a closed hearing on India. Several of the senators questioned State Department officials closely about the deteriorating situation, and most reportedly urged the United States to demand from Britain "an immediate pledge of postwar self-government for India" before it was too late. The Senators' concern was primarily short term. As Assistant Secretary of State Breckinridge Long recorded in his summary of the hearings, their arguments rested on India (and China) "as sources of military strength." The Senators, he wrote, felt unanimously that "the only way to get the people of India to fight was to get them to fight for India." The United States, they felt, must push Britain to grant independence or autonomy and thus energize the Indian populace.[21]

At the hearings State Department officials had to reply with caution, since American policy was still in flux. But privately important officials agreed with many of the criticisms voiced in the public debate. The senators did not know, for example, that the previous week Assistant Secretary Berle in a formal memorandum had urged the administration once again to press the British to make India "a full partner in the United Nations."[22] Venkataramani and Shrivastava have shown that privately Berle agreed with the senators. He feared that British policy would limit India's resistance to Japan and would make the country an insecure base for carrying on the war. Why should colonial people fight, he asked? "After all these people had nothing to defend except their own exploitation." Berle's vision was wider than immediate military realities, for he believed that the age of imperialism was waning and with it England's day was passing. It was therefore a self defeating policy for the United States to stand with Britain on colonial matters. Instead, he thought, the United States ought to base its policy on the promises of the Atlantic Charter. Sooner or later the British would have to get out, and it behooved the United States to take nationalists like Nehru seriously.[23]

Wallace Murray, chief of the department's Office of Near Eastern Affairs, was equally critical of the British and, especially after American entry into the war, continually bombarded his superiors with information unfavorable to British rule in India and often suggested a more energetic United States policy. And in India Thomas Wilson and other American officials repeated their critical assessments of British rule and questioned the loyalty of ordinary Indians toward their rulers.

Yet another source of opinion that, on balance, encouraged the adoption of a policy challenging Britain imperial rule were various State Department advisory committees. These committees, whose membership included State Department officials and prominent outsiders such as Isaiah Bowman, president of Johns Hopkins University, Hamilton Fish Armstrong, editor of *Foreign Affairs*, and Norman H. Davies, president of the American Red Cross, performed the very useful function of looking ahead to the post war period. Not limited by the immediate war time needs, they could consider longer term developments and recommend appropriate American policies. "The predominant opinion in these committees in 1942," observes Christopher Thorne, was "strongly reformist."[24]

Once the United States entered the war, State Department critics of British rule gained a most important ally in the Office of the Coordinator of Information (OCOI). Formed in July 1941, and headed by the flamboyant William J. "Wild Bill" Donovan, the agency's mandate was to gather intelligence and recommend policy choices that would enhance the war effort. India was soon on its list of concerns, for that country's contribution to the war was thought to be far short of what it could be. Intelligence officers quickly concluded that the bitter political disputes between nationalists and the British lay at the heart of the problem. Within a few days of the Pearl Harbor attack "several of the higher officials in the Coordinator's office" concluded that the United States had to help improve the deteriorating political situation on the subcontinent. Murray, responding to OCOI concerns, urged the President to discuss the matter with Churchill, who was then in the United States.[25]

As we have seen Roosevelt did raise the question, only to be lectured harshly by Churchill. But the Prime Minister's attitude did not cause either the OCOI or the State Department to back away. About the time Churchill was telling Roosevelt to stay out of Indian affairs, OCOI analysts were preparing the first of several reports on India that urged the President to intervene. As the Japanese were advancing almost unhindered into Southeast Asia early in 1942, the intelligence analysts, like others observers, concluded that India "might well be the decisive element in the war in southeast Asia." It was there that a stand might have to be made against Japan. India had substantial reserves of manpower and resources and potentially could serve as a major industrial base for the military's needs. It was one of the poorest countries in the world and yet in absolute terms had great wealth.[26]

India could, of course, perform the same role for its would-be conquerors. It "lights a gleam in the eye of the German and the Japanese," the analysts contended, just as in previous centuries the Moguls and Genghis Khan had coveted the subcontinent. In sum, vigorous Indian participation in the war on the Allied side was not merely desirable but crucial. "The Allied cause *requires* that India should now cooperate more vigorously in the war than heretofore," OCOI analysts concluded.

Like most observers, the OCOI analysts were concerned primarily about the immediate military situation. But they also looked to the future. India's nearly 400 million people, raw materials, industry, and international trade made the country a valuable political and economic prize in the postwar world, the OCOI reports implied. Thus the analysts hoped that India would emerge from the war a strong, democratic country. "America should be concerned that India's problems neither interfere now with the conduct of the war nor afterward prevent a stable peace for the benefit of democracy," stated one OCOI report. If the United States could convince Indians that their interests lay with the democracies, it would have done "a service to herself, to India, to Asia and to the world."[27]

The major obstacle to securing both the short- and long-run objectives was the bitter political impasse in India. How to respond to this unfortunate situation depended in part on how the nationalists were perceived. OCOI analysts did not view the nationalists in romantic terms. They felt that Gandhi was in a technological sense a reactionary who longed "for return to the mythical golden age," for example. But they did not find Indian nationalism ultimately threatening. The goals of the movement were constitutional and therefore conservative. Economic issues were secondary, while interest in larger social issues were thought to be of even less importance. "It is not an effort of the proletariat to achieve a social revolution," read one report.

In sum, despite the mysterious workings of Gandhi's mind and the allegedly irrational aspects of Indian philosophy and religion, the nationalists were at heart reasonable. An American representative could convey American concerns to Indian leaders, could listen attentively to what they had to say, could "detect points on which they might be willing to compromise," and thus could help frame a final agreement. All of this was comforting to Americans, who wanted change to come to India (and elsewhere in the colonial world), but who were fearful of revolutionary, radical, irrational change. Soon Louis Johnson would go to India as the President's personal representative and would arrive at precisely the same conclusion: Indian nationalists were reasonable people; one could deal with them.

Therefore, the OCOI analysts could feel comfortable suggesting American political intervention in India, with the President himself pressing Churchill to make further assurances about granting India dominion status. The United States should also undertake informational activities in India, including radio broadcasts (in which "America must never appear to be pleading Britain's cause"), sending American films and speakers, translating American books, and seeing that American magazine and newspaper articles about the "democratic way of life" reached India. The analysts admitted that none of this would guarantee that India would turn its full attention to the war, but they thought the United States was the only outside power that could have significant influence on events since it was trusted by both sides. Soon the American Office of War Information was carrying out the agency's informational suggestions, sometimes to the great irritation of British and Government of India officials.

The OCOI reports confirm the importance of India in American eyes early in 1942. Furthermore, the agency's reports directly influenced the course of American policy because its director had direct access to the President and urged Roosevelt to get involved in Indian affairs. On February 10 Donovan passed along Bajpai's opinion that the President ought to speak to Churchill about India.[28] India was "no longer merely a British domestic question," the director asserted; the United States had a stake in the outcome. He enclosed a letter from Krishnalal Shridharani, a friend of Gandhi who lived in the United States. The author of a popular book, *My India, My America*, and frequent opinion pieces in journals of opinion, Shridharani, like the OCOI reports, contended that India's heart was not in the fight and that it was vital to settle the Indian situation equitably and quickly. This was so not just on grounds of immediate military necessity, but also because the future of Asia lay in the balance. "All Asiatic countries, without a single exception, are more or less distrustful of the Dutch, the French, and the British Imperialisms. And for all of them," he went on, "India has become the acid test of the Allied bona fides." If the West failed, Japan might be able to inspire a full fledged anti-Western revolt which was her only hope of winning the war in the long run.[29]

Worried by reports of this nature, Roosevelt asked the Combined Chiefs of Staff for a detailed report on the military outlook. He then drafted a hard hitting message to Churchill, in which he reflected on the question of colonies generally. Suggesting that the British leaders were old fashioned imperialists, the President wrote that the colonial relationship was out of date. It had "ceased to exist ten or twenty years ago," yet neither the British nor the Dutch had altered "the older policy of master and servant" in their colonies. Only the Americans, by promising the Filipinos independence, had changed. As for India specifically, the President concluded that the Indians "feel that delay follows delay and therefore that there is no real desire in Britain to recognize a world change which has taken deep root in India as well as in other countries." There was in India "too much suspicion and dissatisfaction," with the result that resistance to the Japanese was not nearly as wholehearted as it ought to be.[30]

In the end Roosevelt decided not to send the telegram, but the draft makes clear that the President, perhaps influenced by the more thoughtful critics as well as responding to his own inner senses, was beginning to think of India in terms beyond immediate military needs. Still very worried about the military situation, Roosevelt was also concerned with the shape of the postwar world. It has sometimes been argued that Churchill had a better grasp of the future than Roosevelt. If there is any truth in such assertions, it cannot apply to Asia. Here Roosevelt was far ahead of the Prime Minister. He already sensed that European empires were moribund and would not long survive the war.

Although Roosevelt did not send his telegram to Churchill, he did ask the London embassy to sound out the Prime Minister about India. "From all I can gather," he wrote on February 25, "the British defense will not have sufficiently enthusiastic support from the people of India themselves."[31] Given Churchill's strong feelings about India, even a mere inquiry was bound to create tension (something Roosevelt undoubtedly knew), and Averell Harriman, second in command at the American embassy who had to deliver the message, did not relish confronting the Prime Minister. He later wrote that it was "one of the most difficult assignments" he ever had to undertake.[32]

A factor overlooked in most accounts of the evolution of American policy was the influence of Sir Girja, the agent general for India. Bajpai went to America with the complete confidence of the British and Indian governments. Indeed, they did what they could to enhance his status and freedom of action in Washington, Amery noting that this could pose problems with a less discreet envoy.[33] Yet these officials overlooked, underestimated, or ignored the fact that Bajpai did not want to play the role of a puppet to the British. Some conservative nationalists recognized this from the start. P. Kodandra Rao of the Servants of India Society in Bangalore, for example, congratulated Bajpai on his appointment to Washington and noted that his arrival in America would "hasten the political organization of India, and we shall not be suprised [sic] that from your place in the U.S.A. you did more than we here to promote that consideration." Rao added that he hoped Bajpai would eventually return to "become the Prime Minister of India under Swaraj [self-rule]."[34]

Rao had greater insight into Bajpai's views than his government superiors. For not only did the agent general establish independent contacts with State Department officials, he also took positions in his remarkably frank conversations with them significantly at odds with those of his own government. He questioned and criticized his superiors, challenged the existing pace of constitutional reform in India, urged that something akin to independence be the goal, and indicated that he wanted the United States to intervene at appropriate times to pressure the British into making concessions to nationalist opinion.

Bajpai was particularly interested in seeking American technical assistance to help India develop its war making capacity. Not long after the Americans entered the war, he approached Berle along these lines. Impressed with what might be done, Berle suggested the sending of a technical mission to India to explore the matter.[35] Although at this stage of the discussions Bajpai emphasized the military advantages of such a mission, he had a broader political agenda: increasingly to involve the United States in Indian affairs, where it would inevitably become concerned with politics. Meeting with an OCOI official two days after his meeting with Berle, Bajpai was explicit. He said he would speak not for Britain but "for the interests of India." Even more telling, Bajpai indicated that India's constitutional future ought to be decided before the war was over, a position at odds with current British policy, and "he thought that some third party might be influential in helping to get some better status for India." President Roosevelt could take the lead by speaking "off the record to Mr. Churchill." Had Linlithgow known that his representative in Washington was urging that the United States approach the Prime Minister about India's political status, he would have removed him immediately.[36]

With State Department officials, Bajpai moved more circumspectly but nonetheless steadily toward his goal of increased American involvement in Indian affairs. On January 23, 1942, he urged the Americans to request a seat on the Eastern Group Supply Council, which met in Delhi and whose members had been limited to representatives of British territories in the Pacific. The recent addition of a Dutch representative, Bajpai suggested, would provide a good reason to request that an American join the council.[37] Five days later he urged Berle to request an expanded American place on the recently created British-American Materials Supply Boards, a suggestion that

Berle found "interesting." In the same meeting he again pushed for
the formation of an American technical mission to India.[38]

A few days later Roosevelt authorized the formation of an official
Technical Mission. The Hearst press, usually pro-nationalist, condemned the mission in florid language because there was no promise
of liberty. The assistance would only help the British continue their
domination of India.[39] Hearst, however, failed to understand the
ramifications of the mission. Although increased war production and
efficient allocation of resources was the primary concern, Bajpai had
achieved his goal of increasing American involvement in Indian
affairs without raising the suspicions of his British superiors. As Bajpai hoped, Berle saw a direct connection between the evolving Technical Mission and the political situation. The mission, he asserted,
would not "get very far unless the political situation is handled with
extreme vigor." He urged that the United States seek a joint policy
with Great Britain to make India a "full partner in the United
Nations," that the United States commissioner in New Delhi and the
Indian agent general in Washington be raised to ambassadorial rank,
and that the Indian viceroy "be directed" to convene a constitutional conference. Though Welles was "very reluctant indeed to go as far
in this direction as you suggest,"[40] Bajpai would have been pleased.
The Technical Mission had raised political questions even before it
had been formally approved.

As American policy began to shift toward active involvement in the
Indian question, the British upgraded their efforts to influence
American opinion and prevent any intervention. Particularly after
the United States entered the war, British and Government of India
information and intelligence agents, several of whom were stationed
in the United States, became increasingly concerned about American opinion. In mid-February 1942, as reports of American concern
with Britain's India policy multiplied, Foreign Office and India
Office officials met (not a common experience) to discuss ways of
influencing American opinion. With the British government considering a public pronouncement about India, they hoped to prepare
the ground for a positive American response. Perhaps Halifax could
get Roosevelt to say "some useful words" at his next press conference.
They also hoped that Wendell Willkie, the Republican candidate for

president in 1940 and a strong supporter of lend-lease, might also be convinced to say something on behalf of the British. Perhaps American journalists and commentators (the "first lady of American journalism," *New York Post* columnist Dorothy Thompson, was mentioned specifically) could be influenced to "stress points that we wished."[41]

Urgent requests went forward to India for information about the country's military strength, its contributions to the war effort, Indian morale, the political situation ("with confidential guidance if necessary"), possible changes on the viceroy's Executive Council, and good human interest stories complete with biographies and photographs. It was also thought important to present a positive image of the United States in India. In this regard Reuters, the British news service, was thought to be "extremely inadequate and altogether one-sided, creating the impression here of defeatism, fifth-columning and opposition to Roosevelt in high places." Could not more positive information about Roosevelt's sentiments be presented to Indians?[42]

For purposes of enhancing morale during the war the Government of India wanted to portray a more positive image of the United States. But privately British officials, both in London and New Delhi, were as contemptuous of the American public's understanding of the situation in India as they were of President Roosevelt's. "It would be difficult to exaggerate either the interest that Americans, for recondite reasons, take in India, or their ignorance on the subject," one Foreign Office official wrote. Therefore detailed explanations were not helpful. Instead British publicists should emphasize "plain and simple facts . . . persistently and insistently."[43]

In a sense such advice stood in contrast to a major British defense of their rule in India: that the Indian situation was extremely complicated and not amenable to simple solutions. But the view that American opinion, whether public or official, was naive and extremely ill-informed, was one that virtually all British officials concerned with India shared. As Linlithgow once put it, the "enthusiasms" of American liberals interested in Indian developments were "unimpaired by any restraining considerations of a practical kind."[44]

Although British officials believed that American views of India were shallow in the extreme, many also feared ultimate American intentions toward that country. Thus, while they took the initiative in elevating official Indo-American relations, they were always apprehensive about the long-run implications of the new intimacy. They were especially suspicious of American economic designs, and when early in 1941 the United States renewed discussion about a treaty of commerce and navigation with India (it was originally proposed in 1939), Amery urged Linlithgow to oppose Cordell Hull's efforts to include a most favored nation provision which, Amery thought, would wreck the imperial preference system. "I hope you will fight to the death and sooner refuse any commercial treaty than admit one which accepts a principle hostile to the whole future development and unity of the British Empire," he wrote. The United States was seeking "export hegemony in the world," and regardless of how closely the Americans wished to cooperate politically after the war, "it would be a fatal mistake to give way."[45] He need not have worried. If anything, Linlithgow was more suspicious of American intentions than Amery.

British officials sought political and economic cooperation with the United States during and after the war, but not at the expense of vital imperial interests.[46] The fear of American designs to control the world, especially in an economic sense, was one that was widely shared in British and Indian government circles, not the least by Amery and Linlithgow. It would continually influence their reactions to expressions of American interest about Indian developments.

Labour Party leaders, more sympathetic to Indian nationalist concerns, began to press for a new round of discussions about India's constitutional future. Churchill warned of raising such issues, but Clement Attlee, then the Lord Privy Seal, persisted. Early in February he stated to the Prime Minister that ever since the Japanese victory over the Russians in 1905 notions of European superiority had lost credibility and were in danger of disappearing altogether with the recent Japanese victories in Asia. The time had come to make a major effort to settle the Indian problem. "Now is the time for an act of statesmanship," he wrote. And Linlithgow was "not the man" to bring about a settlement. His "past failures" and his reactionary "mental attitude" precluded him from taking the lead. What was necessary, Attlee thought, was to send a representative to India "to negotiate within wide limits" for a political settlement.[47]

As Attlee drafted his paper, American opinion was on his mind.

"American sentiment has always leant strongly to the idea of Indian freedom," he wrote.[48] Concern with American opinion was growing. Less than two weeks later Foreign Office officials, reading a survey of American newspaper opinion about India, expressed appreciation to Ministry of Information officials that had provided the survey because, as one of them put it, it was "the first indication I have seen of the idea that what we do in India is of direct importance to the U.S. . . . We may expect more pressure to be brought to bear on us."[49] Churchill's comment about American restraint was out of date.

Pressure from Labour and indirectly from the United States showed results, for on February 13, 1942, the War Cabinet approved a scheme to create a Defence of India Council, which would select two representatives to serve on the viceroy's Executive Council. Surprisingly Churchill, who had previously resisted any changes in India's governance, emerged as a strong supporter of the scheme. To the viceroy he acknowledged that his support was based on concern about American opinion.[50] Linlithgow strongly resisted this idea, as he would many others, arguing that the grave military situation in Asia was no reason for "hasty or unsound" action. Significantly, he was concerned that Churchill and the War Cabinet were making their proposal to appease the Americans, something he thought foolish and short sighted. "We must regard morale and fighting value of the army as more important than U.S.A. opinion or that of any minorities in the U.K.," he wrote. This is not to say that Linlithgow discounted entirely the importance of American opinion. The contemplated prosecution of Nehru at that moment would, he wrote, have a "disastrous" impact on American opinion and therefore ought not to be done—this despite his personal contempt for the Indian leader. But the views of foreigners, he insisted, should never influence fundamental considerations.[51]

As Linlithgow feared, however, the British were bending to American pressure. As Amery worked on a draft declaration of policy regarding Indian's future status, the United States loomed paramount in his thought. "I believe if we go as far as this draft we shall have gone a long way to meet American and even Indian criticism," he wrote. Indeed, the American factor was so strong that even Linlithgow could not prevent a British move to settle the Indian question. As Amery put it in a letter to the viceroy, "there is a certain sense of humour in that Winston, after making infinite difficulties for both of us in respect of whatever constructive suggestions we put forward, has now, as is his wont—seen the red light (especially the American red light) overnight." Though he did not note, as he might have, that Linlithgow himself often found "infinite difficulties" with proposed changes, Amery knew this news would be very distasteful and urged the viceroy to "keep fit and keep up your courage. You will need all of it."[52]

Two days later Churchill informed Roosevelt that his government was considering issuing a declaration providing for dominion status for India after the war. The declaration, which was opposed by professionals in the India Office as well as the King, and on which Amery professed only an "open mind," was designed to appeal to Americans. "It has its advantages psychologically in America and in some Indian quarters," Amery wrote.[53]

By the following day the British government had decided not to issue a draft declaration (a partial victory for Linlithgow) but instead to send Sir Stafford Cripps, who had recently resigned as British ambassador to the Soviet Union to replace Attlee as Lord Privy Seal, to India to present a plan to Indian nationalists for a political settlement. American pressure was a major factor—arguably the most important factor—in the British decision to send Cripps. As Amery explained to the viceroy, "The pressure outside, upon Winston from Roosevelt, and upon Attlee & Co. from their own party, *plus* the admission of Cripps to the War Cabinet, suddenly opened the sluice gates, and the thing moved with a rush."[54]

By March 1942, the Roosevelt administration was on the verge of intervening in the Indian situation. Driven initially by concerns of military necessity, even by a sense of panic as the Japanese moved into Burma, broader considerations were also beginning to emerge. Antiimperialists hammered away on the theme of self-determination and urged the administration to be true to American idealism. Others contended that, in any event, the days of colonial rule were virtually at an end, and the United States should adjust its policies to meet the new reality. All of these arguments appealed to the President. Realizing this, the British moved to head off American pressure by sending Cripps to India. Their action, however, came too late.

3 | The Johnson Mission
(March–May 1942)

The Cripps Mission, designed to head off American intervention, came too late. The very day it was announced, Roosevelt sent a long telegram to Churchill that would constitute his most serious, personal intervention in the Indian constitutional question. Drawing on many of the ideas that had been included in his unsent telegram of February 25, the President informed the Prime Minister that he had "given much thought to the problem of India" and had concluded that something of value for the subcontinent might be learned from studying the American experience in the 1780s. As "an obvious stop-gap government," the American states had agreed to unite under the Articles of Confederation. After four years a constitutional convention, representing all states, was called and a more permanent constitution drafted and subsequently adopted. Was there not a useful precedent here for India? Could not there be set up in India a "temporary Dominion Government" representing various "castes, occupations, religions and geographies"? This temporary government would have authority over "public services," but its main responsibility would be to establish a method of setting up "a more permanent government," a process that might take "five or six years or at least until a year after the end of the war." The President hoped that this would diminish internal hostilities, make India loyal to the empire, and provide for "peaceful evolution as against chaotic revolution." Indicative of the seriousness of the President's intervention, he hoped that whatever moves the British government made would be made in such a way "that there should be not criticism in India that it is being made grudgingly or by compulsion."[1]

So that there could be no doubt about the serious nature of Roosevelt's concern, the President met the following day with Bajpai. Doing most of the talking, the President repeated the analogy with the American experience of the 1780s and commented pointedly on how the American decision to grant independence to the Philippine Islands on a specific date had "accelerated realisation of Filipino solidarity. Without explicitly stating the conclusion," Bajpai reported, "the President obviously intended it to be inferred that similar device may lead to comparable result in India."[2]

The President's intervention was not well received in London. Foreign Office comment was uniformly negative and reflected the long standing prejudice about the shallowness of American views on India. One official commented on Roosevelt's "rather lighthearted . . . attempted comparison between incomparables." The same official also thought the allusion to the Philippines was not "altogether happy." Nevile Butler, who was in charge of the North American Division, commented condescendingly that this was "very characteristic" of the President and was similar to the way Theodore Roosevelt had behaved about Egypt. Yet another official found it "a terrifying comment on the likely Roosevelt contribution to the peace, a meandering [?] amateurishness lit by discursive flashes." Yet another was reminded of Sir Owen Seaman's lines on Kier Hardies' visit to India: "And you will learn in 'arf a mo' / What takes a man ten years or so / To know that he will never know."[3] For his part, Churchill privately considered Roosevelt's intervention an "act of madness."[4]

Government of India officials, meanwhile, were beginning to regret that the Americans were now ensconced in New Delhi. In March government officials obtained (by means not made clear in the available records) Commissioner Wilson's confidential assessment of Chiang Kai-shek's recent visit to India. In February Chiang had sent a strongly critical report of British rule to Roosevelt. (The report was another factor in moving Roosevelt toward intervention.)

Wilson agreed with much that Chiang had to say, and Linlithgow, who claimed to have shown the American "every personal attention," seemed almost hurt that Wilson could have sent such a report to the State Department. "I suspect he is a rather stupid man (though very pleasant)," the viceroy wrote, "and that someone on his staff is out to make mischief."[5] It was a typical reaction of the viceroy to any outsider who viewed the situation in India differently than he.

Linlithgow also heard that Louis Johnson was about to replace Wilson, which he correctly assumed indicated the President's increasing interest in Indian developments. Johnson was a lawyer who had his practice in Clarksburg, West Virginia.[6] Soon after his graduation from the University of Virginia law school in 1912 he entered politics and became the Democratic floor leader in the West Virginia House of Delegates. During World War I he served as an infantry captain in Europe. After the war he helped organize the American Legion and rose to become its national commander in 1932. He was a loyal and energetic Democrat—and a very ambitious one.

After Roosevelt's election to his second term, Johnson hoped to be appointed secretary of war but the post went to Harry H. Woodring. Asked to become assistant secretary, Johnson at first refused but changed his mind. He claimed that he was promised that he would soon become secretary and periodically would announce that he was about to move up, but it never happened.

As might be expected, Johnson and Woodring did not get along. In fact, the two men were barely on speaking terms, and Woodring tried very hard never to be out of town when the President scheduled a cabinet meeting. If he were away, Johnson would have to sit in for him. Much as Woodring disliked Johnson, though, he never felt strong enough politically to take the matter up with the President.

In 1940 Woodring was forced to resign because of policy disagreements with Roosevelt. But the President turned not to Johnson but to Henry Stimson, a Republican, and a few weeks later Johnson was forced out to make room for Robert Patterson, Stimson's choice for assistant secretary. Johnson was deeply hurt by this action, and appointment to the Indian mission may have been partly to soothe his feelings. Even so, controversy surrounded the appointment. Vice

President Henry Wallace lobbied hard to block it. Diplomat John Paton Davies thought that Johnson's bombastic qualities made him "uniquely unsuited to deal with the British and the Indians."[7] But Johnson's blunt manner and feisty personality were probably precisely the characteristics Roosevelt sought. If he wanted to impress on the British and the Government of India his anger at British intransigence and his determination to see political change on the subcontinent, he could not have chosen better, though in keeping with his usual style of diplomacy the President did not give Johnson explicit instructions to challenge the British.

Only one day before Roosevelt's intervention with Churchill on March 10 (when the President had drawn an analogy with the Articles of Confederation), the State Department announced that Johnson would chair the Technical Mission to India.[8] Henry F. Grady, a former assistant secretary of state who had previously been mentioned as the probable chairman, was placed in charge of economic surveys.

Officially, the mission was nonpolitical. An apparent press release, clearly intended for foreign consumption, contended that Johnson's mission was to help India "develop into the Far Eastern arsenal of war materials for the United Nations." Johnson would coordinate the work of the various experts.[9] This was also the view presented to the Government of India. To be sure, the Indian government knew as early as March 13 that, in addition to chairing the Technical Mission, Johnson would replace Thomas Wilson as the chief American diplomat in India, Wilson having told this to Linlithgow personally.[10] This indicated that Johnson would bring to India a broader agenda than a survey of India's technical needs. But it was still assumed that his major concern would relate to India's military requirements. On March 19, when the President officially informed Linlithgow of Johnson's appointment, he emphasized his "broad experience with problems relating to military supply" and said nothing about politics. But Bajpai, in his report to British officials, noted significantly, "you may also find him not uninterested in Indian politics."[11]

The British expressed some irritation at the appointment, one Foreign Office official commenting that "it looks as if the Americans are trying to force our hand by anticipating the grant of full dominion status to India." The Government of India formally welcomed Johnson's appointment, "particularly in view of his close association with the President," but behind the scenes officials were reportedly "most disturbed." Olaf K. Caroe, secretary for external affairs, commented condescendingly that the attempt to have Johnson be both head of the Technical Mission and Washington's diplomatic representative in New Delhi "could probably not have been thought of except by the U.S.A." As Caroe's comment suggested, though, most criticism from Government of India officials was about procedure. There was annoyance about premature publicity and a lack of advance consultation about the appointment, particularly about Johnson's rank. But because of the emphasis on technical and military expertise, they generally welcomed the appointment.[12]

Those officials who did suspect that Johnson's appointment had a serious political dimension were correct. In fact, the decision to select Johnson instead of Grady had everything to do with international politics. His work as the President's personal representative, he was told, "would take precedence over his work as Chairman of the [Technical] Mission." Moreover, Johnson's instructions contained no mention of technical matters. Johnson was not instructed to take a hostile attitude toward the British, but he was advised to "take all appropriate measures to foster friendly relations between the United States and India"—not, it should be noted, the Government of India—"and to promote the mutual interests of both countries."[13]

Excited at the chance to get involved in the India imbroglio, Johnson wrote to Berle, "I am impatient to get underway—the more I study the situation the more interesting it becomes."[14]

Cripps, meanwhile, had arrived in New Delhi. An idealistic and somewhat eccentric man, austere, deeply religious, a vegetarian with (according to Averell Harriman) a messiah complex who wanted "the British people to wear the hair shirt for the sake of wearing it," Cripps was a personal friend of Nehru and other nationalists and sympathized deeply with their cause, though Nehru did not always have a high opinion of his judgment. Wilson reported that his appointment found almost unanimous approval in Indian political circles, both Hindu and Muslim.[15] He relished the chance to bring a permanent settlement to the vexing Indian problem, though he recognized the many obstacles involved. His good friend, Agatha Harrison, with whom he had confidentially shared the proposal before he left England, told him that the Indians would not accept. "It is too late," she said. "They would have accepted it six months ago."[16] Told by a distinguished Indian journalist that his mission might succeed "provided the British Cabinet was determined to achieve success," Cripps "smiled but said nothing."[17]

The proposal that the Lord Privy Seal brought to India was significant, although historian Robin J. Moore may exaggerate when he terms it "a large advance in British constitutional policy."[18] Mostly Cripps's own, one that he had put forward three years earlier, it reaffirmed the government's intention to confer dominion status on a new Indian union following the war. A body consisting of elected representatives from each province of British India and appointed representatives from the quasi-independent Indian states would draft a constitution. No province or state would be required to join the new union. Until an acceptable constitution was developed, the British would continue to bear full responsibility for India's defense, but Indian leaders would be invited to participate in some undefined way. They might be asked to serve on the viceroy's Executive Council, "provided this does not embarrass the defence and good government of the country during the present critical time."[19] Cripps was allowed to negotiate with the Indians on the scope of their participation in the government for the duration of the war.

Cripps met with Indian leaders and delivered a radio address urging acceptance of the proposals. But, as Harrison had predicted, rejection seemed likely. Although Jinnah seemed willing to go along (as Amery put it in a letter to Linlithgow, "Jinnah, I should have thought, will be content to realise that he has now got Pakistan"), Congress was divided with Gandhi strongly opposed.[20] On April 2 the Working Committee of Congress rejected the proposals because they were too uncertain about how and when self-determination was to be realized, gave too much encouragement to centrifugal forces in India and not enough to those groups which wanted a unified state, and gave Indians too little authority during the war. The provisions for Indian participation in decisions about defense were especially offensive, the committee contended. They would reduce Indian "responsibility to a farce and a nullity and . . . make it perfectly clear that India is not going to be free in any way."[21]

The rejection incensed Amery. "I am not sure these people really want responsibility," he wrote Linlithgow, "and if we offered them the moon they would probably reject it because of the wrinkles on the surface." Churchill was relieved. Never comfortable with any attempt to turn responsibilities over to the Indians, the Prime Minister congratulated Cripps on his efforts, noted the beneficial public relations impact in the United States and Britain, and assumed, without regrets, that the matter was closed.[22]

But that was not the end of it. For one thing, though the Working Committee had rejected the proposals, it was willing to negotiate. For another, Louis Johnson arrived the day after the committee's rejection and did what he could to facilitate a settlement. Finally, Cripps himself did not want to break off the discussions. To stand fast, he cabled Churchill, "would be a fatal policy" that would ensure failure and open the government to criticism for being rigid and stubborn.[23]

Cripps, therefore, proposed modifications in the formula for defense which he hoped would bring Congress into the government. He offered the British government two alternatives. The first, which he favored, was to turn the defense ministry over to a representative Indian, provided there was a written agreement that the minister would not act contrary to British war policy. The other alternative, which he thought unlikely to be accepted by the nationalists but which he felt the British government would more likely consider, was to transform the existing defense department into a war department, headed by the commander-in-chief, and to create a new defense coordination department to be headed by an Indian. The new department would have responsibility for relatively minor functions, subject to approval of the commander-in-chief.[24]

Fearing opposition to the revisions from officials in London and New Delhi, Cripps asked Johnson, whom he had taken completely into his confidence, to urge Roosevelt to intervene directly with Churchill. Johnson agreed, but Roosevelt, while urging his representative to keep him abreast of developments, declined to approach the Prime Minister.[25] Roosevelt probably felt that another intervention so soon after his telegram of March 10 would not be helpful; furthermore, it was not yet clear that the Cripps negotiations would fail. But in retrospect it was a major miscalculation, one that may have caused the Cripps mission to collapse.[26] In any event, elements of the American government were at that point supporting the original, unmodified Cripps proposals. The State Department's Division of Near Eastern Affairs, for example, supported a radio propaganda campaign, the "principal objective" of which was "to assist the British Government in persuading the Indian people to accept the Cripps proposals."[27]

Johnson too was then supportive of the British initiative, telling Nehru that the United States would "support Great Britain to the end of the war, to the utmost and to preserve the integrity of the British empire." If Congress wanted to retain American sympathy, he added forcefully, it would have to support the war wholeheartedly. Even Linlithgow, inveterately suspicious of foreigners, especially Americans, who involved themselves in Indian constitutional questions, thought Johnson's actions helpful to the British cause. He had, the viceroy wrote, "succeeded in very considerably increasing the pressure upon the Working Committee in favour of accepting the offer."[28]

As it happened, the British government was willing to support Cripps's second alternative,[29] but as Cripps feared it was far too little to satisfy Congress, and the Working Committee quickly objected. "I am more convinced than ever that the new suggestions put forward by Sir Stafford Cripps will create a very bad impression on our people," Nehru wrote to Johnson. "Instead of handing over control of defence generally, they will emphasize that this will not be done."[30]

Fearing a final breakdown, Johnson jumped headlong into the negotiations and suggested further modifications that gave (or at least appeared to give) Indians additional responsibilities in the area of defense. Nehru found Johnson's draft "a more healthy one,"[31] and over several hours Nehru, Johnson and Cripps worked out language that both Johnson and Cripps felt would allow the Congress to enter the government. This "Cripps-Johnson formula," as it came to be called, involved retaining the existing defense department, which would be headed by an Indian; but some of the department's functions would be transferred to a new war department, to be headed by the commander-in-chief. The heart of the matter concerned the powers to be entrusted to the new Indian defense minister.

For a time there was optimism. In addition to the modifications in the defense formula, Cripps had in writing held out the prospect of a "new National Government," thus meeting a key Congress demand if it meant, as the Indians assumed, a genuine cabinet government in which the viceroy would function as a constitutional monarch. Johnson was convinced that Congress would now come into the government, while Indian newspapers reported that there was "every likelihood" that a successful negotiation was at hand.[32]

The viceroy, however, was not cheered by these apparently positive developments. In an angry confrontation with Cripps he complained bitterly about having been frozen out of the discussions and accused Cripps and Johnson of being virtual dupes of the Congress. That Johnson was so deeply involved by now seemed especially dangerous to Linlithgow, for if the government decided it could not support the Cripps-Johnson formula, "my position might well be rendered intolerable, as I ran the risk of being held up to the U.S.A. as an obstacle to a settlement."[33] By this time Johnson had in fact concluded that the viceroy *was* the problem. Having initially lectured Nehru on the need to support the empire, the American had quickly become convinced of the nationalist leader's reasonableness. Linlithgow, by contrast, seemed intent on blocking a settlement of historic proportions.

The viceroy's anger did nothing to lessen Cripps's determination to reach an agreement, nor did Cripps reduce his contacts with Johnson. In fact, immediately after his angry confrontation with Linlithgow, Cripps sent a defiant telegram to Churchill praising the American. "Largely owing to very efficient and wholehearted help of Col. Johnson . . . I have hopes scheme may now succeed," he informed the Prime Minister. "I should like you to thank the President for Col. Johnson's help on behalf of H.M.G., and also personally on my behalf."[34] It was a remarkable telegram, designed to show Churchill his intention not to be deterred by what he regarded as Linlithgow's reactionary views and that he was not bound (as indeed he was not) to secure the viceroy's approval of his proposals. Perhaps he even intended to force Churchill into a premature decision, for if the

Prime Minister thanked Roosevelt, it would be difficult to retreat later.

Churchill was not taken in. Instead of thanking the President, the Prime Minister rebuked the Lord Privy Seal and ordered him not to commit the government in any way pending consultation with the commander-in-chief, Lord Wavell, and the viceroy. Perhaps to Linlithgow's chagrin, Wavell was willing to go along with the Cripps-Johnson formula on defense, provided a few modifications were made. And even the viceroy, despite his immense anger at Cripps and Johnson, contended that he would have reluctantly acquiesced if Congress accepted. The American connection, he suggested, was vital. "Given all the circumstances and the importance of American opinion," he wrote in a draft telegram, "Commander-in-Chief and I feel that we have no choice but to acquiesce in this and take the chance of subsequent trouble rather than the immediate certainty of very unfavourable propaganda position in America."[35]

The suspicion lingers that Linlithgow's "acquiescence" was only for the record, for there is ample support for Nehru's assertion the following month that "in the recent history of India, there has not been such a combination of fiercely anti-Indian freedom elements in the British Government as we have had during the past two years and still have today."[36] Amery and Churchill, Linlithgow knew, were fully aware of his unhappiness, and though a little nervous, the viceroy felt that in a showdown his conservative allies in London would block Cripps's efforts to achieve a settlement that threatened to undermine his prerogatives or that gave too much authority to the Indians, especially in the defense area.

The viceroy's assessment was correct. His private correspondence with Churchill (never revealed to Cripps), combined with Cripps's absence from London, had tipped the balance of forces toward the conservatives. As two Indian scholars put it, "Cripps underestimated the threat that a hostile Linlithgow could pose to his mission."[37] From London, Amery telegraphed his sympathy and support to the viceroy, while the War Cabinet, characterizing Johnson's intervention as "unfortunate," came very close to calling off the negotiations altogether. Churchill's response was even blunter. Cripps, he insisted, had no authority to negotiate at all, only "to try to gain acceptance," a contention not in accord with the mission's conception. All in all, it was a striking, but undeserved, rebuff to the British negotiator.[38] As an American general reportedly said at the time, "Cripps was bitched in the back."[39]

The government's response put Cripps in a most awkward position. The Congress, having been told by Cripps that a genuine national government was possible, was even then giving the proposals serious consideration. At 5:30 that afternoon (April 9), Cripps met for two and one-half hours with Nehru and Azad, where he seems to have informed them that there could be no genuine cabinet government; the viceroy would have a veto. Nehru emerged from the meeting pessimistic. "The omens are bad," he wrote dejectedly to Johnson. "The whole situation that we had tried to build up so laboriously in our minds was without any real foundation."[40]

The following evening the Working Committee rejected the proposals, even as amended by the Cripps-Johnson formula. In a lengthy and eloquent response drafted by Nehru, Congress President Maulana Abul Kalam Azad contended that the proposals promised too little. They "asked for participation in the tasks of today with a view to ensure 'the future freedom of India.' Freedom was for an uncertain future, not for the present." With respect to the defense formula, it was unacceptable because in the final analysis the British were not yet prepared to give real authority to an Indian defense minister. Most fundamentally, there was insufficient movement in terms of governmental structure. "The picture of the government which was so like the old in all essential features, is such that we cannot fit into it," he wrote. Only if Britain allowed a "truly National Government[,] . . . a cabinet government with full power and . . . not merely a continuation of the Viceroy's Executive Council," could the Congress assume responsibility.[41] The talks had come to an end.

Nehru sent a copy of Congress's rejection to Johnson. "I need not tell you how much we wrestled with the problem and explored every possible avenue," he wrote. Nehru accepted the outcome philosophically. "For the present the road is closed to us," he stated. "But I do not believe in any finality in such matters."[42]

Accustomed to failed negotiations, Nehru could be fatalistic. But Johnson was livid, no doubt because he had assured everyone that the Cripps-Johnson formula on defense would bring Congress into the government. The villain, he was certain, was the British government. "London wanted a Congress refusal," he telegraphed to Washington when he learned of the breakdown. England seemed to be writing India off, preferring to lose the country to the enemy for the time being in order to regain control at the peace conference. The United States should reassess its entire policy in the area, Johnson insisted. It should cease association with the British and provide direct aid to India.[43] The cause of the failure was more complex than Johnson allowed, but it was true that Churchill and Linlithgow wanted no settlement that in any way diminished the preeminent role of the viceroy.

The whole affair had a dramatic impact on Johnson. When he first arrived he had lectured Nehru on the need to pull together and stated that the United States would support the British empire to the end. Even Linlithgow had applauded his efforts. Now scarcely a week later he termed Congress's rejection of the amended Cripps proposals "a masterpiece" that would "appeal to free men everywhere." Nehru was "magnificent in his cooperation with me," he observed. "The President would like him and on most things they agree."[44]

Not all American officials agreed with Johnson's assessment. Harry Hopkins, who was in London attempting to secure Churchill's agreement to establish a second front in Europe, looked with horror on Johnson's activity. Shortly before the War Cabinet rejected the Cripps-Johnson modifications, the Prime Minister had read Hopkins a dispatch he claimed to have just received from Linlithgow. It related Johnson's involvement with Cripps in drafting the new defense formula and made it abundantly clear that the viceroy resented Johnson's meddling. Johnson, the dispatch continued, gave the distinct impression that he was acting at the President's behest.

Making matters worse, Johnson's activities were counterproductive because, Churchill continued, Linlithgow had indicated that "he and Cripps could have got Nehru's agreement to the original proposal had not Cripps and Johnson worked out this new arrangement."[45] It is not clear to which dispatch from Linlithgow Churchill was referring, for the available records do not indicate that Linlithgow ever made such a claim. It was in any event patently false, for

Congress had rejected Cripps's original proposals even before John-son arrived and then rejected the Cripps-Johnson formula which was more favorable to them. Either Hopkins misunderstood what the Prime Minister said, or Churchill deliberately misled the American in an effort to make Johnson's actions appear foolish and ill advised, as well as unauthorized.

Hopkins was deeply troubled by what he took to be Johnson's unauthorized action (he wrote that Roosevelt had told him that he "would not be drawn into the Indian business except at the personal request of the Prime Minister and then only if he had an assurance from both India and Britain that any plan that he worked out would be acceptable") and feared the consequences for Anglo-American relations. Without discussing the matter with Roosevelt he assured the Prime Minister that Johnson "was not acting as the representative of the President in mediating the Indian business." In all probability, he continued, Cripps was using Johnson to get Roosevelt identified with the proposals.[46]

Hopkins's assurances had greatly strengthened Churchill's hand. He cabled Cripps (with the humiliating instruction to repeat his message to Linlithgow and Wavell) that Johnson represented the President only on matters relating to the Technical Mission, a claim that was assuredly false. Roosevelt's "message to me, just received from Mr. Hopkins, who is with me as I write," he went on (falsely implying that Roosevelt had actually sent a message personally), "was entirely opposed to anything like U.S. intervention or mediation."[47] He then informed the War Cabinet of his discussion with Hopkins, which made it considerably easier for that body to question the Cripps-Johnson formula and to chastise Cripps for his alleged indiscretions.

Hopkins probably acted as he did because of his profound admiration for Churchill and his deep desire to forge a close Anglo-American relationship to win the war. The previous year he had brought Churchill to tears when he closed some after-dinner remarks with a quotation from the book of Ruth: "Whither thou goest, I will go; and where thou lodgest, I will lodge; thy people shall be my people, and thy God my God." And, he added softly, "even to the end."[48] John-son's actions posed a serious threat to the close relations he thought essential. It is also possible that Hopkins feared Johnson's meddling would hinder chances for an agreement on the second front and other military measures.

Although Hopkins presumably believed that his assessment of the situation was accurate,[49] his actions did a great disservice to President Roosevelt and American policy objectives in India. For the President clearly supported Johnson's action. For several weeks, American policy had been moving toward intervention, which culminated in the President's proposal of March 10. The circumstances surrounding Johnson's appointment represented another stage in this evolving policy.

The ultimate evidence of Roosevelt's true position was his reaction to the breakdown of the talks. Hopkins urged Roosevelt to distance himself from Johnson, defended the British ("all believe that a fair offer was made and that no stone was left unturned to reach agreement"), and urged that the matter be dropped. "Quite apparent that further negotiations with Cripps would be futile," he telegraphed the President. Johnson, of course, attacked the British in the bitterest terms. He accused them of deliberately sabotaging the negotiations and urged the United States to reconsider its association with British policy in India. Cripps and Nehru, he said, could have solved the matter "in five minutes if Cripps had any freedom or authority."[50]

Faced with these contradictory assessments, Roosevelt hesitated not for a moment. In one of the sharpest cables he ever sent to Churchill, the President virtually insisted that the deadlock was due to the failure of the British government "to concede to the Indians the right of self-government." Drawing directly on Johnson's reports the President observed acidly, "I read that an agreement seemed very near last Thursday night," and he urged Churchill to keep Cripps in India to continue the negotiations, something that even Johnson had not suggested. Johnson, not Hopkins, represented Roosevelt on Indian policy.[51]

Churchill was furious. Hopkins described to Secretary of War Stimson "how the string of cuss words lasted for two hours in the middle of the night."[52] The Prime Minister then threatened to resign (though it is likely that he was bluffing),[53] Hopkins calmed him down, and Roosevelt did not pressure him further. Had the President acted earlier, as Johnson had urged him to do on April 5, the results might have been different. Of course no one can be certain that a new Presidential initiative would have made any difference. Churchill might not have acted very differently on April 5 than he did on April 12, and the War Cabinet might still have found reason to question the Cripps-Johnson formula. But at least there would have been no doubt about Roosevelt's true intentions, and there would have been no intrusion by Harry Hopkins, whose actions were of great importance in making British rejection a certainty.

During the few weeks that Johnson remained in India after the collapse of the Cripps Mission, he acted in ways calculated to irritate the British. Within a day after the collapse of the talks, Johnson invited Nehru to visit the United States. Nehru had often been tempted to visit America but had never felt the timing was right. He declined Johnson's invitation, though in the next few weeks many Indians incessantly urged him to reconsider, and the press continued to ask him why he refused to travel to the United States. Although Nehru decided to stay in India, there were continual rumors that he would go. Churchill was so concerned that he telegraphed Hopkins urging that an invitation not be extended.[54]

Johnson also fraternized publicly with Indian nationalists. "I have seen much of your friends," he wrote to Nehru, informing him of a recent dinner at which many members of the Congress's Working Committee were present. Particularly likely to irk the British were Johnson's press conference of April 22 and a radio address to the Indian people the following evening. He pledged to devote unstinting efforts in the future to make Americans more aware of India and vice versa. American interest in Asia, he asserted, was best seen in the Philippines, which the United States had put "on the road to independence." The war, he continued, would determine "whether the government shall belong to the people, as it must if there is to be liberty and dignity for mankind anywhere." And he sensed that India was "achieving a new national self-consciousness, a new popular soul, a new popular will."[55]

When a State Department official learned of these remarks, he noted that Johnson had better be careful lest he "seriously antagonize the civil government." "He probably already has," commented Paul Alling, chief of the division of Near Eastern Affairs. Alling was correct. One British official, for example, wrote to the viceroy expressing his resentment at Johnson's allusion to the Philippines, but he disliked even more the American's "general attitude," which conveyed "the impression that America will compel us to hand over to Congress."[56]

Although the negotiations failed, the Indian nationalists deeply appreciated Johnson's efforts. B. Shiva Rao, a prominent journalist, wrote that Johnson's "friendly and sympathetic interest" kept nationalist resentment at ill-informed, superficial, and patronizing stories in the American press "within due proportions," while his formula for defense arrangements "enabled the negotiations to proceed after the first serious hitch."[57] Nehru himself publicly thanked Johnson "for his friendly approach to our problems," and a week later sent the American a copy of his book, *The Unity of India*, which he characterized modestly as "an odd collection of essays."[58]

When Johnson entered a New Delhi hospital for treatment of a persistent nasal infection, Nehru visited him twice, leaving the American with the impression that Nehru would "continue his efforts to calm Indians, speed production and make them hate Japs." Johnson requested from the Indian leader a statement detailing the background of the current crisis and Congress's position on the situation. Nehru complied with a document of sixteen typewritten pages, which Johnson studied with great care.[59] When it became apparent that Johnson's physical condition required his evacuation to the United States, he shared his plans in confidence and in detail with Indians before informing Government of India officials, and then only in general terms. "Do not fear that I shall lose interest in the matters we have discussed," he wrote to the Bombay industrialist G. D. Birla, a major financier of the nationalist effort.[60]

Meanwhile, the British, already uncomfortable with Johnson's activities, were beginning to fear that his reports and activities might have serious consequences. On May 13 Supreme Court Justice Felix Frankfurter divulged to a British official the substance of Johnson's reports to the President (which contended that the War Cabinet and the viceroy had sabotaged Cripps), and that the President was convinced of their accuracy. This interpretation of events, Frankfurter indicated, "was causing serious distrust in the highest circles and extending to other circles."[61] This information was transmitted immediately to the viceroy, who then wrote Amery that Johnson had not "been altogether a helpful influence here. In fact," he went on, "one might put it rather more strongly than that." He urged Halifax to counter Johnson and indicated that he did not want the American to return to India.[62]

The viceroy's complaints bore fruit almost immediately. Amery asked Churchill to try to prevent Johnson's return to India.[63] Churchill, who had himself just complained to Hopkins about Johnson's "alarmist reports," again telegraphed the President's assistant to urge that Johnson remain in America. The viceroy, he told Hopkins, was "much perturbed" at the thought of Johnson's return to New Delhi. "I know you will remember my many difficulties," he added.[64]

Johnson, meanwhile, underwent treatment at the Mayo Clinic upon his return. He had promised the nationalists he would not forget them, and before he left India he told Nehru that making his acquaintance had been the highlight of his Indian assignment. "I look forward to years of happy friendship with you," he wrote. Their overseas correspondence began almost immediately, with Nehru writing through Lampton Berry, the ranking American diplomat in New Delhi, and ended (for the time being) only when the British imprisoned the Indian leader in August. Johnson responded appreciatively to Nehru's overtures. "I want you to know that I have in no way changed my personal opinion and I shall act in accordance therewith on my return to Washington," he wrote while recuperating in Minnesota.[65]

In short, Johnson's Indian sojourn had a significant impact on the American. He went to India without much knowledge of the situation and certainly without any particular sympathy with the Indian nationalists. His close contacts with British officials in the Indian government, however, soon convinced him that the government was reactionary and unlikely to make needed concessions to Indian opinion, even if it meant losing the war in Asia. By contrast he found Nehru and other nationalists to be idealistic but reasonable, devoted to a cause with which Americans could sympathize. He became a great admirer of them, especially of Nehru, with whom he remained a lifelong friend and correspondent. Although Roosevelt could not have foreseen these developments in detail, he most likely thought that Johnson, with his feisty qualities, would be of value in the President's efforts to bring about political change in India. The Johnson mission suggests the subtlety and shrewdness of Roosevelt's diplomacy, as well as the President's tactical sense of the indirect approach. He could challenge Churchill without directly revealing his own hand.

By the time Nehru visited the United States for the first time in 1949, Johnson had finally achieved his ambition of being secretary of defense under President Harry S. Truman. Nehru accepted Johnson's invitation to spend a day and a half at his West Virginia estate, a fitting tribute to a man who seven years earlier had tried to bring about a settlement in India on terms acceptable to the nationalists.[66]

4 | From the Cripps Mission to the "Quit India" Crisis (April–August 1942)

After the collapse of the Cripps mission, the military situation continued to worsen. By the end of April 1942, the Japanese had cut the Burma road, the only remaining overland supply route to China. Thereafter only a trickle of supplies, transported by air over the dangerous Himalayan route, arrived in China. There was serious fear that loss of the overland supply route would so demoralize the Chinese forces that they would give up, thus allowing Japan to withdraw its forces from China for use elsewhere. Japan also moved a striking force of aircraft carriers and battleships into the Indian Ocean and launched raids against Ceylon. Most of what remained of the British fleet had to withdraw toward Africa. By mid May virtually all of Burma was in enemy hands. The final British withdrawal took place on May 20, and India itself seemed "wide open to attack."[1]

These events, although ominous, were of only secondary concern to the British, whose attention was focused on Hitler. They scarcely registered with the British public (although Churchill himself wanted aggressive action to retake Burma). By contrast the American public considered Japan the primary foe and followed developments in Asia and the Pacific with rapt interest. Even as late as 1943 a majority of Americans thought the war against Japan more important than the European one.[2] To Americans, India seemed more vital than ever for the war effort. If Japan could be stopped there, India could provide a base from which to supply China and begin the drive to roll back the Japanese.

While the Roosevelt administration had adopted a Europe first strategy, it feared a possible link up of Japanese and German forces in India or the Middle East and had to take into account public anger at Japan. (For example, it diverted more supplies to the Pacific than might have been justified purely on a military basis.) In addition, American officials feared that Japan, with its appeal to Asian solidarity, would succeed in transforming the war into a racial crusade. This would complicate efforts to win the war and to build a stable peace that would favor American ideological and material interests. Thus it became even more important than ever to keep China and India in the war on the Allied side.[3]

With Japan "thundering at the gates," as the *New Republic* put it, the Americans had placed great hope on a successful outcome of the Cripps negotiations, which had been followed avidly. For a time reports about the talks even "overshadowed war news, and achieved in the daily press the treatment usually reserved in more peaceful times for football scores, film stars' activities, murders and disasters."[4] An agreement in India would have several advantages. First of all, it would hopefully enlist the full cooperation of Indians in the war effort and thus secure the subcontinent to the Allies. The *New York Times*, which between March 30 and April 12 ran no fewer than five editorials on the negotiations, expressed near hysteria about the importance of India, stating that "within India after all the greatest battle of this war is taking place." The future of Asia lay in the balance. As the *Times* suggested, the importance of an Indian settlement went beyond the immediate military situation. A successful outcome could pave the way for a general settlement of the colonial issue. The *New Republic* was convinced that the negotiations might well "shape the destinies of white men as well as brown, black as well as yellow, for generations to come."[5]

Because of the perceived importance of India and the Cripps mission, Americans were in little mood, as one journal put it, to "tolerate sabotage by either side in reaching an immediate settlement."[6] American publications were particularly worried that the Indians might reject the British proposal for what seemed like insubstantial reasons. Even some journals that usually favored the nationalist cause were at pains to warn the Indians to be careful. Freda Kirchwey, editor and publisher of *The Nation*, urged them not to succumb to the temptation to take advantage of Britain's hour of desperation and hold out for concessions of minor significance. "Hesitation and delay may prove fatal," Kirchwey wrote.[7]

With the mission's failure, fear replaced hope. That India would contribute in a major way to the war was no longer certain. Indeed, relations between Indians and the British were at their lowest point in years, and there were fears of civil disorder, perhaps even civil war. Whom did the Americans blame for this distressing situation, and how did they respond?

The British thought that the Indian National Congress's rejection of Cripps's terms had resulted in a major propaganda victory in the United States. Amery, for example, wrote in May 1942, that the aftereffects of the mission were "excellent in America."[8] A British survey of American press reaction noted that "one of the chief fruits of the Cripps mission" was the "cessation of American press attacks on British policy."[9]

The British assessment was generally accurate. Given what appeared to be a genuinely desperate military situation, with Japan thought to be on the verge of invading the subcontinent, many American publications were not persuaded that the nationalists had good reasons for rejecting the proposals. Sending Cripps had been a master stroke for the British, for the Lord Privy Seal had unquestioned credentials as a long time sympathizer with the Indian cause. There was general agreement that he had negotiated in good faith. Even the *Nation* thought that the Indians had "fumbled" the opportunity presented by the proposals.[10]

The British were nevertheless nervous about American opinion, and with some reason. *The Christian Century* had never thought much of the Cripps proposals and blamed the British when the mission failed, for example. More troubling to the British, most journals of opinion concluded that the British had waited much too long to attempt a solution (the *New York Times* complained that Britain acted only when "the enemy was at India's very gates") and thus shared some responsibility for the mission's failure.[11]

Furthermore, official American opinion was much less supportive of the British. The idea that the British government had sabotaged Cripps just when he was on the brink of success—in short, the Louis Johnson version of events—persisted, in spite of a generally favorable press reaction and strenuous British efforts to down the story. Graham Spry, for example, met with this version time and time again in his discussions with American officials.[12] Wallace Murray told Bajpai that he thought that "the sinister distrust of British promises . . . was justified by the slow and grudging character of past British attitude to Indian pleas for freedom."[13] Most significantly, the President himself believed that the War Cabinet, together with Linlithgow and Halifax, had conspired to prevent any agreement. When Spry met with him personally, Roosevelt raised the Cripps Mission immediately. Discussing "American constitutional history with a rather delightful and almost boyish relish," Roosevelt reiterated his earlier suggestion that the Articles of Confederation provided a useful model for settling the Indian situation. He then asked Spry directly whether last minute instructions to Cripps had caused the mission to fail.[14]

Although Spry and other British officials denied in the most emphatic terms that the British government was in any way responsible for the failure of the Cripps mission—Spry told Roosevelt that there was "no truth whatsoever" in such contentions—they were not persuasive. Roosevelt, though glad to hear Spry's denial, gave no hint as to whether he believed him. The matter was "obviously . . . on his mind and he had raised the issue himself, very pointedly and early in the interview," Spry reported to his government.[15] Spry was right not to assume that he had persuaded the President, for the next month Roosevelt complained that the "negative results" of the Cripps mission could have been avoided if only the British had followed his advice. "The trouble with the British," he was quoted as saying, "is they don't know how to play poker. They haven't played it in India." Even more astonishing, Harry Hopkins commented that "it was a pity that Cripps' mission had been torpedoed" by the War Cabinet.[16]

The persistence of American suspicions about British intentions is a tribute to Johnson's influence. Churchill and Linlithgow dismissed him as a man with little standing. (Had not Harry Hopkins himself told the Prime Minister that Johnson carried "no special weight with

President"?)[17] But privately the British worried that they might have misjudged his influence on American policymakers and feared he could do serious harm to their cause.[18] Halifax thought Cripps himself ought to come to the United States as an "antidote" to Johnson.[19] Cripps did not come (a terrible blunder, according to one British official, who thought Roosevelt would have taken a completely different view of India if he had come),[20] but the Lord Privy Seal did deliver a radio address to the American public on July 27, 1942. Needless to say, there was no indication in Cripps's remarks that British officials might have undercut the mission.[21]

Meanwhile the Technical Mission, now headed by Henry F. Grady, which commenced while the Cripps negotiations were under way, threatened to become another source of tension between the United States and the British.[22] Sir Girja's efforts to involve the United States ever more deeply in Indian affairs was bearing fruit. There was concern that the British would object to the mission because, wanting to control the Indian markets in the postwar world, they would not welcome efforts that would make India self-sufficient during the war. But in fact both the Government of India and the British government were enthusiastic about the mission, with the former even offering to pay all of the delegation's expenses while in India.[23] Indian industrialists, on the other hand, expressed reservations. Having achieved some success in ending domination by British businesses, they feared that the United States might be positioning itself to replace the British. To them, the Technical Mission was one means of creating "vested American interests in the Indian industrial field." As Thomas Wilson put it wittily, the Indian industrialists were opposed to the exploitation of India by any business interests—except their own.[24] In addition to fearing possible American competition, many Indian industrialists sympathized with the broader nationalist movement and, in the absence of a political settlement, were not that concerned with making India's contribution to the war more effective, particularly if it would cause them any inconvenience.

That the Technical Mission could not operate in a political vacuum was immediately evident. Simply put, a poor political situation detracted from Indian's potential contribution to the war. Johnson reported that the "industrial, military, and political situation" was "much more serious that I was advised before arrival." But he was convinced that Indian war production could be dramatically increased. What was needed, he felt, was an Indian "war production board" to coordinate efforts. Highly critical of the Government of India (the Indian Civil Service was "absolutely dead and Supply Member of [Viceroy's] Executive Council does not favor any change from present peace time production"), Johnson wanted Indian industrialists to be fully represented on the board and insisted, above all, that it not be dominated by the government. He also thought it was crucial that he be involved personally in the board's formation, a suggestion not likely to be well received by Linlithgow.[25]

Grady took a less confrontational approach with the Government of India. His relations with Johnson, never good, deteriorated to the point that the two men were scarcely on speaking terms.[26] The viceroy was almost euphoric about Grady. When the governor of Bombay reported that the American had characterized Indian industrialists as "a hopeless crowd," the viceroy commented, "splendid." "!Good." When Grady allegedly indicated that conversations with Gandhi had convinced him that the mahatma's talk was "hog wash," Linlithgow wrote, "!Better still."[27]

That there were serious tensions between Johnson and Grady (which British intelligence sources had astutely discovered) is evident. The disagreements were mirrored in the Technical Mission itself. Arthur W. Herrington, president of the American Society of Automotive Engineers and a member of the mission close to Johnson, wrote to Nehru that he disagreed with his colleagues "in a good many respects."[28] But Linlithgow and Amery exaggerated the differences about what was required in India. Thus, while the Technical Mission did not go as far as Johnson wanted, it did recommend that there be some kind of a centralized authority to oversee war production, the lack of which was Johnson's major complaint.

As it became apparent that the Technical Mission would not be without criticism of the Government of India's efforts (Averell Harriman characterized the mission's preliminary report as "a severe condemnation of the lack of coordinated organization of the Indian Government"),[29] British officials, following a by now well established pattern, began to revise their views of Grady. His reputation with the

British never reached the depths that Johnson (or later William Phillips) would reach, but the euphoria was gone. Thus, while the mission's preliminary report was acknowledged to be helpful in intent, the viceroy considered it "at the same time a little woolly and amateurish in some respects, and not free from inconsistencies." Amery characterized it as "a very general document" that scarcely compared to a series of reports about India's needs prepared previously by Sir Alexander Roger. A deeper understanding of local conditions would likely demonstrate that "many things" in the report were "unrealisable."[30]

In spite of doubts about the Technical Mission's recommendation and partial disillusionment with Grady, the Government of India announced that it had "decided to implement its [the Technical Mission's] recommendations to the maximum extent possible." The need for better coordination of war production would be addressed by a new committee drawn from the Viceroy's Executive Council, to be called The War Resources Committee of the Executive Council. The committee's decisions would be binding on all authorities in India. Although Johnson's reaction to the Indian government's announcement was not recorded, it cannot have been complimentary, for the new committee was composed entirely of government officials; indeed all were members of the viceroy's Executive Council.[31]

The Technical Mission's final report, issued in August, applauded the decision to appoint a government committee to address the shortcomings that the mission had identified. But its overall tone was strongly critical. "The chief problems," wrote Frank Waring, the mission's executive officer, included "the inadequate organization of the Government and industries of India for war," congestion in the ports, an overburdened railway system, and the need to stimulate production of war materials. The Government of India and Indian industries "were not organized on a war basis. There was no single governmental official or group of officials with the responsibility of directing and coordinating the entire industrial war effort."[32]

With the issuance of the final report, pressure developed for its immediate implementation. Grady himself urged "prompt and decisive action."[33] K. C. Mahindra of the Indian Supply Mission in New York was particularly visible. An industrialist charged with obtaining supplies for India, Mahindra was actually more interested in the Indian political situation and, if not a Congress supporter, held views at variance with the British. Like Bajpai, he saw political advantages that might flow from implementing the Technical Mission's recommendations. In addition, Mahindra urged a new Presidential initiative, in which Roosevelt would offer to "examine present political conditions in India" (precisely what Grady had urged him not to do). Waring, who was also anxious to see a political settlement in India, immediately forwarded Mahindra's letter to Hopkins with his opinion that Mahindra's ideas were "sufficiently important and timely to merit your attention."[34]

No serious American objections were raised about the mission's recommendation, and all seemed poised for their implementation. On September 11 the Government of India and the American government issued a joint statement indicating that the Government of India had already implemented some of the recommendations, while others, including the sending of American experts to India, were about to be instituted.[35]

The optimism of the joint statement was premature, for less than a week later the United States Joint Chiefs of Staff recommended against implementation. Although the joint chiefs had earlier expressed their support in principle, a more detailed review had concluded that a diversion of supplies and resources to India could not be justified.[36] On October 29 Hull informed Bajpai, Mahindra, and the Government of India that demands for resources elsewhere made it impossible to implement the program.[37]

Hull's explanation revealed only part of the truth, for the decision was based on a combination of military and political assessments. On August 18, nine days after the most serious British crackdown yet on Indian nationalists had begun, Bajpai received Grady who told him that (in the words of Halifax) "failing quick restoration of order certain American military circles might use conditions as argument against proceeding with implementation of the report." Grady added that Welles too thought this was possible.[38] In October Bajpai reported more definitively that ranking American military officers opposed implementation of the report until internal conditions in India changed, presumably in the direction that the United States wanted. Possible Japanese invasion, attacks by sea, or sabotage were unacceptable risks. Berle told Bajpai that, although the State Department had not been consulted, its own reports were such that it could not argue against the decision. "He seemed reluctant to discuss the matter in detail," Bajpai added.[39]

The Technical Mission had come to naught. It had produced useful reports, and the Government of India had acted on some of its recommendations. But the hopes of Bajpai, Mahindra, and Johnson, that implementation of the recommendations would draw the United States more fully into questions about India's political future, were not realized (although the decision not to go forward was in part a political one, a way of expressing dissatisfaction with British policy in India). Nor were Grady's, who hoped to make India contribute more effectively to the war effort. Finally, the Government of India, which saw practical advantages to be gained in the way of additional supplies and advisers, was not to receive them.

While the Technical Mission conducted its investigations and prepared its reports, American diplomats were increasingly apprehensive about the political situation in India. The failure of the Cripps mission had very significantly increased tensions. Gandhi, who had previously decided not to encourage mass movements for the remainder of the war, changed his mind and began to argue that the British should leave India at once and that there should be no Allied troops, including American soldiers, on Indian soil as long as India was not free. American aid would inevitably mean American influence, perhaps on top of unwanted British influence, he contended. "It is a tremendous price to pay for the possible success of Allied arms," he wrote.[40] These positions put Gandhi at odds with Nehru who, despite the failure of the Cripps mission, wanted to assist the Allies. He encouraged sending American troops to India and even proposed resorting to guerrilla warfare in the event of a Japanese invasion.

These contrasting views were the subject of intense debate at a meeting of the Congress Working Committee in Allahabad from April 29 to May 2. Agreement was reached on a compromise resolution (drafted by Nehru) that attacked fascism, as well as imperialism, and that promised nonviolent noncooperation with any invader. Most important was the demand that Britain must leave and India must be independent. On this Gandhi and Nehru were agreed, though another of the Congress inner circle, Chakravarty Rajagopalachari, refused to support the resolution and openly complained that the policy was insufficiently strong against the Japanese. There was also criticism of the presence of American troops in India. Gandhi's original draft characterized the presence of foreign troops as "a crying shame . . . proof of the immorality that British imperialism is." And even the final, much watered down resolution complained about the danger of having foreign armies on Indian soil when so little use had been made of India's own manpower.[41]

As the Congress moved toward confrontation with the British, American opinion was a matter of concern to both sides. Gandhi seemed the least concerned. In May he told reporters that the United States should have stayed out of World War II, criticized American racial practices, and asserted that Americans were "worshipers of Mammon." In June he termed the presence of American troops in India "a bad job," characterized the United States as "a partner in Britain's guilt," and again attacked American racism.[42]

A careful reading of Gandhi's comments revealed that most objections to working with the United States would disappear the moment India achieved its freedom, particularly if the United States used its leverage to pressure the British. In June, for example, Gandhi told an American reporter that American and Allied troops could operate in India if independence was granted, the point being that decisions about India's defense would then be Indian decisions, not British ones.[43]

Other statements were more obviously intended to influence American opinion. In mid-June Gandhi addressed a lengthy letter to Chiang Kai-shek, a copy of which Nehru immediately sent to the American mission in New Delhi, in which Gandhi not only repeated his determination to resist the Japanese but also said he would allow Allied forces to use India as a base of operations. In his cover letter to the American mission Nehru called particular attention to these points. "Asia, or any other large part of the world, dominated by fascism or Nazism," he wrote, "is an intolerable thought to me, and I should like India to do her utmost to combat this." And two weeks later Gandhi wrote directly to the President repeating his position, including his offer to allow Allied troops on Indian soil to resist the Japanese. In August, shortly before the British crackdown, Gandhi addressed a statement to Americans in which he wrote that he had more foreign friends in the United States than anywhere else in the Western world, paid homage to Thoreau, complained that the British had distorted Congress positions, and again insisted that a British withdrawal would aid the war effort.[44]

At the same time, however, Gandhi continued to insist that the United States shared the guilt of imperialism because it had made common cause with England. And it was really Nehru who took the lead in trying to woo American opinion. He kept up an intensive correspondence with Louis Johnson and maintained close ties with the American mission in New Delhi. He did his best to explain that Gandhi's comments were neither pro-Japanese nor anti-American. He told Johnson that the mahatma's policy was resistance to the Japanese and denied suggestions that his writings were in any way pro-Japanese.[45] When Johnson responded that Gandhi's statements were still being interpreted as opposing Allied war aims, Nehru replied that Gandhi wanted "to do everything in his power to prevent a Japanese invasion and occupation of India." Independence, he argued, was the key to a strong Indian commitment to the Allied cause.[46] Furthermore, at Nehru's urging the Working Committee of the Congress passed a resolution at its important meeting in Wardha on July 14 which explicitly stated that the Allies could station troops in India to resist possible Japanese aggression. Although the committee also demanded the ouster of the British, the resolutions were surprisingly mild and meant to appeal to the Americans.

Nehru also responded to Sir Stafford's radio broadcast to the United States of July 27. Cripps's address had not only absolved the British of responsibility for the demise of his mission to India, it also attacked Gandhi and the Congress for endangering the British and American war effort by giving "aid and comfort" to the enemy. The broadcast was "so full of misrepresentations of the Congress attitude that I am amazed," Nehru stated. A free India, he maintained, would provide the best possible defense against external aggression and

would help China, Russia, the other Allies, and "the cause of freedom" much more than an India under British rule. Cripps, he concluded, had "injured Indo-British relations more than any other Eng-
lishman could have done."[47] Clearly Nehru thought American opinion worth cultivating. He told reporters that the United States "did
not want to exploit India in any manner," and he was privately critical of Gandhi's "insensitiveness to America." Gandhi had the heart of
most Indians, he admitted, but in the summer of 1942 he had
"ignored too much the wider international aspects."[48]

Whether American opinion could be explained solely by Gandhi's
lack of sensitivity is open to question, but there is little doubt that
public opinion continued to be nearly as critical of the nationalists as
it had been in the immediate aftermath of the collapse of the Cripps
mission. When, for example, Gandhi indicated that he would allow
Allied troops to remain in an independent India to fight the Japanese, *Newsweek* mocked the mahatma with his "gnarled walnut head"
who "graciously accorded" the United Nations "the privilege of
defending India against the Japanese."[49]

In the popular mind, the main concern was the impact the nationalist resistance to British rule would have on the war at a time when
a Japanese invasion of India still seemed certain. In May the *New York
Times* urged Americans to "deplore the kind of political pressure"
that the Congress was attempting to put on the British.[50] Time magazine summarized well the press's reaction to the nationalists at this
time. "Ever since India turned down Britain's offer of post-war independence," *Time* stated, "the U. S. press has cracked down on India's
political leaders."[51] Official British observers in the United States
confirmed the drift of newspaper opinion, one British official
reporting in July that Gandhi had "obtained an almost consistently
bad press" in recent weeks.[52]

Eventually Nehru himself became disillusioned with American
opinion. Just before the arrest of Congress leaders early in August, he
received clear indications that, despite his efforts, American opinion
still tended to condemn the nationalists for hindering the war. J. J.
Singh sent him an unvarnished account of American newspaper
opinion, and Lampton Berry confirmed that account in a letter
hand delivered to Nehru on August 4. "As far as I have been able to

ascertain," Berry wrote, "the American press comment which has appeared here represents the unanimous reaction of the American press."[53]

The Americans' attacks on the nationalist perspective angered Nehru. "There is a great deal of criticism in America," he told the All India Congress Committee on August 7. "May I, with all respect, suggest to the great people of America that they have all gone wrong in regard to India." Repeating criticism that had not appeared in his correspondence in recent years, the nationalist leader accused Americans of viewing India only as an appendage of Britain. Even those who were benevolent were tainted with a sense of racial superiority. The Americans believed the Indians were a "benighted backward people," he told the Congress. "They have always considered themselves . . . to be infinitely better than us." His earlier, critical views of the United States were on the ascendant once again.[54]

Congress leaders blamed most of their problems with American opinion on the British who, they were convinced, had a much more effective propaganda apparatus at work in the United States than they did. As Gandhi once put it, "British propaganda is so well organized in America against the Indian cause that the few friends India has there have no chance of being effectively heard."[55]

Interestingly, the British held something of a mirror image of who influenced American perceptions of Indian developments. Although their reports showed that at the moment most Americans were critical of the nationalists, the British feared, as Graham Spry put it, that in the long run "the trend of American opinion on British relations with India is towards sympathy for the more extreme and usually the Congress party points of view." Government of India officials had similar perceptions, feeling that American reporters who came to India gravitated to Congress sources and that Congress held the upper hand in American public opinion. Many who shared these views blamed the situation on their own inadequate informational activities. One report noted that British propaganda in America had improved but added condescendingly that it was still too sophisticated and "does not get down to the mental capacity of the average American citizen."[56]

With a possible civil disobedience movement and a government crackdown in the wings, Government of India officials thought it imperative to improve their publicity and propaganda in the United States. There was initial enthusiasm for a magazine containing "about 2 per cent of judiciously presented propaganda." Other ideas included making a "talkie" with Linlithgow surrounded by his Indian cabinet, with American commentator Lowell Thomas introducing the film; wooing Herbert Mathews, the *New York Times* correspondent in India; sending religious representatives to address American religious gatherings, Indian professors to American universities, Indian lawyers to the American Bar Association, Indian women to American women's clubs, and Indian Rotarians to American Rotarian meetings. "Eminent Americans" might be invited to tour India (they should be kept off the Indian trains, however, because riding the trains "would have a very bad effect on their outlook and possibly mar the whole tour!") In the end the idea of a magazine was shelved, as were other long range propaganda devices. Evelyn Wrench, the Government of India's American relations officer, was charged with increasing his contacts with American journalists, and certain unspecified short term projects were to be pursued.[57]

Officials were also concerned about the opinions of Americans who resided in India. Based on intercepted mail, government officials concluded that Americans in India were about evenly divided among pro-British, pro-Congress, and impartial sentiments, with the pro-Congress Americans having a slight preponderance. The survey of opinion did not include missionaries, however, who were, the government thought, unanimously pro-Congress. This they attributed to their "narrow" and "partial" educations and their "entirely emotional" attitudes.[58]

If missionaries publicly expressed pro-Congress views, they were liable to expulsion, or if they left temporarily, were barred from returning. For example, H. E. Buell, a Methodist, and E. A. Becker, a Presbyterian, were teachers at Christian College in Lucknow who returned to the United States in 1941. Because the Government of India was unhappy with their pacifist convictions, it refused to issue them a certificate enabling them to return without objection and in 1942 requested that British passport officials deny them travel facilities should they desire to return to India. There was similar concern with the organization of an Indian branch of the pacifist Fellowship of Reconciliation. The new branch was predominantly American, many members having "German sounding names." The government refused to allow the Fellowship to publish its newsletter. For the time being the government would do no more than watch the group carefully, but should it persist in its views the government "would be compelled to take drastic action" against the organization and individual members.[59]

Meanwhile, official American opinion was divided. Many officials criticized Gandhi's talk of mass protest designed to push the British out once and for all. (George Merrell gloated that the American mission had learned of Gandhi's plans well before the British did.) To the mission this seemed a dangerous prospect, for the ensuing chaos would make a Japanese assault more likely and in general hinder Allied war aims in Asia. Like most of the American press, American diplomats in the Indian capital were initially highly critical of Gandhi and Nehru.[60] Some State Department officials agreed. A memo from the Office of Near East Affairs, for example, noting that a Gandhi-led civil disobedience campaign would amount to an "insurrection," seemed almost to welcome the probable imprisonment of nationalist leaders. Secretary Hull himself expressed irritation with Gandhi, telling Bajpai that the mahatma was "evidently doing all in his power to play into the hands of the Japanese by preaching nonresistance and that no practical steps of resistance were being advocated by the other leaders, including Nehru."[61]

Other American officials blamed the British for the impasse. Johnson and Herrington, for example, told the State Department that if many Indians viewed Japan "in a friendly light" it was only because their distrust of the British was so deep. P. W. Bradford, the manager of the Calcutta Branch of the American Express Company, told American officials that anti-British feeling was so widespread in India because the British were apparently continuing their "stupid practice of antagonizing even those Indians whose interests tended to make them loyal." Wallace Murray, noting that Bradford's testimony supported that of Johnson and Herrington, forwarded the report to Berle, Welles, and Hull.[62] Roosevelt, too, remained critical of the British. Vice President Wallace recorded in his diary that the President had "a very profound concern about India and a definite belief that England has not handled India properly."[63] In sum, although the unfolding drama in India attracted increased American attention (in June, Hull directed the New Delhi office to send even more reports on developments there), there was no consensus on what action, if any, the United States ought to take. Perhaps, as Paul Alling put it, "we should let the Indian situation rest" for the moment.[64]

In the meantime the British were debating how to deal with the Americans. Although there was no disagreement on the need to improve their publicity and propaganda in the United States, there was no consensus over how and when to move against the nationalists or whether it was wise to prepare the United States specifically for a government crackdown which would include the arrest of nationalist leaders. Generally speaking, Government of India officials wanted an aggressive campaign to prepare the Americans for probable action against the nationalists. They were tempted to share with the Americans materials gathered in a secret police raid on the Congress headquarters in Allahabad on May 26, during which they had seized various draft documents related to the resolutions that the All Indian Congress Committee had approved in early May. Especially interesting to the authorities were Gandhi's drafts, which were more extreme than the resolutions eventually adopted. Such information, thought government officials (correctly as it turned out), would enhance anti-nationalist feelings in the United States.[65]

British officials in Washington disagreed. They warned their government that, while American opinion at the moment viewed Gandhi as unreasonable, his arrest would probably shift attention back to British repression. There still remained a strong undercurrent of feeling that the British ought to do more to solve the crisis and could not merely stand fast on the rejected Cripps proposals. Consequently they warned against any precipitate action. Even after the Working Committee's resolution of July 14 demanding a British withdrawal, Bajpai, noting that the usually friendly radio commentator Raymond Gram Swing had stated that the Cripps proposals did not go far enough, urged a cautious approach lest strong anti-British sentiments reemerge.[66]

The advice of British officials in the United States had little immediate impact. On July 13 Amery sought, and received, Churchill's permission authorizing Gandhi's arrest for interfering with the war effort. "I don't believe the effect in America would be serious," he wrote, "anyhow, nothing like as serious as the effect of hesitation and weakness." The viceroy, even more anxious to move, scribbled "O.K.!" in the margin of Amery's cable authorizing the mahatma's detention. American opinion, Linlithgow insisted, was more favorable to the government than reports from the United States indicated.[67]

Eventually, though, the cautionary advice had its effect. Linlithgow demurred from taking action against the Congress leaders until after the All India Congress Committee met on August 7 to consider ratifying the Working Committee's Quit India resolutions. Amery, too, swayed by reports of probable negative reactions in the United States, suggested that the viceroy move carefully, and flatteringly (if not quite accurately) congratulated Linlithgow on his policy of "not taking drastic action prematurely." However, he added ominously, once Gandhi "and his clique mean real mischief, the sooner you pounce on them the better." Even after the AICC ratified the resolutions on August 7, British officials in Washington continued to fear the consequences of a crackdown. To arrest the leaders on the basis of resolutions only, Bajpai wrote, would have a very detrimental impact on American opinion. Better to wait until Congress actually defied the law and hindered the war effort, he thought.[68]

In the short period of time between the Working Committee's resolutions of July 14 and the scheduled meeting of the All India Congress Committee on August 7, a last ditch diplomatic solution to the crisis involving an important American role was briefly explored. The nationalists might not go through with their civil disobedience campaign to drive the British out provided that Britain made an unequivocal promise of immediate postwar independence, and provided President Roosevelt or the United Nations guaranteed the promise. Nehru first mentioned such a possibility (though without great enthusiasm) at a press conference on July 17. Four days later Maulana Azad indicated that a United Nations guarantee of India's independence would receive "the fullest consideration." Off the record Azad was even more forthcoming. If the United Nations or Roosevelt acting on his own would guarantee a British promise of independence and arbitrate differences that would arise in the interim, Azad would guarantee "that he will get Congress to accept offer and agree beforehand to accept whatever interim plan is submitted by United Nations or President Roosevelt alone."[69]

Azad's offer created a burst of enthusiasm in the American mission. "Without actually being on the ground here, it is difficult if not impossible to appreciate how distrust and hatred of the British has developed even during the last 3 months," Merrell wrote. An "entirely new approach" of the sort Nehru and Azad had suggested was in order. The mission therefore drafted a Presidential statement guaranteeing postwar independence and offering to submit a plan for an interim government until the end of the war. "It is believed that President's declaration would be all but irresistible," Merrell thought.[70]

For a time there was considerable momentum toward a Presidential initiative along these lines. Only four days after Azad's offer, Chiang Kai-shek sent Roosevelt a long emotional telegram urging the British to take the courageous step of freeing India. (J. B. Kripalani, general secretary of the Congress from 1934 until 1946, recalled that Chiang "pleaded more earnestly than anyone else for the freedom of India.") When Chiang's ambassador in Washington delivered the letter to the State Department, he stated explicitly that China wanted the United States to help guarantee a settlement.[71]

Rather surprisingly, Sumner Welles endorsed Chiang's ideas. Objecting to the President's proposal to share Chiang's confidential telegram with Churchill, Welles suggested that American and Chinese intermediaries might be able to arrange a settlement.[72] But Roosevelt shared Chiang's letter with Churchill and asked for his comments. The Prime Minister replied immediately. He would resign, he implied, rather than go beyond the Cripps offer, and he urged the President "to dissuade Chiang Kai-shek from his completely misinformed activities."[73]

What Roosevelt's purpose was in sharing the generalissimo's confidential communication with Churchill can only be surmised. He may have wanted to remind Churchill indirectly that British policy in India worried him and that he was still unconvinced by British accounts of the reasons for the failure of the Cripps mission. At the same time, however, he seems to have concluded that Gandhi's actions did pose a threat to American hopes to use India as a base from which to supply China and eventually launch counterattacks on Japanese positions in Southeast Asia. Robert Sherwood, for example, wrote to him, "we can have no sympathy with a policy which would aid our enemies."[74] Even Eleanor Roosevelt, normally an outspoken supporter of the nationalist cause, had written in June how she "deeply deplored the refusal of the [Cripps] proposals by Congress." "My basic belief," she stated, "is that there is no chance for India's freedom or for anybody else's freedom if the Axis win the war."[75] For the time being, winning the war took precedence over other considerations.

Furthermore, despite his disagreements with Churchill over India and American complaints about British military incompetence, the President was firmly committed at this point to maintaining the Grand Alliance. That summer, for the first and only time during the war, he had overruled his military advisers who wanted to break with the British over their unwillingness to approve an invasion of Europe. And when the British suffered serious military defeats in North Africa (25,000 men were captured at the important battle of Tobruk in Libya, for example) Roosevelt responded by promising new supplies. Furthermore, his ideas on the postwar world had not solidified. As historian William Roger Louis states, "in the summer of 1942 Roosevelt preserved flexibility on the colonial issue."[76] Events in India probably contributed to the President's uncertainty.

On August 1 Roosevelt replied to Gandhi's conciliatory letter. The tone further indicated that for the moment the President was not prepared to support the nationalists against the British. The military situation worldwide was simply too threatening to permit serious breeches among the Allies. Instead he urged the mahatma to "make common cause against a common enemy" and sent him a recent address by Cordell Hull, in which the secretary suggested that those who refused to fight were almost as dangerous as those who actively took up arms against the forces of democracy. The speech, the President told Gandhi, had his "complete approval."[77]

With the war going badly almost everywhere, the President was not ready to cross swords with the Prime Minister. To Chiang he said nothing about possible American intervention or even support for

Gandhi's goals. Repeating the sentiments he had expressed to Gandhi, he stated that Indian leaders should join the fight against the Japanese. Given the feelings of the British government that the Cripps proposals were fair and their unwillingness to countenance any outside interference, intervention would only "tend to create that very crisis in India which it is your hope and my hope may yet be averted," Roosevelt wrote to the Chinese leader.[78] All of this suggests that at a moment when the British were on the defensive in various theaters, Roosevelt would not pressure them about India, particularly when Gandhi appeared to be criticizing the Americans while taking an unrealistic posture toward the Japanese. He rejected a proposal to give priority to the Pacific. "Defeat of Germany," Roosevelt wrote, "means the defeat of Japan, probably without firing a shot or losing a life."[79] Nothing more was heard about an American or United Nations guarantee of postwar independence for India.

In any event, the crisis in India that Roosevelt professed to fear was already at hand. His failure to support a guarantee or otherwise take action did nothing to prevent it.

At times Linlithgow seemed genuinely to think that the Congress leadership might distance itself from Gandhi and at the August 7 meeting of the All India Congress Committee draw back from the Quit India resolution. But other evidence indicates a desire for confrontation. Central to the confrontational thesis was the viceroy's decision to publish some of the documents obtained the previous May in the police raid on Congress headquarters. The government had used these documents to bolster its anti-Congress arguments but had not published them. Now Linlithgow weighed the advisability of releasing them just before the All India Congress Committee met on August 7. Supposedly the revelation of Gandhi's "defeatist" and "pro-Japanese" positions would erode the mahatma's support.

Possible publication of the documents appears to have been considered in a serious way only a week or so before the Congress meeting, and a number of officials thought the idea provocative. Amery himself advised against publication and suggested that the documents would be better used subsequently to help justify the crackdown. In Washington, Bajpai accepted the view that publication of the documents would damage the Congress's reputation in the United States (as indeed it did), but the British officials in Washington were aghast that no one had thought to inform the American government in advance. Frantically Ronald Campbell sought permission to advise Roosevelt and Hull of the impending action, a request the Foreign Office supported.[80] But by then it was too late. The documents were published on August 5, and the only debate remaining concerned how to explain this to the Americans.

The Foreign Office decided to have Campbell see Hull, while Attlee sent a message to the President. Noting apologetically that the Foreign Office had learned of the Government of India's decision only "at the last moment," Attlee not only justified publication as best he could but also informed the President that if the All India Congress Committee endorsed the Working Committee's resolutions, the government would arrest all individuals who were capable of organizing a mass movement.[81]

It is difficult to believe that Linlithgow actually hoped that publication of the documents would help prevent a confrontation. In fact, the action eliminated any chance of a cooperative approach. Nehru, reported to be in a "white hot rage" over the government's action, indicated that there was no choice now but to go ahead with civil disobedience. More likely the viceroy sought to goad Congress into action precisely so that he could arrest and put away his tormentors among the nationalists. Then England could fight the war without having to worry about India's political future. British authorities began arresting Indian leaders on August 9. They came for Gandhi at 5:00 a.m. Soon, over 60,000 nationalists were incarcerated.[82]

With a Japanese invasion of India still thought to be probable, another crisis was at hand in India. In the United States public opinion leaned strongly against the nationalists. In May they had rejected what many Americans considered a fair offer, extended to them by a tried and true friend of Indian nationalism, Sir Stafford Cripps. Gandhi had made a number of comments which seemed to indicate that he would not resist the Japanese and had encouraged the Congress to declare a revolution against continued British rule in India. American troops, he had indicated, were not welcome. Even Roosevelt, who did not blame the nationalists for rejecting the Cripps proposals, objected to their current campaign to throw the British out and had urged Gandhi to join the common effort to defeat fascism. Nehru had tried valiantly to counter this trend and explained that Gandhi's views had been misunderstood, but in the end he confessed his failure to alter American views and condemned them. The trend of American opinion in the summer of 1942 suggested that the British had achieved one of their major aims of sending Cripps to New Delhi.

The British were nevertheless astute in understanding that their victory in the propaganda war might be temporary. President Roosevelt and several important officials, for example, still believed that the British, not the Indians, were to blame for the failure of the Cripps mission. While the President might object to Congress's attempt to cause turmoil in India, he might well expect the British to reopen negotiations soon. Even the defenders of the British in the American press acknowledged that the British were partially to blame for the failure of the Cripps mission, and some were beginning to insist that the British could not merely stand on the Cripps proposals and refuse to negotiate further. Finally, there was, as Graham Spry and others observed, a general tendency among Americans to favor Indian freedom. For the moment irritation, even anger, at Indian actions that appeared to hinder the war effort was on the ascendant. But a change of course could bring underlying antiimperialist sentiments back with a rush.

The arrest of the nationalist leaders and the repression that soon followed posed such a possibility. The immediate reaction of American diplomats on the scene to the British action suggested that the British might be in trouble with American opinion. The crackdown only succeeded in lowering the government "still further in Indian public esteem," reported Merrell, "at a moment when constructive statesmanship is the crying need of the hour."[83]

5 | "Quit India" Arrests to the Appointment of William Phillips (August 1942–January 1943)

The August crisis threatened to change American public opinion about India. Initially, however, those newspapers and journals that had usually supported Britain continued to do so. Thus the *Christian Science Monitor* blamed Gandhi for the ensuing violence and suggested that the Indian leaders had brought on the current crisis for their own political aggrandizement. The *New York Times* contended that Gandhi was knowingly advocating anarchy and therefore deserved no toleration whatsoever. *Newsweek* complained that Gandhi was risking India even as the "Japs stand at the gates" and contended that "for the Axis, it was a field day." Influential columnist Raymond Clapper accused Gandhi of "stabbing us in the back." The *Saturday Evening Post* found the nationalist action deplorable and inscrutable. In an editorial appropriately entitled, "Does Mother India Know Best?" the *Post* found Gandhi's "mental habits" and those of other Congress leaders "mysterious." "Perhaps the only Americans who could be expected to understand them are those irreconcilables who think the way to beat Hitler is first to topple over the American Government," stated the magazine.[1]

In one of the few debates in the American Congress about India, several Senators rose to object to suggestions that India ought to be granted immediate independence. Senator George W. Norris (Ind.-

Nebraska), for example, predicted "one of the greatest Civil Wars in all history" if that were done. Even some senators who had supported India in the past, such as Senators Claude Pepper (D-Florida) and Tom Connally (D-Texas), the latter chairman of the Foreign Relations Committee, now argued that discussion of new political arrangements in India had to await the end of the war.[2]

The *Christian Century* found press coverage of events in India entirely too one-sided. "Not for a long time has the American press given as shabby a performance as in its treatment of the recent tragic developments in India," it observed. But some magazines and newspapers did support the nationalists. As might be expected, the *Christian Century* itself characterized the arrest of the nationalists as "the most serious blow struck at the four freedoms in any of the United Nations since the outbreak of the war." *Time* magazine correspondent William Fisher suggested that Britain could settle the Indian political problem if it really wanted to, and on August 24 the magazine put Nehru on its cover and made the imprisoned Indian leader the subject of a lengthy and positive story. The Raleigh, North Carolina, *News and Observer*, edited by Woodrow Wilson's secretary of the navy, Josephus Daniels, was unremitting in its criticism of the British action. And in Congress Senators Elbert Thomas (D-Utah) and Robert R. Reynolds (D-North Carolina) called for Indian independence, both on grounds of immediate military necessity and ideological consistency with the Atlantic Charter.[3]

But if the public reaction was in one sense predictable, there was nevertheless a significant shift in opinion. There was more criticism of the British for their past failures and for their unwillingness to move beyond the positions embodied in the Cripps negotiations and to reopen negotiations with the nationalists. Even the *Saturday Evening Post* thought it might have been best "if the English had departed years ago" and acknowledged that the British had acted arrogantly and should have extended more authority to the Indians during the war.[4]

The *New York Times* argued in a similar fashion. On August 11 the *Times* insisted that once the immediate crisis was over the British had to lead the people toward democracy. In the following weeks the newspaper criticized the British for whipping prisoners and argued that they needed to be magnanimous and convince the people that they intended earnestly to move toward freedom for India. Americans ought seriously to try and understand the Indians' motives, contended the *Times*, for India was very important, and Americans ought to think about India as much as they might think about Hawaii or crop reports.[5]

Further antagonizing even friendly American opinion was Prime Minister Churchill's speech in the House of Commons on September 10. Over the cries of "nonsense" from opposition MPs, the Prime Minister asserted that Congress was not in the least representative of India, that it had abandoned its nonviolent approach, and that it was probably infiltrated by Japanese fifth column elements. One book accurately characterizes the address as "a slashing attack on the Indian Congress."[6]

The speech appears to have had a significant impact on the American public generally. The *New York Times* sharply criticized Churchill's decision to stay blindly with the Cripps proposals. Americans "must view with disappointment his seeming insistence that force is the only answer to the Indian question." The *Saturday Evening Post*, previously among the strongest supporters of British action in India, now demurred. Similarly, the *San Francisco News*, which had strongly criticized Gandhi, now attacked Churchill with equal vigor.[7] British Ministry of Information personnel reported from the United States that "housewife radio comment" about India, previously sparse, had steadily increased after Churchill's speech. More ominous, previously friendly radio commentators were either silent or had turned against the British, John Hughes of the Mutual Network being a prime example. Halifax reported that the famous radio commentator Raymond Gram Swing, who normally favored the British, was "seriously disturbed" by British actions in India. American opinion, the ambassador told the Foreign Office, was "becoming very restive."[8] Within a few days of Churchill's speech, a Gallup poll showed that 43 percent of Americans favored complete independence for India, while only 17.2 percent were opposed. (The poll so irritated the British that they wondered if it might not be possible to have all polling about India suspended.)[9]

Bajpai's assessment was similar to Halifax's. Even Americans friendly to the British perspective felt that Churchill's remarks were unhelpful because they implied that there would be no further efforts to find a settlement, he reported. One British official, reading Bajpai's dispatch, minuted that American censors were no longer able or willing to keep American opinion about British rule in India under control.[10] Alec H. Joyce, the India Office's adviser on publicity, also discerned a growing belief in the United States that the British were not committed to finding a political solution.[11] Even Amery, who in parliamentary debate had repeated many of Churchill's points,[12] soon concluded that the Prime Minister's comments had been "a bad boomerang" which in the United States had "undone almost all the good work that Gandhi had previously been doing for us."[13]

Bearing out Amery's observation, the *New York Times* of October 1 offered two specific suggestions. It urged the Churchill government to establish explicitly "its firm intention to grant India the opportunity for self-government when the war is over" and pointedly observed that Churchill had not done this in his speech. Secondly, it called on the British to facilitate meetings between Hindu and Muslim leaders, including those who had been imprisoned, so that they could discuss India's future. Neither suggestion was likely to be received well in London or New Delhi. *Life* magazine addressed a full-page open letter to the "People of England" which pleaded for political concessions. The Americans were fighting for principles, the magazine stated, which the very existence of the British empire contradicted. "In order to have our own freedom we are learning that others must have freedom," stated the letter. If the British insisted on fighting for the empire, *Life* predicted that Britain would lose the war "because you will lose us." According to British historian Henry Butterfield Ryan, the open letter "was taken very seriously in London."[14]

As Americans became disenchanted with British policy there were more and more calls for American intervention to end the Indian crisis. "India is an acid test of the sincerity of America's purpose in fighting this costly war," Louis Fischer, whose career will be discussed in more detail below, wrote. Editorially, *The Nation* (which unlike Fischer criticized Gandhi as well as the British), supported Fischer's call for intervention, begging Roosevelt to mediate the Indian conflict. "It is, we believe, the last and only hope of averting a tremendous defeat," the journal's editors contended.[15] Similarly Senator Reynolds publicly urged the administration to intervene, as did the United Automobile Workers Union and the Greater New York Industrial Council, which represented 500,000 Congress of Industrial Organizations (CIO) members in New York City. The *Saturday Evening Post* did not specifically call for American intervention, but it implied as much by stating that "India is now more than a British imperial issue. The whole Allied cause is involved in her survival."[16] A number of important private citizens concurred. Clarence Poe, editor of the *Progressive Farmer*, Walter White of the National Association for the Advancement of Colored People, and prominent church leader E. Stanley Jones all urged the President to disassociate the United States from British imperialism and to intervene.[17]

After Churchill's and Amery's speeches, calls for American intervention multiplied. British analysts concluded that "most" radio commentators were now urging American mediation.[18] Of particular importance, because of the attention the British paid to them, were two articles in the *Washington Post* by columnist Ernest K. Lindley. On September 11 Lindley argued that, despite the exasperating actions of Indian leaders, the United States remained committed to self-determination. Moving ever so cautiously toward advocating American intervention, Lindley wrote that "informed observers" felt that renewed negotiations now had a chance of success but were unlikely to take place without American and Chinese intercession. Three days later, after Churchill's and Amery's uncompromising speeches had been fully reported, Lindley returned to the theme but with more force. Noting that American officials were unhappy at the speeches, Lindley predicted that the policy of repression that they advocated would result in a "harvest of bitterness even greater than that which already is visible." Contending that American policy must be based "on our immediate primary interest in winning the war," the columnist argued that the American government "would be remiss in its duty to its own people as well as to the allied cause if it did not exert its influence in behalf of the treatment of the Indian problem which will best serve to win the war." Appointment of a skilled American diplomat like William Phillips or Joseph Grew to try and bring about a settlement, Lindley thought, ought to be considered. The Lindley articles were especially troubling to British officials because they felt they were officially inspired and reflected the administration's growing irritation with British policy.[19]

Adding to the pressure for intervention was a full page advertisement in the *New York Times*, signed by fifty-seven prominent people, calling for American mediation as a way to ensure stronger Indian participation in the war effort. Several were well known leaders in the antiimperialist cause, but others, including former Republican Presidential candidate Alfred M. Landon, Henry I. Harriman, former president of the United States Chamber of Commerce, and radio commentator John Hughes were less closely identified with the cause of Indian independence.[20] The advertisement received considerable publicity in India and heartened Nehru and other imprisoned nationalist leaders.[21]

The day after the appeal appeared in the *New York Times*, the India League of America called one of its most successful rallies. More than 2,000 persons "jammed the meeting place," and police had to turn away hundreds more who wanted to attend. The crowd adopted a resolution calling on Roosevelt and Chiang Kai-shek to intervene and get talks started once again between the British and the nationalists.[22]

The *New York Times* chided those who spoke at the rally as one sided (prompting an angry reply from Pearl Buck), but the *Times* itself had already edged close to an interventionist position. Never quite asking the administration to intervene, the newspaper commented on September 23 that it was unfortunate that Indians seemed to be losing faith in the British and that the issue of Indian defense was one in which the United States had a legitimate interest. "After Burma and Malaya," the editorial stated in a telling observation, "do we need any further proof that the distrust of a native population can be a costly handicap in the defense of any Oriental area against Japanese attack?" The reports of the *Times*' own correspondent in India, Herbert L. Matthews, also provided ample grounds for intervention, as Pearl Buck pointed out in her rejoinder to the *Times*. On October 1, for example, Matthews reported that Indians with whom he had spoken had come to feel that "white men will stick

together, that the United States is interested in economic exploitation of India after the war, and that the only real friends the people
of India have are the Chinese." If India was important to the United
States for winning the war, as the *Times* believed, perhaps the time
had come for intervention. The *Saturday Evening Post* had arrived at
a similar conclusion. "We have a real interest in India," stated the
magazine's editorial after Churchill's defiant speech, "and a claim to
be admitted to British councils on this emergency."[23]

In sum, it was clear that American opinion had turned. Criticism
of Britain's India policy had abated after the Cripps mission and was
even muted in the immediate aftermath of the crackdown. But now
fears that Britain's actions might strengthen the Japanese, as well as
idealistic concerns that American support for self-determination not
be shown to be hypocritical, had resulted in what the British Ministry
of Information described at the end of September as "a new landslide
of anti-British feeling."[24]

The British followed the change in American opinion closely and
with considerable apprehension. When the United Auto Workers
passed its resolution supporting India's independence, for example,
the embassy suggested that British labor unions be asked to respond.[25]
Particularly dangerous in terms of its negative impact on American
opinion, the embassy thought, was the Indian government's use of
whipping as a form of punishment. In the United States, where whipping was thought to be "suitable only for slaves," the practice would
have "serious repercussions," Bajpai predicted.[26] Soon Amery wrote to
Linlithgow that many Americans believed the Indian authorities were
"employing methods more commonly associated with the Hun."[27]
The impact that whipping had on American opinion was significant
enough to be discussed by the War Cabinet, which issued a specific set
of instructions to Amery. Although the cabinet did express concern
about the conditions under which whipping was permitted, its primary interest was to try to prevent or at least limit the publicity attendant
on the practice.[28] The War Cabinet set the tone for future discussion
of the matter: whip if you must, but keep it quiet. "Care should be
taken to avoid publicity," Amery wrote.[29]

Rather than explain the transformation in American opinion as a
reasonable response to real events, the British Ministry of Informa-

tion asserted that the change was due to "skillful and industrious Congress propaganda" which appealed strongly to "middle-class liberal-evangelically minded provincials" who had learned about India from "protestant missionaries narrowly educated like themselves." Regrettably, such people were said to be an important factor in American politics.[30] Whatever the reasons, if the trend continued it could cause much damage to Anglo-American relations.

The new wave of American concern about India was reflected in the desire of several prominent Americans to visit India and, in some cases, to assist directly in bringing about a settlement of the crisis. Linlithgow referred to them disparaging as "peripatetic Americans." Those who caused the British particular concern in the immediate aftermath of the August crisis were Sherwood Eddy, Louis Fischer, Wendell Willkie, and Lauchlin Currie.

On August 30, 1942 Sherwood Eddy spoke with Ambassador Halifax about his hope to visit India. On the basis of the Ministry of Information's opinion about liberal evangelicals and missionaries, Eddy was immediately suspect. A committed Protestant, Eddy had lived in India from 1896 to 1911 where he was in charge of student work for the Young Men's Christian Association. Subsequently, as the Y's Secretary for Asia he remained in close touch with Indian developments; he could scarcely be described as ignorant about India (though British officials would do so). He was close to both Gandhi and Nehru but was married to an English woman, had worked with British troops during World War I, and considered himself as much pro-British as pro-Indian. Eddy confided to the British ambassador that British rule of India was "the finest instance in all history of the government of one people by another." He hoped he could bring about a settlement of the Indian problem and prepared a specific plan, which he shared with Harry Hopkins and perhaps with the President as well. Later he sent it to the viceroy. Halifax, who as viceroy in the 1920s had once entrusted Eddy with an important communication for Gandhi, found the American "very sympathetic to our difficulties" and reported that he had promised to exercise restraint if allowed to go to India. Eddy said that the ambassador also promised to send a letter of introduction to Linlithgow if Eddy could arrange transportation to the subcontinent.[31]

Linlithgow, however—never one to pay much attention to Foreign Office opinion in any event—immediately telegraphed Churchill about the "threats" of visits from Eddy (and Wendell Willkie) and urged the Prime Minister to stop them. Both Amery and Churchill tried to get the viceroy to be less intransigent. "Eddy is the kind of person who might be greatly influenced by a talk with [B. R.] Ambedkar [leader of the Untouchables] about the position of the Untouchables," Amery wrote. Churchill, noting that Eddy was reportedly friendly, told the viceroy that he always made a point of seeing such Americans "and making sure that they get a good show, and the results have always been most satisfactory." But the viceroy was not easily influenced, even by the Prime Minister. He could not welcome Eddy, he responded, because Congress leaders would use his presence as "a means of escaping from the impasse in which by their own folly and wickedness they have landed themselves."[32]

Faced with such resistance the India Office, the Foreign Office, and the Prime Minister gave in. In light of the viceroy's "deliberate opinion," Churchill ordered Anthony Eden and Amery to discourage Eddy's proposed visit. Shortly thereafter Halifax asked Hull to dissuade Eddy from visiting India, which the secretary did. While the American was "generally friendly," Halifax told the secretary of state, he was "not at all well informed."[33] But it is doubtful if anyone in the British government except Linlithgow was convinced that this was the right course. Many felt the viceroy, by refusing to cultivate important Americans, had only himself to blame for the deterioration of American opinion.[34]

Wendell Willkie posed a more difficult problem because of his importance. A liberal Democrat turned Republican because of his dislike of the New Deal, he had been the Republican candidate for President in 1940. Unlike many Republicans, he was a strong internationalist and supported the Selective Service Act and assistance to the British. Rumors of a possible Willkie visit to India surfaced late in July 1942, when it was reported that Roosevelt wanted Willkie to make a good will visit to the Middle East and Asia. In India, it was thought, Willkie would try to bring about a political settlement to encourage enthusiastic Indian participation in the war. It was precisely the kind of rumor that the sensitive ears of Linlithgow were sure to hear. Sensing that a Willkie visit would give "very direct encouragement to Congress," Linlithgow sought confirmation of the rumor and punishment for Reuters for reporting it.[35] If there was truth to the rumor, Linlithgow wanted the visit discouraged.

As with Eddy, officials in London thought that if Willkie did want to come to India it was best to receive him courteously and cultivate him in the hope of influencing him. Thus Amery replied that if Linlithgow insisted he would try and prevent Willkie from visiting, but "it might not be a bad thing" for Willkie to meet the viceroy and form "his own impressions of the situation." The Foreign Office, for its part, did not think it could reasonably stop Willkie from passing through India on his way to China, which was the normal route, if that was his intention.[36]

By mid August it appeared that Willkie would not go to India after all, much to the viceroy's relief. "Of course I fully realise that one has to handle these important Americans with great care," Linlithgow wrote, but if they asked to see Gandhi or other prisoners, he would be "badly struck."[37] Soon, however, it was reported Willkie did plan at least to pass through India on his way to China, and Linlithgow was livid when he learned the news. He was engaged daily with the "most serious rebellion since that of 1857" and did not need any more "peripatetic Americans" to bother him, he wrote to Churchill. "Their zeal in teaching us our business is in inverse ratio to their understanding of even the most elementary of the problems with which we have to deal." He hoped Halifax would ensure that Willkie and other "well meaning sentimentalists" did not come to India.[38]

Amery and Eden thought that Linlithgow was only hurting himself by resisting such visits. The War Cabinet agreed and asked Linlithgow to afford not merely "reasonable facilities" to prominent American visitors but to take "every opportunity of enabling them to obtain a better understanding of the [government's] position." To do so, the cabinet concluded, "might have an important effect on public opinion in America." The Prime Minister personally urged Linlithgow to try and "captivate" Americans who came to India and, if necessary, to try and "convert" them. He noted that he himself had had "great success" with Willkie, whom he considered a "good dining companion."[39]

In the end, Willkie did not go to India. It may be that India was omitted from the itinerary because Roosevelt, as Venkataramani and Shrivastava put it, "was loath to permit the inquisitive Willkie to take a look into Churchill's Indian cupboard." But if the viceroy had encouraged him to come, an Indian stopover could have been arranged. Instead, Willkie went to China by way of the Middle East, the Soviet Union, and Central Asia, where he learned first hand of Asian indignation at British imperialism in India. In Chungking he called for universal freedom and an end to empires and challenged the powers to make their war aims clear.[40]

When he returned to the United States Willkie reported to the American people in an address carried by all of the major radio networks. An estimated thirty-six million Americans heard him criticize imperial rule and the "wishy-washy" attitude of the American government toward India. Millions of Asians were uncertain about how the United States would deal with colonialism after the war, he asserted. "They cannot tell from our vague and vacillating talk whether or not we really do stand for freedom or what we mean by freedom."[41] Later he wrote *One World*, an influential account of his trip, which discussed the growth of nationalism in colonial areas and the need for the West to respond sympathetically.

The Prime Minister privately flailed Willkie. He reminded Churchill of "a Newfoundland dog in a small parlour, which had wiped its paws on a young lady's blouse and swept off the tea cups with its tail," a description that William Phillips, soon to take up his duties as the President's personal representative in India, who was present, thought "not bad." When Phillips later reminded Churchill of his characterization of Willkie, he said, "Oh, Lord! I hope that will never get to Willkie." But he remained angry.[42] Foreign Office officials, however, blamed Willkie's unhappy sentiments on the viceroy. His failure to welcome the American to New Delhi, where he might have heard the British side of the story first hand, was a major error of judgment, thought Nevile Butler. Instead of a more balanced view of the Indian situation, Willkie had therefore "taken his colour from Chiang Kai-shek."[43]

Willkie's attack on colonialism in fact was an important factor (and so acknowledged by Churchill himself) in forcing both the

United States and Great Britain to consider issuing a joint statement about the future of colonial areas. It was not something the Prime Minister wanted to do, and Willkie's continued outspoken sentiments about colonialism did not improve his reputation with Churchill. Shortly after Willkie wrote an article for the London *Times* that called for a clear statement of war aims, Phillips informed the President that Churchill "was bitter about Willkie" and had come to feel that he was "fundamentally hostile to Britain, and therefore a danger in the present circumstances."[44] If intellectually Churchill thought Linlithgow was short sighted in not working with Willkie, emotionally he had come to agree with his rigid viceroy.

But Amery continued to feel that the viceroy's action was self-defeating. In May 1943, after reading *One World*, Amery concluded that the American was "a very impressionable person and very susceptible to courtesy." Had he been courted earlier, he might have written a favorable account of British rule in India, the secretary thought. Perhaps even now Linlithgow ought to invite him to visit India and "help him to understand the real nature of the problem." The viceroy was unmoved. "You may take it from me that in no circumstances will I be prepared to send an invitation to him or to encourage any other American public man to come here!" he replied tartly.[45]

It will never be known, of course, whether Willkie's attitude might have been different if he had been invited to visit India and treated courteously by the viceroy. What can be said with certainty is that nationalist Indians took comfort in Willkie's words. Rajagopalachari, for example, sent a message of appreciation to Willkie through the American mission. Nehru, in prison, probably was unaware of Willkie's speeches in the fall of 1942, but he was much taken by *One World*, which he was able to read late in 1943. From his prison cell he wrote that it was "a remarkably good" book which he found "exhilarating." Willkie's willingness to risk his standing in his own party by his uncompromising statements about world freedom greatly impressed the Indian leader, and he recommended it to his daughter, Indira.[46]

Willkie's premature death in 1944 (he was fifty-two years of age) came as a shock. Nehru's always ambivalent attitudes about the United States had become more critical because of the American attitude during the Quit India movement. But Willkie's book revived his faith in the potential of the country. The American "gave us hope for the future," he wrote. "Why do good men die and the undeserving live on and on?"[47]

In 1944 a member of the Indian Council of States asked the government, during a formal debate in the legislature, whether it had "directly or indirectly" attempted to influence Roosevelt to discourage a Willkie visit to India. Although the viceroy eventually disallowed the question (and hence it was not answered), the government had prepared a response in which it would have stated that it had not discouraged Willkie from visiting.[48]

Probably the most persistently irritating of the peripatetic Americans was journalist Louis Fischer. Born into poverty in Philadelphia in 1896, Fischer was attracted to the Soviet experiment and visited the USSR often. In the 1930s he deliberately downplayed the hardships of collectivization of Soviet agriculture and Joseph Stalin's purge trials. But the trials raised his doubts, and his faith in the Soviet Union collapsed entirely in the wake of the Nazi-Soviet Nonaggression Pact of 1939. Having rejected faith in Stalin, Fischer transferred his allegiance to Gandhi and his philosophy of nonviolence. In 1950 he published an important biography of the mahatma.[49]

In the summer of 1942 Fischer spent eight weeks in India and returned to the United States only days before the crackdown with predictably strong feelings about developments there. He aggressively and repeatedly charged that Stafford Cripps had promised the nationalists a national government, only to be short circuited by Churchill, Linlithgow, and the War Cabinet. He told President Roosevelt that Gandhi wanted to be dissuaded from the launching the civil disobedience campaign. The mahatma, he reported, had tried to be conciliatory but Linlithgow was simply not interested in seeking a settlement.[50]

British officials dismissed Fischer as an "extreme leftist" and the magazine for which he wrote, *The Nation*, as of interest only to a small group of left wing intellectuals. But they nevertheless feared that he would damage their cause. After a meeting with the journalist, Halifax concluded that he would "no doubt continue to give us all the

trouble he can."[51] Halifax was right. Fischer continued to write articles, pamphlets, and books strongly critical of British rule, several of
which the Government of India attempted to ban (not always successfully.)[52] He also allegedly insulted Begum Shah Nawaz, a Government of India sympathizer, by telling her that her few weeks in the
United States "had done her country more harm . . . than anyone
else could claim to have done in an indefinite period." The Begum
reportedly was delighted with Fischer's remarks.[53]

To some officials in the Government of India, Fischer was more
than an irritant. Gilbert Laithwaite, the viceroy's secretary, characterized him as "a dangerous . . . high grade international revolutionary."[54] The head of the Home Department, parroting Laithwaite, also
thought him "a dangerous international revolutionary who is utterly
unscrupulous."[55] But the India Office was not impressed. One official characterized the Home Department's telegram as "hysterical,"
while another thought descriptions of Fischer's alleged revolutionary propensities "nonsense." Amery's reply was tart. Fischer was only
a "tiresome journalist" who trumpeted Congress's position. If any
action was required in India, it ought to be taken unobtrusively. Halifax, too, thought the allegation that Fischer was an international revolutionary was silly, though he agreed that if Fischer applied for a visa
it should be quietly denied.[56]

The fourth "peripatetic American," Lauchlin Currie, was in a
slightly different category because he was a government official. A
special assistant to the President and Roosevelt's personal representative to China, Currie found himself in India on his way back to the
United States from China just as the crackdown began in August.
While there he visited the viceroy. They did not discuss Indian politics, but (according to Linlithgow) Currie later met confidentially
with Shiva Rao (described by the viceroy as "the most insidious of our
Congress newspaper men"), who gave him a memorandum, presumably to be transmitted to the President. The viceroy considered Currie's action a betrayal of his hospitality, but Eden, Halifax, and others
considered Linlithgow's failure to discuss politics with Currie irresponsible. As Eden put it, Americans would continue to flirt with
Congress leaders "unless and until we take them into our confidence." Nevile Butler put it even more strongly. The viceroy, he

wrote, "really has largely himself to thank" if Currie returned with a one-sided view of events. A weary Linlithgow concluded, however, that the Americans were "a difficult people."[57]

Meanwhile the American government, like the public, was increasingly worried by the arrests and the subsequent disturbances. The war was a major reason. In the fall of 1942 the military situation in Asia did not appear much improved. Although we now know that the Japanese never had serious plans to move beyond Burma and that by the end of the summer their fleet had withdrawn from the Indian Ocean never to return, this was not known to the Allies. An invasion of India was still thought possible.[58] By early October the Allies had learned that the Japanese were constructing air fields and hangars in Burma capable of housing hundreds of aircraft and had begun to increase their air warfare capacity. The British were forced to postpone their attempts to move back into Burma (Operation ARAKIM). It was now scheduled for the fall or winter of 1943. Even when it became clear a few months later that the Japanese advance had stopped, Japanese forces were still dangerous for they remained in control of vast areas of Southeast Asia and the Pacific.

India's importance in winning the war had not diminished. The country remained the only base from which to ship supplies to China and would be the location from which the reconquest of Burma and parts of Southeast Asia would be launched (important in part to open a better supply route to China). For these reasons the American military presence in India was steadily increasing. In addition, as the Russian armies became engaged in severe fighting with the Germans in the southern parts of the Soviet Union, India took on significance as a potential supply route to Iran and Russia, particularly if the Russian armies were defeated. India was, in sum, ideally situated, a country from which the Allies could move east or west as the military situation demanded.

India was also important for political reasons, for the United States was determined to thwart Japan's efforts to unite Asians into a racial bloc against the West which, if successful, would prolong the war and increase the difficulties of making a peace that would serve American ideological and material interests. Finally, Roosevelt continued to want to transform colonial relationships after the war. An India in turmoil, its leaders jailed and its populace sullen, did not bode well for any of these military and political goals.[59]

From the very beginning of the August crisis the Roosevelt administration made its discomfort with Britain clear. The government pointedly asked the British if they had prepared a specific and succinct statement of "essential conditions and preparations" that needed to be met for India to achieve an independent government. It repeated its insistence that the Atlantic Charter had universal applicability and tried to get the British to agree. It inquired as to whether there was any prospect of renewed talks. After the uncompromising addresses by Churchill and Amery, Hull complained to Halifax that the situation in India was "entirely static and at a standstill" and that future British speeches about India ought to be "more moderate and sympathetic" and indicate that the British were still committed to finding a road to Indian independence once the violence of the moment ended.[60] It is also likely, as we have seen, that the decision in October not to implement the Technical Mission's recommendations reflected the administration's irritation at the unsettled political conditions in India.

On the other hand, shortly before the crackdown Roosevelt had thrown his weight against Gandhi, having decided that at a time when England's back was to the wall on several fighting fronts, Anglo-American solidarity would have to take precedence over his personal sympathies for the nationalists' objectives. Even after the arrests began he continued to feel that close ties with the British remained essential. This remained the President's view for several more weeks. In late September he wrote to Senator George Norris that the United States "must not get into a serious dispute with Great Britain. Even in relation to Indian affairs," he continued, "any handling of the matter which affected the British ability to cope with the Japanese would be bad service to India—for unless India is defended talk about independence now or later becomes pretty futile." He also continued to express his irritation with the timing of the civil disobedience campaign, which he still felt played into Japanese hands.[61] In sum, the government's response to the crisis was a cautious one. The United States, *Newsweek* predicted, "would maintain a hands-off policy," even if the British made no concessions to the Indians.[62]

However, pressures began to crowd in on the President almost immediately, to which he was not immune. Much of the public debate was aimed at enlisting his intervention, as were letters from private citizens. Additional pressure emerged from within the government. Secretary of the Interior Harold Ickes, for example, immediately urged intervention; and only two days after the arrests began Currie telegraphed the President from New Delhi to inform him that Congress supporters increasingly identified the United States with the British. Currie asserted that this perception endangered Roosevelt's "moral leadership in Asia and therefore America's ability to exert its influence for acceptable and just settlements in postwar Asia." Fearing in particular a clash between Indians and American troops, Currie hoped that the President would issue public instructions to American troops emphasizing that they were in India to support China and would not become involved in Indian politics. The President immediately adopted Currie's suggestion, thus distancing himself a bit from the British.[63]

The American mission in New Delhi also criticized the British actions in strong language. Merrell, in fact, could hardly believe that the government would arrest nationalist leaders before receiving a letter from Gandhi aimed at defusing the situation. To do so, he cabled, would "further deeply antagonize people of this country and possibly discredit Government even among moderates." When the arrests came anyway, Merrell characterized them as "hasty" and predicted that they would result in more violence.[64] Norris S. Haselton was equally critical. Four weeks after the arrests had begun he told Hull that he did not believe official casualty figures (the 300 reported killed was "absolutely ridiculous"), that the government had "no desire whatever to reach a settlement," and that the Muslims were as supportive of the civil disobedience as were the Hindus.[65]

Additional pressure to intervene came from foreign leaders. Chiang Kai-shek issued another emotional appeal for American intervention, while the President of Mexico, Avila Camacho, conveyed the deep concern of the Mexican people and himself about developments and wondered if joint American-Soviet mediation might be useful. (The forcefulness of the Mexican appeal must have been undercut, however, when Ambassador Don Francisco Castillo Nájera told Welles that he thought "Gandhi was secretly working with the Japanese.")[66]

Another important, and often overlooked, source of pressure on the American administration was certain official Indians. At considerable risk to their positions (and perhaps even their personal freedom), these Indians urged the United States to pressure the British. K. C. Mahindra of the Indian Supply Mission, for example, suggested that Roosevelt ought to "examine present political conditions in India" and get Britain to endorse his interpretation of the Atlantic Charter. Though not uncritical of the Indian nationalist leaders and their supporters among the industrialists, Mahindra blamed their inadequacies on the frustrations of living in a repressive atmosphere. Once they got to a "free table" they would act responsibly, he felt certain.[67] A further indication of Mahindra's uncomfortableness with his own government was that the next day he wrote to Louis Johnson expressing his interest in meeting him, "the sooner the better."[68]

Sir Girja's position was considerably more sensitive than Mahindra's, yet this direct representative of the Government of India made it clear to American officials that he disapproved of his government's policy. Three days after the crackdown he asked to see Berle. Appearing "obviously shaken and unhappy about the events of the past few days," he criticized British intransigence. "It was difficult to see that much could be done until their views had developed further," he told Berle. The assistant secretary, in fact, found himself offering defenses of the British position![69]

This is not to suggest that Bajpai had become an ardent nationalist. He had been very critical of Gandhi and the position of the Working Committee of Congress during the Cripps negotiations, and he was equally upset with the Quit India campaign, which included some violence. But he clearly considered the British intransigent and hoped for American intervention. His discomfort with British policy was evident when he continued in the next several weeks to press the American government to appoint a new presidential representative to India to replace Johnson, and more particularly in the reasons why he wanted a new American representative in New Delhi. Such a person, he felt, "could be of extreme importance in the situation," a conclusion with which Linlithgow would surely have disagreed. "Only in

that way," Berle reported him as saying, could the United States "have
any real data on what was going on," an indication that Bajpai had little faith in the official pronouncements of his own government. Bajpai also told Paul Alling in an amazingly frank comment that Linlithgow had been in India for so long that he was "probably more or
less out of touch with outside opinion, particularly American opinion." In fact, Bajpai confided to the American that the situation
would not be resolved as long as Linlithgow remained viceroy and
Amery secretary of state for India. As for Churchill's bellicose speech
defending the British position in India, Bajpai told Berle it was a "disastrous" address. "Sir Girja struck me as a very unhappy man," Berle
commented.[70]

By the middle of October, both Mahindra and Bajpai were profoundly discouraged. They were particularly upset at Linlithgow's
reaction to Halifax's suggestion that perhaps the time had come to
reopen negotiations. Linlithgow, in an unusual move, had responded directly to Halifax telling him to stop providing unsolicited advice
and for a change to use his talents to defend the Government of
India. Mahindra told Berle that Linlithgow's cables "would have
made your blood boil." The current British government, he was convinced, did not want to solve the Indian problem. Bajpai, meanwhile,
told Murray that he would no longer be "an apologist of British policy." If the British were stalling about approving a successor to Johnson, he said, the United States ought to ask for an end to the Indian
agency general in Washington. Sir Girja was ready to leave.[71]

Although the British were not aware of how freely Indian officials
had spoken with Americans, they knew of the mounting pressures on
the Roosevelt administration to take strong action. Aside from their
own close watch on American public opinion, Harry Hopkins told
the ambassador that there was considerable pressure both within and
without the government for the President to do something about
India. The British were most worried about the critical reports from
American diplomats in India, about which they were well informed.[72]
The British received their information about the dispatches from a
secret American source in the United States who was not in the State
Department.[73] Whatever the source, the knowledge of what American officials in India were reporting to Washington caused consider-

able concern that the administration would move toward intervention. As was so often the case, the British attacked the character of those who criticized British policy in India. In a retrospective analysis Government of India officials described Merrell as having virtually no "strength of character," while Haselton, either because he was ambitious or because he "was affected by the poisonous outpourings of the extremely hostile representatives of the American press then in India," was essentially a Congress dupe.[74]

The British worried that Roosevelt secretly welcomed the pressure to intervene, pointing to the Lindley columns in the *Washington Post* which they thought bore "signs of official inspiration."[75] But on balance they found little yet to complain of in the formal American stance. The British pinned their hopes on the President's determination to maintain close Anglo-American ties, despite tensions over India. They took particular comfort in an emotional speech that Secretary Hull delivered shortly before the British crackdown began. In addition to portraying the enemy as utterly barbaric, Hull condemned those who refused to fight as being "unworthy of liberty." After the crackdown British officials decided to "make the most" of the secretary's comments.[76]

The British could also take comfort in the Roosevelt administration's responses to Chiang's pleas for intervention. To do nothing, Chiang cabled shortly after the arrests began, would cause the United Nations forces to "lose much of their spiritual significance." As he had before, Roosevelt asked for Churchill's reaction before replying. The President doubtless enjoyed sharing Chiang's critical cable with Churchill, and the Prime Minister's response was predictable and immediate. In an angry tone he accused Chiang of being ill informed. "All Chiang's talk of Congress leaders wishing us to quit in order that they may help the Allies is eye-wash," he protested. All they wanted was power, and Gandhi, he stated incorrectly, was willing to negotiate the passage of Japanese troops through India to link up with Hitler. In a final mark of disdain, Churchill suggested that Madame Chiang was behind the message.[77]

When Chiang persisted and asked to send messages directly to imprisoned Congress leaders, Churchill was outraged. Congress did not represent India, he insisted, and Gandhi would probably allow

PACKING SLIP:
Amazon Marketplace Item: Quest for Freedom : The United States and
India's Independence--[Paperback...

Listing ID: 0204J661322
Purchased on: 09-24-2001 13:45:27
Shipped by: eyeore211@yahoo.com
Shipping address:

Ship to: Paul Teed
Address Line 1: 5824 Sturgeon Creek Pkwy
Address Line 2:
City: Midland

the Japanese to drive on through India in return for a pledge to suppress the Muslims. He concluded with a strong warning to Chiang
not to interfere in British or Indian affairs and specifically not to try
to correspond with Congress members. To do so would estrange
"powerful sections of British opinion." He added with emotion that
he would never accept Roosevelt's mediation.[78]

Churchill's strong responses to Chiang appeared to bolster the
Roosevelt administration's inclination not to intervene in Indian
affairs, or so the British concluded. Bajpai had it "on unimpeachable
authority" that the government would not yield to Chinese pressure
or to the "sentimental approach of certain liberal elements." Berle
told him that Chinese pressure only made things worse.[79] The British
were also pleased to hear from Vice President Wallace that Gandhi
was near the top of his list of "bad men," in the same category with
the likes of Benito Mussolini, Pierre Laval, and Vidkun Quisling, and
that the arrest of the nationalists was justified.[80] Wallace, it appeared,
would not pose a serious threat to British policies, at least in the short
run.

The British, however, knew that the situation could change. Thus
one Foreign Office official questioned Bajpai's assurance that the
United States would reject Chinese efforts to involve it in a mediation
attempt. Some Americans, the official observed perceptively, might
regard mediation as a way of assisting the Allies, not hindering them.
The British minister himself thought Roosevelt might be tempted to
intervene if conditions changed. In his view the crucial variant was
Roosevelt's desire "to avoid odium" in Indian eyes.[81]

As American public opinion turned against Britain, the British
considered how they might stem the tide. Several suggestions were
canvassed in the weeks following the crackdown. The British had
long emphasized the inability of the Indians to agree among themselves and of the general need to preserve order. If the British left,
they said, chaos would result.[82] After the events of August a Foreign
Office official, Basil Newton, suggested a new twist on this old theme:
Americans ought to be reminded, he wrote, of the chaos that had
befallen China when the Manchus fell. Even though such an
approach almost invited perhaps embarrassing comparisons of
British and Manchu rule, it received "thorough discussion" in the

Foreign Office, which formally recommended it to the Ministry of Information with the proviso that care be taken not to offend the Chinese.[83]

More promising was a proposal put forward by the Canadian radio commentator Leonard Brockington. Speaking in London to the Dominion high commissioners, Brockington urged the British to emphasize ideals and idealism. Americans had used idealistic language so much that at times the United States seemed the sole repository of good intentions, he stated. A related suggestion was to avoid using the word "empire," which the "abysmally ignorant" Americans misconstrued. "Commonwealth" was much preferable, and the British ought to indicate how much the they had accomplished for the British Commonwealth—more, for example, than the United States had for Latin America, despite more than fifty years of Pan-Americanism.[84]

The idea of emphasizing idealism commended itself to British leaders. Attlee asserted, for example, that "in many respects America was now preaching what statesmen in Great Britain had not only preached but practised for the last generation or more." Alexander Cadogan, permanent under secretary for foreign affairs, wrote that a favorable American view of the British empire was crucial to postwar collaboration, a major Foreign Office goal. "Unless they come generally to regard our ideas and practice in the field of the administration of backward peoples and dependent areas as no less advanced than their own," he wrote, "they may be unwilling to remain in partnership with us and other nations in the establishment of a stable world system after the war."[85]

Though presumably not privy to British discussions about idealism, Secretary of State Hull encouraged such an approach. Speaking off the record to Ambassador Halifax, Hull, who was less outspoken than some of his colleagues about the need to end colonial rule quickly, urged the British to emphasize idealism, to repeat often the country's contribution to freedom in the Commonwealth, and to indicate that it intended to do the same in India once the immediate emergency was over. The British should always combine "some note of sympathy and hope and untiring pursuit of our ideal," Hull told Halifax, even if for the moment they had to place priority on restoring order.[86]

But more than new emphases were called for. There had to be more effective propagandizing as well. Even before the August emergency Graham Spry had filed his critical report of British propaganda efforts in the United States. After the crackdown, officials had to respond. Amery, in a memorandum prepared for the War Cabinet, agreed with Spry that publicity in America needed to be improved. Though he saw no need for dramatic innovations, he urged closer coordination, and more particularly a clearer division of responsibility, between the British Information Service and the Indian Agency General.[87] The British also gave serious consideration to enlisting the active support of the dominions, especially Canada. While the British were somewhat irritated with Canada for being too cautious in its contacts with American officials, they nevertheless grudging appreciated that Canadians would sometimes get a better hearing in Washington than a British representative could, and so were generally enthusiastic about enlisting the dominions in support of British policy toward India.[88]

Indicating the seriousness with which the British government viewed American opinion was the decision to have Secretary Amery broadcast about India directly to the United States.[89] On October 20, 1942, broadcaster Edward R. Murrow interviewed the secretary of state for India. Amery fielded questions about the Atlantic Charter (contending sophistically that Churchill had not excluded India from the Charter's provisions), about the Cripps mission (he denied categorically that London had overruled Cripps), about the nature of British rule, and about the Indian contribution to the war effort.

Probably Amery's least persuasive answer came in response to Murrow's question about whether a successful conclusion of the war would result in an early solution of the Indian problem. Amery responded with the conventional British line that the issue was one of "immense complexity and difficulty" which only the British truly understood: that outside intervention ought to be avoided, that there was no clear solution in sight, and that until there was one the British were obligated to protect India from external aggression and internal chaos.[90]

Amery's performance was less than stellar. The British Information Service found only one reference to his talk in the American press or on radio, and that, in the magazine *P.M.*, accused the secretary of hedging and dodging questions about India's status. Foreign Office administrators commented that a previous speech by a different British official had been superior to Amery's efforts—"a good deal better," minuted Nevile Butler.[91]

The most important of the various British initiatives to counter the drift of American opinion about India was to encourage the appointment of a new representative in New Delhi. Thomas Wilson, the first American commissioner to India, had left shortly before Louis Johnson arrived as the President's personal representative. When Johnson returned home, both posts were vacant.[92] British intelligence soon learned that the reports of the lower ranking Americans who remained in India were often critical of the British. A new, well respected American representative in India with the proper temperament and views, and of sufficiently high standing to influence American policy, would decrease the possibility of American involvement.

The roots of British thought about American representation in India in the post-Johnson era went back to May 1942, when Halifax and the President discussed the advisability of sending an American to India to conduct an impartial investigation of conditions. Halifax thought that such an inquiry might counteract the "well-intentioned but ignorant drift of thought in intellectual circles here." Some time later he asked Hull's opinion about sending an impartial commission to India to report on conditions there.[93]

By the time of the August crisis nothing had happened, and the British began to press for new American representation in New Delhi.[94] Only three days after the crackdown Sir Girja urged the Americans expeditiously to name a replacement for Johnson.[95] Although Bajpai's reasons for wanting the appointment differed from those of his superiors, the Foreign Office also wanted an appointment made. Halifax, in a variation of his previous recommendation to dispatch an American investigatory team to India, suggested to Amery that the President send three "persons of high calibre" to India on a fact finding mission. Amery disliked the proposal and, as an alternative, the Foreign Office (Nevile Butler appears to have originated the idea) suggested sending "an American of really good calibre" to New Delhi who could "be counted on to send back to Washington reports based on information from real sources."[96]

Amery was slow to respond. Three weeks later he sought Linlithgow's views. To the viceroy he mulled over the advantages and disadvantages of having in New Delhi an American of high status "in whom both we and the President could have confidence and who would be sufficiently well-known figure to command confidence of American public." Amery, sensing how Linlithgow would react, acknowledged that "a big man" might not be willing to remain long in India and might be tempted to get involved in Indian politics. On the other hand, a person of lesser stature would not command sufficient attention from the administration. On balance the secretary supported the idea of sending a prominent American representative to New Delhi.[97]

Linlithgow quickly concurred in the need for a suitable American representative in India and professed his desire that "a man of substance" be appointed. He wanted "a Foreign Service Officer of reputation and controlled ambitions" who would spend years in India and travel extensively. Although wanting someone of "experience and quality," he was more cautious than the secretary. He did not want a person of really high standing, he stated, lest the appointee be discontented with a posting to New Delhi, and he adamantly opposed a non-career person.[98]

After sending his telegram to Secretary Amery, the viceroy read two recent dispatches from Halifax and Bajpai, both of whom reported a serious deterioration in the state of American opinion, official as well as unofficial, about India. Both pointed to Lindley's columns, which criticized the British government's apparent lack of interest in finding a solution to India's political problems. Lindley also suggested sending a high ranking American to India to mediate, and he specifically mentioned Joseph Grew, the former ambassador to Japan, and William Phillips, a former ambassador to Italy.[99]

Linlithgow, still smarting from the Johnson mission, bristled at the thought of allowing any foreign mediation of the Indian question. Although he still professed to want a new American representative, the Lindley piece strengthened his determination not to receive a representative "of really high standing," and he objected specifically to both Grew and Phillips. Nothing could be worse, he telegraphed Amery the same day, than to send to India "the type of American representative discussed by Halifax and Bajpai." Instead, the government should "stand firm . . . and take what may come to us if we do." Three days later Linlithgow was still fuming. In a lengthy letter to Amery he lashed out at the diplomats for their tendency "to think that the Americans are invariably right" while the Government of India was "invariably wrong."[100]

The viceroy's unwillingness to make new initiatives to break the Indian deadlock, his obvious irritation with Halifax and the Foreign Office, and his lukewarm responses to proposals to replace Johnson, led Bajpai (who was increasingly disgusted with his own government) to fear that the British did not want the vacancy filled.[101] But on this point the agent general was mistaken. The Foreign Office was especially anxious to see the position filled, and even Linlithgow, despite his anger at the thought of American mediation, had given his approval to the appointment of the right kind of American. At the end of September, therefore, Eden was able to inform Halifax that the British wanted the vacant commissionership filled as soon as possible. Britain should press the initiative, Eden urged, so that British ideas of the kind of representative would be considered. Despite Linlithgow's reservations, the British government wanted "someone of substance . . . a Foreign Service officer of high standing" who had the President's confidence, who would remain in India for the duration of the war, and who would travel extensively throughout the subcontinent. A mediator, however, would not be acceptable. On October 2 Halifax informed the State Department that the British wanted the position filled as soon as possible, and Welles responded that he was submitting the names of Grew and Phillips for the President's consideration.[102]

Although Halifax and the Foreign Office welcomed this news, it was apparent that Linlithgow was not yet reconciled to a representative of the stature of Grew or Phillips. "Someone of level of Wilson would suit me perfectly well, and be all we really need," he wrote to Amery. When he learned that Grew and Phillips had been nominated, he complained that Halifax had moved too quickly. The problem with former ambassadors, he asserted in a telling comment, was that they would expect results.[103]

The British government responded to the viceroy's position in two ways. Amery urged him to accept either Phillips or Grew. Though someone like Wilson could carry on the day to day work, someone of more stature was needed to have the ear of the President. Both Grew and Phillips were "level-headed, disinterested and experienced men, the best type of American gentlemen." At the end of distinguished careers, they would not advocate policy out of personal ambition. They were, in fact, the best hope the British had "of keeping U.S. Government straight regarding India." At the same time Eden instructed Halifax not to commit himself to either Grew or Phillips until the viceroy had agreed. And in a further effort to placate Linlithgow, Eden ordered the ambassador to press the State Department again on the question of mediation. Linlithgow soon gave in, all the while complaining that he was forced to do so because developments had proceeded too quickly in Washington. How unfortunate, he added wistfully, that they had not been able to secure someone like Cornelius Van H. Engert, the notoriously pro-British American minister in Kabul, Afghanistan.[104]

As between Grew and Phillips, the British expressed a slight but nevertheless distinct preference for Grew. Campbell claimed that Phillips had a certain suspiciousness of British intentions that came from being a New Englander, while a Foreign Office official, who knew both Americans, commented mysteriously that Phillips was "not altogether friendly just now."[105] Having pressured the State Department to name a person of the sort represented by Grew and Phillips, however, the British could not press this preference strongly. Instead, they noted that Grew would be especially good and that they would hate to lose Phillips from his current assignment in London. But on November 14 Secretary Hull informed Halifax that the President had selected Phillips and that he would soon leave for India.[106]

If the British had not gotten their very first choice, they were nevertheless pleased that Phillips had been chosen. Only Linlithgow was less than enthusiastic, and the Foreign Office set out to convince him. Enlisting the aid of three British diplomats who were acquainted with Phillips, the Foreign Office asked them to write a letter about the American that would be sent to India.[107] The result was an effusive letter from the Earl of Perth, who had known Phillips since 1917 and had been posted with him in Rome in the 1930s. "I can hardly conceive a better appointment or one which is likely to be more helpful to our cause in India," he wrote. "The Viceroy can tell him all his troubles and need not be afraid that Phillips will ever be indiscreet." Halifax told Linlithgow bluntly that he was lucky to get Phillips, "an extremely good man." Amery, too, after visiting with Phillips, gave the American high marks. And in the end Linlithgow at least acknowledged that he was encouraged by the reports he had received about Phillips.[108]

Although the initiative for the appointment came mostly from the British, the State Department and the President were open to making an appointment at the appropriate time. Consistent with his cautious approach to India after the August crisis, Roosevelt did not make up his mind until the very end of October. Even then he did not inform Phillips until November 4 and delayed telling the British for ten more days.[109] The President had responded to the cumulative effect of pressure from public and journalistic opinion, members of his own government, the Chinese, and disaffected official Indians in the United States who wanted a more forceful role in India. He also had to respond to Willkie's criticism of the administration's "wishy-washy" attitude about India.[110] It also seems clear that despite his desire for close Anglo-American relations, the President, like the State Department and the public generally, found Churchill's intransigence unhelpful in the context of the war and unacceptable for his postwar hopes to end traditional colonialism. Thus on October 27, the day after Willkie's critical radio address, Roosevelt reaffirmed that the Atlantic Charter "applies to all humanity" and took the unusual step of allowing himself to be quoted directly. This was a significant change from the previous summer when, on the first anniversary of the charter he had deliberately avoided pressing his views that the document had universal applicability.[111] But the most important factor was that the British government itself wanted the position filled, if for quite different reasons.

At first glance the selection of Phillips is puzzling. Although not as ignorant of Indian matters as Sumner Welles thought ("Mr. Phillips has not the slightest familiarity with the Indian picture," he once wrote Hull), he was not an authority on South Asian matters. The President's request, Phillips wrote at the time, came like a bomb striking London. "I am amazed and dumbfounded by the suggestion that I try to solve India's problems," he wrote.[112] Previous accounts have speculated that Roosevelt chose Phillips because his status as a distinguished American statesman would demonstrate that India now commanded American attention, and there is no doubt that Phillips brought considerable prestige to the position. He was, in fact, one of the most respected and influential diplomats of his time, having twice served as undersecretary of state (1922–24 and 1933–36), and as ambassador to Belgium, Canada, and Italy, the last during the tumultuous rule of Benito Mussolini.[113]

More significantly, Phillips, along with his close friend Joseph Grew and a few other like-minded men, had converted the foreign service during the previous decades from a mostly amateurish operation into a professional career service staffed by a talented, elite corps of experts. Having come into the diplomatic corps at a time when Theodore Roosevelt was inspiring young men of means to enter the government, Phillips signed on in 1903 as an unpaid private secretary to Joseph Choate, then ambassador to Great Britain. In 1907 he joined the State Department, where he stimulated the creation of the Division of Far Eastern Affairs, the first geographical bureau in the department, and proceeded to improve the consular service in China.[114] Always insistent that diplomacy was too important to be left to amateurs and politicians, Phillips as undersecretary in Franklin Roosevelt's administration tried to guard the service from the President's inclination to appoint deserving Democrats to important diplomatic posts.[115]

Although Phillips never fully trusted Roosevelt, he was good friends with the President. Coming from similar aristocratic backgrounds, the two men had known each other for nearly thirty years. Caroline Phillips had known Eleanor and Franklin even longer and was one of the few persons who addressed letters to the President as "Dear Franklin."[116] Presumably because of Phillips's distinguished career, his close personal relationship with the President, and his reputation as a cautious diplomat who would carry out his responsibilities with tact, Wallace Murray, George Merrell, and Cordell Hull all apparently mentioned him as an ideal person to go to India even before the August crisis.[117]

Phillips's background also fit the Foreign Office's requirements almost to a tee. As professionals, Phillips and his associates looked to the European diplomatic establishments as the ideal models. They "steeped themselves in the cosmopolitan culture of the European courts," writes one authority.[118] Muckraking journalist Drew Pearson was convinced that they "held the British Foreign Office in reverence about as if it were the Deity."[119] Assistant Secretary of State Breckinridge Long characterized Phillips personally as "always an Anglophile—of marked degree." His great desire in life, according to Long, was to become ambassador to Great Britain.[120]

Moreover, the careerists' attitudes resembled those of "tory aristocrats." They disdained the masses ("the occasional necessity for mingling with the proletariat," observed historian Martin Weil, "aroused sheer revulsion") and were horrified at the Bolshevik revolution with its assaults on the old-fashioned decencies, which they embodied. As undersecretary, Phillips had fiercely resisted Roosevelt's move to recognize the Soviet Union, and when the President persisted he attempted to stiffen the conditions for recognition. Caroline Phillips considered any diplomatic dealing with the Communist regime to be morally reprehensible.[121]

Finally, the State Department was racially arrogant. Most foreign service officers had "little respect for members of those races customarily dismissed by Anglo-Saxons as inferior." Blacks who managed to get into the service were immediately shipped out to Liberia. Journalist I. F. Stone even thought the diplomats had "strong leanings toward fascism," and indeed Sherwood Eddy asserted that Phillips had "leaned towards Ciano and Mussolini in Italy."[122]

In sum, someone less likely than William Phillips to sympathize with the Indian nationalist leaders, much less with the masses, could scarcely be imagined. Phillips himself was certain that the British played a vital role in his appointment because he "had been sympathetic with the British and had many contacts in England. I dare say," he told an interviewer in 1951, "they felt that because of this I would take the British side of the Indian problems."[123]

That was certainly the perception at the time. Eddy predicted that

Phillips would incline "heavily towards Churchill and the Viceroy" and would "never lean toward Gandhi, Nehru, or India." And some American liberals, while pleased that Roosevelt was again engaged with India, viewed Phillips's appointment with alarm. "Why does Roosevelt intrust to a typical diplomatic stuffed-shirt like Phillips the delicate job of representing our position in India?" asked the editor of *The Nation*, Freda Kirchwey? I. F. Stone recalled that "we were appalled" about the Phillips appointment. Stone expected the British to "take him into camp. He is not the kind of person one expects to get too far away from the better clubs." On the other hand, Britain's supporters in the United States were pleased. "Nothing could be more helpful for giving our British friends the assurance that we shall do no undue meddling there," one of Roosevelt's friends wrote commending the President's decision to appoint Phillips. "It was another inspiration."[124] Such people were correct about British perceptions but wrong about Phillips's independence of mind and probably about Roosevelt's ultimate intentions.

With Roosevelt's decision to appoint Phillips, the only issue unresolved concerned his rank. From the start the British had assumed that the new representative would be the American commissioner in New Delhi. They did not want another personal representative of the President, partly because of the unhappy memories of the previous personal representative, and partly because the title implied a short term appointment. Furthermore, Phillips's status entitled him to the rank of ambassador, and Linlithgow, who was already reluctant to accept another Presidential personal representative, was not about to have an American ambassador accredited to his government. Among his concerns was a fear that increasing the status of the American representative in India would create pressure, encouraged by Bajpai and Halifax, to raise the status of the Indian agency general in Washington. To prevent the appointment of an ambassador to New Delhi, the viceroy was willing to appeal to Churchill if necessary.[125]

Initially the Americans seemed willing to accommodate the British. Sumner Welles suggested that Phillips be designated the "United States Commissioner with personal rank of Ambassador." Whereas Johnson had absolutely refused to accept the title of commissioner because it was not sufficiently dignified, there is no evidence that Phillips protested. But State Department officials soon came to realize that commissioners had to be confirmed by the Senate, while personal representatives did not. Senate confirmation would delay Phillips's appointment and could result in embarrassing questions in the Senate which both the administration and the British wanted to avoid. Furthermore Murray persuasively argued that William Phillips was not Louis Johnson, and that just because Johnson had the title personal representative was insufficient grounds to deny the same designation to Phillips.[126]

The time had come to retreat. "I doubt whether we can do better than what is now proposed without seeming to reflect on Mr. Phillips and good intentions of the President," Halifax cabled. Linlithgow reluctantly agreed to receive Phillips as the President's personal representative and even agreed to have him hold the *personal* rank of ambassador, as long as it was made clear that the rank was based on his past service.[127] Although Linlithgow continued to feel that the rank was important (he would continue to express irritation at the tendency of the British Information Service to refer to Phillips as ambassador to India), his main concern was to be assured that Phillips would not try to mediate the Indian dispute.

The arrest of the Indian nationalist leaders, then, had resulted in a deterioration of Anglo-American relations. There was a clear change in American attitudes, as indignation at British intransigence replaced previous anger at the nationalists' rejection of the Cripps proposals. A feeling grew that renewed American intervention in India was required to resolve the impasse, both to improve the military situation and to ensure that American ideological objectives for the postwar world would be achieved. At first the President, devoted to close Anglo-American relations at a time when the British were on the defensive in many theatres, resisted calls for a change in policy. But many within the administration pressed for a more active role, as did the disaffected Indian officials and important public figures like Wendell Willkie.

The British government did what it could to counter the growing pressures on the administration to change its policy. Its most important tactic was to ask that a new American representative of high standing be sent to India who would, hopefully, come to appreciate the complexity of the Indian situation and take the British perspective of events there. By the end of October the President had decided to send William Phillips. The Phillips appointment generally pleased the British, but they wanted firm assurances that he would not try to mediate the Indian dispute. Although the British embassy exerted all of its influence to commit the United States government to a noninterventionist posture prior to Phillips's departure for India, it was not successful. The extent to which the President and his new personal representative would remain aloof from Indian politics remained to be seen.

6 | William Phillips's Mission to India (January–June 1943)

By the time William Phillips left London for India in December 1942, the Allied war effort was beginning to show significant results. On November 2 the British scored a major victory over the German forces in North Africa at El Alamein, and Field Marshall Erwin Rommel was in retreat. Also in November General Dwight D. Eisenhower landed in North Africa, occupied Morocco and Algeria, and advanced into Tunisia. The heroic Russian forces finally outlasted the Germans at Stalingrad, virtually annihilating an entire German army in the process, and were beginning a counteroffensive. In the Pacific the Americans, aided by Australians and New Zealanders, had stopped the Japanese advance. American forces landed on Guadalcanal in June, and after a fierce six-month-long battle took possession of the island in January 1943. A similar Allied victory took place in Papua. "Everywhere," states the official British history of the Pacific war, "the Allies' star was in the ascendant."[1]

Progress in the India-Burma theatre, however, was still negligible. Particularly disheartening was the complete failure of the Arakan campaign, the first British attempt to retake portions of Burma, most notably the coastal city of Akyab. Begun in September, the campaign encountered strong Japanese resistance and faltered well short of its goal. In February 1943, the Japanese began a counteroffensive, which ended in May in a complete rout of the British. Partially off-setting the humiliating Arakan campaign were the remarkable Chindit incursions into Burma early in 1943. Though without much strategic or immediate military value, these long-range penetration operations demonstrated that it was possible to infiltrate forces deep into occupied Burma. Their successes built up morale and provided experience that would be valuable later on.[2] Also on the positive side, some one hundred new airfields had been completed in India, with 120 more under construction. In December the Americans began construction of the Ledo Road to China, meant to replace the Burma Road that was now under Japan's control. Most heartening of all, by January 1943, the Allies had concluded that Japanese forces in Burma were on the defensive. An invasion of India was now thought to be unlikely.

How all of these developments might affect American policy toward India was not yet clear. In a military sense, India had been considered important partly because it was to serve as the base from which the Allies would advance into Burma and Southeast Asia. As it began to appear that victory over Japan would come via the Pacific, India lost some of its military significance. Even the British began to talk of bypassing Burma with its difficult fighting terrain. But India remained important as a base from which to supply China. Well into 1944 the Americans continued to consider China of considerable importance and put heroic efforts into building the Ledo road to supply Chiang Kai-shek. In sum, India continued to be important militarily, but its significance was beginning to fade. This reality tended to make the British less vulnerable to outside pressure over their India policy. As *Newsweek* put it in February 1943, "support in the form of enlistments and war production did not mean as much to the British as it would have meant last spring or summer." These developments weakened Congress's leverage, since it was more difficult to argue that popular support for the war in India was central to victory.[3]

Even if China and India lost some of their military value, they retained considerable political significance in American eyes. The Japanese had appealed to Asian racial unity, and the United States still feared the impact of such an appeal, partly for military reasons, but increasingly for reasons having to do with the shape of the post-war world. *New York Times* correspondent Herbert Matthews was not entirely correct when he asserted that ultimately nothing mattered to the British or American governments except winning the war.[4] Americans wanted the promises of the Atlantic Charter realized and were increasingly insisting that specific dates be set for colonial independence. Some Americans also saw economic advantages in a postwar Asia free of European control. Roosevelt's own critical views of European imperialism hardened early in 1943 after he viewed first hand British and French colonies in Africa. At the Casablanca conference in January he made clear his sympathy with colonial demands for independence. During that year he spoke out strongly against allowing the French to return to Indochina, and at the Cairo and Teheran summit conferences in November the President lined up Chiang and Stalin against the British on the colonial issue.[5]

To counter the Japanese appeals to racial unity and demonstrate the American commitment to Asian independence, it was very important to keep China and India in the war on the Allied side. Keeping China in the war was "the best insurance that the present war does not become a race war," wrote one State Department official. The same could have been said of India which, in any event, continued to be important as a base from which to supply China. From this perspective, the American tie to England was a liability, since Churchill had shown no indication that he anticipated changes in imperial arrangements. Indeed, after the British victory at El Alamein the Prime Minister became even more insistent about retaining British colonies, which only convinced the United States Joint Chiefs of Staff that Britain's military strategy of attacks on the periphery were intended primarily to retain the empire.[6] Some Americans even thought it best to discourage British participation in the war against Japan, lest the United States be tainted by perceptions that it was part of an imperialist alliance. The same reasoning could also apply to American policy toward India. Perhaps the United States should clearly disassociate itself from the British there.[7]

There was as yet no clear American policy, however. It was not even entirely certain what Roosevelt had in mind in sending Phillips to India. With the military situation improving, perhaps the President, thinking ahead to the postwar shape of the world, intended to use Phillips, as he had Johnson, to intervene in the Indian political situation and pressure the British to reopen talks with the nationalist leaders whom they had jailed. On the other hand, with India losing some of its military significance and with public interest about India declining in 1943, perhaps the President would be inclined to defer to the British there. If so, then Phillips was sent mostly because the British wanted him in New Delhi to observe events and, hopefully, come to understand Indian complexities and take a sympathetic view of British difficulties there. Perhaps also he was sent merely to assuage American public opinion.[8] What is most likely is that Roosevelt expected Phillips to make recommendations on how to resolve the Indian political situation but was for the moment keeping his options open on what actions, if any, to take.

Initially it looked as if the President was deferring to the British, for he refused to allow his new personal representative, who was in London, to return to the United States for consultations before proceeding to India. Roosevelt's refusal baffled Phillips, who very much wanted to come to Washington to gain a fuller understanding of Indian developments and American policy toward the subcontinent. State Department officials, too, wanted him to return, but to their "great regret," as Murray put it, Roosevelt asked Phillips to proceed directly to India. If he was not to return to Washington, at the very least the ambassador desired expert assistance and asked if academic advisers on India might accompany him because the Indian situation was "so filled with dynamite." But the President remained unmoved. When Phillips went to India he was accompanied not by university experts but by Major Richard P. Heppner of the OSS office in London and "an incompetent sergeant whom army headquarters in London had foisted off on me as a secretary." Heppner, as it developed, was a great help to Phillips, "a most agreeable and efficient companion" and "a splendid representative of America." But he was not an authority on India.[9]

Why Roosevelt refused to allow Phillips to return to the United States or take advisers with him remains unclear. India's lessening importance militarily, Churchill's adamant feelings about India, and perhaps also a residual feeling that Gandhi was hurting the Allied cause, might account for the President's decision. If Phillips returned to Washington, Roosevelt knew he would be exposed to the pro-nationalist views of some State Department officials, Louis Johnson, influential private citizens, and organized pressure groups such as J. J. Singh's India League of America. In any event, the decision to proceed directly to India further alleviated British concerns and reinforced their hopes that Phillips would not turn out to be another Louis Johnson. When officials in the British embassy learned that Phillips would soon be proceeding to New Delhi, they were delighted. They wanted a good American "rapporteur in India as soon as possible."[10]

On the other hand, there is evidence that the President ultimately expected Phillips to do more than observe and report. When Phillips first learned informally of his appointment, he assumed he would have a very activist role, for he was almost overwhelmed at the thought "that I try to solve India's problems."[11] Communications from Washington were not at first very explicit about his responsibilities, however, suggesting that Roosevelt was keeping his options open. Hull's cable informing Phillips of the President's desire to appoint him characterized the assignment as profoundly important, but it gave him no clear guidance. In his reply Phillips said he would try hard to carry out the President's purposes, but he asked the State Department and the President for additional information about "the scope of the duties they expect from me."[12] Having heard nothing a week later he still assumed that he was "to unravel problems in India."[13]

Finally on November 20, 1942, Hull responded to Phillips's request with a lengthy but ambiguous telegram. The United States favored "freedom for all dependent peoples at the earliest date practicable," he wrote. American actions in the Philippines provided the best model. At the same time the administration had not taken sides in the struggle between the British and the Indians and wanted to remain friends with both. Therefore, the United States could not pressure the British. But Phillips could "in a friendly spirit talk bluntly and earnestly" to British officials about India. Such an approach might result in a settlement, Hull went on, thus giving the impression that Phillips was free to pursue a settlement so long as he refrained from "objectionable pressure." Indeed, he was specifically urged to "encourage both sides or either side" toward "a practical settlement."[14]

Although ambiguous, Hull's instructions were significantly different from what the British wanted. They gave Phillips leeway to pursue a settlement and make recommendations to each side, an impression that must have been reinforced by Hull's enclosure of a memorandum he had submitted to the President for applying and implementing the promises of the Atlantic Charter. Perhaps after all the President was again willing to countenance some pressure on the British.[15]

Further evidence that the President intended Phillips to play an active role in Indian politics was the British failure, despite strenuous efforts, to get commitments in advance that would restrict the scope of Phillips's activities. About November 18 Campbell asked the State Department to include in its public announcement of Phillips's appointment a specific disclaimer of any intention to conduct negotiations. "What is really required," wrote Nevile Butler, "is that . . . the U. S. authorities should make it perfectly clear to their own press when the appointment is announced that Mr. Phillips is not being sent in any mediatory capacity." Welles declined to do this (although according to Halifax he pledged to clarify the matter if "undesirable speculation" developed).[16]

Welles's refusal worried the Foreign Office. Considering the matter "urgent," Foreign Secretary Anthony Eden hoped that the President could be persuaded to deny publicly that there would be any interference in the Indian problem. After further discussions the United States and the British agreed on December 10 that a question would be planted at Secretary Hull's press conference. A reporter would ask if Phillips would be carrying to India "a special plan or formula for the solution of the Indian problem," to which the response would be that there was "absolutely no truth in such rumors." The plan was carried out the next day, except that it was the President himself who stated that Phillips was not carrying any special plans to settle the Indian problem.[17]

Although the British had agreed to this public announcement of Phillips's duties, they could not have been entirely pleased, for the statement did not indicate that Phillips would not at some point make suggestions, urge intervention, or offer to mediate. The Foreign Office decided not to press the matter further, however, but to hope for the best. "As we have had to give the President and State Department a good deal of trouble on this matter," Eden wrote to Halifax, "I should be glad if you would convey in general terms our thanks for their helpfulness."[18]

Meanwhile, Phillips approached his mission with great seriousness and almost as much vigor as his younger predecessor. In the weeks remaining before his departure, Phillips, although not allowed to return to Washington, was determined to learn as much about India as he could by speaking with a large number of persons in England of various views. "I need not assure you how eagerly I am looking forward to my new assignment," he wrote to Berle.[19]

Phillips quickly met with the highest British officials who had Indian responsibilities. He saw Amery and Eden at least twice and met with the Prime Minister on three occasions, once for more than two hours. All defended Britain's India policy and blamed the Indians for their failure to overcome their own profound differences. Churchill, as might be expected, spoke glowingly about British accomplishments in India, insisted that there would be no change in the form of government during the war, and evidenced a certain amount of irritation over the treatment of India in the American press. Phillips found Eden "astonishingly friendly." The foreign minister confided to him the name of the next viceroy (a closely guarded secret) and, when they had finished talking, personally saw Phillips to the stairs. "Nothing could have been more personal and in a way intimate," he wrote. "Naturally I fell for it."[20] Phillips also met with private citizens, including anti-Congress Indians and one maharaja, who generally took the British line.

Despite the courtesies, Phillips and British officials spoke from different assumptions and remembered the conversations in slightly but significantly different ways. The British assumed that Phillips understood that he would not attempt to mediate or intervene. Phillips doubtless encouraged them when he told reporters that he was going to India to keep Washington "advised on Indian affairs" and to coordinate the activities of American civilian agencies operating in India.[21] But in fact Phillips expected to be involved to some degree in finding a solution to India's problems. Phillips's interviews with Amery illustrate the different perspectives well.

Phillips first called on Amery on November 24, and for an hour the two men reviewed Indian developments. In his account of the meeting, Amery wrote that he emphasized the viceroy's fear of American mediation. Phillips, he stated, "emphatically disclaimed" any intention of mediating. Although Amery had objected to mediation, he did suggest that Phillips might explain to the Indians how the American Federalists had overcome their divisions to devise the Constitution and that he might try to get the Indians to come together in a similar fashion. He also said the there would be no objection to the American "meeting any and everybody in the ordinary course," though he probably would not meet Congress leaders in the immediate future. Phillips, he wrote, "said that he had no desire" to meet them.[22]

Phillips's account, by contrast, envisioned a more activist role for himself. He claimed that he pointed out to Amery "the new and vivid interest" of the United States in India. "Anything I could do to help the British solve the problem would be one of the principal objects of my Mission," he told the secretary, which strongly suggested something more than a passive posture. Furthermore, in marked contrast to Amery's account, Phillips's record mentioned nothing at all about the British government's central concern: that he not attempt to mediate. On the question of whom he might meet, Phillips's account, like Amery's, indicated that he would be "free to come in touch with anyone whom I desire to meet," but his account did not confirm Amery's assertion that Phillips had expressed no interest in seeing Congress leaders. Phillips told the President, in fact, that Amery "encouraged me to do everything I can" to get the Indian leaders to come together for discussions.[23]

From his conversations, Phillips also discerned that not all Britons agreed with Churchill's intentions to retain the empire unchanged. Even within the British establishment, Phillips found important distinctions. Amery for example admitted that Churchill was "very emotional on the subject [of India], sometimes harking back to his subaltern days."[24] Phillips quickly learned that the viceroy was a controversial figure. Sir Eric Miéville, the King's private secretary, who had spent five and one-half years as secretary to a former viceroy, made disparaging comments about Linlithgow.[25] Cripps called the viceroy "impossible" and confided that he had begged Churchill to recall him. Lady Willingdon, widow of Lord Willingdon who had succeeded Halifax as viceroy in 1931 (he served until 1936), was similarly critical of Linlithgow. In order to gain the confidence of the Indians, she told Phillips, it was necessary to gain both their respect and their love. Due to his "stiffness and formality" Linlithgow had not gone beyond gaining respect.[26]

Phillips also conferred with Sir Ramaswami Mudaliar, the Indian representative on the British War Council, who was about to leave for Canada to attend a meeting of the Institute of Pacific Relations where he was expected to (and did) counter the arguments of pro-Congress forces. But Mudaliar was nevertheless critical of the Government of India, complaining that there was no reason why all the major posts in the government were in the hands of Englishmen. The viceroy's Executive Council, he argued, should be entirely Indianized. He also wanted a guaranteed promise of independence at the end of the war.[27]

A potentially damaging interview with a government official occurred when Phillips met with H. V. Hodson, who had just resigned as reforms commissioner in the Government of India to become minister of production in the British government. Hodson had had a falling out with the viceroy, and government officials feared what he might say. However, Hodson seems to have said nothing with which the government would have disagreed; he offered strongly negative assessments of Gandhi and Nehru, for example. Of all the people to whom Phillips spoke, the American found Hodson the best informed on constitutional issues.[28]

British officials must also have been nervous about what Stafford Cripps might say to Phillips. In the event Cripps presented to the ambassador a confidential proposal that involved calling a conference under the auspices of the International Labor Organization to deal with the Indian question. Only Roosevelt could bring this about, Cripps told Phillips. This was not a plan the current government would readily endorse, and there was no point in even discussing it with Amery, Cripps said.[29]

Phillips also spoke to nongovernmental Britons and Indians of various political persuasions. Indeed, he sought out conflicting opinions. Soon after receiving his notice of appointment, for example, Phillips attended a three hour roundtable discussion at the Charing Cross Hotel with nine prominent Englishmen, most of them in the Indian Civil Service or with business interests in India. Most participants strongly defended British rule and rejected an American role in bringing about a settlement. Sir Herbert Emerson was particularly emphatic "against any interference whatsoever by the Americans." But Edward Thompson, an Oxford University historian and former missionary in India, disputed his colleagues and even offered the heretical suggestion that there should be an Indian government at the center and that the next viceroy should be an Indian.[30]

Some of the people to whom Phillips spoke were even more outspoken than Thompson. A prominent British cleric strongly disagreed with those who belittled the Congress. It was an important organization and had widespread support, he told Phillips. The Indian correspondent for *Time* magazine spoke to him of the Indian desire for freedom, asked him if he expected to see Gandhi and Nehru (he couldn't be certain, Phillips replied), and noted a growing tendency in India to believe that the United States supported British policy toward India.[31]

But easily the most important dissenter with whom Phillips spoke was V. K. Krishna Menon, head of the India League and Nehru's spokesperson in London. So sensitive was Phillips about his contact with Menon (which Ambassador Winant's office had arranged) that he referred to him in his diary as "Mr. M." Menon told him that the government had no real interest in a solution to the Indian problem and that the Cripps proposals were no longer relevant. What was needed, he asserted, was a provisional government in which the viceroy would serve as a constitutional monarch. "Mr. M.," Phillips wrote blandly, "was clearly out of sympathy with the attitude of the British Government towards India."[32]

As Phillips listened to the various arguments, he found certain aspects of the British position persuasive. He accepted the British view about how complex the Indian situation was. Divisions between Muslims and Hindus were bitter and deep, he concluded, and Gandhi and Congress did not represent the views of all Hindus. Phillips was even attracted to the argument of some of Gandhi's critics that the Congress was in some ways a fascist organization. He put some credence in the British view that many, perhaps most, Indians believed London's assurances about India's future, despite the public expressions of skepticism from their leaders. And, of considerable significance, he was at first inclined to blame the Indians themselves for the divisions. "Until the political groups are willing to sit down and talk things over amongs [sic] themselves, I wonder how much help we can be," he wrote.[33]

However, it was apparent by the time Phillips left London that he would not be a stooge of the British government. He had listened attentively to dissenting opinions and found merit in some of them. He liked Cripps's idea of an international conference called by Roosevelt. He also decided to send to the President the suggestions of Menon ("a highly intelligent Indian, a friend of Nehru") about forming a new Allied Command in the Indian theatre and a possible reorganization of the Indian government.[34]

In sum, Phillips would go to India rightly believing that he had "the confidence of the British." But he had worked extremely hard to acquaint himself with Indian realities (Hodson, for example, found Phillips "intensely interested" in what he had to say) and had been exposed to antigovernment perspectives. He would take to India an open mind.[35]

Late in December Phillips traveled to New Delhi by way of Nigeria and Egypt. Although Cairo was not directly en route, he thought it important to stop over and pay his respects to the Indian troops training in Egypt. The pilot nearly ran out of fuel approaching the Egyptian capital, but Phillips was glad he had come. There he quickly encountered India's cultural divisions. At the troop encampment near the pyramids were two large water jars, one for Hindus, the other for Muslims, although the water came from the same tap.[36]

Now that Phillips was coming to India, Linlithgow pledged himself to receive the American cordially and establish close ties with him. Upon Phillips's arrival the viceroy hosted a spectacular dinner in his honor, complete with Indian bagpipe players and numerous servants. "Every two guests had a waiter," Phillips wrote. "As we entered the dining-room, the servants, dressed in crimson and gold, were lined up on both sides of the table and presented a most brilliant color scheme." Phillips wondered if he was "being mistaken for royalty." More substantively, Linlithgow assured the new representative that he could go anywhere he wished and speak with anyone he desired. (Phillips's account did not indicate that the viceroy had placed any limitations on whom he might interview.) "He could not have been kinder or more reassuring," Phillips wrote.[37]

Arrival in India seemed only to enhance Phillips's enthusiasm for his mission. "This is certainly the most interesting and absorbing assignment that I have ever had," he wrote to Hull, "and I only hope that something constructive may develop from it."[38]

The British, who had placed such high expectations on Phillips, were initially very pleased with his conduct. Upon his arrival in New Delhi on January 8, 1943, Phillips had spoken "with impeccable correctness," observed one Foreign Office official, and even the skeptical Linlithgow was impressed. It was "impossible to imagine a greater contrast to Johnson," he reported. Phillips had excellent manners, was friendly, and "seems to me better really than anything we could reasonably have hoped for."[39]

The euphoria lasted scarcely two weeks. On January 26, 1943, Phillips met with Linlithgow for their first substantive discussion. Phillips told the viceroy frankly that the Indians had lost confidence in British promises. He thought there was a chance the Indians might attempt a new initiative to break the deadlock, but in view of their distrust the first move had to come from the government, and it had to go beyond the Cripps proposals. Phillips wanted to know if there was any possibility of the government reopening talks with the Indians and also whether a provisional government might be established to give the Indians practical experience in government before a new constitution was drafted.[40]

Linlithgow did not take overt exception to Phillips's remarks, although he suggested that the American needed more time in India to appreciate the complexity of the situation. But in actuality the viceroy was extremely distressed. Amery received the full force of Linlithgow's wrath. Seeing Phillips's comments about possible agreement among the Indians and the establishment of a provisional government as indicating that the viceroy was somehow to share power with Phillips or the American government, Linlithgow made it clear that he would resign first. Phillips, he now thought, "regards himself as charged with a mission." The American was skeptical of British policy and was anxious to right it, Linlithgow asserted, "and that is not a position we can accept or acquiesce in." He asked Amery to bring this matter to the attention of the War Cabinet so that he could refute Phillips with the full backing of the British government.[41]

All of this was bad enough, but the viceroy was incensed when Phillips contended that, in his efforts to bring together the Indian parties, he was only doing what Amery had suggested he attempt. Linlithgow could not believe that Amery could have encouraged Phillips in this direction.[42] But it seems evident that Amery had done just that. Phillips's accounts of their various meetings are unambiguous on that point, while Amery himself wrote after their first meeting that it "would be all to the good" for Phillips to encourage the Indians to overcome their differences.[43] Nevertheless, Amery denied that Phillips was acting with his approval. Although he acknowledged telling Phillips that he might remind the Indians that the American and Dominion constitutions had evolved through discussion and agreement, he expressed amazement that Phillips could have understood this as "a suggestion that he should himself take part in bringing them together."[44]

Given Phillips's strong, detailed, and repeated recollections, however, it is almost certain that Amery, pleased as he was to have Phillips as the new American representative, had in fact said that he would welcome Phillips's efforts to bring the Indian parties together. But it is also likely that the two men spoke from different premises and thus Phillips may have read into Amery's comments more than was intended. Phillips assumed that his role was to be more than merely reportorial—his instructions after all explicitly empowered him to "encourage both sides or either side" toward "a practical settlement"—while Amery assumed the American representative would not seek to mediate or intervene in the Indian situation.

Whatever the truth, Linlithgow was right to sense a change in Phillips's behavior. When he first arrived Phillips was inclined to accept the British viewpoint that the Indians were responsible for their own divisions and that little could be done until they were will-ing to come together.[45] However, he soon discerned disturbing signs to the contrary. The day after his arrival in the Indian capital, for example, Phillips telegraphed to Hull that reports of a massacre by Indian police and military personnel at Chimur several months ear-lier were almost surely accurate. The government had suppressed news about the event, and Professor J. B. Bhansali, a member of Gandhi's ashram at Sevagram, was in the sixtieth day of a fast to protest the coverup. The British had already taken action against one American, William M. TenBroeck, who had written to fellow Ameri-cans in India protesting the atrocities and the government's refusal to allow mention in the press of Bhansali's fast. Phillips probably knew, or later learned, about the TenBroeck affair since the Ameri-can consul in Bombay had formally advised TenBroeck not to inter-fere in Indian political matters.[46] In any event, Phillips felt compelled to speak with the viceroy and the governor of Bombay about the Bhansali matter, and, perhaps as a result, shortly thereafter the gov-ernment agreed to an unofficial investigation, and Bhansali ended his fast.[47]

Despite the resolution of the Bhansali matter, Phillips quickly con-cluded that Government officials in India were much more intransi-gent than their counterparts in England. In London he had encoun-tered what he assumed to be a sincere spirit of compromise accom-panied by frustration at the failure of the Indian leaders to cooperate. Here was a problem about which Phillips could be helpful, they had said. But in India he discovered almost no interest in compromise and none at all in his being involved in a solution. Englishmen in New Delhi were "for the most part extremely conservative."[48]

Phillips also became persuaded that the Indians, while deeply divided among themselves, all wanted the British out. British colonial officials, on the other hand, could not "really envisage a free India fit to govern itself." It was no wonder that Britain's promises of eventu-al dominion status were simply not believed. "The heart of the prob-lem," he telegraphed to Hull, "seem to me the lack of faith in the promises of the British Government."[49]

By the time he approached Linlithgow Phillips had also conclud-ed, with great reluctance, that the British were pursuing a policy of

divide and rule. They inhibited discussions among the various factions, arrested leaders just when agreement with their opponents
seemed possible, and supported different factions at various times to
prevent an accord. Several factors influenced the ambassador's conclusion about British policy. Most Indians with whom Phillips spoke
(and the leading Congress newspaper reported that "during the first
month of his stay he has met more Indians than many who have spent
years in the country")[50] claimed that Britain deliberately maintained
communal division. Among those to express this view was Madhao
Shrihari Aney, an Indian member of the viceroy's Executive Council
whom the viceroy had praised for his role in the Bhansali matter.
Although Phillips was at first skeptical, he was struck with Aney's
comment that just when a meeting between Gandhi and Jinnah
seemed about to materialize, the government arrested the Hindu
leader. "I did not pursue this line further," Phillips recorded, "but it
seemed an important admission from a member of the Viceroy's
Council." Five days later Devadas Gandhi, son of the mahatma, told
him the same thing. Three days after that the journalist Shiva Rao
contended that the real block to a solution was the viceroy who "on
various occasions had made an agreement impossible between the
Muslims and the Hindus."[51]

An intensive review of the correspondence between the American
mission in New Delhi and the State Department for the weeks preced-
ing Phillips's arrival provided additional evidence that the Government of India had consciously obstructed Indian unity. In particular,
the viceroy had refused to permit Indians to consult with the jailed
Gandhi about a plan to resolve Hindu-Muslim differences, a consultation that apparently had Jinnah's full endorsement. The American
mission termed the refusal "incredible," the result, everyone agreed, of
the government's lack of interest in a settlement. As a result of the
viceroy's refusal, Phillips related, a conference of moderate, nonparty
leaders met at Allahabad on December 12–13, 1942, to work out proposals for the settlement of some of India's most serious problems,
notably the treacherous question of a separate Muslim state of Pakistan. If formulae could be agreed upon, they would seek permission
to share them with the imprisoned Indian leaders. But just when agreement was reached, Linlithgow poured cold water on the conference

with a speech in Calcutta which "all competent observers" saw as a blatant effort to sabotage possible agreement among the Indians.[52]

Phillips was incensed that he had misread British intentions. On January 26, the day he spoke with Linlithgow, he wrote that the British had long insisted publicly that it was up to the Indians to propose solutions for India's problems, particularly since the Cripps mission had come to naught. Important Indian moderates had taken the government at its word, it seemed to Phillips, only to have the viceroy pull the rug out from under them. "It is difficult to escape the conclusion that the Viceroy's speech was calculated to . . . sabotage all efforts designed to bring about a general settlement," Phillips advised Hull. The Indian moderates, he added, were "reported in a state of utter hopelessness and despair."[53]

Phillips's views may also have been influenced by John Paton Davies, a foreign service officer assigned to General Joseph Stilwell, the commander of American forces in China and India. Davies toured India in the fall of 1942, speaking to prominent Indians, Britons, and American State Department officials. He completed his lengthy report for Stilwell on January 23, 1943, and forwarded a copy to Phillips the next day. Whether it arrived or was read before Phillips wrote his important dispatch of January 26 or spoke with the viceroy is not clear. But Davies's conclusions were remarkably similar to the ambassador's, and later when Phillips transmitted copies of Davies's report to Washington he stated that it provided an "excellent summary."[54] In his personal reply to Davies, Phillips termed his memorandum "a splendid presentation," one which he took "particular pleasure" in forwarding to the State Department.[55]

The viceroy hoped that extensive travel would deepen Phillips's knowledge about Indian conditions. The American agreed, and immediately embarked on a previously planned tour of the northern provinces. But the suspicions of the Government of India were now thoroughly aroused. Government officials tried to keep a record of every person with whom Phillips spoke and even considered retaliating against some. For example, when officials intercepted a letter from Shambas P. Gidwani, the president of the Sindh Provincial Hindu Mahasabha, which described the topics he had discussed with Phillips, they considered cutting off his government pension.[56]

On the trip Phillips met with numerous Indians of various persuasions, from a wealthy landlord who described the "horror of Congress rule" and who feared the loss of his jewels in such an eventuality, to members of the Indian Communist Party, the Nawab of Mamdot, and members of the Muslim League. By far the most spectacular of Phillips's interviews, however, was with Lala Dunichand Ambalvi, an imprisoned Congress leader in the Punjab.[57]

Phillips's interview with Dunichand heightened his interest in meeting Gandhi himself. He had wanted to see "the most powerful Hindu in India" since his arrival but had demurred because Gandhi was under detention. But now that he had spoken with those leaders of all Indian parties who had not been detained and with one imprisoned Congress leader, Phillips felt the time had come to approach the viceroy for permission to see Gandhi. (More than two years later Dunichand recalled his conversation with Phillips and its larger consequences with considerable, and well justified, pride. To Rajendra Prasad, he sent a copy of the memorandum he had presented to Phillips, adding, "I thought I had done a bit of service at the time when the whole country was stunned.")[58]

Meanwhile the British were frantically trying to explain, and counter, Phillips's unexpected activism. The most common explanation was that Phillips was acting under orders from Roosevelt. Amery raised the possibility in a letter to Linlithgow, and Foreign Office officials came to the same conclusion independently. "We must assume that we are dealing with the President in this business," wrote Angus C. E. Malcolm.[59]

Amery urged Linlithgow to dispel Phillips's belief that he was acting in accordance with British wishes. Amery also suggested that Linlithgow tell Phillips frankly why talks among the Indian parties would not be productive under present conditions.[60] Thus when Phillips asked to see Linlithgow on February 7 the viceroy was prepared to deal with him, although there is no indication that he expected Phillips to ask to meet Gandhi. In the interview, Phillips raised the question of seeing Gandhi first, but the viceroy instead addressed the larger question of Phillips's intentions. British officials in London had informed him, Linlithgow said, that no one there expected Phillips to intervene. At that point Phillips, irritated at being challenged about his responsibilities, interrupted to say that he had never used the word intervention, which Linlithgow acknowledged. He was there to report his impressions of the Indian situation to the President, he said, to which Linlithgow, relieved, said, "I am glad that we understand each other."[61]

With respect to Gandhi, Linlithgow informed Phillips confidentially that the mahatma was about to begin a "fast to capacity" to mark the sixth month anniversary of his arrest. "He gave me the impression that he felt bitterly towards Gandhi," Phillips wrote. When Phillips expressed sympathy for the viceroy's position, Linlithgow "became more human" and the conversation, initially difficult, "ended pleasantly," even though Phillips failed to get permission to see the mahatma. The viceroy thought the interview had gone very well. "Phillips's reaction was all that could be desired," he reported to Amery.[62]

Because Linlithgow was so pleased with his performance, he personally kept Phillips closely informed of the progress of Gandhi's fast and his government's actions with respect to it.[63] Phillips appreciated the viceroy's gesture, but he considered the government's hardline response to the fast as further evidence of the bankruptcy of British policy. Linlithgow's letters revealed a rigid mind dedicated to preserving the status quo. "One looks in vain for any hint of official willingness to seek a reasonable compromise," Phillips wrote, whereas Gandhi's letters to the viceroy had "their usual ring of sincerity."[64] That the viceroy's Executive Council had voted to support Linlithgow's policy by the narrowest of margins (6–5) was further evidence, Phillips thought, of how little support the viceroy had in India.[65] Three Indian members of the council soon resigned.

As the fast continued, prominent Indians (including at least one member of the viceroy's Executive Council) asked Phillips to do something, or at least say something, that would indicate American concern for Gandhi's health and a lack of support for British repression. Without instructions, however, there was little he could do except suffer the growing criticism in silence.[66] "I wish the Department would give me some hint as to their own views," Phillips wrote, "but, of course, they never do this in ticklish times."[67]

Increasingly sympathetic to the nationalist position and the reasonableness of its leaders, especially when compared with the rigid and unimaginative British posture, besieged by the international press and prominent Indians, Phillips agonized over the ramifications if Gandhi should die with the United States having remained silent. The Atlantic Charter and various pronouncements by the President, he felt, meant that the United States had already "assumed a degree of responsibility which should be recognized by us now, in the present crisis." Wallace Murray told Welles that Phillips's recent telegrams had been "obviously written in considerable distress," and he requested that some specific guidance be sent to New Delhi. But Welles demurred.[68]

In the United States the *New Republic* complained that British policy was "the work of men of inferior minds" and lacked realism, common sense, imagination, and any sense of humanity. But Gandhi's fast did not arouse great popular concern, partly because the British exercised rigid censorship to prevent news from reaching the outside world (which produced vigorous complaints from American correspondents in India), and partly because important war news elsewhere had pushed Indian events out of mind. The nationalist cause was "weakened by Allied victories in Africa, Russia, and the Pacific," reported *Newsweek*.[69] "So far so good," wrote a Foreign Office official. "If the Russians can go on filling the headlines until the fast is over we may yet get through all right."[70]

Eventually Phillips's daily, sometimes twice daily, telegrams did have some effect. Murray continued to argue that the ambassador's pleas should not be ignored, and on February 16 Hull summoned Halifax to his office and told him that he was disturbed at the possible consequences if Gandhi should die. He also asked, according to his memorandum of the conversation, if the British might "find it possible and advisable to consider certain additions to the Cripps proposals."[71]

Halifax's report to London (inexplicably not sent until February 18) differed from Hull's account in important respects. Indeed, about the only point of agreement was that Hull had expressed concern about Gandhi's possible demise. Halifax's dispatch mentioned nothing about additions to the Cripps proposals and instead reported that he had used the occasion to emphasize how important it was that Phillips not intervene on behalf of the United States. Hull, he stated, "warmly agreed" and said the British, had they seen Phillips's instructions, would "not have wished to change a word." According to Halifax the secretary even urged the British to go on the offensive and argue aggressively that winning the war was what was really important. Giving Gandhi leadership "would be fatal to any Indian war effort." If Gandhi really represented the Indian majority, Hull allegedly asserted, then "God help India!"[72] Hull's account of the conversation included nothing at all about Phillips, advice to the British on how to argue their case, or Gandhi's views of the war.

It is probable that Halifax's account was the more accurate one. Hull's memorandum was for the record, and if he said the things alleged he would not likely have recorded them. On the other hand, Halifax's telegram was for his government; it is inconceivable that he would have fabricated any portion of his report. Although Hull could be critical of the British empire, in particular its closed trading arrangements, during the war he sought close Anglo-American ties. After the Indians had rejected the Cripps proposals, for example, he had thought criticism of British rule in India harmful to the Allied war effort. During the following months Halifax's reports of his conversations with the secretary indicated that Hull continued to feel that maintaining close Anglo-American ties was his top priority, not only for military reasons but also for the sake of the postwar world. "We cannot have a serious breach," Hull wrote.[73] At times Hull even asked Halifax's advice on how best to respond to questions from the press about India, points that the secretary did not usually include in his own records of the conversations. However, during Foreign Secretary Eden's visit to Washington in March 1943, Hull did record his position clearly. He reminded Eden that he had made "every effort to prevent this [Indian] question from becoming a matter of serious contention and general discussion here."[74] Phillips's reports may have forced Hull to summon Halifax, but the secretary of state was less concerned than the President's personal representative about the nature of British rule in India.

The same day that Hull conveyed to Halifax his concerns about Gandhi, the secretary received yet another telegram from Phillips. This one asked for permission to approach Linlithgow, if Gandhi's life appeared to be in danger, to "express our deep concern over the political crisis." This would "help to correct the impression, based on our inactivity and the presence of American troops, that we have been giving support to the Viceroy's position."[75]

Whether Hull on his own would have acceded to Phillips's request is doubtful, but the next day the President, who often ignored Hull, agreed that Phillips could approach the viceroy "and express our deep concern over the political crisis." He was also permitted to voice the administration's hope that "some means may be found to avert the worsening of the situation which would almost certainly follow Gandhi's death."[76]

On February 18 Phillips met Linlithgow in the viceroy's library and communicated to him the message he had received from Washington. Linlithgow indicated that the British government was solidly behind the present policy. While Gandhi's death would create some problems, after six months "a new and improved situation would develop." As Phillips put it in his report to Washington, government officials "faced with equanimity the possibility of Gandhi's death."[77] Linlithgow's own account of the conversation was even stronger on this point: "the prospect of a settlement would be greatly enhanced by the disappearance of Gandhi" who had "torpedoed" all previous attempts to resolve the situation. (Not all Government of India officials agreed. The British governor of Bombay, for example, wrote that he and most governors thought Gandhi's death while in British detention would make an eventual settlement with the Indians almost impossible.) But the viceroy did not think Gandhi would die in any event because he was convinced that he had skillfully devised ways of mixing glucose and fruit juices with water, a mixture that would sustain life for long periods of time.[78]

Phillips felt discouraged. "I left with the impression that the Viceroy had made up his mind and would not be moved from his position," he wrote. The next day, February 19, Phillips urged Roosevelt to "exert friendly pressure on the British Government through Halifax," presumably to release Gandhi.[79]

Phillips also telephoned the viceroy to ask permission to tell the press that they had met. He had not originally planned to do this, believing it best to keep the entire matter confidential. But as the pressure from the press increased by the hour, he changed his mind. There was developing a sense that the United States failed to "appreciate the seriousness of the situation." Because the viceroy was ill, Phillips's request was handled by a close adviser, who told the American that he thought a public disclosure would be "disastrous," and the viceroy himself soon concurred. His only suggestion was for Phillips to tell the press that Linlithgow was keeping him fully informed of developments, a suggestion that Phillips considered "worse than saying nothing at all."[80]

Phillips's action meanwhile led to a furious flurry of telegrams, discussions, and recriminations among British officials. Linlithgow felt justified in his initial resistance to having someone of Phillips's stature in New Delhi, telling Amery bluntly that it was "a great mistake" and that he regretted setting aside his own serious reservations "in deference to your view and Eden's." Amery remonstrated that the problem was not who represented the United States in New Delhi but the President's determination to intervene in Britain's internal affairs.[81]

It was in fact the President that the British came to feel was responsible for their problems. At first they were baffled by the apparent inconsistency between Hull's reassuring conversation with Halifax and the telegram to Phillips two days later authorizing him to express American concern over the Indian political situation. But Amery quickly surmised that the President, probably influenced by Madame Chiang Kai-shek and Eleanor Roosevelt, had intervened and "overpersuaded Hull."[82]

The British were right to focus their attention on the President, who had in effect overruled Hull. But they were not aware of how strongly Phillips himself had pressed for Presidential intervention. They saw him as the messenger dutifully carrying out his orders, and they even pitied him. But they were determined that the American action had to be strongly resisted. American intervention was "intolerable," Amery wrote to Churchill. The President ought to be told "that his people must keep off the grass."[83] Eden, who was going to Washington anyway, added India to the list of concerns he would take up with the Americans.

In the meantime Halifax sought an appointment with the secretary of state. As he was meeting with Hull on February 20, the President interrupted their discussion with a telephone call about India. It was evident that Roosevelt would not easily back away from the challenge he had raised. Presumably responding to Phillips's anguished telegram of the previous day, which urged the President to intervene, Roosevelt ordered Hull to tell Halifax that he was deeply concerned over the damage that would be done if Gandhi died. Quoting Roosevelt, Hull told Halifax that the President's "biggest desire is not to see the fellow die in prison." Hull thought he had made this point "unmistakably clear to the ambassador."[84]

The British were quickly made aware of the President's views but ultimately decided not to respond to them, probably concluding that, with the Allies doing better in the war and India's position less important than previously, the United States would not press them further. In the Foreign Office there was, however, an undercurrent of sympathy with Roosevelt, at least insofar as he was implicitly critical of the viceroy's rigidity. "President Roosevelt is a past master at not letting difficult situations come to a head," wrote Nevile Butler, "and he will inevitably feel that the Viceroy has been clumsy in allowing Gandhi to martyrize himself."[85]

The British also hoped to keep knowledge of the American expression of concern about Gandhi confidential. Linlithgow had reacted strongly when Phillips had asked for permission to mention his visit to the press, and Amery supported him. To have it known that the Government of India had turned down a Presidential request would, he believed, have extraordinarily serious consequences for Anglo-American relations.[86] Halifax asked Hull to see to it that Phillips made no public statements about having seen the viceroy about Gandhi.[87] Just what transpired on the issue of Phillips keeping quiet is uncertain because the two accounts differ. Halifax reported that the secretary of state, while not giving a definite answer, "appeared to agree." Hull, however, wrote that he complained forcefully about the "very difficult and unsatisfactory situation" in which Phillips found himself. The President, he told Halifax, had stated that Phillips would "not be expected to remain quiet and nonvocal." Halifax, he asserted, did not take issue with his remarks.[88] At the very least, Hull made no commitment to ask Phillips to keep his approach to the viceroy under wraps, and there is no indication that he ever asked Phillips to say nothing.

The American press reported Halifax's meeting with Hull and indicated that the United States had expressed concern about Gandhi's fast.[89] But the report generated surprisingly little comment in the British or Indian governments, perhaps because the press did not report Phillips's approach to the viceroy and because the same reports indicated that the United States was not intervening in Indian affairs.

The British, including Linlithgow, continued to think that Phillips was privately pro-British and had been forced into his actions by Roosevelt (and Madame Chiang). But they were mistaken. The crisis only caused Phillips to increase the pressure for forceful American actions.

To this point Phillips thought the United States ought to press for change in India primarily to keep India as a reliable base for the war against Japan. He had gone out of his way to praise Davies's analysis of conditions in India, for example, and Davies began his report by examining the military situation. Davies concluded that with the threat of an invasion by the Japanese or the Germans now unlikely, India was not for the time being a serious military problem for the United States. But he feared that a deteriorating economic situation or a fast by Gandhi "could produce disturbances sufficient to disrupt the war effort." When in the context of Gandhi's fast Phillips first explained his own thinking on the situation, he wrote that "the safeguarding of our own position in India as a military base against Japan" was an important consideration.[90]

Phillips also wanted the United States to exert pressure on the British so that the United States would be better placed to establish favorable relations with India after the war. He was equally concerned that idealistic American pronouncements not be viewed as hypocritical. The Atlantic Charter and statements from the President in support of oppressed people meant that the United States had "assumed a degree of responsibility which should be recognized by us," he wrote. For the moment Indians still had hope in the United States, but that could change, particularly if Gandhi died.[91]

The military situation, postwar relations with India, and fear of the

United States being portrayed as a hypocritical country continued to concern Phillips. But more and more the ambassador looked ahead to the post colonial world and the role the United States would play. Influenced in part by conversations with Rajagopalachari who "emphasized over and over again the extreme importance of averting a white against colored complex in the East," the ambassador pointed to the powerful forces of nationalism that were sweeping Asia and would soon dramatically transform long standing colonial arrangements. The United States had to see beyond immediate wartime necessities, even beyond India, and ally itself more fully than it had with these forces. In the immediate context this meant that it must make clear to the world that it did not support current British actions in India and that it was attempting to modify British policy. Since working through Linlithgow was impossible, could not Washington approach Ambassador Halifax, who as viceroy had taken a more flexible approach than Linlithgow? Could not the United States prevail upon the King to make a dramatic gesture of conciliation by ordering Gandhi's unconditional release? "There is no time to be lost," he warned. If Gandhi died, "white prestige in the east" would virtually disappear and with it the opportunity for the United States to seize the leadership for a new age.[92]

In this mood Phillips sent a personal letter to the President, his second in less than two weeks. All Indians, he stated, even those who disliked Gandhi or his tactics, supported the mahatma in the present crisis. Many looked to the United States for help. "I have been literally besieged by callers and overwhelmed by telegrams from all parts of India, asking whether there could not be something done from Washington or by me to relieve the present deadlock," he wrote. The viceroy was insensitive to "the pathos in the appeal of these millions for freedom for their own country. . . . Perhaps," wrote Phillips in a telling analogy, "he is a 'chip off the old block' that Americans knew something about in 1772."[93]

It soon appeared that Gandhi would survive his fast, which was scheduled to end on March 3. Hardliners in the British government congratulated themselves on their effective handling of the matter. In the viceroy's view the Americans had been duped. "Those who lately so fondly allowed their heart-strings to be plucked had better begin preparing themselves for [the] realisation that it was really their legs being pulled," he wrote. To the Prime Minister Linlithgow wrote that Gandhi was "the world's most successful humbug." Churchill agreed. The mahatma had no intention of dying, the Prime Minister wrote, and in the last week had probably eaten better meals than he. "What fools we should have been to flinch before all this bluff and sob-stuff." (Both ignored the fact that Gandhi had said from the beginning this was to be a fast "according to capacity," not a fast to death.) When the fast ended, Linlithgow was determined that it would make no difference in government policy. If Gandhi survived, Linlithgow informed Bajpai, "we shall close down on interviews and return as soon as possible to the *status quo ante.*"[94]

Phillips, however, was not content to allow a return to business as usual if he could prevent it. The day Gandhi ended his fast he made an ambitious proposal directly to Roosevelt for American intervention. Harking back to Cripps's earlier proposal for a multilateral conference on India, and drawing more specifically on an idea advanced to him only a week before by Sir Abduhl Hamid, a former prime minister of the Indian state of Kapurthala, Phillips suggested a mechanism for getting the Indian political leaders together to discuss the future. The President of the United States, with British approval, would call an international conference on the Indian problem. The United States, Great Britain, the Soviet Union, and China would be the major participants. An American would preside. Simultaneously, the British would "give a fresh assurance" of their intention to grant India independence and to establish a provisional government for the duration of the war. Phillips envisaged his proposal as a means of enhancing American prestige in the eyes of colonial peoples. Even if it were rejected, he wrote, at least the United States would "have taken a step in furthering the ideals of the Atlantic Charter."[95]

Phillips then left for a month-long tour of central and southern India, during which he met with literally hundreds of prominent Indian leaders, including Jinnah. Everywhere he found substantial, deep-rooted, and growing anti-British sentiment. "There is everywhere a feeling of frustration, discouragement, and helplessness," he reported to the President.[96] His tour left Phillips even more frustrated with the Government of India, which he was now sure wanted no reasonable solution to the political crisis.

One incident in particular demonstrated the government's inflexibility, Phillips thought. While visiting Bombay, he learned that a number of nationalists had written to the viceroy requesting permission for a small delegation to meet with Gandhi. The groups would attempt to obtain Gandhi's written assurances that he deplored violence and sabotage, assurances which might in turn lead to new negotiations. Phillips was afraid that the viceroy would reject the proposal and urged his own government to attempt to stop a rejection. Murray, noting Churchill's "sterile and negative attitude," told Welles that he would be "delighted" to see the President endorse Phillips's idea, but the State Department was not willing to do so, particularly since the Prime Minister had so recently rejected American concerns about Gandhi's fate. When the viceroy did in fact turn down the Indians' request to see Gandhi, Phillips was incensed. "The continued refusal to allow mediators access to Gandhi," he telegraphed the State Department, "leaves one with the suspicion that authorities have no desire to see deadlock ended."[97]

His tour and the government's rigid attitude convinced Phillips that he must once again attempt to see Gandhi, as well as Nehru, if only to convince the world that the United States did not support British policy in India. In February, at the height of the crisis created by the President's challenge to British policy, Roosevelt had asked Phillips to return to Washington in April or May to report personally to him, and the ambassador wanted to attempt to speak with Gandhi before he left India. He asked the State Department to support his appeal.[98]

All of Phillips's requests for a more active American role met with a sympathetic response from some elements in the State Department. Most in tune with the ambassador's thought was Murray. The Indian situation, he argued, provided "a test of our sincerity and honesty of purpose." If the United States gave the impression that it was "more interested in the creation of sonorous phrases than in the implementation of the principles enunciated in those phrases," Murray went on, "we can expect a harvest of hate and contempt the like of which our imperialistically minded ally has never known." The ability of the United States to contribute to settlements in the Middle and Far East, he wrote, would be seriously compromised. Consequently he actively supported Phillips's idea of an international conference to allow the Indians to plan for the future.[99]

Murray's efforts to embolden the State Department produced few results. When he argued that intervention in India provided a test of American sincerity, Welles's oblique response was that such action was not a "test of liberalism."[100] Prior to Phillips's request to see Gandhi, the only positive action came from the President. Although he did not endorse Phillips's suggestion regarding an international conference, he respected his emissary's view. Passing Phillips's letter along to Harry Hopkins, he commented that it was "amazing radical for a man like Bill" (a good commentary on Phillips's evolving thought), but added significantly that Phillips "has been there fairly long now and has his feet on the ground." Roosevelt asked if Hopkins could speak to Eden, who was then in the United States, about Phillips's idea or even show the letter to him.[101] (Hopkins wrote that he did show the letter to Eden, but if he did the Foreign Secretary seems to have kept the information to himself, since there is no reference to it in Foreign Office records. Perhaps he said nothing because he knew how Churchill and Linlithgow would react.) The President, it was clear, was still willing to make his discomfort about India's policy known to the British, although he tried to avoid direct conflict with Churchill.

Phillips's renewed request to see Gandhi and Nehru threatened to bring the United States government into just such a direct confrontation. Given the Government of India's strong reaction when Phillips had tried to see Gandhi before, its feeling that any questions about British policy had to be addressed through diplomatic representatives in either Washington or London, and the general view that India was no business of the United States, Phillips's request was bound to cause great controversy. Much to Phillips's annoyance,[102] State Department officials took nearly two weeks to make up their mind. Initially a cable was drafted giving official support to Phillips's request to see Gandhi. Murray argued forcefully that it ought to go out, even though the British would not like it. But Welles disagreed, and Hull refused to allow the telegram to be sent.[103] Hull felt strongly that postwar planning for Europe, the Middle East, and elsewhere required close Anglo-American ties. In the recent meetings with Eden Hull had repeatedly made this point and emphasized the need for both Allies to refrain from criticizing the policies of the other. A few days later, therefore, another draft telegram to Phillips allowed the ambassador to approach the viceroy but without official support, which "would undoubtedly be misinterpreted by the British Government." The ambassador would be allowed to make his request only on a personal basis.[104]

Meanwhile Phillips found more and more evidence of Indian disenchantment with British rule. For example, on April 8 a prominent Indian woman from Hyderabad who had spent many years in England and had been "an enthusiastic supporter" of British rule, now admitted to Phillips that she was completely disillusioned. "She spoke with deep sincerity," Phillips wrote. The same day Howard Donovan, the American consul in Bombay, confirmed this trend of opinion when he reported growing "frustration and bitterness" over the viceroy's refusal to discuss the Indian leaders' request to meet Gandhi. There was a perception, he wrote, that the British would not allow Indian self-government for years to come.[105]

Increasing expressions of disillusionment about American intentions were equally troubling to Phillips. Donovan had alluded to Indian concern about possible postwar Anglo-American commercial domination, and about the same time an important Muslim newspaper commented about how "the early beliefs in American professions of freedom and democracy are slowly giving way to fears in India of a triumphant American imperialism in the postwar era."[106] Consequently when Hull finally replied to Phillips's request to ask Linlithgow for interviews with Gandhi and Nehru (the ambassador had asked three times for a response) and indicated that the State Department would not associate itself officially with such a request, Phillips was angered. He characterized Hull's note as "rather a curt message" and complained that it had arrived a few hours after the viceroy had left town for his vacation. The following day Indian journalists, aware of Phillips's imminent departure for the United States but not privy to his attempts to see the imprisoned Indian leaders, strongly criticized him for not visiting them. "More and more the feeling was crystallizing that America and Britain were one in holding India down to its present position," he wrote. A visit to Gandhi was becoming the acid test of American intentions.[107]

Angry with the State Department, sympathetic with the Indians, and stung by unfair press criticism, Phillips penned a testy and gloomy letter to the President which, he feared, would not be well received. He flayed the British failure to extend the principles of the Atlantic Charter to India. "There is to be no change," he wrote, "no effort to open the door to negotiation among the leaders, no preparation for the future until after the war, and that date is so uncertain that I believe the Indians generally feel there will be no material changes in their favor even after the war." Indians were also increasingly cynical of American professions of freedom for the oppressed. "America has allowed such moments [when it was expected to speak out in favor of freedom] to slip by in silence," he wrote. American silence on the Indian question had a larger significance as well. "Color consciousness is also appearing more and more and under present conditions is bound to develop," he stated. "We have, therefore, a vast block of Oriental peoples who have many things in common, including a growing dislike and distrust of the Occidental." For these reasons, Phillips continued, he placed great importance on asking Linlithgow for permission to see Gandhi. "If the record shows that I have never made a serious effort to obtain the views of the Congress Party from Gandhi," he wrote, "then indeed my future usefulness here is at an end."[108]

Despite the lack of official support and the lateness of the hour, Phillips determined to press for an interview. Taking advantage of an invitation to visit the viceroy in the hill station of Dehra Dun, the ambassador made his request. Linlithgow himself reported that Phillips's representations were forceful: "he pressed me very strongly while here on two occasions to be allowed to go to see Gandhi."[109]

As it happened, the viceroy was prepared for Phillips's request, had indeed been expecting it for some time. Six weeks earlier Cornelius Van H. Engert, the American minister in Kabul, Afghanistan, was on leave in New Delhi. The British considered him so friendly that the viceroy invited Engert to stay with him, an invitation which reportedly flattered the American diplomat very much. While he was in the Indian capital, Engert reviewed the correspondence between the American mission and Washington, ostensibly because it would be useful to him in his work in Kabul. He found that many of the dispatches, particularly those written by Haselton, were critical of the British in India, and in what can at best be characterized as an improper action, promptly informed Olaf Caroe, secretary for external affairs of the Government of India, about what he had seen. He believed that the negative views among the mission's personnel helped explain Phillips's activities.[110]

Engert, who was acquainted with Phillips, tried to convince him of the righteousness of the British side. Shortly after the latter's arrival in New Delhi, Engert had sent him a British paper on the constitutional issue in India which argued against any negotiation with the nationalists. Engert himself warned Phillips that India "would very quickly revert to anarchy if the paternal hand were removed too suddenly."[111] When he came to New Delhi, Engert visited Phillips and apparently learned something of the ambassador's plans. He then passed this information on to the Government of India. Emphasizing that he did not want his actions "to get back to his own people," Engert told the Indian government that Phillips would soon return to report personally to the President and that before he went he would be instructed to see Gandhi.[112] (In light of Engert's known espionage, it seems likely that he was one source of other American dispatches that from time to time turned up in the hands of the Government of India.)[113]

Linlithgow lost no time in forwarding this interesting material to London and indicated, characteristically, that he was determined to resist Phillips's anticipated request to see Gandhi. He asked for support from his superiors and received it. Seeing "nothing but infinite harm to Anglo-American relations" if the United States intervened, Amery wrote to Eden that it appeared that the President had "not given up the idea of somehow or other using Phillips as a negotiator or mediator," and asked him to dissuade the President from this course during his forthcoming trip to the United States. Churchill also pledged his support. If necessary, the Prime Minister promised to speak with Hopkins or even Roosevelt directly.[114] In 1945, an India Office official recalled that Engert's information about Phillips's intention to ask to see Gandhi was "decidedly useful."[115]

Thus, when Phillips approached the viceroy (he brought up the matter while they were riding elephants during a hunt for tigers), Linlithgow could respond without panic because he expected the question and knew the British government would stand firm. His dispatches lacked the anger that had characterized his telegrams when Phillips had made his first request in January. He was even relaxed enough to conclude that Phillips's mission had been "of real use" and might help reduce any misconceptions. But he would not permit interviews with Gandhi or Nehru. No one could talk to them in the present circumstances. To allow Phillips to do so would give Gandhi the victory he was hoping for. He reminded Phillips that Gandhi was under detention for sparking a very serious rebellion and had "seriously interfered with war effort."[116]

In reporting to London the viceroy also offered an intriguing, but inaccurate, analysis of Phillips who, he was convinced, was seeking a compromise solution because it was natural for a diplomat to want concrete results. Although he professed to like Phillips personally and thought that the American had become increasingly aware of India's complexities, he felt that Phillips's "intellectual quality is a good deal lower than his personal charm," a typical Linlithgow judgment on those who disagreed with him. He also thought Phillips rather sentimental and thus likely to be impressed by the Congress viewpoint. (One Foreign Office official objected to Linlithgow's criticism of Phillips's mentality. "I wonder," he wrote, ". . . whether we shouldn't all be better off if Ld. Linlithgow were himself a little less inflexible.")[117]

Linlithgow did make one concession. This time he permitted Phillips to say to the press that he had requested an interview with Gandhi and had been turned down.[118]

Phillips was pleased with his final performance. At his press conference his statement that he had been denied the necessary facilities to see the mahatma "made a sensation," he thought. "All the correspondents seemed delighted and the American correspondents expressed themselves enthusiastically about the way in which the atmosphere had been cleared." All of the Indian newspapers, except the British backed *Statesman*, gave Phillips's comments front page exposure. A survey of American newspaper, magazine, and radio opinion by the British Information Service concluded that most commentators and editorial opinion praised Phillips and criticized the viceroy's decision.[119]

The ambassador thus saved his own honor and reputation. He also restored temporarily American prestige in India, for a personal representative of the President, a distinguished diplomat, had at least attempted to get first hand the views of the revered mahatma. Phillips was "returning to America as a friend of India and not as a supporter of the imperialist cause," wrote the editor of the *National Call*, a Congress newspaper.[120] More than one attempt was made in the Indian Legislative Assembly to introduce motions to permit Phillips to see Gandhi, but the viceroy invariably disallowed them.[121] In spite of the adverse publicity, the viceroy too approved of Phillips's statement. It was "all quite correct," he wrote.[122]

Phillips had also succeeded in one other respect: Linlithgow and the British still wanted to believe that he was acting only at the behest of his government and, indeed, was speaking for the President (who Linlithgow thought at times was "afflicted with just a touch of exaltation!")[123] His actions, they felt, did not represent his personal feelings which, they thought, were more favorable to the British.

To be sure, the American had not invoked any higher authority when he asked to see Gandhi, but neither had he pointed out that the State Department had denied his request to speak with the full backing of the government. Consequently, when Halifax finally mentioned the matter to the President over lunch, he seemed taken aback when the President did not dissent from his assertion that the viceroy been "absolutely right" to refuse Phillips. Indeed, Roosevelt "appeared to agree" with Halifax. Only Nevile Butler questioned the assumption that Phillips had acted on behalf of the President. Maybe Wallace Murray was the culprit, he suggested. But, he added presciently, "the Viceroy's refusal will be stored up against us."[124]

Linlithgow and the India Office were not pleased that Phillips saw so many Congress supporters and received deputations from political parties, but they assumed he was acting under direct or indirect orders. Therefore, the appropriate place to complain was in Washington. Eden, who was going there for other reasons, was approached. Perhaps he could raise the matter with Hull. Eden, however, seems not to have done so. "I have had a private letter from Sir R. Lumley with warmest praise of Mr. Phillips who has been staying with him in Bombay," he wrote. "I do not see that any action by me is called for."[125]

The British belief that at heart Phillips himself remained a supporter of their policy was shaken by comments Phillips made to Viscount Philip Swinton, the British Resident Minister in Accra, Gold Coast (later Ghana). During a stopover in the African colony on his return to Washington, the American unburdened himself and expressed what Swinton characterized as "some very definite and rather alarmist views." Phillips told the resident minister that beneath the surface in India there was considerable unrest, that the British and Indian governments were "increasingly unpopular" and not trusted by "any section of the community." Things were so bad, the ambassador said, that he doubted if India was any longer a safe base for operations against the Japanese. He hoped the British would make a new attempt to bring about a settlement.[126]

Phillips's incautious comments appeared to make clear that the ambassador shared the critical views of Murray and others. They further tended to contradict the viceroy's final assessment of the ambassador, that by the time Phillips departed he had come to appreciate the complexity of the Indian situation. They also called into question Linlithgow's belief that he had made some impression on the ambassador's views. The British, who considered Swinton's report sufficiently important to bring it to the attention of high level officials, including Churchill, in general diminished its importance; Amery remarked that Phillips had momentarily been too impressed by "the excitable Indian politicians." Only a little later, when Phillips made very similar and frank comments to Halifax, was there general disillusionment with the ambassador. He had "let himself be stuffed with just the kind of views the Indian politicians want to get across to the President," Amery wrote to Linlithgow.[127]

When Phillips arrived home he immediately reported to the President. Although Roosevelt received him "in his usual friendly way," the President did most of the talking, as he often did when he preferred not to deal directly with unpleasant business. Phillips left the meeting "far from satisfied" since he had been unable to make a complete report. Consequently he wrote yet another lengthy letter to the President. If the United States did nothing to change British policy in India, he contended, there would likely develop antiwhite sentiment not only among the "hundreds of millions of subject people" in India but also throughout all of Asia.[128]

Perhaps Phillips's eloquence moved the President, for Roosevelt subsequently invited the diplomat to join him for dinner at the White House. Afterwards, the two friends talked alone until past midnight about India, with Phillips urging more American involvement. Finally the President agreed to take action. As Phillips recorded it, "he would recommend to Churchill that he send Eden to India to explore the situation, to talk to leaders of *all* parties and groups, Gandhi included, and report to Churchill his findings."[129]

Roosevelt's subsequent action illustrates well how the President dealt with the Indian question in the years after the Cripps Mission. Prime Minister Churchill was then in Washington, but instead of approaching him about India directly, Roosevelt spoke to Lord Beaverbrook, the British minister of supply, who said he would take the matter up with Churchill. The President seemed optimistic, telling Phillips that if Eden did go to India, he wanted Phillips to return there too. The ambassador, however, was pessimistic, given Churchill's attitudes. He did not think Roosevelt's action was very forceful. "It was merely an example of Rooseveltian impulse, so characteristic of him," Phillips recalled.[130] Eden did not go to India. But once again the President had indicated his displeasure with British rigidity.

In addition to the indirect approach through Beaverbrook, Roosevelt personally asked the Prime Minister to speak with Phillips. Churchill was no doubt aware of what Phillips would say, for the previous week Phillips had spoken very frankly with Halifax about the Indians' "increasing bitterness and total loss of confidence in British purpose."[131] When Phillips called on Churchill the morning following his meeting with the President, he told the Prime Minister of the "unanimous cry for independence" he had found in India. Indians distrusted British intentions, he said, and he urged the British quickly to transfer more power to them.[132]

Phillips's remarks aroused Churchill to a fury. He prophesied a bloodbath if the British left and made it clear that there would be no changes for the duration of the war. His personal assessment of Phillips typified the reaction of British defenders of the status quo in India when confronted by those who advocated change. Echoing the views of Linlithgow and Amery, Churchill concluded that Phillips was "a weak agreeable man" who was "very ill-informed" about British advances in India. He would, Churchill feared, "do a certain amount of harm" because of his friendship with the President.[133]

Phillips's discussion with Churchill served to indicate to the Prime Minister that the President did not approve British policy in India. On the other hand, Churchill's reaction served another Presidential purpose: to remind Phillips how difficult it could be to deal with the Prime Minister on Indian affairs. "It was helpless to argue," Phillips wrote of Churchill. "It is only too clear he has a complex on India from which he will not and cannot be shaken." When Eleanor Roosevelt asked him how the interview had gone, he replied "badly." And when he reported to the President he said that he now understood the President's problems in discussing India with the Prime Minister. As for Roosevelt, he was "rather amused" at what had taken place, although he also said that he was glad Phillips had spoken frankly to Churchill.[134]

Phillips had also intimated to Churchill that he probably would not return to India, which pleased both Churchill and Linlithgow. "The viceroy will have a quieter life," observed an India Office official. Others in the British government, noting that Roosevelt had said that Phillips would not return "unless and until something happened," thought that the decision represented a further distancing of the United States from the British. They regretted that Phillips would not return. Even Linlithgow, while not wanting an American representative of high status, continued to want a "Wilson-type" to be stationed in the Indian capital. The difficulty with that was, as Roland T. Peel, the official in charge of the external affairs division of the India Office, wrote, that Roosevelt had no interest in such an arrangement. The choice was essentially someone like Phillips or no one at all. "So long as the President continues to take such a close personal interest in Indian affairs," Peel wrote, "I fear we shall have exactly the same difficulties recurring at intervals."[135]

This difference of opinion over what kind of American representative to have in India accentuated the disagreement between the
viceroy and the London authorities, especially those in the Foreign
Office. Not only had the viceroy been too insensitive to Phillips (and
also to American newspaper correspondents in New Delhi), the latter felt, but they took serious issue with his position that the United
States had no legitimate ground to say anything about events in
India. There was a basis for American expressions of concern, they
felt, and if the Government of India continued to react unsympa-
thetically every time the United States raised issues, it would "cause
India to bedevil Anglo-American relations somewhat as Ireland did
in 1919/20."[136]

Phillips never returned to New Delhi, but his India assignment had
a dramatic impact on the normally reserved diplomat. He became
committed to the cause of change in India. Indicative of Phillips's attitude was his decision not to accept the post of American minister to
Canada. To do so, the ambassador felt, would indicate to the Indians
that the President had lost interest in the subcontinent.[137]

Phillips also tried to convince Secretary of War Henry Stimson
that the unsettled political situation in India had significant negative
military consequences. It was important, he argued, to have friendly
populations around American bases.[138] He also continued to correspond with the President about Indian affairs but did not think it
wise to return to India until there was some prospect of political
change, and so after an extended vacation Phillips went to London
in September 1943, where he served as a political adviser to the
supreme allied command.

The Phillips mission demonstrated the limits of the Roosevelt's
commitment to decolonization. On the one hand, the administration preferred to see a peaceful end to colonial rule, and Roosevelt
was not willing to allow the British to continue their rigid approach
to India without challenge. His general support for Phillips, his willingness to respond to Phillips's entreaties by expressing (against the
advice of his secretary of state) his concern about Gandhi's health,
his personal request that Churchill speak with the ambassador, and
his recommendation that Eden go to India, all suggest that Roosevelt's commitment to change in India was real. Later, when the

British demanded that the administration disassociate itself from some of Phillips's views which were leaked to the press, Roosevelt stood firm. His decision not to send Phillips back to India—and more important his decision not to send anyone else in his place—also indicated quietly his disagreement with the British. Such actions are also consistent with Roosevelt's strongly stated opposition to continued colonial rule in Southeast Asia and his growing interest in international trusteeships. On the other hand, the administration would not offer strong support for Phillips's request to see Gandhi. Above all, after the collapse of the Cripps Mission all of the President's initiatives about India were indirect. Never again did he confront Churchill directly over the Indian question.

Roosevelt's approach of distancing himself from the British without going so far as to cause a break in Anglo-American relations reflected the general ambivalence of American policy toward India in 1943. From the beginning a major factor had been India's potential contribution to the war. By 1943 India's importance as a military factor had lessened noticeably, as Davies had reported. There was less reason from a purely military perspective to confront the British over India. The case for American pressure, therefore, had to be based on other reasons, such as those Phillips emphasized. Failure to solve the Indian problem might "constitute a threat to the peace of the postwar world," as Wallace Murray put it later. It was important to American interests that the United States not be identified with British imperial policy and that, instead, Asian nationalists be convinced that the United States was sincerely supporting their aspirations toward independence. Yet even then, Murray observed, the United States would take care not to let any differences jeopardize Anglo-American friendship.[139] It was a delicate balance.

Phillips himself had shown a remarkable ability to grow intellectually. A career diplomat of the old school, nearing retirement, a man not given to rhetorical excess nor previously identified with the anticolonial viewpoint, indeed a man assumed to be sympathetic to the British and with little previous interest in or knowledge about the colonial world, Phillips became an eloquent advocate for the oppressed. Perhaps he had inherited something from his great-uncle Wendell Phillips, the outspoken nineteenth-century abolitionist. Per-

haps like so many other Americans who had spent time in India he
found Indian culture irresistible. "The four months in India were
certainly among the most interesting ones I have ever spent," he
wrote several months after leaving New Delhi.[140]

Phillips's growth also derived from a realistic assessment of the
future of the colonial world, however. His Indian experience brought
home to him in dramatic fashion the strength of Asian nationalism
generally, a force that, he realized, would destroy the entire prewar
political structure. The "pretty good club" that had reshaped the foreign service over the previous decades was aristocratic, racially arrogant, and drawn to Europe. But its members also prided themselves
on their realism. Drawing on America's long-established tradition of
support for self-determination, Phillips urged his government to
grasp the leadership for the future.

It was a truly remarkable transformation, entirely unexpected by
the State Department, the British, and perhaps also by the President.
As Murray understated it in the fall of 1943, Phillips's "views on India
came as a great surprise to a number of officials in the Department
who felt sure he would react otherwise."[141] Although he was unable
to convince his government that in the case of India idealism was in
the long run the highest realism, it was a noble effort.

Phillips's blunt reports from India cost him the pleasure of retiring with his many British friendships intact. Later, he hoped the
British had forgiven him, but doubts remained. "I hope memories
are short," he stated in 1951, "and that I have been forgiven for the
practical reason that public opinion in this country very strongly supported my views about India; and then," he concluded, almost wistfully, "with the change of British Government, the very situation I
hoped for took place. India won her independence."[142]

7 | American Disillusionment Grows (June 1943–September 1944)

By the time William Phillips returned to the United States, the war was going well for the Allies.[1] They were on the offensive in North Africa and in Russia, and the Japanese advance in the Pacific had been halted. Admiral Isoroku Yamamoto's daring attempt to destroy the American fleet in the South Pacific while he still had the resources to do so had failed. In April 1943, American fighter pilots shot down Yamamoto's bomber as it flew to Bougainville, and the admiral, one of Japan's most outstanding naval figures, died. It was a serious blow to Japanese morale. In the meantime, the Allies prepared to launch a major offensive through the Pacific. It began on June 30, 1943.

Although the main military thrust against Japan was now in the Pacific, India still remained important militarily, for the Americans were determined to keep China in the war. The President personally supported General Claire Chennault's plan (which Chiang Kai-shek also backed) to build up his air force in China. Chennault claimed that he could destroy enough shipping in six months to force the Japanese out of China altogether. The plan called for substantially increased supplies shipped from India. This depended on part on reopening the Burma road, which in turn required aggressive military action to neutralize Japanese forces there. Consequently, in May

1943, the Combined Chiefs of Staff recommended a concentration of available resources in the India-Burma theatre and renewed air and ground operations into Burma once the monsoons ended. In June the Allies announced that a new South-East Asia Command would soon be created to carry out the Combined Chiefs' plans.

Although Churchill had gone along with the plans, he and his new commander of the Indian Army, General Claude Auchinleck, soon had second thoughts. There were serious administrative and supply problems, and they concluded, as Wavell had earlier, that it would be preferable to attack Sumatra rather than get bogged down in Burma. In any event they argued that, even with an offer of substantial American military assistance, nothing could be attempted on the ground until the following year. Strategic bombings of Burma, however, increased substantially. Although it is difficult to assess the immediate military impact of the bombing, by late 1943 the Allies were better situated to maintain air superiority over Burma during any later ground operations.

The Americans, President Roosevelt in particular, rejected the notion of a peripheral attack on Sumatra. They continued to want to supply forces in China at an accelerated rate. Therefore at the Trident conference in August, it was agreed that air operations over Burma would continue, that plans would proceed for an amphibious invasion of Burma the following spring, that India would continue to be built up as a base for later operations in Southeast Asia, and that the airlift to China would be increased. At the same conference the Allies established the separate South-East Asia Command (SEAC) to be headed by Admiral Louis Mountbatten. Stilwell was named deputy commander.

Despite the encouraging war news, throughout this period there were American criticisms of British military prowess, their failure to fight in Burma being a major grievance. American military officers in the China-India theatre were, in general, highly critical of the British. Especially noteworthy in this respect was Stilwell, whom historian Christopher Thorne characterizes as having "fierce anti-British sentiments." In the spring of 1944 Bajpai reported that comments in the American press about the British military performance had reached a "hostile peak."[2] Stilwell and others also complained about fighting a war to save the British empire, a view that was reflected in growing interallied tension over SEAC's mission. The Americans thought that SEAC's primary purpose was to support operations in China, while the British, who found Roosevelt's interest in China utterly baffling, viewed it as a way of restoring European prestige and colonies in Southeast Asia.

Another source of discouragement to American officials was the unwillingness of the British government to modify its policy toward India. Encouraged by the Allied successes, aware that a Japanese invasion of India was now much less likely, and believing that the domestic situation in India was well in hand, the Churchill government, fully supported by Linlithgow in New Delhi, refused to make concessions to the nationalists. There were even hints that the British government might renege on commitments it had already made to India.[3]

By October 1943, American officials were depressed about the future. Lampton Berry, whom Murray described as the most highly regarded American political officer then in India, reported that he had never "seen such utter hopelessness among Indians of all shades of opinion." They were all in a "complete state of depression" and felt that the British had no intention of ever handing over power to them. Merrell added that even the moderates had "now lapsed into a silence of utter hopelessness."[4]

One such disillusioned moderate was Samuel Evans Stokes, an American who had lived in India since 1904 and who was the only American ever to have served on the All India Congress Committee. Over the years, Stokes, though a through-going nationalist who had spent time in jail as a guest of the Government of India, found himself urging a moderate course of limited cooperation with Britain. When World War II broke out he advocated cooperation with the British to defeat the Nazis and thus found himself at odds with Gandhi and Nehru. But the British crackdown in August 1942, changed his mind. He wrote to Eden, Wavell, and others insisting that the British accept immediately the nationalist demand for a genuine responsible government at the center. One American relative sent a copy of Stokes's demand to President Roosevelt.[5]

Along with the growing anger and despair among Indians, the

American mission discerned increasing disillusionment with the United States. The perceived failure of Phillips to influence his government toward meaningful intervention was often cited as a major cause of this disappointment. In February 1944, the President issued a statement making it clear that the American task in India was to defeat the Japanese. He did suggest that after victory freedoms might be expanded, but his meaning was obscure and did little to decrease Indian disillusionment with the United States.[6] For example, the distinguished conservative Indian nationalist, K. M. Munshi, told the American consul at Bombay that nationalists had "become completely disillusioned with respect to the possibility of intervention on their behalf by the United States." Most believed, Munshi continued, that the United States was now in the hands of the "enemy," a victim of "British sophistry." Significantly, Munshi's views, while important in themselves, were by no means unusual.[7]

William Phillips, too, saw little prospects for improvement. On August 5, 1943, in an address the Harvard Defense Group, he foresaw "the lid blowing off in India" unless the British made concessions to the nationalists. Although the ground rule for Phillips's address was that his remarks were to remain "within four walls," a British informer in the audience reported them to British authorities. The ambassador's remarks, minuted a Foreign Office official, were "neither helpful nor constructive."[8]

In September 1943, Phillips was assigned to work as a political adviser with the Supreme Allied Command in London, but he still retained his title as the President's personal representative to India and continued to follow Indian developments closely. For the next several months he saw little reason for optimism. He feared India was ready to turn away from the West. Phillips, who foresaw more clearly than most the colonial upheavals that would rack Asia in the wake of World War II, sensed there would be considerable trouble for the United States if it could not influence events in India and elsewhere.[9]

Phillips did what he could to bring about a change. He spoke frankly and repeatedly to Englishmen who he sensed were sympathetic with his perspective. Halifax, who talked to Phillips with surprising frankness while in London, wanted a new initiative to settle the Indian deadlock, something he had denied when he had spoken with Phillips in Washington only a few months earlier. Lady Mount-batten was both well informed about India and "strongly, if not bit-terly, opposed to the British Government's policy." Lord Lytton, author of the famous Lytton Report for the League of Nations that had condemned Japan's occupation of Manchuria, thought Linlith-gow should have let Phillips see Gandhi.[10] Most significantly, Phillips went to see Lord Archibald Wavell, commander in chief of British forces in India who had been designated to succeed Linlithgow, and indicated that both he and the President hoped there would be another attempt to resolve the Indian deadlock. He came away encouraged. But although there was disagreement in Britain with the government's approach, no one Phillips met was able to influence policy. As for the occasional official comments about changes in pol-icy, he wrote, they were "merely pleasant words."[11]

Phillips was especially perturbed when those who supported British policy in India pointed to the inability of Indians to resolve their differences. In Phillips's view, the British were obstructing Indian efforts to get together while doing all they could to prevent agreement. It was only with difficulty that he was able to restrain himself. When he took the visiting Wallace Murray to meet Amery, for example, the secretary "found it necessary to pull out the usual stuff that there was nothing that could be done until the political parties agreed to cooperate." Amery knew full well, Phillips went on, "that permission to cooperate was forbidden by the Government of India but he is probably so accustomed to saying it that it came out automatically."[12]

Contributing further to the negative views of British policy in India was a fact-finding visit to India by five United States senators representing the Senate's Military Affairs Committee and another special committee on national defense. Although not happy, Linlith-gow agreed that the senators should be allowed to come.[13] The sena-tors were not impressed with what they found, and the Government of India feared that the American mission had given them a biased briefing.[14] One of the five was Albert B. "Happy" Chandler of Ken-tucky, who would soon cause great embarrassment to the British over their treatment of William Phillips. A little later when William Dono-van indicated he wanted to go to India, Halifax urged that he be welcomed. "If he were to come back with a helpful report from India and the Pacific," the ambassador explained, "this might be a great value here, especially after the 5 Senators."[15]

There was some momentary optimism among the Americans when, in July 1943, the British announced that Wavell would replace Linlithgow as viceroy later in the year. (Linlithgow subsequently became chairman of Midland Bank, Ltd.) A graduate of Sandhurst, Wavell was near the end of his distinguished military career. He had served in the Boer War, was wounded in France in World War I, and thereafter had risen through the military ranks, serving in the Middle East. He was assigned to India in 1941 and achieved the rank of field marshal in 1943. Despite Wavell's accomplishments, there was little joy in either India or Britain at the appointment of a man reputed to be worn out, unimaginative, and slow. But the British hoped that news of the appointment would result in a cessation of American criticism, at least until Wavell's ideas about policy became clear.[16]

Unlike Linlithgow, Wavell seemed to have some genuine sympathy for India's aspirations and also appeared to want Phillips to come back to India. "There was nothing in his attitude to indicate the same rigidity of policy as that of Lord Linlithgow," Phillips advised Roosevelt. Phillips's optimism was only relative, however. Linlithgow was so rigid that almost anyone was bound to be an improvement. To his diary Phillips confided the limits of his optimism. Wavell was without cordiality, slow of speech, inarticulate, unapproachable, and "spent" (a view that mirrored Louis Johnson's evaluation the previous year that Wavell was "tired, discouraged and depressed"). Still, Phillips acknowledged that he felt "a little bit more hopeful" about the new viceroy.[17] Once Wavell took over in October 1943, the American mission found him only a slight improvement over Linlithgow.[18] In sum, the official American perception of Wavell in 1943 and early in 1944 was that he was a bit less rigid than Linlithgow but was not the one to initiate meaningful change.

In fact, behind the scenes Wavell was encouraging much more constructive attitudes about the Indian deadlock than Linlithgow ever had, and his approach to the Americans was much less confrontational as well. For example, he wanted his instructions to allow him to "examine whether a fresh attempt" to settle the political situation would be worthwhile. The War Cabinet feared the consequences of such an approach (one probable result would be more American pressure) and toned down the language. Wavell's final instructions, drafted by Churchill and approved by the War Cabinet, placed consideration of the constitutional question last. The new viceroy could suggest solutions to the political deadlock, but he was to "beware above all things lest the achievement of victory and the ending of the miseries of war should be retarded by undue concentration on political issues while the enemy is at the gate."[19] Proposals for even modest advances would result in skeptical scrutiny in London.

Still, the new administration would be significantly different, although it took some time for Americans to understand this. Shortly before Wavell took office, the retiring viceroy told him that Britain would have to remain in India for thirty years. "We could not for the peace of the world allow chaos in India," Linlithgow said.[20] Wavell cordially disagreed. While willing to defend the empire's accomplishments, he preferred to address its shortcomings. He would soon test the limits of his instructions.

If the Americans saw little evidence of positive change in British policy or relations with the United States over the India question, the British assessment of Anglo-American relations after Phillips's return to Washington was decidedly more positive. Churchill claimed that the Indian nationalist leaders had discredited themselves in the eyes of the United States and that there was no longer any American pressure for changes in Indian political arrangements.[21] But in reality official relations between the United States and Britain over India were desultory at best. Bajpai, though he agreed that the State Department had little desire to interfere in Indian affairs, warned that "it would be wrong to assume that the Administration has lost interest in the country's political future."[22]

The tensions between the American and British approaches to India were revealed in the sometimes tense communications between the American mission in New Delhi and the Government of India. In August 1943, when the Government of India requested information about certain mission procedures, for example, the Americans responded that the completeness of their reply would depend on how fully its own inquiries were dealt with. "It is clear that relations are not good," commented one British official in November, after reading this correspondence. The American reply, he thought, was "rather nasty, not to say ill-bred."[23]

The growing American presence in India also contributed at times to ill feelings between the British and the Americans. The few American diplomats in the major cities were now joined by increasing numbers of soldiers and representatives of various wartime organizations, such as the Office of Strategic Services, Lend Lease, the Office of War Information, the Bureau of Economic Warfare, and so forth. The presence of the additional Americans, particularly the military forces, provided a rationale for expressing more official American interest in Indian developments. As William Phillips told Wavell, "we were more than ever interested [in India] now because of the presence of American forces."[24] Linlithgow had long predicted that this would happen and consequently had never welcomed foreigners very warmly. When the authorities in London overruled his objections and insisted that the American agencies be allowed to operate in India, the viceroy tried to limit the number of personnel and to keep their rank low. The level of suspicion is clear from the numerous government documents analyzing each agency, often in meticulous detail, that had an office in India, and the duties, background, and personal views of Americans posted there. The result was considerable friction and even hostility between Americans in India and the Government of India.

Phillips, for example, encountered the Government of India's obstructionism whenever he tried to increase the size of the American mission in India.[25] He also found that he had to press the government "continually" for permission to establish a branch of the Office of Strategic Services. Linlithgow admitted that he planned to "stone-wall" on the matter and eventually insisted on referring the matter to London.[26]

Linlithgow's primary reason for resisting the growing American presence in India was that he felt with absolute certainty that many, perhaps most, of the Americans were part of an American conspiracy to dominate the postwar world politically and especially economically. Even before American entry into the war he and Amery had opposed a treaty of commerce and navigation with the United States because of Cordell Hull's insistence on free trade, which they assumed would wreck the existing system of imperial preferences and result in American economic domination of India.[27] Negotiations on the treaty were therefore postponed and never completed while Linlithgow was viceroy. When the American Technical Mission came to India in 1942, Linlithgow feared that its stated purpose of helping with the war effort was nothing but a mask for its true intention, which was to gather information useful for American business in the postwar era. The viceroy even found reason to question the activities of the American Naval Liaison Officer in Bombay, whom he accused of attempting to secure commercial information of no value to the war effort, "but of obvious importance in preparation for postwar commercial penetration by the United States."[28]

Consequently, Linlithgow was most concerned with those Americans and agencies which had anything to do with economics. The Bureau of Economic Warfare, the Lend Lease Mission, and economic counselors attached to the mission were targets of his dark suspicions. Amery shared some of the viceroy's fears, especially regarding Lend Lease. As early as January 1942, he stated that Cordell Hull's free trade views dated "back to somewhere round 1860" and that the secretary of state intended to use Lend Lease "as a lever for compelling us to adopt the same ideas and more particularly to pledge ourselves to abandoning Imperial Preference."[29]

When Lend Lease finally began to operate in India in April 1943, the mission's director, F. W. Ecker, felt he had to go out of his way to deny that he intended to position the United States for future economic advantage. Lend Lease, he wrote, was "not in any way an effort to establish American economic interests in India." Its only purpose was to assist India to defeat the Axis powers.[30]

Sometimes Linlithgow's suspicions were too much even for his cohorts in the India Office. When he complained that an American economic adviser, Eric Beecroft, had well known anti-British inclinations and was unqualified for his position, and also that Simon Swerling, another economic counselor, who he said had a close relationship with Birla Brothers, a chief Congress industrial supporter, he found no support in London. Paul Patrick had interviewed Beecroft

thoroughly and was unable "to detect any signs of the cloven hoof."
The American was not, Patrick thought, "a snake in the grass."[31]

The operations of the first wartime American agency to receive a
permanent position in India, the Office of War Information (OWI),
also aroused the viceroy's suspicions. As a result of an agreement
negotiated with British and Government of India officials in March
1942, Robert Aura Smith, then the director of the United States Foreign Information Service in the Far East, arrived to open the first
OWI office in New Delhi. Subsequently, other offices were opened in
Bombay and Calcutta.[32]

Initially, relations between the OWI and the Government of India
were generally good.[33] Later, suspicions of the agency mounted. By
March 1943, on the basis on intercepted correspondence, Government of India investigators had determined that three OWI employ-
ees (two of them women married to Britons) held "marked anti-
British views." The government also objected to certain agency publications. But the most offensive of the OWI activities involved the
advertisements, prepared by the J. Walter Thompson Agency in New
York, for publication in Indian newspapers. The advertisements,
which included pictures of the Statue of Liberty and proclaimed
that the United States was fighting to extend fundamental liberties,
were deemed "unfortunate in their application to India in present
circumstances."[34]

Some officials, notably the viceroy, thought that a clandestine
OWI objective was to prepare the ground for American domination
in the postwar world. Praising American democratic ideals, presenting the strengths of the American economy, and emphasizing the
American contribution to defeating the Axis powers (without giving
much credit at all to the other United Nations) was part of a con-
scious effort to enhance the postwar American position in India, they
thought.[35]

As it happened, some American officials agreed that some OWI
activities were unnecessarily offensive to the British and wanted to
bring the agency under tighter control. Among these was William
Phillips, whose instructions included achieving better coordination
of the activities of American agencies in India. Phillips was critical of
the organization and its director. "I hope Smith is the cooperative

type," he wrote, "because I fear that I am not in sympathy with much of his output in the past."[36] Phillips feared that, in addition to the advertisements angering government officials, the United States would be unable to fulfill the promises they contained, thus setting the stage for later disillusionment. Phillips saw that the OWI ran no more advertisements.[37]

Perhaps as a result of reforms Phillips instituted, the British embassy in Washington reached an agreement with the American government allowing the OWI to continue to operate in India. Linlithgow, as usual, complained that the Foreign Office was "weak-kneed" and that it was vital to "stand up to the United States" to avoid "being trampled." But even some India Office officials thought Linlithgow was misinformed at best, and perhaps paranoid. "The general feeling," wrote one India Office official, ". . . was that the Government of India are being unnecessarily and undesirably stiff and suspicious."[38]

In July 1943, Smith was transferred to Australia and Ralph Block arrived shortly thereafter to take over the work of the OWI in India, much to Phillips's delight. Block was being sent, wrote OWI director Elmer Davis, "to remedy the conditions which have brought criticism in the past."[39]

When Block arrived he found a warm welcome at the American mission, even a sense of relief that he had arrived to take charge.[40] Once there, Block reorganized the OWI operations along professional lines, with the emphasis on disseminating information about the United States. He also established good working relationships with the Government of India (this was much easier after Wavell replaced Linlithgow in October 1943). The new director claimed that he took pains to "avoid associating United States actions with the imperialistic policies of Great Britain,"[41] but he even cooperated with government censorship. He wanted to exercise great care, he told the government, "in keeping OWI in India completely free of any possible infringement upon the internal affairs of India."[42]

Suspicions about the OWI never disappeared, however. Some government officials feared that OWI libraries might house objectionable publications, for example.[43] One government press adviser thought the OWI was the source for the publication in India of a leaked Phillips letter, as well as a letter from Chiang Kai-shek to Roosevelt, both of which first appeared in India in the Indian communist newspaper, *The People's War*.[44] Likewise, rumors continued to flourish that the OWI and other American agencies and individuals were intent on finding commercial possibilities for postwar India. "Though there is little or nothing tangible at present," wrote one official as late as November 1944, "there is a certain amount of suspicion that USOWI in India are interested in commercial intelligence."[45]

Such suspicions about the OWI were unfounded, at least under Block's cooperative direction. With respect to the OWI being the source for the Phillips and Chiang Kai-shek letters, Caroe himself thought otherwise. Block, he said, had provided "the most positive assurances that his self-imposed charter keeps him rigidly away from Indian politics." More likely suspects, he thought, were Mahindra or Chaman Lal, an Indian journalist and sometime intelligence source.[46] As for the selection of periodicals in OWI libraries, it was "similar to that which might be seen in any English club."[47]

The increasingly significant American military presence in India also resulted in its share of complications. Gandhi and some elements within the nationalist leadership had always opposed the introduction of American troops on grounds that there was sufficient manpower available in India and, more fundamentally, that the decision to invite foreign troops to India was taken by an illegitimate government.[48] Some anti-government Britons agreed; Evelyn Wood wrote to Nehru that he feared American troops were being sent to India to help repress the nationalists.[49]

The presence of the American troops also resulted in some friction with Indians for more mundane reasons: there appears to have been a fairly large number of crimes of violence against civilians. Further inflaming public opinion were the results of trials. Often the accused soldiers were either acquitted or given very light sentences. In addition the amount of compensation, even for the families of homicide victims, was small. To its credit, the Government of India found this situation intolerable and pursued the incidents with great determination, often obtaining positive results.[50]

But, although there was some friction, on balance the American military presence seems to have been welcomed by Indians. "Indians like Americans," *New York Times* correspondent Herbert Matthews wrote in a feature about American soldiers in India. They paid well and treated the Indians "like human beings," Matthews reported. In January 1944, the American Naval Liaison Officer reported that there was a perception that the American military personnel were undermining British rule, not intentionally, but because of "their friendly and easy treatment of Indians." The Indians appreciated this and even more so the lack of deference that Americans showed to British officials. One particularly appreciated story concerned Louis Johnson, who allegedly once pounded the table and said to the viceroy, "let's get down to brass tacks, Linlithgow."[51]

Such reports seem reasonably accurate, for Nehru's account of the flood of Americans into India was similar:

> They were very much in a hurry, eager to get things done, ignorant of the ways and ceremonies of the Government of India and not particularly anxious to learn them. Intolerant of delay, they pushed aside obstructions and red-tape methods and upset the even tenor of life in New Delhi. They were not even careful of the dress they should wear on particular occasions and sometimes offended against the rigid rules of protocol and official procedure. While the help they were bringing was very welcome, they were not liked in the highest official circles and relations were strained. Indians liked them on the whole; their energy and enthusiasm for the work in hand were infectious, and contrasted with the lack of these qualities in British official circles in India. Their forthrightness and freedom from official constraints were appreciated. There was much silent amusement at the underlying friction between the newcomers and the official class, and many true or imagined stories of this were repeated.[52]

As Nehru suggested, relations between American and British soldiers were not always cordial. For one thing, the Americans enjoyed substantially higher pay. Their 200 rupees per month "would be a veritable fortune to a British Tommy," wrote one correspondent. Indian "tongawallas" (horsecart drivers) always preferred American soldiers over the British because the Americans paid four times as much, and sometimes the police had to step in to force the drivers to accept customers on a first come first served basis. Even American privates had servants. By all accounts American soldiers also had much better amenities than their British counterparts. The army provided modern sanitation, hot showers, good food, radios, movies, and social clubs, for example.[53] W. F. Rivers, an American businessman living in Bombay, complained that American soldiers were "spoiled and pampered," especially when compared to the average British Tommy who was "accustomed to the lean and hard and truly spartan existence." There is no question that the higher pay and better facilities irritated the British. When Government of India authorities intercepted Rivers's letter, one official commented that Rivers was "one of our best publicists in India." His letters home "present the British case better than we ourselves present it."[54]

At a higher level, the British kept careful track of important American military commanders assigned to India, most of whom they came to dislike. With Phillips's departure, the British surmised that effectively the chief of the American mission would be Stilwell, commanding general of American forces in China, Burma, and India. This would probably be an improvement, they thought, since Stilwell would take less interest in political matters. They were concerned that Stilwell's political adviser, John Paton Davies, might be tempted to become involved, but even if he did he would not have the stature that Phillips did. Typical of British thoroughness, though, they instigated an investigation of Davies's background and concluded that he bore watching.[55]

As they did with so many Americans, the British eventually came to dislike Stilwell and Davies. The immediate cause was a report by an American general, Patrick Hurley, who in January 1944 told the British representative in Baghdad, Sir K. Cornwallis, that American troops in India disliked India "intensely," complained that they were forced to fight for British imperialism, and disbelieved British assurances of help against the Japanese.[56]

Cornwallis could not have envisioned the amount of attention his dispatch recounting Hurley's remarks would cause. Foreign Office officials, who wrote extended comments, thought Hurley's account accurate, since they had received similar reports before. Some officials placed primary blame on conditions in India. The American soldiers were understandably shocked by the "poverty, hunger and dirt" that they encountered. Anti-American feelings among the British in

India surely added to their resentment.[57] However, most officials were inclined to place the blame for the undesirable attitudes among American soldiers directly on Stilwell. His increasingly negative view of India, they felt, had percolated to his troops. When another American general, Albert Wedemeyer, was shown a copy of Cornwallis's report, he commented that "troops are always inclined to take the spirit of their general." And that, stated a Foreign Office official, "puts the whole thing in a nutshell."[58]

British defeats in the Assam-Burma region in the spring of 1944, reinforced the image of hapless British-Indian troops. Bajpai reported that even normally friendly newspapers like the *New York Herald Tribune* and the *Washington Post* were criticizing the British military.[59] The defeats were only temporary setbacks, as it developed, and in June 1944, the British and Indian forces finally won an important victory. This came about as a result of a Japanese decision to mount a limited but important invasion of Assam. Assuming that the Allies were planning an invasion of Burma, the Japanese determined that the best way to protect their position there was to attack British forces near the Assam-Burma border and capture the important British bases near Imphal. A victory there, they reasoned, would go far toward offsetting their defeats in the Pacific. They launched their attack in March 1944, but after ferocious fighting at Imphal and Kohima were thrown back. In June the British decisively defeated them, thus achieving sweet revenge for the humiliations inflicted in 1942.[60]

This does not seem to have changed American opinion materially, however. In August 1944, Wedemeyer lunched with Phillips in London and not only told the ambassador that he agreed with Phillips's views of the Indian political situation, but also that he was "very dubious" about the ability of the Indian army and was concerned about tensions between American and British forces.[61] In August Wavell reported that Stilwell was "most definitely anti-British," as were many of his subordinates.[62] When in November 1944, Stilwell was removed because of an impasse with Chiang Kai-shek, Amery was no doubt correct when he wrote to Wavell that it "must be a great relief to all of you" that Stilwell had gone.[63] But whether this resulted in a change of the generally negative American perception of the Indian army may be questioned. In December Wavell felt it necessary to try to have Mountbatten elicit some positive statements from American military leaders aimed at "contradicting the insulting references to the Indian Army that are now so common in America."[64]

The British also came to distrust Davies. On September 9, 1944, Drew Pearson intimated that he had Davies's report on the Indian situation completed for Stilwell in January 1943, a copy of which Davies had sent to Phillips. Pearson claimed that its assessment of the British in India was damaging, as indeed it was.[65] The story put the British on their guard, and they could not have been surprised when on November 8, 1944, Pearson published portions of the report. The Davies report, wrote an India Office official, "seems typical American nonsense about the Indian situation." Nonsense or not, government censors prevented Pearson's column from appearing in the Indian press.[66]

Given Linlithgow's fundamental suspicion of foreigners, especially Americans, in India, it is not surprising that there were few attempts to court those Americans who were there. This was a matter of considerable criticism from Halifax and the Foreign Office and even on occasion, in more muted form, from the India Office. The viceroy's critics claimed that he was responsible, at least in part, for the negative image that Americans often had of India. But with Churchill to back him, Linlithgow felt little need to change.

The Government of India did, however, include an American Relations Officer, Sir Evelyn Wrench, whose job it was to work with the Americans. Though sometimes himself criticized for not being up to the job, Wrench did try to be friendly to the Americans and present to them a positive view of the government.

Wrench's primary efforts to influence Americans seem to have been with parties. Beginning in the middle of 1942, as the Quit India crisis grew, Wrench arranged informal gatherings where American officials and journalists could meet prominent Indians and learn first hand how complicated the situation really was. By the end of 1943, with a new and less rigid viceroy in charge, Wrench had ambitions of inviting such luminaries as Rajagopalachari and Jinnah. The India Office politely suggested he not invite Rajagopalachari because his pamphlet, *The Way Out,* was suspect. But he did arrange for Jinnah to meet with more than fifty Americans, including three generals and many other lower ranking military officers and diplomats. The event, he felt, was a great success. "Jinnah stood up to an hour and three quarters of cross examination and came out of the ordeal very well," he reported. Jinnah also stated that when Pakistan was established, he intended to work closely with the British Commonwealth. "I was glad to hear these sentiments expressed before our American friends!" Wrench wrote.[67] It is, however, difficult to judge if Wrench's parties had any significant impact on American attitudes.

If the increasing number of Americans in India resulted in tensions and irritations between the United States and Britain and provided an enhanced basis for the American government to express its views about Indian developments, the British could take considerable comfort in the low level of interest in Indian matters among the American public at large. To be sure, there were still calls for Indian independence and criticism of the United States for not doing more. In August 1943, for example, about 1,500 people heard Representative Clare Boothe Luce attack the Roosevelt administration's "pontius pilate silence" about India.[68] But the reality was that popular interest in India had declined precipitously. *New Republic* writer Kate Mitchell was discouraged that people regarded the Indian question with "complacency or disinterest."[69] Press coverage of Indian developments dropped dramatically. From July 1941, through June 1943, approximately 136 articles about the Indian political situation had appeared in American popular magazines. From July 1943, through April 1945, only eighteen were published. Of these, six were in the *Christian Century.*[70] In 1943 reports of Indian developments in the *New York Times* dropped by more than 50 percent when compared with the previous year. In 1944 the number of reports dropped another 50 percent.

As always, the British followed trends in American opinion with care. Aside from considerable American concern over a major famine in Bengal (discussed below), British observers in the United States, including Bajpai, the British Ministry of Information, Sir Frederick Puckle (the director-general of the Central Board of Information of the Government of India), and others, confirmed that

India had largely dropped from public view. As Bajpai put it in March 1944, "while the war lasts, the Indian problem will remain in the background, unless a new famine, epidemics, internal commotion or set-backs in Burma can be used to conjure up visions of danger to the U.S. forces now stationed in India."[71]

Even the most persistent critics of Britain's India policy seemed to have lost their fervor. Puckle called on the editors of the often anti-British *New Republic* and found no hostility. Editor Richard Walsh even invited him to dinner with his wife, Pearl Buck. Puckle also called on Edward Clark Carter, general secretary of the Institute of Pacific Relations. Carter and the Institute had been so critical of British policy that Linlithgow had tried (unsuccessfully) to deny Carter a visa to visit India.[72] But Puckle found "no trace of the highly critical attitude" which Carter had reportedly voiced previously. Most important, Puckle found a changed attitude at the Luce publications of *Time, Life,* and *Fortune.* Their editors, Puckle wrote, demonstrated "more knowledge of the facts and a much greater disposition to acknowledge the difficulties of the problems of India" than when he had met with them a year earlier.[73]

An important exception to the lack of American public interest in India in this period was the tragic Bengal famine of 1943–44, which resulted in the deaths of hundreds of thousands; perhaps as many as three million died.[74] As early as the fall of 1942 American representatives in India and newspapers reported food shortages in India, which were sometimes linked in part to the demands for food from the newly arriving American troops. In March 1943, the resignation of the Bengal premier and his cabinet received some attention, but for the next five months the food situation in India was mentioned only once in the *New York Times.* In August the newspaper reported that Calcutta officials had appealed to the United States for assistance, but nothing more appeared for an additional month.[75] By late September, however, in spite of severe censorship, reports were reaching the American public of starvation and food riots. On October 4, 1943, *Newsweek* reported that so many people were collapsing on the sidewalks of Calcutta "that at times the authorities despaired of being able to collect and cremate the bodies."[76]

Before the famine received attention in the press, American officials were well aware that a tragedy loomed. In July, for example, the United States Board of Economic Warfare presented a report that predicted hundreds of thousands of deaths from starvation. By the fall of 1943 the State Department had comprehensive reports and even photographs of the gruesome developments in Bengal.[77] The British, however, insisted that nothing was amiss, and, with the exception of Murray and a few other middle level officials, few American government officials displayed much sense of urgency about sending food to the stricken area.

One high level official who did want action was William Phillips, still officially President Roosevelt's personal representative to India, who brought the matter directly to the President's attention on September 9, 1943. Arguing that the famine posed a strategic problem for the United States because of American troop concentrations in the area, Phillips complained that the British were not addressing what was becoming a very serious problem. In the countryside, there was increased sympathy for the Japanese. And everywhere in the affected area lawbreaking was common as desperate people sought to obtain food in any way they could. Combined with the political deadlock, Phillips argued, the famine posed a potentially disastrous situation for American interests in the area. "The remedy, if there is one," he argued, "is for the British to open the door to negotiations and to do everything possible to lessen the famine conditions in the province of Bengal."[78]

Roosevelt took no action, however, and had he attempted to intervene the British would surely have reacted with resentment. When Phillips asked Amery if there was any way the United States could help, the secretary of state for India blandly told Phillips that he did not think there was much the United States could do to alleviate conditions. The American government seemed not to want to embarrass the British over the famine. When a private committee was formed to address Bengal's needs, Berle urged Louis Johnson not to get involved.[79]

However, public attention to the famine steadily increased. While acknowledging a multitude of causes for the famine, including the Japanese occupation of Southeast Asia, a region which in peacetime had provided some rice to India, most comment was critical of the

British for not having anticipated the shortages and of the American government for having done nothing to bring relief to the hungry. In October *Time* asserted that the famine demonstrated that "the Raj has failed" and complained that no influential Americans had called for famine relief. Harold E. Fey, an editor at the *Christian Century*, accused both the British and American governments of hiding the truth. Americans knew more about internal conditions in Germany, an enemy country, Fey complained, than about India, theoretically one of the Allies.[80] *The Nation* was equally critical, accusing Linlithgow of failing "to take even the most elementary steps to meet the crisis." In December *Life* published vivid photographs of starving Indians. The magazine's photographer, William Vandivert, was reportedly deeply shaken by what he had seen.[81] A few commentators noted a relationship between the imprisonment of the nationalists and the failure to address the famine. The *New Republic*, for example, speculated that the Indians themselves might have handled the situation better "except that nearly all their best leaders were in jail."[82]

British authorities charted the changes in American opinion carefully. At the end of September 1943, Bajpai reported that there had been little discussion of the situation in the American press. A month later he noted that comment was beginning to appear. By the end of November he discerned a big upsurge in interest, and by the end of the year the agent general reported that the famine had produced "lurid headlines" and "sharp criticism" of the British authorities. When Puckle attended a luncheon in New York organized by the British Information Service, he reported that there were many questions about the famine. The usual British line about American criticisms was that much of it was not genuine. Rather, anti-British forces were using the food shortages as another reason to press for Indian independence. But Bajpai reported that the critics also included "some highly respected and friendly figures" and concluded that the best way to reduce criticism was to deal effectively with the famine.[83]

Critical commentary in the American press slackened in 1944, as the famine appeared to ease, although the *Christian Century* contended that optimistic estimates of the situation were politically motivated and should be discounted.[84] Another reason for the decline in criticism were the actions of the new viceroy. Two days after Wavell took office on October 20, 1943, he established a Relief Distress Fund, and then, in stark contrast to Linlithgow, who never visited the stricken area, the viceroy and his wife immediately flew to Calcutta to see the devastation first hand.[85] The famine was "one of the greatest disasters that has befallen any people under British rule," he wrote to Amery. It had done "incalculable" damage to Britain's reputation, both in India and abroad. (From his prison, Nehru wrote that the British attitude, particularly Amery's, toward the famine was the thing that "has embittered me most.") Churchill's insistence that India could take care of itself was "statistically fallacious." If His Majesty's Government failed to respond, warned the viceroy, it was risking a catastrophe, not only to the Bengalis, but also to its international position.[86]

When the British government stalled again, Wavell reminded Amery that he had provided warnings months ago which London "has chosen deliberately to disregard." The government's decision not to approach the United States for assistance was almost beyond belief, he stated. A week later he pleaded with London to contract for one million tons of wheat available in Australia and to use American ships to transport it.[87]

Finally Amery threw his support to the viceroy in the War Cabinet, and "Winston was at last seriously perturbed" and agreed that something had to be done. The Prime Minister finally asked Roosevelt to provide one million tons of surplus wheat and the shipping necessary to get it to Bengal. Wavell was delighted and took credit for the change. The decision was "a considerable success for my persistency," he wrote.[88] Churchill did approach the President, but nothing happened. The Joint Chiefs recommended against the British request because they did not want to divert shipping. The President went along without protest and expressed his deep regrets to the Prime Minister.[89] There was further discussion of appealing to the Americans to reconsider, but in the end the War Cabinet decided not to press the issue. Wavell would have to rely on his own resources.[90] Although of little help to the starving, at least the viceroy's good name was intact. As a writer in the normally critical *Christian Century* put it, Wavell was "the person whose reputation has suffered least."[91]

By the summer 1944, discussion of the famine and criticism of

Britain's handling of it had virtually disappeared, though as a residual factor in the overall attitude toward India it remained. For the
moment, however, the British felt quite satisfied with most aspects of
American opinion.[92] Nevertheless, the British were well aware that
American criticism could reemerge almost overnight, particularly in
an election year, as indeed it already had with respect to British military failures that spring.

Some British officials, including Wavell, thought that raising the
status of the Indian agent general in Washington would be an excellent way to help keep American opinion in line. This was not a new
idea. Bajpai's status had been an issue ever since July 1941, when the
Americans had agreed to receive an Indian representative. In the
beginning, Linlithgow, always suspicious of the Foreign Office and
the British embassy in Washington, had argued for a relatively independent status and rank of minister for the new representative.

Within the year Ambassador Halifax had come to agree with Linlithgow that India's representative ought to head an independent
mission. But now Linlithgow changed his mind and objected to any
attempts to elevate Bajpai's status. He professed to like Bajpai very
much but felt that the agent general's keen interest "in his own status and position" lay behind the pressure for change. More basic to
Linlithgow's change of heart was his fear that the United States
would demand some kind of reciprocity. He felt greatly abused over
the assignment of Louis Johnson some months before and was, at the
moment, fighting efforts by Halifax and the London authorities to
try to secure the appointment of a high level American to New
Delhi.[93]

Linlithgow's opposition put the matter on hold, but it was not forgotten because Halifax, Eden, and even Amery supported the effort
to enhance Bajpai's status. With the appointment of Wavell as viceroy
a change in Bajpai's status could be reconsidered in a serious way.
Amery clearly thought the matter important. He mentioned it to
Wavell in July 1943 (as did Halifax the next month), and then formally raised it in October, shortly before Wavell assumed his new
post, noting the strong support for the idea from Halifax and Eden.
Wavell's response indicated that his tenure as viceroy would be very
different from his predecessor's. The difficulties that Linlithgow had

seen in raising Bajpai's status "were somewhat over-stressed," wrote Wavell. In spite of the "constitutional anomaly," he fully supported the attempt to upgrade the agent general's status.[94]

The change of heart from New Delhi set off a furious debate. Sir Olaf Caroe, the Government of India's secretary of external affairs (who was not in India when Wavell made his decision), protested strongly and urged the India Office to make his objections known to the viceroy.[95] India Office bureaucrats weighed in with their opposition. Roland Peel, head of the external affairs division, thought the arguments against it were "overwhelming." Another outspoken dissenter, David T. Monteath, permanent under-secretary at the India Office, wrote that his opposition to raising Bajpai's status had not abated. "I dislike this proposal intensely," he wrote.[96] It was left for F. F. Turnbull (whom Agatha Harrison, one of Gandhi's British supporters, once described as "a rather pinched person") and Monteath to put the negative case before Amery, which they did at length. Amery rejected their objections out of hand. "I seem to remember most of them as urged against Dominion representation between 1920 and 1926," he responded. But he did ask that a number of practical matters be investigated further before submitting a proposal for the War Cabinet.[97]

In the meantime Wavell's view prevailed in New Delhi. Although the viceroy was not unaware of the criticism directed at the agent general (he noted sardonically that Bajpai's style of life was "most extravagant" and that in India he "insisted on having everything of the best, and has several expensive hobbies"), he convinced his colleagues, including Caroe, that there were many advantages to the move.[98]

Late in February 1944, all questions had been answered to Amery's satisfaction, and when Eden offered to join him in making a formal proposal to the government to raise Bajpai's status, Amery quickly accepted.[99] The War Cabinet discussed the matter on June 9. Opinion was hostile. The United States, it was feared, would press for diplomatic representation in India. If the new Indian minister took positions at odds with the British, it would prove embarrassing. There was not enough business between the United States and India to justify the move. In the end Eden, who had suggested that he and

Amery introduce the plan jointly, backed away, confessing that after all he was "not himself enthusiastic about the proposal." Finally, it was decided to postpone action until Halifax could address the cabinet in person.[100]

In the meantime Wavell, who was not privy to the War Cabinet debate, waited impatiently. His Majesty's Government was "being maddeningly slow" in making a final decision on a matter that he thought had for all intents and purposes been settled six months previously.[101] But the viceroy underestimated the Prime Minister's strong feelings.

On August 3 Halifax argued his case before the cabinet, but without success. The cabinet voted to shelve the proposal, though it allowed for its reconsideration six months hence. The cabinet's action discouraged Bajpai, and he nearly resigned. Wavell was angry. "I suppose it is just part of Winston's general hate against India," he wrote.[102] Soon, revelations of lax security in Bajpai's office would doom the idea altogether for another year.

If Wavell's efforts to better Indo-American relations by raising Bajpai's status had come to naught, another of his actions resulted in a very positive response in the United States, if not from the British government. On May 6, 1944, Wavell released Gandhi unconditionally, ostensibly because of his deteriorating health. The move "awakened hope that the Anglo-Indian deadlock may soon be broken," stated the *Christian Century*.[103]

Over the next several weeks, American journals of opinion seconded the *Christian Century*'s hopes.[104] In London, William Phillips, sensing that Gandhi's health was only an excuse for the viceroy's decision, was exhilarated. "It is a most important moment in Indian affairs," he wrote in his diary. Now if Gandhi and Jinnah could get together, he thought, the political problems might yet be solved. Phillips felt that Wavell's action presaged real movement. But of one thing Phillips was not sure: how far would the British government go in allowing Wavell to seek a settlement?[105]

Phillips's skepticism was well founded. On June 17 Gandhi asked Wavell for permission to consult with the Congress's Working Committee and also offered to meet with the viceroy. Subsequently he offered to repudiate mass civil disobedience and cooperate with the war effort, provided Britain would declare India independent and form a national government at the center. Wavell clearly wanted to engage the mahatma in discussions, if not negotiations. But he faced an uphill battle as long as Churchill remained at the helm. The return to politics of the "naked faqir," as Churchill once called Gandhi, angered the Prime Minister. With almost brutal sarcasm, he asked Wavell how it was that Gandhi's health had so quickly improved after his release that he could resume an active role in politics?[106] While this bitter internal debate raged, Wavell could make no response to Gandhi's requests.

When nothing had happened by late July, and with a Parliamentary debate about to begin over India, Phillips urged the United States to express its concern about India. Either Phillips could call on Amery to urge that the Indian parties be brought together, or even better the President could raise the question with Churchill, he suggested.[107]

Whatever chance there was of the State Department authorizing Phillips to approach Amery vanished three days after the ambassador made his suggestion when syndicated columnist Drew Pearson published Phillips's letter to the President of May 14, 1943. In that report, written after his homecoming interview with Roosevelt, Phillips offered several negative assessments of Britain's contributions to the war against Japan and their rule in India. He charged that Britain would offer only "token assistance" in the war against Japan, that the Indians felt they had no stake in the war, that Churchill had stated that the Atlantic Charter did not apply to India, that the Indian army was "purely mercenary," that the general population was bitter and demoralized, and that all Indians, in spite of their divisions, wanted independence. The time had come for the British to act, Phillips told the President. The King should publicly set a specific date after the end of the war for independence, and in the interim the British should permit a provisional government at the center and transfer significant powers to it.[108]

When Pearson's column appeared, Phillips immediately realized he could no longer serve as an effective American representative on Indian matters. He also feared that the disclosure would give Hull a convenient excuse to take no action on his request for American intervention. To Phillips's surprise, however, the secretary of state authorized Ambassador Winant to say to the British government that a settlement of the Indian problem would help win the war in Asia and "is of great importance to the future peace of the world." Winant did mention the matter to Eden, but when Phillips asked about it he found the ambassador "very non-communicative" and concluded that he had not taken any energetic steps.[109]

Whatever Winant may have said seems not to have been a matter of discussion among the British, suggesting that Phillips's assessment of the ambassador's action was correct. It certainly had no effect on the outcome. As the authorities debated a response to Gandhi, Churchill expressed his "grave uneasiness" that Wavell should be having any contact with Gandhi at all because Gandhi "had consistently been a bitter enemy of this country."[110] Eventually the War Cabinet, over Amery's strong objections, authorized a response so negative that Wavell and the British embassy in Washington considered it "hostile and provocative" and one that would have a very bad effect on opinion in the United States and elsewhere.[111]

On August 16 Wavell told Gandhi that there would be no discussions on the bases Gandhi suggested. Only if the various communal groups cooperated to establish a transitional government *within* the existing constitution could there be negotiations. But the viceroy was bitter that he had been forced to send this to Gandhi.[112]

As Wavell predicted, the reaction to his letter was very strong and very negative. Even the Muslim press was critical, contending that even if all Indian groups agreed to a common program, the British government would find a way to obstruct progress. "Some day we have got to negotiate with these people, not necessarily Gandhi perhaps," Wavell wrote, "and this letter has destroyed at one blow a reputation that had been accorded me in the Congress press of being at least straightforward and courteous in my correspondence with Congress."[113]

As for the American response, it was much as Wavell predicted. The day after Wavell's letter to Gandhi, Lampton Berry, back in Washington, stopped by to see his friend Frederick Puckle, the British publicist, and commented that he thought the British were being "unnecessarily and perhaps dangerously stiff" in their response to Gandhi's proposals. "He thought it was a pity that the Viceroy did not see Gandhi," Puckle reported, in part because it gave the impression that the "white nations" would make no concessions to nationalist sentiment in Asia. Although Berry's visit was ostensibly social, it may have been, as Puckle thought, intended to convey State Department views of the British decision. Certainly his expressed concern about keeping India loyal to the West represented the President's thinking.[114] In any event, Berry's views were seconded the next day by Wallace Murray, who privately attacked Wavell for refusing to talk to Gandhi and for not allowing him to visit the Working Committee, in spite of Gandhi's disavowal of civil disobedience and his condemnation of violence in the Quit India campaign. The viceroy's "refusal even to have a talk with Gandhi in the face of these declarations speaks for itself," he wrote to Phillips.[115] There was also a significant public reaction among Americans interested in India. Shortly before Wavell's response to Gandhi, more than one hundred prominent Americans signed an appeal urging serious consideration of Gandhi's suggestions for a settlement, an appeal that at least one Foreign Office official thought should "not be taken lightly."[116]

At exactly this time, however, most American attention about India was focused on what was really a less significant, but more sensational, incident: the unauthorized disclosure of the Phillips letter and related documents. Pearson's publication of Phillips's letter to Roosevelt angered the British. The very day the letter appeared, Campbell called on Secretary Hull to protest, arguing that Phillips's report would "create an extremely bad impression in London and in India." He called Hull's attention in particular to Phillips's comments about the low morale of the Indian army and to his assertion that Britain would provide little assistance against the Japanese. Hull, who was not even aware of Pearson's column (he never read Pearson, he said), pledged an early response.[117] Two days later Berle orally expressed the government's "sincere regret" that the letter had leaked and promised an investigation. Hull was reportedly "extremely angry" about the matter.[118]

The matter might have ended there, but the British government insisted on more than expressions of regret that the letter had leaked. They wanted the United States government to "disassociate" itself from Phillips's statements.[119] Campbell spoke with Undersecretary of State Edward R. Stettinius, Jr. (Hull being absent) and asked if Roosevelt or Hull would comment on three specific opinions expressed by Phillips: his "damaging reference" to the Indian army's morale, the "unfair reference" to Britain's role in the war against Japan, and Churchill's alleged failure to include India in the purview of the Atlantic Charter. Later the same day Campbell wrote again to the State Department asking the United States government to disassociate itself from Phillips's opinions, "the sooner . . . the better."[120]

Much to the irritation of the British, the State Department did not move with dispatch. It took five days for the department to consider the matter. Officials in the Office of European Affairs joined those in the Office of Near East and African Affairs in recommending against acceding to the British request, for the simple reason that they agreed with Phillips's views. It is unlikely that Hull himself concurred entirely with substance of Phillips's report, but the secretary did agree that the department should not repudiate Phillips. To the President he stated that the department considered it "impossible" to comply with the British request.[121]

Although the British knew nothing of these developments, there were hints that the Americans would not accede to their request. On August 10, for example, two British officials met with Harry Hopkins who told them that the President was angry about the claims of colonial sovereigns in general.[122] When the British had heard nothing for a month after their original protest, Halifax again approached the State Department. This time he dropped the request that the United States disassociate itself from Phillips's statement that Churchill had excluded India from the promises contained in the Atlantic Charter, but he continued to think that it was "essential and urgent" that the administration disavow Phillips's assertions about the morale of the Indian army and British contributions to the war against Japan.[123]

Hull promised to bring Halifax's request to Roosevelt's attention, but when there was no early response the Foreign Office began to wonder if there would ever be a satisfactory reply. Three weeks later Hull held out a glimmer of hope by telling Halifax that the President "was readily receptive" to commenting on the points raised, but Roosevelt never did disassociate himself or his administration from Phillips's observations and probably never intended to do so. "How can I say anything," he told Phillips later, "since every word of your report is true?"[124] It was yet another indirect way for the President to express his disagreement with British policy and his support for independence of colonial areas. Eventually some British officials reluctantly recognized this. As one Foreign Office official, A. C. E. Malcolm, put it, Roosevelt "rather agrees with Mr. Phillips than otherwise."[125]

Aside from his essential agreement with Phillips's views, there were other reasons why the President chose not to disavow Phillips's sentiments. The two men and their families had of course been close personal friends for decades. Malcolm again was one of the first British officials to understand this. "If we thought we were going to get Mr. Roosevelt to disavow his old friend Mr. Phillips on a subject like British policy in India, in a difficult election year," he wrote, "we must be crazy."[126]

Another reason for Roosevelt's caution were the sensational charges that the British had forced Phillips to resign from his London post and would not welcome him back in India. Such accusations, if true, were unlikely to go down well with the President. Although the State Department announced that Phillips would be returning to Washington for "urgent family reasons," many people not unnaturally assumed that the leaked letter was the real cause of his return.[127] And, in fact, the timing of Phillips's return *was* affected by the disclosures. Phillips's relationship with the Foreign Office was now beyond repair, and he knew this would affect his working relationships in London. Publication of his letter had already prevented him from presenting the administration's concerns about Indian developments. Sensing the coolness of his English colleagues, Phillips decided that he would advance the date for his return.[128]

But what convinced many people that the British had forced Phillips out was Pearson's dramatic charge on August 28 that the British had declared the ambassador *persona non grata* in London and India. He also wrote that Foreign Secretary Eden had stated in a telegram that India was "more important than a thousand Phillips [*sic*]."[129] The same day Happy Chandler repeated the *persona non grata* charge on the Senate floor,[130] and shortly thereafter in the House of Representatives Calvin D. Johnson, a Republican from Illinois, introduced a retaliatory motion declaring Bajpai and Campbell *personae non gratae.*

Chandler's and Pearson's charges, and Johnson's motion, increased British anger that the Roosevelt administration had not disavowed Phillips's sentiments earlier. Had it done so, London thought, Chandler and Pearson might not have made their allegations.

The British redoubled their efforts to get a satisfactory statement from the administration. They insisted that Halifax add to his demands an administration statement denying the charge that Phillips was *persona non grata.* Halifax was also ordered to reinstitute the item he had previously dropped: Phillips's charge that Churchill had excluded India from the provisions of the Atlantic Charter. The British Government was also beginning to feel that Halifax had muffed the job. Eden reprimanded him, saying that he "regret[ed]" that the ambassador had not issued his own statement saying that Pearson's new charges were almost entirely inaccurate. "Something fairly full-blooded" that all the papers would print, was required, he said in another dispatch. Halifax strongly defended his handling of the entire matter, including his decision not to press the Atlantic Charter point. But the next day he issued a strong statement denying that the British government had ever asked for Phillips's removal or declared him *persona non grata.*[131]

Halifax also spoke again with Hull, who promised to arrange for a senator to respond to Chandler's allegations,[132] and Hull asked Assistant Secretary Breckinridge Long to follow up. Long sent copies of Halifax's denial to Sol Bloom, chairman of the House Committee on Foreign Affairs, and Senate Majority Leader Tom Connally. To both he emphasized the harm the incident was causing to Anglo-American relations. Bloom then denied the *persona non grata* charge, and Connally was preparing to do the same when Chandler, who had shrewdly waited for the various denials to be made, reemerged and cited a telegram that Sir Olaf Caroe, secretary for external affairs of the Government of India, had sent to Amery, which described Phillips as *persona non grata.* "We could not again receive him," Caroe was quoted as stating. Connally decided that it would be "inopportune" to issue his planned statement.[133] (Two days later Caroe privately admitted that the telegram Chandler had cited, dated August 16, 1944, was accurate, although he was personally "shattered" that it had been made public.)[134]

Halifax then told Long that the American response had been inadequate. Hull himself had to condemn Chandler, the ambassador insisted.[135] Long took the matter to Hull, who in turn referred it to the President. On September 5 Hull held a press conference at which he said only that Phillips's resignation from his London post was not the result of the leaked letter nor was it demanded by the British. To the British, Hull's performance was, as Nevile Butler put it, "disappointing."[136] Publicly from the Americans the British had only expressions of regret that the Phillips letter had leaked and that they had never received an official request for Phillips's removal.

The British were not yet willing to throw in the towel, however. Eden ordered Halifax to press the administration for a "maximum response," including a reply to the much belabored Atlantic Charter question (which Halifax had not raised again, in spite of the Foreign Minister's strongly worded insistence that he do so).[137] In London, the Foreign Office, claiming the Pearson leaks were unprecedented, urged Winant "to make it quite clear to Mr. Hull" that these events had caused "great concern" in Britain. They thought Hull's statement about the incident "exceedingly luke-warm" and requested that the President or some other high official make a speech defending the British contribution to the Pacific war.[138]

Halifax saw Hull again on September 9, but the secretary offered little more than a Presidential expression of regret that the Phillips letter had leaked. Increasingly the British realized that there would be no statement unless the Prime Minister himself approached the President. Finally Churchill ended the matter. The incident was not important enough to trouble the President with, he stated to Halifax. However, the Prime Minister probably also sensed that Roosevelt would not have acceded to his request. "This seems to put the lid on any hopes we might have had of getting a statement out of the Americans," commented one India Office official with evident disappointment.[139] There would be no repudiation of Phillips from the administration.[140]

Yet another reason for Roosevelt not to accede to the British request to distance his administration from Phillips was the very positive reaction of Indian nationalists to what Phillips had written. At first the British tried to keep news of the disclosures out of the Indian press and even received help from American diplomatic and military authorities in India who knew that the State Department was upset at Pearson.[141] But within a few weeks they gave up when it became apparent that sooner or later the news would get in. By late August it was all over the Indian papers. As Wavell wrote in September, "the Congress newspapers have had a series of field-days."[142] All facets of the dispute received front page attention in the Indian press, and many editorials praised Phillips and the United States. "No leading article in the columns of a nationalist newspaper in India could have put in more forceful language India's case against Britain," stated the *Hindustan Standard* of Calcutta.[143] Even moderates were impressed with what Phillips had written. Bhola N. Pande, for example, a good friend of the leading Indian Liberal Sir Tej Bahadur Sapru, followed the Phillips affair closely and concluded that Phillips's views were "for the best of this country. His exposition of the situation may be regarded as prejudicial in the present day conditions," Pande went on, "but some day the world will realise the truth of his words."[144] Howard Donovan, the American consul in Bombay, summed it up well: Nationalist Indians were "jubilant over the Phillips letter," and the incident tended to enhance American prestige in India.[145]

The publicity resulted in notice being given of several motions and questions that would be raised in the Indian Legislative Assembly (the lower house) and the Council of States (the upper house). Wavell (who now, like most Government of India officials, considered Phillips "very light weight" with "no assets beyond good manners")[146] eventually decided to disallow the motions on the grounds that to discuss them would be detrimental to the public interest,[147] but he was inclined to make a statement about the Phillips affair to clarify the Government of India's position. In his draft statement, Wavell admitted that the Government of India had informed the British government that it did not want to receive Phillips again because of the statements disclosed by Pearson. In other words,

Wavell proposed to confirm the existence of the Caroe telegram.[148] Foreign Office officials, however, did not want Wavell to make any statement. It would reopen a very sensitive matter that might cause Roosevelt to reaffirm that Phillips was still his personal representative to India and would give Pearson ample material to cause trouble. They also objected to acknowledging the existence of the Caroe telegram. The use of the term *persona non grata* had been a mistake, they claimed, and acknowledging it would only provide evidence for the charge that the British were penalizing Phillips for reporting the situation as he saw it.[149]

The India Office and the Foreign Office then prepared a new draft statement which did not admit the authenticity of the Caroe telegram and which, they thought, was less provocative. Halifax feared that even the watered down version would irritate the United States and cause the President to reaffirm Phillips's position. The issue was temporarily delayed when Wavell agreed to defer any statement until after the American elections.[150] By then interest had declined, and in the end the Government of India did not confirm the authenticity of the Caroe telegram. Although Pearson had published the text of the dispatch, it was not until 1973 that the British finally acknowledged that the telegram existed when they allowed it to be published in the *Transfer of Power* volumes.[151]

Publication of the Phillips letter also tended, from the nationalist perspective, to counter a less positive view of the American role in India. Shortly after Wavell released Gandhi, the American mission in New Delhi asked what it ought to do with the letter that President Roosevelt had written to Gandhi shortly before the mahatma's arrest in August 1942. The letter was in reply to one that Gandhi had written some weeks earlier. Because Roosevelt's reply had arrived after Gandhi's incarceration, it had remained in the American mission undelivered. Now that Gandhi had been released, Merrell in New Delhi recommended against forwarding the undelivered letter, which contained outdated sentiments, and suggested instead that Roosevelt send a new one urging a dialogue with Jinnah. But Hull and Roosevelt disagreed and instructed Merrell to arrange for delivery of the letter.[152]

Merrell first gave Caroe a copy of the letter and said that Lampton

Berry, who would soon return to the United States and who wanted
to visit with Gandhi before he left, would deliver it to Gandhi. But
before Berry left New Delhi, nationalist newspapers got wind of the
Roosevelt letter and published "exceedingly accurate details" about
Berry's plans, from which they erroneously concluded that the
American had instructions to negotiate with the mahatma. Berry
thereupon canceled his plans to visit Gandhi and, after carrying Roosevelt's letter to Bombay, turned it over to the Congress industrialist
G. D. Birla for delivery. Birla handed the letter to Gandhi on June 24,
1944.[153]

This incident is important partly because on July 6 Pearson published a misleading account about it, in which he alleged that the
Government of India had prevented delivery of the original letter,
and partly because of the nationalist reaction. The letter, written in
the weeks after the failure of the Cripps Mission and in the context
of Gandhi's threat to lead a civil disobedience campaign to demand
that the British quit India, urged the mahatma to cooperate with the
British. This led Pearson to charge, with some force, that the President had, in effect, sold out the nationalists in favor of the British. It
was a theme that the nationalists themselves picked up. Not only did
Roosevelt's letter appear to demonstrate the President's support of
the British position, but also the administration's failure even to ask
the British to deliver the letter was further evidence of a weak American approach. These matters, along with the later American failure
to make strong representations to the British in support of Phillips's
efforts to see the imprisoned Gandhi, added up, as Howard Donovan
put it, to a perception of a "spineless attitude adopted by the United
States when it clashes with Great Britain on such matters." All in all,
Donovan concluded, the incident had hurt American prestige in
India.[154] Although Donovan did not say so, the mission's original recommendation not to deliver the letter made more sense than Hull's
to send it forward.

Why Roosevelt agreed to have the letter delivered is unclear.
Venkataramani and Shrivastava, in the most complete account of the
incident, contend that it was Hull who influenced Roosevelt. Determined not to have any further correspondence between Roosevelt
and Gandhi, but at the same time wanting the record to show that the

President had replied to Gandhi's letter, Hull concluded that the best course was to deliver the original letter with an explanation for the delay. A new letter would only invite the exchange of correspondence that Hull wished to avoid.[155] The explanation rings true, for the sentiments expressed in the letter did not represent Roosevelt's current thinking, which was again moving strongly away from supporting imperial possessions in the postwar era. Hull's recommendation, based on a desire to show for the record that the President had responded to Gandhi in 1942, probably appealed to a busy and tired President who had more pressing concerns on his mind.

The controversy over Roosevelt's letter to Gandhi developed only days before Drew Pearson published Phillips's letter. Indian perceptions of a weak American position in the former matter helped ensure that the President would not give in to British pressure to repudiate Phillips.

From the summer of 1943 into the fall of 1944, there was no strongly stated American position on Indian developments. Some American actions pointed to an American determination to support the British in India. The administration failed to press the British strongly to modify their overall position toward India or even to release Gandhi and the other nationalists from prison. Roosevelt's public statement on India in February 1944, which emphasized that winning the war came above all else, indicated his reluctance to challenge Churchill at this point. Likewise, the administration did not make a strong response to the Bengal famine. Wavell was more outspoken on this than was the United States. When Churchill finally did request American ships to relieve the famine, Roosevelt declined to help.

On the other hand, American officials in India were highly critical of the British and the Government of India, as was William Phillips, who continued to take an active interest in India after his transfer to London. Phillips in particular continued to make the case—and did so directly to the President—that the United States must distance itself more than it already had from British imperialism. While concerned with the immediate military situation, he emphasized the need to keep India in the western fold for the future. His reasons had historical, idealistic, and practical bases.

On a personal level, there is every reason to think that Roosevelt agreed with Phillips. The President's ideas on colonies generally were definitely moving toward eventual independence. Although he envisaged a period of transition during which former colonies would be under some form of international trusteeship (his interest in trusteeship in fact peaked during this period),[156] the end result in almost all cases, Roosevelt thought, should be full independence. Although he was reluctant to challenge Churchill on India, particularly since Allied military successes made the Prime Minister even more intransigent than ever, he continued to make his discomfort with British policy clear. His decision not to send Phillips back to India, while insisting that Phillips retain his title of the President's personal representative to India, was one indication of his displeasure at British policy, something that some British officials understood. More telling was his refusal to repudiate Phillips's strong views when Pearson published them, in spite of his personal contempt for the columnist and immense pressure from the British that he do so. Churchill's decision not to press the President on this point probably resulted from the Prime Minister's awareness that the President would not back down. The next year the United States would once again ask publicly that the Indian issue be resolved and would offer its assistance toward that end.

8 | Renewed American Interest in India
(September 1944–December 1945)

The unauthorized disclosure of the Phillips letter, the Caroe *persona non grata* telegram, and subsequently some additional confidential diplomatic dispatches as well, mostly by Drew Pearson, were serious matters that complicated Anglo-American relations, even as they enhanced the image of the United States in India. Consequently, there were intensive investigations in three countries on three continents to find the source or sources of the disclosures.

The Phillips letter almost certainly came from someone with State Department connections. Suspicion immediately focused on Sumner Welles, who had recently been forced to resign. Other suspects have included unnamed officials sympathetic to William Phillips, and even President Roosevelt. Tantalizing, but inclusive, evidence implicates Louis Johnson. The British Secret Service has also been suspected. The most likely possibility is that as yet undiscovered State Department officials, or perhaps Johnson, gave a copy of the letter to a disaffected Indian in the United States, probably Obaidur Rahman who had worked in Bajpai's office. Chaman Lal, a disgruntled sometime intelligence agent for the Government of India who also had access to Bajpai's office, had a copy of the letter months before Pearson published it. In all probability, either Rahman or Lal passed the letter to Anup Singh (one of the few Indian nationalists living in the United States to whom Lal had access), who in turn gave it to Pearson.

The Caroe telegram came from the agent general's office. Bajpai and British investigators concluded independently that the embassy's third secretary, Major Altaf Qadir, was the culprit, and he was quickly reassigned to active military duty in Italy. Qadir may have been involved (Bajpai had long warned his superiors of Qadir's unreliability), but the case against him was weak. Investigators also thought that K. C. Mahindra, director of the Indian Supply Mission, played a part in the leakages, but he was almost certainly innocent. Rahman and Lal are the most likely suspects, and Bajpai was privately criticized for lax security.[1]

That so many Indians were central figures in the drama illustrates the strength of Indian nationalism and the difficulties the British had in controlling it. Although most of the leaders of the Congress were still incarcerated, nationalism had not been suppressed. Hardly any Indians in Washington, including those in official positions (presumably the most likely to identify with the British) were unaffected by nationalist sentiments. Thus, although Mahindra may not have had a hand in disclosing the documents, he undoubtedly had bitter anti-British attitudes. So did Qadir. Even the trusted Bajpai harbored mildly nationalistic attitudes (and some have even suspected that he had a hand in the leakages.) To the British and Indian governments, of course, Mahindra, Qadir, and Rahman were traitors. To Indian nationalists, however, they were patriots who risked their careers (and, in the case of Qadir, who was sent to the front, his life) to promote a noble cause.

Among the major consequences of the leaks incident, differences among the Government of India, the India Office, and the Foreign Office became greatly accentuated. Anti-Indian prejudices within the Foreign Office increased markedly. Not only were efforts by the Indian authorities to get the Foreign Office to accept Indians into the foreign service in Asia put on hold, but also new regulations were drafted forbidding Indians from occupying positions where Foreign Office ciphers were available. Despite vigorous protests from the India Office that these regulations were racially discriminatory, they were allowed to stand.[2]

While the ramifications of the leaked Phillips letters were being debated and as investigators scurried about to pinpoint responsibility, the military situation in Asia continued to improve on all fronts. In the Pacific, the American advance proceeded apace. A debate between Admirals Ernest J. King and Chester W. Nimitz, who wanted to bypass the Philippines, and General Douglas MacArthur, who insisted that the United States was honor-bound to recapture the commonwealth, was settled in favor of MacArthur. By October 20, 1944, American soldiers were on Leyte. Very heavy fighting lay ahead, for the Japanese knew that they had to stop the American advance in the Philippines or face disaster. But by the end of December all Japanese resistance on Leyte had ceased. In January the assault on Luzon began. By March 4, 1945, after several additional weeks of desperate resistance, during which much of Manila was reduced to rubble, the Philippine capital was in American hands. Three weeks later after ferocious fighting Iwojima fell to the Americans, and Japan was more vulnerable than ever before to air attacks on the home islands and an invasion.[3]

At the same time British forces, under the inspired leadership of General Sir William Slim, followed up on their successful defense of Imphal by attacking the Japanese forces retreating into Burma. By early May 1945, Rangoon had been captured. The once formidable Japanese armies in Burma had been destroyed, and all that remained were mopping up operations. The victories in Burma improved the image of Britain. The advance on Mandalay "caught American imagination," wrote the leading British publicist in the United States, while the Burma campaign as a whole was "the best piece of British propaganda about India which has yet appeared."[4] Gratifying as these military advances were, however, many Americans, both military and civilian, remained very suspicious that Britain's only interest in Asia was to restore its colonies.

As for India, it had provided the base for British operations in Burma, and it continued its longtime role as the location from which to supply Allied forces in China. But by 1945 even Roosevelt had been forced to concede that China—or at least Chiang Kai-shek's China—could not play its assigned role as one of the "Four Policemen." Increasingly Roosevelt ignored Chiang and at the Yalta conference in February 1945, made decisions affecting China without informing, much less consulting, the Chinese leader. India, then, in late 1944 and 1945 lost much of its military significance in American eyes. It did, however, continue to be an important factor in the Southeast Asia theater. In fact in October 1944, the Combined Chiefs of Staff issued orders to expand India's capacity. After the fall of Rangoon India served as a base for Operation ZIPPER, the attack on Swettenham (now Port Klang) and Fort Dickson, Malaya, which was to prepare the way for the reconquest of Singapore.

More important to India's future was the general state of Anglo-American relations which, by late 1944, were experiencing considerable strain over a variety of issues. Very serious differences remained over economic policy, for example, with the British still committed to some form of protection and the Americans wanting open markets, competition, and free trade. This was seen in strenuous negotiations over civil aviation rights, the President even threatening to scuttle lend lease assistance unless the British gave in to American demands. Even more emotional were British efforts to establish close ties with the regime in Argentina that the Americans considered virtually fascist and their interference in Italian politics without consulting the United States. There was genuine anger at harsh British occupation policies in Greece, especially after Pearson published Churchill's order that Athens was to be treated as a "conquered city" rather than as an Allied capital. Serious differences were also beginning to develop over how to deal with the Soviet Union.[5]

Such criticisms of Britain, which peaked at the beginning of the new year (one scholar describes Anglo-American relations at this time as the "wartime nadir"), had important implications for India. When a particularly critical and widely discussed article about American policy appeared in the respected British journal, *The Economist*, Representative Emanuel Celler (D.-N.Y.) asked why Americans should not criticize British policy in India. Shortly thereafter Arthur Vandenberg (R.-Michigan), the influential ranking minority member on the Senate Foreign Relations Committee, asserted that the time had come to stand by the ideals of the Atlantic Charter.[6]

Even more directly important to India's future were American views about the future of the European empires. Roosevelt continued to be critical of the French rule in Indochina and was determined to prevent the French from reoccupying the area after the war. His views on the futures of the Dutch and British empires were less clear, and he said different things to different people at different times about both. In January 1944, for example, he mentioned breezily to Halifax that the British need not fear his trusteeship plan because it would not apply to their colonies. They and the Dutch, he said, had "done a good job" in their colonies.[7] But the overall direction of his thought in 1944 and into 1945 was still strongly toward ending empire, including the British empire.

At the Cairo and Teheran conferences in November 1943, Roosevelt ignored the British on colonial matters, instead discussing his anticolonial ideas with Chiang and Stalin. In December 1944, he told the Australian minister to Washington that he wanted the British "to give up Malaya and Burma unconditionally as he was giving up the Philippines." In January 1945, he emphasized to Oliver Stanley, Britain's colonial secretary, the need for timetables for independence. "No other specific point," writes historian William Roger Louis, "so well illuminates the real difference between Roosevelt's approach to the colonial question and that of the British and Europeans." Two days later Stanley made it clear to State Department officials that Britain's goal was not independence but self-government. The differences between Roosevelt and the British government were becoming sharper and suggested that Roosevelt would pressure the British over India. As Harold Macmillan put it retrospectively, "the British Empire was a bugbear to him . . . and the liquidation of the British Empire was, whether consciously or unconsciously, one of his aims."[8]

In the context of sharp tensions in Anglo-American relations, calls for a more clearly idealistic foreign policy, and the President's continuing devotion to anticolonialism, American diplomats discerned new political stirrings in India. In particular, the Indian National Congress was again debating whether it ought to cooperate with Wavell's administration to the extent of reentering the provincial and central legislatures.[9] The United States was interested in this development because it could lead eventually to a settlement of the political impasse. But American diplomats on the scene were not optimistic about a successful outcome. Gandhi, they believed, was worn out and fading fast. Some predicted his death within months. Jinnah had little to offer, they felt. Furthermore, they saw no change in Britain's hard line approach to the nationalists. To be sure some constructive ideas were being pressed by people like Sir Mirza M. Ismail, the Prime Minister of Jaipur state, and the Liberals around Sapru. Ismail, for example, recommended freeing all imprisoned Indian leaders, appointing representative Indians to the viceroy's Executive Council, and forming a committee to draft a new constitution. But Ismail himself held out little hope of forward movement since Wavell was "worn out," and the Europeans around the viceroy and in the Indian Civil Service were uninterested in change. On the latter point, Sir Henry Twynam, Governor of the Central Provinces and Berar, impressed an American vice-consul as being "very conservative." The governor did "not try to hide his antipathy towards Indians in general."[10] All in all, there was little reason for hope.[11]

Despite these pessimistic assessments, the United States government determined to keep the pressure on Britain for change. On January 29, 1945, Acting Secretary of State Joseph Grew stated publicly that the United States had continued to follow Indian affairs sympathetically, hoped progress would be made, and stood ready to assist in bringing about a settlement.[12] The statement, while responsive to immediate Indian developments, should also be seen in the context of Anglo-American tensions and criticisms that the United States should be doing more to promote freedom in the colonies.

It was perhaps not coincidental that less than a month after Grew's statement, Merrell indicated that it would not be wise for William Phillips to resign from his post as the President's representative to India, even though he had not been in New Delhi for nearly two years. Merrell feared that nationalists would interpret a resignation as "a definite indication that the United States had ceased to have an interest in the Indian political problem."[13] Further indicative of official American concern with Indian developments, a few days later President Roosevelt addressed the sensitive issue of Indian immigration and called for an end to the discrimination against Indians, who were ineligible for citizenship. Stating that the immigration statutes provoked "ill-feeling" and served "no useful purpose," Roosevelt concluded that they were "incongruous and inconsistent with the dignity of both of our people."[14]

In India, the nationalist press found some hope in the new American interest. The *Hindustan Times* noted (incorrectly) that Grew's statement was the first public comment on India since 1943, and while it might not mean much, perhaps the United States had finally "got tired of being bullied by Britain." Maybe the Americans would yet line up with the nationalists. Nationalist Indians in the United States also took heart. Krishnalal Shridharani thought Grew's statement "very hopeful," while Anup Singh, the man who gave the Phillips letter to Pearson, found Grew's remarks "very encouraging" and indicating that the United States would intervene "at the appropriate moment."[15]

A particularly important voice for Indian nationalism then in the United States was Nehru's sister, Vijayalakshmi Pandit. Urged by Gandhi to come, she had arrived in December 1944, to visit her two daughters, who had enrolled in Wellesley College the previous year. Amery had tried to prevent her daughters from going to the United States, but the Government of India had already given them passports and they had left before Amery could stop them. In 1944, though with obvious reluctance, Amery granted a passport to Pandit herself since the viceroy, Halifax, and Bajpai all supported her application. Even the British Information Services in the United States felt that to deny the recently widowed Pandit a passport to visit her daughters would create a much worse impression than any anti-British statements that she might make while in the United States. The matter was considered sufficiently serious, however, that Amery had to explain it in detail to the War Cabinet's India Committee.[16]

Once in the United States Pandit attracted considerable attention. In January Eleanor Roosevelt invited her for tea, and a few weeks later William Phillips, still technically Roosevelt's personal representative to India, gave a dinner in her honor.[17] As expected she was an outspoken and vocal supporter of the nationalist cause and urged the United States to do more. Her comments about American inaction, in fact, probably contributed to the State Department's decision to issue its statement of January 29. Like other nationalists, Pandit found the statement "helpful," although she complained that it did not go far enough.[18]

Shortly after the American offer to assist in settling the Indian problem, Roosevelt joined Churchill and Stalin at the important Yalta Conference where issues of fundamental importance were to be debated and, in some cases, settled. To the disappointment of Phillips and other friends of the Indian nationalists, India was not directly discussed. But issues with potential implications for India were. Yalta is usually analyzed in the context of the Cold War and Western-Soviet relations. But at the conference American disputes with the British were nearly as serious as with the Russians. The Declaration on Liberated Europe, for example, which the Americans proposed and pushed at the conference, was aimed initially as much at the British as the Russians. Although the British were eventually assured that the declaration did not apply to their empire, the sentiments contained in the document, which sounded very much like the Atlantic Charter, indicated that the President still thought that self-determination was an important part of the nation's postwar goals. The *New York Times* thought the declaration the most important result of the conference.[19]

Roosevelt also urged Churchill to reduce the empire's trade preferences (which, if done, would have resulted in more American influence in the colonies) and shrewdly lined up Stalin on his side of the colonial question. He even told the startled dictator that he hoped Churchill would restore Hong Kong to China.[20] Most significantly the President outmaneuvered an unprepared Churchill on the trusteeship issue. It has sometimes been alleged that the President's declining health affected his ability to deal forcefully with the complex issues at Yalta. Such an interpretation cannot apply to the colonial issue, which Roosevelt handled with consummate skill.

The trusteeship formula that emerged from the Yalta talks was an American one. It is sometimes argued that the formula adopted at Yalta represented an American retreat on the colonial question because it applied only to former Axis territories and League of Nations mandates.[21] Indeed, Churchill went along only when assured that it did not apply to the British empire. It is true that the formula did not directly endanger European colonialism. But it laid the basis for future attacks on empire because it applied to the mandates (including British mandates) and because it provided for the voluntary transfer of territory into a trusteeship system. There would now be a basis for challenging British colonial rule. As William Roger Louis writes, Churchill had unwittingly "given the future international organization the basis for putting the British Empire 'in the dock.'" The British Colonial Office recognized this and complained that the Foreign Office had appeased the Americans. The British Empire did not die at Yalta, but it was seriously, perhaps mortally, wounded.[22]

In the immediate aftermath of the Yalta Conference Roosevelt continued to indicate that he would press the British on the colonial question. On the return voyage he told aides that at Yalta he had had as many problems with the British as with the Russians and pointed particularly to the question of imperialism. The President "showed his eagerness to apply the principles of the Atlantic Charter to all the colonial peoples" in the Pacific region. Churchill, he told reporters, was "mid-Victorian" in his thinking about colonial rule, and the President agreed that the Prime Minister's ideas were "inconsistent with the policy of self-determination." "In this area," wrote his speech writer, "the President knew that he and Churchill were going to have deep-seated differences of opinion."[23] Churchill's efforts to hang on to India, it would appear, would face a serious challenge from the President once the war was over.

Shortly after the President returned from the Yalta conference, William Phillips argued forcefully that the time had come for the American government once again to press the British "to make a further prominent effort at this time to reach agreement with the Indians." Phillips probably sensed that American intervention might be of value because of Lord Wavell's impending trip to London. The Americans assumed that, with the European war winding down, the Americans making dramatic progress in the Pacific, and the United Nations Organization meeting in San Francisco coming up in a few weeks, the viceroy was returning for a serious discussion about the future of India.[24]

In fact, there had already been some behind-the-scenes movement in England. Over the Christmas holidays Amery had come to the rather startling conclusion that, rather than wait for the Indians to agree on a constitution prior to granting self-government, it made more sense to reverse the order. They should be given self-government under the existing constitution, "and then let them consider at leisure how they can amend it." Wavell was delighted. "Some light dawning at last!" he scribbled on Amery's letter. The following day Amery urged the War Cabinet's India Committee to reconsider its approach to India. Without using the dreaded word "independence," Amery contended that what India "most passionately desires is not a particular constitution . . . , but freedom from a status of subordination to an outside authority."[25] The situation, he later argued, was analogous to that in America at time of the American Revolution when the failure of the British to give way in time lost the United States forever to the British empire. Only timely concessions resulted in other British colonies retaining some ties to the mother country. To keep India in the Commonwealth (this had become Amery's overriding concern), then, required that the country be made a free and equal member of the Commonwealth soon, and treaty negotiations to regulate relations between the new India and Britain should begin. Among other considerations, Amery noted that if his recommendations were adopted the Americans would realize "that we had done our best in a difficult situation."[26]

Amery's efforts were not known to the Americans and, in the face of Churchill's intransigence and opposition within the government, produced no immediate results.[27] Wavell's return to England in March did produce some optimism, but early American reports from India were not very hopeful. Merrell discovered that, while nationalist Indians hoped for progress, Government of India officials curiously did not expect any breakthroughs. The officials' view seemed to be accurate: Ambassador Winant soon reported from London that Wavell and Churchill had discussed India's future but no radical change in the situation could be expected.[28]

Had the Americans understood the deep contempt with which Churchill viewed Wavell and his ideas for constitutional advance in India, they would have been less puzzled. Wavell had been kept waiting for months before his return to London was approved. In fact, the government had wanted to postpone his visit again, until June, and only acquiesced in a March visit after the viceroy protested in the strongest possible terms.[29]

Despite the pessimistic reports from India, the State Department continued to expect something to happen. Dean Acheson, noting unspecified "accumulating evidence" that pointed "to possible important developments concerning India," asked Merrell about several aspects of the Indian political situation, including whether it might be true that Sir Francis Mudie, home minister in the Government of India, was on his way to London to discuss a release of political prisoners. But unfortunately Mudie was going to London for other reasons.[30]

Only in April, shortly before Roosevelt's death, did American diplomats learn to their surprise that Wavell had not been summoned to London after all but had gone on his own initiative, where he had received a "frigid reception" from Churchill. The American press had been right, as Puckle put it, to portray the viceroy "as sitting *dharma* on the steps of 10 Downing Street."[31] It was now suddenly clear why Government of India officials had not expected much to change as a result of the viceroy's trip.

Exactly what the President thought about India in the last few weeks of his life (he died on April 12) can only be inferred, and then not with certainty. On the colonialism issue generally, Roosevelt seems to have retreated very little from his long standing belief that colonialism was wrong and was one of the causes of the war. Just as the Americans had promised freedom to the Philippines, Roosevelt felt that the European colonies should become independent after a period of transition. His strong feelings expressed at Yalta and on the return voyage persisted. In mid-March he asked Bernard Baruch to travel to London to try and smooth over relations with Britain. The only specific guidance he gave to the financier was to try to get Churchill to restore Hong Kong to China—not, it would appear, an indication that Roosevelt intended to retreat on the colonial issue.[32] About the same time in a conversation with Charles Taussig, a trusted adviser on the trusteeship question, Roosevelt commented that the American goal was to help Asians "achieve independence." When Taussig asked the President whether he would settle for self-government in Indochina, Roosevelt replied "no—it must be independence."[33]

Roosevelt's last recorded comment on the British empire seems to have occurred on March 24 when, according to Ambassador to China Patrick Hurley, the President threatened to appeal to the King and to Parliament if Churchill continued to refuse to return Hong Kong to China. When Hurley accused the French and the Dutch, as well as the British, of conspiring to prevent the establishment of a United Nations trusteeship in Indochina, Roosevelt assured him that the forthcoming conference in San Francisco to establish the United Nations Organization would, in Hurley's words, "make effective the right of colonial people to choose the form of government under which they *will live* as soon as in the opinion of the United Nations they are qualified for independence."[34]

While these anticolonial expressions are instructive in understanding the President's general feelings about empire, they did not mention India explicitly. Making judgments about Roosevelt's final views about India even more difficult is Eleanor Roosevelt's reaction to the activities of the Indian nationalists in the United States. Pandit in particular had been attracting considerable attention with her strong attacks on the British government. In her first month in North America, for example, she made her views known as a prominent participant in the Institute of Pacific Relations Conference, spoke on a CBS national radio program about India, addressed the National Press Club, and met with New York Mayor Fiorello LaGuardia.[35] The *Christian Science Monitor* ran an interview with her, as did the *Washington Star*, in which she complained about British intransigence. In March she joined Owen Lattimore, a prominent Asian scholar, on a Town Hall radio broadcast to discuss colonial empire as a threat to world peace. Perhaps her most notorious statement was that India was one big concentration camp, a comment that resulted in a Parliamentary question in London.[36]

On April 4, 1945, Eleanor Roosevelt wrote to Secretary Stettinius to complain about the activities of Indian nationalists in the United States. Pandit, Shridharani, and Anup Singh, she stated, provided only one point of view. While she thought most Americans sympathized with their perspective, she thought it dangerous to "stir up feeling against Great Britain" at this particular time and complained, almost as the British did, that these nationalists were anti-British and made the Indian problem seem simple when in fact it was complicated. "Even our own minority problems cannot be compared to it," she wrote. Her solution was most unusual for a person so closely identified with the defense of civil liberties: would it not be best to prevent the Indian nationalists from touring the country and speaking, she asked?[37]

Eleanor Roosevelt's letter can only be described as shocking. She was normally sympathetic to Indian freedom and had over the years been identified with that cause. Moreover, it is at least questionable whether she would have written to the secretary of state without first clearing her letter with the President. Conceivably the President was now backing away quickly from his former anticolonialist stance, as some historians have suggested he was doing during these weeks with respect to Indochina.[38] More plausibly, the letter was further evidence that in the last weeks of his life Roosevelt, angered at Soviet intransigence particularly over Poland, was revising his cooperative approach with the Soviet Union. This in turn meant working closely with the British, something that Churchill had been urging insistently. Eleanor Roosevelt's letter was written, after all, the day after the President expressed great anger at Stalin's accusation that the United States was negotiating with the Germans behind his back.[39]

But even if the President had approved his wife's letter, it is unlikely that it signaled a dramatic shift in his views about India. It may be that Roosevelt thought that strong criticism of the British might derail potentially fruitful negotiations then going on between Wavell and the Prime Minister, or that tensions over India might make more difficult his efforts to forge international trusteeships to govern other colonial areas, particularly since Pandit intended to lead an unofficial delegation to the forthcoming San Francisco conference. Some other Americans had voiced the fear that excessive sympathy for India would be used not merely to berate Britain but also to undermine the final peace settlement as a whole.[40] In sum, Eleanor Roosevelt's letter probably indicates a momentary irritation with Indian nationalists in the United States, not a fundamental criticism of their objectives or a reversal of American policy toward India.

In any event, the letter had no influence on policy. After discussing his reply with Phillips, Stettinius disputed Eleanor Roosevelt
at several points. Although the secretary agreed that some of Pandit's
remarks had made a bad impression, Phillips had already indirectly
told the Indian leader that such comments were hurting her cause in
the United States. Regardless, however, Stettinius had no intention of
interfering with Pandit's activities. In the first place, he stated, the
British had made no objection to Pandit and had, after all, provided
her with a passport. In addition, both the British embassy and the
Indian agency general had information services that were not only
capable of refuting the nationalists in this particular case but on a
continuing basis also had a much broader distribution network than
the nationalists. Furthermore, the United States was, and would continue to be, concerned that Asians would identify it with the European imperialism. Suggesting that the State Department, at any rate,
still assumed that the President wanted the United States to keep its
distance from the imperial powers, Stettinius stated that interference
with Pandit's activities would indicate to the Indians that the United
States was "conspiring with the British to prevent the expression here
of India's aspirations for self-government." Finally, "our tradition of
free speech" made efforts to restrict Pandit's activities unwise, he
wrote.[41] Whether there was more significance to Eleanor Roosevelt's
letter soon became moot. Five days after Stettinius's reply, Franklin
Roosevelt died of a cerebral hemorrhage.

Whatever the President might have thought of Pandit, her activities in the United States thoroughly irritated the British. In February
Amery described her comments as "egregious nonsense." He feared
that, given her admittedly attractive personality, the naive Americans
would accept her version of reality. In April, shortly after Roosevelt's
death, she enjoyed considerable publicity when she attended the San
Francisco conference (critics of her contingent termed it "the Unofficial Bleeding Hearts Delegation"), and the following month she
addressed the California state legislature.[42]

Despite their displeasure with Pandit, British authorities did not
act against her. Perhaps Agatha Harrison played a role here, for she
pleaded with the government not to try and counteract Pandit's
remarks. Pandit was a woman of integrity, she argued. Furthermore,

the British held all of the propaganda advantages—"an almost clear field," Harrison thought—and Pandit's opportunity to discuss British repression "was the price we must pay for our handling of the situation."[43]

Also, upon reflection the British were not unduly alarmed about Pandit's influence. Bajpai reported that she had received "fairly wide coverage" in the press but less than might have been expected. Her expressed indifference about the war's outcome, Bajpai thought, would not go down well with American audiences.[44] As for her activities in San Francisco, Bajpai reported that publicity about her and other nationalists in attendance was mostly confined to San Francisco newspapers (the *New York Times* took no notice of her activities there) and did not distract in any way from the recognition accorded the official Indian delegation, headed by the respected Sir Ramaswami Mudaliar.[45] In sum, as Stettinius responded to Eleanor Roosevelt, the British did not find Pandit's activities so threatening as to require extraordinary measures to silence her.

Nationalists, on the other hand, felt that Pandit had presented their case very well. Nehru wrote to her in July that she had done "a splendid job" in America and that her work there "has been very greatly appreciated here by all kinds of people." Indian Industrialist G. L. Mehta even thought that a trip to the United States by the recently released Nehru was unnecessary now since "the general propaganda has already been done effectively by Mrs. Pandit."[46]

Whatever the precise impact of Pandit's visit to the United States, Stettinius was correct in contending, as Harrison had in private, that the British had ample means to counteract Pandit if they wished. Chaman Lal made headlines in India when he charged that there were 10,000 British propagandists in the United States, charges that led to embarrassing questions being raised in the Indian legislature. Lal's figures were highly exaggerated, but a more respected observer, G. L. Mehta, after a visit to the United States accused the British and Indian governments of carrying on "tendentious propaganda" against the Indian national movement and spending millions of dollars for this purpose. Government officials attempted to refute Mehta's charges, but unquestionably the combined activities of the British Information Services and the Indian Information Services (the latter run out of Bajpai's office) had considerably more resources for propaganda and publicity work and a much more effective distribution network than the financially strapped and amateurish nationalist organizations in the United States.[47]

The British government itself, while it complained about nationalist publicity, kept track of nationalist spokespersons in the United States and regularly denied passports to committed nationalists, thus tacitly acknowledging its own overwhelming superiority in the propaganda field. Its response (or, more accurately, its lack of response) to J. J. Singh and his India League of America illustrated this. British intelligence agents followed Singh's activities closely and read his monthly magazine, *India Today*. They often considered responding to what they regarded as unfair or inaccurate assertions. But in the end they almost never made a direct response, having decided that the league, which was the most significant of the nationalist pressure groups in the United States, was not important enough to merit any response.[48]

There are many examples of British and Government of India propaganda activities. In 1944 and 1945 the most successful was the extensive lecture tour of Colonel Himatsinhji, an Indian military leader. Arriving in August 1944, just as Drew Pearson was publishing the Phillips letter that, among other things, criticized the Indian armed forces, Himatsinhji proceeded to laud the Indian army's contribution to the war effort. In the ensuing months, he crisscrossed the country, speaking to at least 100 meetings. He made ten radio broadcasts, inspired editorials in the *Washington Post* and the *New York Times*, and got Hanson Baldwin, the *Times*'s well known military analyst, to make favorable comments about the Indian army. The British were extremely pleased with the colonel's performance. He "has done a splendid job in the United States," wrote an official with the British Information Services, "and has helped enormously to improve American understanding of India and the Indian war effort. . . . We shall all be extremely sorry to lose him."[49]

The British case also reached the American public with the publication of two important books about India. In 1944 Oxford University Press published Sir Reginald Coupland's exhaustive work, *The Indian Problem*, which supported the British government's views of developments in the subcontinent. The American journal *Amerasia* challenged the study and concluded that it was written with the approval of the British government. According to one scholar Coupland's work had a "marked influence on American scholarly thought" about India which eventually influenced popular attitudes about the country. More clearly propaganda was Beverly Nichols's *Verdict on India*, which also appeared in 1944. A kind of updated, "British version of *Mother India*," Nichols's strongly pro-British views reached a wide American public when in February 1945, it was published in condensed form in *Reader's Digest*.[50]

The sudden elevation of Harry S. Truman to the presidency in April 1945 created considerable uncertainty about the direction of American foreign policy. Experienced almost exclusively in domestic politics, Truman suffered from the further disadvantage that Roosevelt had made almost no effort to acquaint him with foreign policy issues. Hopkins told Halifax shortly after Roosevelt's death that there was now "a completely new situation." The British, he added, would be "starting from scratch." In fact, however, Truman continued the essentials of Roosevelt's approach to most foreign policy questions, though with his own more businesslike, less personal, less dramatic style. As one Foreign Office official observed in January 1946, "the Truman Administration are pursuing the Rooseveltian policies clumsily but pretty consistently."[51]

British irritation with Truman stemmed fundamentally from the fact that the United States was now a much stronger power and often took positions contrary to those of the British, at times without even consulting them. Serious differences arose over the end of lend-lease assistance, a postwar loan, policy toward Japan and the Pacific, atomic energy, Palestine, and how to deal with the Soviet Union. At times, in fact, Truman complained that he had more problems with Britain than with Stalin's Russia. Stalin's growing intransigence, evident particularly at the London conference of Foreign Ministers in September, forced the United States and Britain closer together. But distrust continued, with Stettinius and others observing in the fall that relations were noticeably cooler than they had been at Yalta or even the San Francisco conference.[52] Such distrust suggested that Truman might be no less committed than Roosevelt to seeing the British depart from India.

On the other hand, most observers believe that Truman was much less personally committed to an antiimperialist stance than was his predecessor. Before he had become President, for example, Truman had given indications of his sympathies with the British empire. Halifax reported that at a dinner at the British embassy Truman "spoke out about India with trenchant good sense."[53] Truman's ideas about colonialism have not been subjected to the same scrutiny that Roosevelt's have been, however, and any assessments must be regarded as preliminary. Ultimately he must be judged by the actions and policies he allowed to go forward, and many of his decisions do suggest a less than firm devotion to self-determination. For example, he contributed to the restoration of British rule in Hong Kong when, over the sharp objections of the Chinese, he permitted the British to accept the surrender of Japanese troops there. He did this despite his knowledge that Roosevelt thought that the colony ought to be returned to China.[54] Truman also moved quickly to reverse Roosevelt's determination to keep the French from returning to Indochina unless they were prepared ultimately to grant the colony independence.[55] Roosevelt had never been so clearly opposed to Dutch colonial rule, but it was Truman who at Potsdam made the decision to transfer responsibility for the Dutch East Indies to the British, thus assuring that the Dutch would attempt to restore their rule there.[56] There were elements in the American government, notably in the State Department's Division of Far Eastern Affairs, that continued to argue that American interests, as well as American idealism, were best served by opposing colonial rule. But they could no longer count on a sympathetic hearing in the White House.

Still, the American anticolonial tradition was not dead. British and Government of India officials in the United States certainly believed, and regretted, that it was very much alive in 1945. At the end of March, for example, Bajpai reported a general anxiety among Americans about fighting to restore the old order in Asia. There was "virtual unanimity," he reported, that "the Colonial system must be abolished as soon as possible." Americans were again speaking of the Philippines as the proper model.[57] Bajpai, of course, was contemptuous (at least publicly) of the American attitude. In May growing pressure from the British to see imperial rule restored in Southeast Asia resulted in murmurs of disapproval. The chief political adviser to the Supreme Allied Command, for example, reported worriedly that the British favored the greatest possible Dutch and French participation in the reconquest of Southeast Asia. The British concern was not military but political, he stated. This, he thought, accounted for Admiral Mountbatten's "tenacity" in attempting to transfer Indochina from the Chiang Kai-shek's China theatre to his own South-East Asia Command. In June Joseph E. Davies returned from an important mission to London to discuss world affairs with Churchill and reported that the Prime Minister was a great man but was "still the King's Minister who will not liquidate the Empire."[58]

The British, in turn, felt that the United States was not supportive enough of European efforts to restore their colonial rule in Southeast Asia. By early fall Bajpai was criticizing the American "hands off" approach to nationalist movements in Java and Indochina as being irresponsible. The United States wanted to see freedom extended, he wrote, but was unwilling "to assume responsibility for the maintenance of order in countries where the struggle for freedom threatens to establish anarchy."[59]

Perhaps as a result of the continuing uneasiness about the empires, the Truman administration's policy toward India differed little from that of his predecessor. Both Roosevelt and Truman hoped that a peaceful solution would be found that would be satisfactory to the nationalists, both were willing to pressure the British on this point, and both were willing to involve the United States in the process. Aside from continuing ideological discomfort over imperialism, it is not entirely clear why this was so. For one thing, initially the Truman administration understandably had to focus on European and Pacific developments, leaving possible modifications in Indian policy for later consideration. For another, it was not until 1946 that the Truman administration committed itself to a close alignment with the British in world affairs. Also, the Indian nationalist movement was strong and had considerable sympathy in the United States. There was much less organized support in the United States for the Indonesians or Indochinese, for example. In addition, the Indian nationalist movement, if sometimes irritating and at other times incomprehensible to Americans, seemed in general to be reasonable and relatively moderate. It stood strongly against the communists, for example. Nationalist leadership of an independent India might well be able to bring stability to the country, and stability would serve American strategic and economic interests. Finally, the situation in India was considerably different from that in Southeast Asia, where the French and the Dutch seemed intent on doing almost anything to regain control of former colonies. By contrast the British government, even under Conservative rule, was in 1945 thinking of ways to give up power in India, although first the Conservative and later the Labour governments hoped that India would remain in the Commonwealth and continue to serve British economic and strategic interests.

Just as Truman was taking over, in London Wavell threatened to resign if he could not return to India with authority to work for a settlement.[60] The confrontation on principle that Amery had once warned him might eventually come, had arrived. The news of Wavell's willingness to challenge the Prime Minister, coming at a time when American policy was still uncertain because of Truman's recent accession to power, caused Phillips to recommend stronger American action. "If only for purposes of record," he wrote, "it seems to me highly important that we should take advantage of this moment to informally express our interest and our hope for an amelioration of the unhappy conditions throughout India." He wanted Stettinius to speak directly to Eden and urge "another effort to break the Indian deadlock."[61]

Phillips's behind-the-scenes effort bore fruit almost immediately. With the President's approval Stettinius spoke with Eden, who was attending the San Francisco conference. Eden remained noncommittal, although Stettinius felt he had "made some headway with him." Three weeks later Grew himself followed up when Eden was in Washington, telling the foreign secretary in strong language that Anglo-American prestige in Asia would be much enhanced if a settlement could be found for the Indian dilemma. Eden, however, had little to offer, saying only that he doubted a settlement could be reached as long as Gandhi lived.[62] Although American pressure made little difference at this point, the approaches by Stettinius and Grew made it clear that the United States still wanted change in India. The contrast with Indochina, where the administration was already in full retreat from Roosevelt's earlier hopes to oust the French, was striking.

In the meantime, Wavell appeared to be having little success. At the end of April Lord Auchinleck, British commander in chief in India, hurriedly left New Delhi for London, reportedly to lend support to the beleaguered viceroy. One British newspaper noted that, while the viceroy was having difficulty finding anyone important to listen to him, his trip was not entirely in vain since he had managed to lower his golf handicap to seven.[63]

Such reports underestimated Wavell's persistence. He was determined to take back to India a reasonable negotiating position that stood a chance of success. By early June he had a plan in hand. The United States was sufficiently interested in the details for Grew to order Merrell to try to obtain a copy of the plan from a sympathetic Indian official. By June 10 a copy was on its way to Washington.[64] Four days later Amery made the plan public with a statement to the House of Commons.

After fighting tooth and nail, Wavell had extracted several concessions from a reluctant Churchill. The government stated that the Cripps offer of 1942 still stood. A final constitutional arrangement would require the approval of the major Indian communities, and the new offer did not attempt to impose a solution. But in the interim the British offered to Indianize the viceroy's Executive Council, except for the position of commander in chief, with an equal portion of Muslims and Hindus. Nominees would come from the major political groupings in the country. Significantly, the British agreed that India's foreign affairs would be in the hands of an Indian, and India would have fully accredited representatives abroad. American pressure was one reason for the plan, though matters related to the war were probably more important.[65]

State Department officials welcomed the plan but were cautious. Lampton Berry, who subjected the Wavell proposals to a detailed analysis, did not think they went far enough but at the same time thought "the Indians would be very unwise to reject them." Although the viceroy still retained his veto, Berry felt that it would become meaningless with an Executive Council composed of representative Indians. Another potential problem concerned representation. Berry regretted that the plan provided for a balance between Muslims and Hindus, rather than a balance between Congress and the Muslim League. (This in fact turned out to be the plan's major flaw.) But for the moment Berry was hopeful. Even the nationalist Indian press had been restrained—"a good sign," he felt.[66]

Public reaction in the United States to the new plan was generally favorable. Both the Associated Press and United Press termed the proposals "sweeping." There was a recognition that the plan did not advance much beyond the Cripps's proposals, but most American publications urged the Indians to accept it nevertheless, *Amerasia* being a notable exception. Even the *Nation* thought the nationalists would be well advised to respond favorably and then press on for complete independence.[67] British and Indian government analysts confirmed the positive American response. Bajpai found support among the public at large and in official circles. Even "habitual critics," he reported, praised the plan. The decision to release the imprisoned nationalist leaders added to perceptions of British sincerity. Later, American reaction was more guarded, and, as it turned out, caution was the appropriate response.[68]

American diplomats in India found that most Indians were encouraged by the Wavell plan. Although it did not promise immediate independence and therefore was likely to disappoint some nationalists like Nehru (who wrote to his sister that there were some "obvious" difficulties with the plan), there was a general feeling that Gandhi would accept it and would be able to overcome whatever opposition might be mounted to the proposals. Jinnah also seemed likely to accept since it was, as Mahadev Desai put it, "the best offer Muslims will ever receive." Only the Hindu Mahasabha, a fervent defender of Hindu communal interests, seemed likely to offer serious opposition.[69] Meanwhile, Wavell invited the interested parties to join him for discussions in Simla, the summer capital, on June 25, 1945.

The announcement of the Simla conference encouraged the State Department, and Grew suggested that the American mission send an officer to Simla to observe the talks. Merrell (no doubt with great reluctance given the intense heat of New Delhi in the summer) ultimately decided that it would not be wise for the Americans to have an official presence at Simla in the cool Himalayan foothills. It might be misunderstood by the nationalists and could embarrass the American mission and the Government of India, he felt. However, he arranged for Wavell's assistant private secretary, who would remain in New Delhi during the talks, to keep him intimately informed of developments at Simla.[70]

As the conference approached, Merrell kept an interested State Department informed. There were potentially serious problems, the most significant being Jinnah's insistence on the right to name all Muslim representatives. But the Americans discerned an atmosphere of good will which they hoped would produce a settlement. At least all of the parties had agreed to attend.[71] Furthermore, Wavell, wanting to establish a favorable atmosphere for the conference, made every effort to provide the best possible amenities for the participants. They enjoyed the best available travel arrangements to Simla, for example, and their accommodations, once in the summer capital, were not only comfortable but were also, as Merrell put it, "in many instances almost luxurious." Lord and Lady Wavell also went out of their way to behave informally toward the Indians (a marked contrast from Linlithgow), a gesture that was greatly appreciated. "Lady Wavell has been particularly helpful," Merrell reported. She invited Gandhi for tea. On another occasion, Wavell insisted that Gandhi "make use of a Viceregal ricksha [*sic*] and chaprassis in returning to his home after an informal chat." Even the suspicious but ever more popular Nehru seemed hopeful that the conference would succeed.[72]

The State Department followed the conference carefully,[73] and for a time all went well. By mid-July, however, the conference appeared to have reached an impasse. While Congress was cooperative and had agreed to submit a list of fifteen names to the viceroy for his Executive Council, Jinnah was unwilling to do so unless he was assured that he could name *all* of the Muslim members.[74] Since the Congress considered itself a multicommunal organization, however, it felt it could name Muslim members of Congress if it wished to and had included some on its list. Barring an unexpected concession by Jinnah, Lampton Berry felt the viceroy had only two choices. He could declare the conference a failure and continue to govern as before. Or he could form a new Executive Council composed of members of Congress and some of the minority parties. Berry thought the latter solution would be representative of 80 percent of the population and clearly hoped that Wavell would follow this course.[75]

Suddenly the mood had changed. Pessimistic reports began to pour into Washington.[76] Patrick told an American official in London that he and many in the British government were unenthusiastic about the plan anyway (thus giving credence to those who thought the whole proposal was only intended to benefit the Conservatives in the upcoming elections) and were not surprised that it had failed. He even expressed a certain irritation with the Americans, who had insisted that the British "do something" about India, but now that Wavell had tried to "do something" it remained to be seen if anything positive would result. Even if the plan were eventually accepted, a bureaucratic paralysis would probably ensue, he thought. Patrick was especially critical of Jinnah and doubted if much progress could be made while the Muslim League leader remained a major figure.[77]

By the next day a negative reaction was in some quarters setting in. Jinnah now said that Wavell's plan "was a snare," while others stated that it had been nothing more than an electioneering ploy. To many Hindus the plan, drawn in such a way that Jinnah would not accept it in the end, was further evidence of Britain's divide and rule policy.[78]

The final outcome did lend support to the latter charge. Faced with Jinnah's intransigence, the British had two choices which Berry had astutely discerned: either pronounce total failure, or constitute an Executive Council consisting of Congress and other representatives and leave the Muslim League out of the government for the moment. Congress was willing to accept this latter outcome. But in the end Wavell declared the conference a failure and personally accepted responsibility. He thus laid himself open to criticism. As Berry put it later in an excellent analysis of Indian politics, "all of the Indian parties other than the Muslim League resented Wavell's willingness to allow the League alone to veto what would have resulted otherwise in an amicable settlement."[79]

Nevertheless, this failure was different from the superficially similar collapse of the Cripps Mission in 1942. While the latter had resulted in the most bitter feelings on all sides, now the mood was very different. On the Muslim side, in spite of Jinnah's comment that Wavell's plan was a "snare," it was apparent that the viceroy had not ignored the Muslim leader, and therefore the Muslim League was reportedly very pleased. As for the Congress, there was considerable irritation with Wavell for not standing up to Jinnah, and some complaints about a policy of divide and rule. But the Americans felt nevertheless that Congress and the government were still on good terms generally. In response to a specific request from Grew about Indian attitudes toward the British, Merrell reported that, while "ulterior motives were pretty generally suspected," there was a feeling that the British "were actually at last doing something" to break the deadlock. As a result the nationalists were "for the time being more disposed to trust British bona fides." Only the Hindu Mahasabha was deeply dissatisfied, complaining that Congress seemed determined to sacrifice Hindu interests in order to find an agreement with the Muslim League.[80]

As for the Americans, there is surprisingly little direct evidence about how the State Department felt about the collapse of the talks. Doubtless the Potsdam Conference, then in session, and the almost overwhelming problems of postwar Europe, distracted American attention away from South Asia. The American press generally blamed Jinnah for the collapse.[81] A Government of India review of American press coverage concluded optimistically that the failure had convinced many Americans that "the problem is not an easy one and that differences among the Indians themselves are at least as responsible for the breakdown as any shortcomings of the British." The British also concluded that Americans were deeply sympathetic to Wavell personally.[82]

As the British reported, the Americans on the ground were not uniformly positive in their assessments of Indian leaders. They believed that Jinnah was most responsible for the collapse of the Simla talks, but they could also be critical of Gandhi, Nehru, and the Congress. In fact, there had been an increase in critical comment in recent months.

The most critical (and least influential) of the official Americans was Roy E. B. Bower, the consul at Madras, who consistently portrayed Indians in an unflattering light and insisted that they were not yet capable of self-government. Bower contended in lengthy dispatches that the police were untrustworthy, traders were dishonest, and bribery was rampant. If India were run as Pearl Buck wanted it run, he wrote, she would soon be calling for American oversight. More fundamentally, and in language reminiscent of Katherine Mayo, Bower found the culture sadly deficient. Individuals would not assume responsibility, partly because of their emotional temperament and partly because the caste system made it easy to avoid taking responsibility; and if Indians did assume responsibility, they could not sustain it. "Almost always at the end a European is called upon to take charge. . . . The house is not kept in repair even when the owner has had the gumption to build it." Indians also exhibited "a beggar attitude, a sort of self-pity." It was, he admitted, "an unkind thought, but effective compassion is not provoked by beggary." India's cultural deficiencies, he felt, made it unlikely that India would ever be an important power.[83]

Another of Bower's themes, deriving from his perception of a deficient character, was that Congress was a fascist organization, very similar to the German Nazi Party. The parallels, he felt, were clear. Both worshipped a single leader, identified the party with the state, had a small inner circle that demanded complete obedience from the masses, and were bankrolled by big business. The Congress, like the Nazis, controlled important newspapers, made "demagogic appeals and extravagant promises," used the old Jacobin trick of accusing their opponents of their own offenses, and used half truths to confuse people. "Above all" in both cases the "party organization" was a "private government beyond the reach of electors or of law." In the midst of the Simla negotiations, Bower contended that Congress's slogan was "Ein Fuehrer, ein Volk, ein Reich." And in September he reported that the "fascist" Congress wanted "dictatorial powers or none at all," a startling statement in view of Congress's acceptance of the Wavell plan, which called for power sharing among India's political and communal groups.[84]

Given these alleged Indian deficiencies, Bower strongly defended

British rule and hoped it would continue for the indefinite future. Even more startling was his belief that most Indians wanted European oversight. For years, most American diplomats had reported that, however deeply divided Indians might be among themselves, they were united in wanting the British out. Bower felt otherwise. They were "neither ready nor willing to assume full responsibility," he wrote. "Under one form or another there may be European courts of last resort for years to come, not because of European imperialism but because India wants it so."[85]

No other American diplomat in India was as remotely critical of Congress or Indian culture as was Bower, but he had something of an ally in George D. LaMont of the American consulate in Bombay. When LaMont sent to Washington copies of correspondence between Gandhi and P. C. Joshi, the Indian communist leader, he acknowledged that the letters made it clear that Gandhi was not a communist. But he had little respect for the political astuteness of Gandhi and other Indian leaders. The Gandhi-Joshi correspondence, he wrote, was "typical of the loose, theoretic, political verbosity indulged in by most Indian political leaders." Later, LaMont characterized J. B. Kripalani, then the general secretary of the Congress party, as an ignorant "zealot" who was "embittered and fanatical as is typical of all too many of Gandhi's followers."[86]

Such views were not typical of the American diplomatic community (although it may be significant that they surfaced in such extreme form in 1945 after Roosevelt had died), and they had little if any impact on policy. More typical (and considerably more influential) was LaMont's superior at Bombay, Consul General Howard Donovan. Like many Americans, Donovan had always found Gandhi somewhat mystifying, and he once predicted that there could be no settlement as long as he (and Jinnah) were alive.[87] But his first meeting with the mahatma (an unplanned encounter), in April 1945, modified his view. Gandhi was then conserving his strength by not speaking during daylight hours, so his responses to Donovan's questions were in writing. In spite of the strangeness of the proceedings, Donovan found himself attracted to the great man. He had a "pleasant manner," a "sense of humor," and an "engaging personality." The traits made "it easier to understand the hold which he exercises over his countrymen."[88]

Donovan still believed, however, that it was exceedingly difficult to understand how Gandhi's mind operated. As the Indian parties were considering Wavell's proposals, for example, Donovan wrote, "it is hopeless to endeavor to forecast the workings of his mind." Later, when Gandhi enigmatically stated that he had yet another fast in mind but was not certain for what reason or for how long, Donovan's Western, logical mind revolted. "I cannot but feel somewhat discouraged regarding India's political future when I read such rubbish as this," he wrote to the secretary of state.[89]

Donovan could also be critical of the Congress leadership generally. On one occasion he characterized their statements as "extravagant, inaccurate and often ridiculous." Nehru, he thought, was the worst offender. On the other hand, he admired the Congress's ability to resist communist infiltration and termed the opposition to the communists by Gandhi, Vallabhbhai Patel, and other Indian leaders "astute." Nehru's strong attacks on the communists, who had supported British rule during the war, were particularly effective, he thought. But he later complained about Nehru's "provocative, ill-informed, and unbalanced statements on political and economic matters" and thought his efforts to blame the Bombay police for a recent riot "ridiculous." Donovan was more inclined to blame the disturbance on the weather.[90]

The leading American diplomat in India, George Merrell, who was in charge of the mission in New Delhi, was more sensitive to the nationalist perspective and the Indian context generally. His reporting tended to be careful, balanced, and accurate. The British liked him and were pleased when he was finally appointed commissioner in January 1945.[91] But it is significant that he never adopted as his own the strong views of Bower. And in marked contrast to Donovan, he generally thought highly of Nehru. During the Simla talks, for example, he reported that the Indian leader's pronouncements "have been judicious, moderate, and reveal a progressive spirit." Merrell called particular attention to one of Nehru's addresses, "India Wants Freedom for All Oppressed Nations," which he characterized as "a calm and reasoned statement."[92]

Although the Simla talks had failed, one portion of Wavell's proposals—placing an Indian in charge of the country's foreign relations and raising the status of India's diplomats abroad—was actively pursued. Bajpai had long wanted a higher status and, in January 1945, asked the State Department to recognize him as chief of a mission. In the absence of any agreement with the British, the State Department demurred, and Bajpai said he intended to take the matter up with his own government. Wavell, of course, had long been trying to raise Bajpai's status but had been overruled by the War Cabinet. Like Bajpai, he too tried to bring the matter up again in January 1945, but the leaks in the agent general's office made it inopportune to pursue the matter. "I think the Drew Pearson business ought to be given more time to be forgotten," commented the deputy undersecretary of the Indian Office.[93] David Monteath agreed, explaining that Wavell was not yet aware of all of the "ripples and reflections" that the scandal had caused. In February the Government of India advised the Americans that it could not accredit Bajpai as chief of mission because of the confused constitutional status of India.[94]

The accession of Truman to the presidency momentarily revived the issue, for Bajpai was at first denied personal access to Truman. This disturbed the Government of India, but the matter was temporarily resolved when Truman agreed to accord the agent general the same courtesies that Roosevelt had.[95] By that time raising the status of Bajpai had become an integral part of Wavell's plan to resolve the Indian constitutional deadlock.

Shortly after the Simla conference failed, the Conservative government in Britain lost the elections, and the Labour Party, led by Clement R. Attlee, took over. Although the new Labour government was on record as favoring a transfer of power in India, it wanted India to be a dominion and retain close economic and military ties to Great Britain. Thus the changes in policy were less dramatic than might have been expected.[96] The new government did, however, expect to bring about a settlement. In August Wavell was summoned back to London, where he found Labour leaders including the new secretary of state for India, Lord Pethick-Lawrence, and Foreign Secretary Ernest Bevin, very anxious to see progress made in India. They announced that legislative elections would soon be held in India. Indicative of the changed atmosphere, the Government of India decided that it no longer needed to keep track of Pandit's activities.[97]

Even Labour, however, had to be convinced that it made sense to change Bajpai's status. In August, Wavell told Pethick-Lawrence that Bajpai should be made a fully accredited minister. Bureaucrats in the India Office raised objections, but Arthur Henderson, the India Office's parliamentary undersecretary, recommended that the change be made.[98]

Wavell returned to the matter on September 23. "I know it is illogical for India to appoint Ministers of her own abroad at present," he admitted, "but logical arrangements are not always right." By then Pethick-Lawrence had already made the case to the cabinet.[99] Bevin agreed, and on October 29 Halifax (also a long supporter of the move) spoke with new United States Secretary of State James F. Byrnes about raising Bajpai's status. Byrnes responded that it seemed "quite all right," and the British planned to go ahead. But a few days later the Americans decided that the matter ought to be put on hold pending a resolution of India's constitutional situation.[100]

Interestingly, the State Department's legal adviser, Green H. Hackworth, found no legal impediment to receiving an Indian minister.[101] The American refusal at this point to receive ministers from India was thus a policy decision reflecting the government's sensitivity to Indian nationalist criticism that the United States supported continuing British rule. Despite the change of government in London, which in general made it easier for the United States to cooperate with Britain on Indian matters, the administration continued to keep the pressure on England to bring about real change in India.

The British were unwilling to accept the American decision without a fight, however. Bajpai protested, and Halifax told Byrnes that he "greatly regretted the attitude of the State Department." Raising the stakes even higher, Prime Minister Attlee, then in Washington, mentioned the issue to President Truman. Both Truman and Byrnes seemed impressed by Attlee's presentation but expressed concern about the logic of the situation. Attlee replied that the entire British Commonwealth was illogical.[102] The real American concern, however, was political. The United States feared the reaction of the Indian nationalists (who were at that very time especially critical of American policy toward colonialism in general) if it accorded full diplomatic recognition to a country whose policy was still, in the final analysis, subject to British control.[103]

The American concern about nationalist opinion was not entirely unanticipated. Not only had India Office officials predicted it, but Loy Henderson and Lampton Berry had also hinted as much to Bajpai some weeks before.[104] Nevertheless, the British were still hopeful. Byrnes reportedly thought the matter was not an insurmountable barrier, but by the end of the year there had been no change in the American position.

The Foreign Office, keeping the pressure on, ordered Halifax to let Byrnes know that the Chinese had agreed to raise the status of the Indian representative in Chunking. The tactic did not work. On January 12, 1946, the United States stated that it could not reconsider its position until India's constitutional position was clearer.[105] It fact, playing the China card rather backfired. The British intended to go forward and raise the status of the Indian agent general in Chunking, but now the Government of India objected. If there was a change in India's diplomatic status in China, the Indian government pointed out, there would inevitably be embarrassing questions about why the same step had not been taken in the United States, which would only embitter the political debate in India. Pethick-Lawrence agreed, and the matter was postponed.[106] The American response to British efforts to raise Bajpai's status was an irritation rather than a cause of any significant deterioration in relations between the two countries. But the Government of India authorities could not but have taken some pleasure shortly thereafter in refusing an American request to establish a consular section at the New Delhi mission, "pending the outcome of expected constitutional developments."[107]

The American unwillingness to upgrade relations between the United States and India resulted from American determination to keep the pressure on the British for a peaceful settlement of the Indian problem and, more directly, because of the country's sensitivity to Indian charges that the United States supported the imperialist countries and was in fact one of them. In this sense British reactionaries like former viceroy Lord Linlithgow and Indian nationalists shared one thing in common: both were at one time or another suspicious of American intentions in the postwar world. Linlithgow regularly accused the Americans of plotting to wrest away Britain's economic advantages in India and elsewhere. Indian nationalists were more ambivalent, since they were drawn to the anticolonial traditions of the United States and had found the President's emissaries, Johnson and Phillips, to be sympathetic to their cause. But as the war drew toward its conclusion, they also worried about the influence of an expansive American capitalism and its impact on American policy. In spite of its antiimperialist traditions, an American imperial policy was possible, they feared.

On the day Roosevelt died, Merrell sent a copy of an editorial from the *Hindustan Times* which claimed that "certain influential sections" of American opinion were "reviving annexationist policies." The editorial focused on American efforts to keep permanently some of the Japanese islands in the Pacific. This was a "disappointing," even "alarming" development, for it contradicted promises in the Atlantic Charter. Merrell complained that the editorial was unbalanced, but what was more significant was his statement that the editorial was not at all unusual. Rather it was "just another example of the anti-American propaganda . . . which has appeared in the Indian press." At the end of April, M. D. Japhteth, who was in charge of United Artists' publicity department in Bombay, complained about American silence on the independence question. United States propaganda in India had emphasized the country's devotion to such ideals as life, liberty, and happiness for all people, but he saw no support for these ideals in American policy toward India.[108]

Indian nationalists' concern for self-determination extended to other colonial regions in Asia. They were especially sensitive to developments in Indonesia, the Dutch East Indies. In August, for example, Merrell to his great surprise found "great bitterness . . . exhibited against the Dutch." Angry as the people were about British control of India, Indians felt that the British rule had been "far better than Dutch."[109]

Anger about Dutch efforts to regain control of the East Indies after the war was one of the few sentiments that both Jinnah and Nehru shared. In October Jinnah expressed his wholehearted support for the "Indonesian struggle for freedom," and added that the struggles of the Indonesian and Indochinese nationalists had "great-ly stimulated nationalist feeling in Bombay." He was especially angry at the use of Indian troops in both Java and Indochina, who served under British command, and he condemned the "so-called civilized big powers" who lusted after imperialism. About the same time Nehru proclaimed, "freedom is indivisible. It crops up separately whether in Java or whether in Indochina or India or elsewhere. But basically it is the same."[110]

American ambivalence about developments in Southeast Asia boded ill for good relations with Indian nationalists. By October 1945, Indian criticism had developed to the point that Secretary of State Byrnes urged President Truman to see Nehru's sister and express his "sympathy with the aspirations of self-government of all dependent countries, including India."[111] A few days later Truman delivered an address aimed at quelling criticism from Asian nation-alists. Truman's "Twelve Commandants" reiterated some of the ide-alism found in the Atlantic Charter. Among other things, the Presi-dent insisted that the United States sought "no territorial expansion or selfish advantage," and that all people "who are prepared for self-government" should be allowed to choose their own form of gov-ernment "without interference from any foreign source." This, he emphasized, was a universal principle.[112] Although Truman was not devoted to anticolonialism in the same sense that Roosevelt had been, he nevertheless appreciated the need to try and keep Asian opinion friendly toward the West. It is probably not coincidental that Truman delivered his speech shortly after the Soviet Union had exhibited its most intransigent attitude yet at the London meeting of foreign ministers.

Truman's speech had only a limited impact on Indian opinion, how-ever, which generally found it inadequate. Donovan reported that "at best" the speech was "received with doubtful credence." Gandhi termed it an "insufficient answer to the people of India." Nehru, inter-estingly, saw some positive elements in the address, and he generally welcomed it. The United States was comparatively "free from the bur-den of an imperialist past," he stated, and Asians admired America. Nehru hoped that actions would follow from Truman's words. Perhaps American subservience to Britain would come to an end.[113]

Still, Nehru admitted to a certain skepticism. He asserted that the United States exhibited "a passive and sometimes active support of British policy" in India. And he was openly critical of the American stance in both Indochina and Indonesia. Referring to the American insistence that the Dutch remove American labels from lend-lease guns before using them in Indonesia, Nehru used biting language. It was "poor consolation" to the Indonesians, he said, to know that they were being shot down with unlabeled American weapons.[114]

There was little change in nationalist perceptions of the Truman administration for the rest of the year. Furthermore, nationalists noted approvingly that the Soviet Union, alone among the world's major powers, had taken an unequivocal stand against colonialism. As tensions with the Soviet Union mounted, this was a charge to which the Truman administration was sensitive. Perhaps the Americans could take some very limited comfort when at the end of December Nehru told an Indian audience that both the Soviet Union and the United States were "powerfully expansionist." But he added that he thought that the United States preferred to see the British empire continue in some form, and he accused it of seeming to "underwrite" the empire. This, he warned, was a very dangerous course, for even the atomic bomb could not suppress the "revolt of millions" in the colonial world. Donovan promptly telegraphed Nehru's comments to Washington and commented that they constituted "one of the strongest criticisms of American policy toward India which has been made publicly by Indian nationalists leaders for some time."[115] Three weeks later Nehru backed away from his remarks. "I did not mean that American policy as a whole was committed in that direction," he stated to an American journalist, only that there were "some trends" in that direction.[116] But there was no question that the drift of American foreign policy deeply disturbed the emerging Indian leader.

In sum, the American approach to India under Truman continued the basic patterns established by Roosevelt. As under Roosevelt, the United States satisfied neither side. The British, even under a Labour government, found the United States insufficiently supportive of their objectives in Asia, while the Indian nationalists felt that the

United States was far too favorable toward the British and other imperialist powers in Asia. Both views contained elements of truth, although by late 1945 there was perhaps more truth in the nationalist perspective. As tensions grew with the Soviet Union and the United States began to expand its influence throughout Asia and much of the rest of the world, the Americans increasingly found it important to be on good (though not necessarily equal) terms with their European allies.

9 | To Independence
(January 1946–August 1947)

The years 1946 and 1947 are justifiably singled out as a time of crucial development in the history of American foreign policy. It was a time when, with the Cold War having unmistakably begun, the United States increasingly stood firm against Soviet demands and expansive tendencies. "I'm tired of babying the Soviets," Truman exclaimed in exasperation at one point. The last significant agreements with the Soviet Union occurred in January 1946, when the two countries settled a variety of issues relating to eastern Europe. But Secretary Byrnes, who had conducted the American negotiations, was criticized for appeasing the Russians, and thereafter cooperation between the two superpowers virtually ceased. In February Stalin delivered a belligerent speech implying that coexistence with the West was impossible. The same month George Kennan sent his influential "Long Telegram" from Moscow which concluded that internal imperatives determined Soviet foreign policy, imperatives that could not be influenced by the actions of other countries. From this important analysis many American officials concluded that the only option open to the United States was to be patient but firm and make no concessions. In March Winston Churchill delivered his famous "Iron Curtain" speech at Westminster College in Missouri. In 1947 the United States adopted the Truman Doctrine designed to stop communist expansion in Greece and Turkey and possibly beyond. Later in the year Truman's new Secretary of State, George C. Marshall, proposed a far reaching plan to rehabilitate Europe's economy in the face of a potential communist threat, and Kennan eloquently, if not always with precision, provided the philosophical bases of the policy of containment in his famous "X" article, "The Sources of Soviet Conduct." Containment was now the new American strategy.

What precisely the new strategy encompassed has been the subject of vigorous discussion. In his influential book, *Strategies of Containment,* John L. Gaddis contends that until 1950 the United States generally concentrated its attention and resources on preventing Soviet domination of certain specific areas of the world deemed vital to American security, rather than acting to contain communism on all fronts with equal vigor. Even this limited response represented a significant change from the days when the United States defined its security interests as scarcely extending beyond the Western hemisphere, but it was not a commitment to global action. "Universalism was abandoned," Gaddis writes. Of particular interest to the study of Indo-American relations, Gaddis contends that the Truman administration concluded that the Asian mainland, including India, was not one of those vital areas requiring an American response. Its loss to Soviet control would not endanger American security, at least not immediately.[1]

Other scholars argue that by spring 1946, and perhaps even earlier, the United States defined its security requirements in virtually world wide terms. As Daniel Yergin put it in 1977 in his study of the origins of the national security state, "America's interests and responsibilities were unrestricted and global."[2] More recent studies of American military and defense planning concur, contending that the Americans sought to preserve "a favorable balance of power in Eurasia." This required "defense in depth," which meant military hegemony over the Atlantic and Pacific oceans. This in turn necessitated a far flung series of military bases, air transit rights, and landing rights to discourage attacks on the United States, preserve access to important raw materials of Asia, safeguard the lanes of trade, and allow for air strikes (should they ever become necessary) on the Soviet industrial infrastructure. In October 1945, the Joint Chiefs and their civilian secretaries approved the first system of overseas bases in the postwar era. This new strategic thinking represented, as historian Mark Stoler writes, "a revolution in the definition and scope of American foreign and defense policies."[3]

Yet other writers contend that American policy was too inconsistent and makeshift to categorize at all with confidence. American policy was "guided not by very carefully devised grand strategy, but by daily expedients contrived to cope with current problems," concludes one historian. Robert J. McMahon in his study of early American policy toward Pakistan finds strategic considerations vital to understanding American postwar expansion, yet observes that American policy "was driven by a remarkably imprecise and inchoate formulation of the nation's strategic needs."[4]

It does seem clear that the Cold War had important ramifications for Anglo-American relations and ultimately for Indo-American relations. Generally speaking, the Cold War pushed the United States and Britain closer together. At the beginning of the 1946, for example, Truman's proposal for a substantial reconstruction loan to Britain was in trouble with a skeptical Congress. But in the end threatening Russian actions ensured its passage. Americans hoped (vainly as it soon developed) that British power in the postwar world would not be substantially reduced, and because of fears of the Soviet Union American military cooperation with Britain became closer than ever before in peacetime (though to some extent the cooperation was carried out without the knowledge of American civilian officials). In keeping with American desires to create a world wide system of in depth defense, the United States approached the British about acquiring military air and landing rights, as well as bases, in some British territories.[5]

The Cold War and a broadened view of what constituted American security interests also tended to mute American criticism of the British empire (as well as the empires of other European powers), which could serve to help contain the Soviet Union. In March 1946, Admiral William D. Leahy, whom Truman had retained as a close adviser, stated that "defeat or disintegration of the British Empire would eliminate from Eurasia the last bulwark of resistance between the United States and Soviet expansion." Loy Henderson, director of the State Department's Office of Near Eastern and African Affairs, later admitted that he never allowed his subordinates to "press the British for independence for the empire—greater self government, yes; but not independence."[6]

Cold War factors inevitably affected American policy toward India. The United States unquestionably feared a confrontation with the Soviet Union in the Middle East, and a stable, friendly India could provide personnel and even bases from which to stem Soviet advances. As part of the larger strategy of "defense in depth," American military and defense officials made a top secret approach to Britain regarding military bases in India. They wanted the British to retain two bases in India, one near Calcutta, the other near Karachi. It also appears that the United States wanted air bases of its own in India. In addition the Americans wanted military air transit rights from North Africa across India (Karachi, Delhi, and Calcutta were specifically mentioned) and thence to Southeast Asia.[7] In effect India, closely tied to Britain, could be part of a quasi alliance to contain the Soviet Union.[8]

At one level the American desire for transit rights and for British and American bases in India complemented British strategic thinking. Like the Truman administration, the Attlee government sought to contain the Soviet Union. In pursuit of this objective it wanted bases east of Suez and intended that India, as a dominion with a strong army, would provide bases and be a close ally. The United States supported these objectives, as well as Britain's hope to remain an important world power. There was, however, an important distinction between American and British strategic thinking: the British wanted to project their power in Asia not only to contain the Soviet Union but also to compete with the Americans. Consequently, they declined the American requests for bases as they affected India, arguing (with a certain irony) that any military arrangements with India would have to be negotiated after a grant of dominion status to India.[9]

The Cold War affected American policy toward India in other ways as well. Whereas Indian communism had been a matter of only the most limited interest to the Americans during the war, there was now considerable concern that communism was growing apace on the subcontinent and that the Soviet Union might be seeking influence in the region. Some State Department officials, without much evidence, were certain that communist agitation lay behind the several tragic riots that plagued the subcontinent. Also without evidence, some (though not the highest level officials) thought that the Soviet Union had undue influence with Nehru and the interim government which took office in September 1946. Finally, because the Cold War significantly, and tragically, affected American policies toward the European colonies in Southeast Asia, relations with Indian leaders, who took strong exception to American support for the European colonial regimes in Asia, were often strained.

The efforts to acquire military bases, transit routes, and landing rights, as well as the interest the United States took in the degree of communist and Soviet influence in India, lend support to those who posit an early commitment to global containment. The United States wanted India to remain loyal to the West and out of the Soviet orb. Had it concluded that the interim Indian government was under Soviet control, it probably would have altered its policy in an effort to keep India under western influence. The issue never arose in extreme form, however, because the United States sensibly concluded that the leaders of both India and what was to become Pakistan were relatively moderate and would keep their countries independent of Soviet influence.

On the other hand, global security concerns did not determine many aspects of American policy in the immediate postwar period. The intensifying Cold War did not, for example, determine all aspects of Anglo-American relations. As historian Robert Hathaway observes, "American policy, except in those areas where Russian obstinacy forced Washington into close partnership with the United Kingdom, displayed the same chariness toward the British as it had in the years before the war."[10]

Concern with imperialism was one issue that was not entirely defined by the new Cold War. Although criticism of the British empire lessened, it did not disappear. Anger at British imperialism erupted during the debate over the proposed British loan. Walter White of the NAACP, for example, wrote to President Truman asking for pledges that any money lent to Britain not be used "to perpetuate imperialism or to deny any colonials of British Empire full freedom and justice." The strongly negative response among the American public to Churchill's strident Iron Curtain speech resulted in part from continuing dislike of the empire. One correspondent complained to the President that Churchill's "long history of exploitation of the population of India and Palestine speak far more eloquently than the words spoken at Missouri." In the Senate Claude Pepper complained about possible American support for British imperialism, while Arthur Capper (R-Kansas) assailed Churchill's call for closer Anglo-American ties as "a bid for us to furnish forces to help hold Gibraltar, Malta, Suez, Singapore, India and all the British colonial possessions." Despite the considerable deterioration in relations with the Soviet Union in 1946, a poll at the end of the year indicated that Americans considered the British only slightly less imperialistic than the Russians.[11]

India stands out as a place where the Cold War and the new strategic thinking were of only middling significance as a determinant of American policy.[12] The effort to secure bases was the direct result of the new concern with global security, but most elements of American policy toward India had been formulated well before the Cold War, and unlike in Indochina, for example, they continued in their essentials until independence was achieved in August 1947. American concern not to be closely identified with European colonialism was one such long standing policy. On February 1, 1946, Secretary Byrnes sent to the American officials in New Delhi a draft "Policy and Information Statement" on India which called attention to American efforts "to disassociate our policies and actions in Asia from those of the Colonial powers." The document also addressed continuing American interest in mediating the Indian conflict.[13] Similarly, the next month, Lampton Berry, who knew American policy toward India intimately, observed that the United States had pressured the British to achieve a satisfactory settlement in India because India provided "the acid test of the liberal professions of the Western Powers." A settlement, he explained, was "in the interests of the prestige of the Western Powers, and indeed of the white races, in that part of the world."[14] While the Cold War added a new dimension to such concerns, the policy itself was developed well before tensions with the

Soviet Union were even on the horizon. Louis Johnson, William Phillips, and even Franklin Roosevelt had made similar comments.

Likewise, American hopes that India would achieve its independence with a minimum of violence and rancor were hardly new. Nor was the desire that an independent India be a united India the result of postwar strategic thinking. The United States consistently supported a united India. During the war there was a growing appreciation in Washington that a satisfactory settlement would have to take into account Jinnah and the Muslim League. But this did not translate into support for political division.[15] The Cold War provided another rationale for supporting a peaceful transfer of power to a united India, but the policy did not result from the Cold War.

Lampton Berry's analysis of American policy toward India in March 1946, provides a fascinating example of how older strains in American policy merged with newer Cold War considerations. Dean Acheson was about to meet with Ambassador Halifax to discuss India, and Berry suggested that the undersecretary remind Halifax about "our traditional interest in seeing a solution of the Indian political problem." He noted, as many others had, that American and western prestige in Asia depended on a settlement satisfactory to the nationalists. Though a traditional American concern, Berry contended that the lack of a solution was now a matter of even more importance, for it affected world wide interests. The United States wanted to maintain British power to help contain the Soviet Union, which in part depended on British access to India's military reserves. This necessitated a strenuous effort to achieve a settlement that would allow the British and Indian governments to remain on good terms. Even then, however, the British could not rely on the Indian army "unless the Indian leaders are made aware that Britain is less of a threat to India than is the Soviet Union." Berry thought India was vital to the defense of the Middle East, where he feared a showdown with the Soviet Union might occur even before a settlement in India was found. Finally, Berry feared that failure to find a settlement soon would result in violent disturbances which would "sap the strength of the whole Empire, militarily and economically. The Soviet Union," he observed, "will certainly endeavor to use this situation to its own advantage."[16] In sum, Cold War considerations added a new dimension—perhaps at times a new urgency—to traditional policies; generally speaking they did not determine new policy directions.

The year 1946 did not open on an auspicious note for American relations with Indian nationalists. Nehru had just delivered his strongest criticism of United States foreign policy yet, and Consul-General Donovan reported that the "great majority of Indians" agreed with his remarks. More moderate Indians, he reported, were merely "disappointed" with the United States for having failed to force the British to solve the Indian situation. The perception was growing that the United States had joined Britain's imperial policy in Asia.[17]

In mid-January, responding to a request from the State Department, Donovan composed a lengthy analysis of Indian attitudes toward the United States. During the war, he argued, Indians had admired the United States both as a leading industrial power and as a champion of democracy and self-determination. But after the war the perceived failure of the United States to put more pressure on the British or to stop British intervention against nationalist forces in Indonesia and Indochina led to strong criticism of the United States. In a perceptive analysis, Donovan pointed out that Indians expected more from the United States precisely because of its outspoken support for self-determination and democracy. And when the United States failed to live up to its professed ideals, they were disappointed and angry. Two weeks later a Bombay newspaper reported angrily that British troops had used American tear gas grenades to suppress disturbances. The report was probably true.[18]

Soon anti-American demonstrations and riots broke out. In February rioters attacked an American army convoy; three soldiers had to be hospitalized. A mob of 400 sacked an American Methodist church and burned its jeep. In Bombay mobs burned a car belonging to the United States Liquidation Commission and broke windows of National City Bank. Rioters attacked an American army lieutenant and the United States naval liaison officer. The American consul's car was stoned and a jeep belonging to the consulate was attacked with clubs. No Americans were killed ("a miracle," wrote Donovan), but there were several narrow escapes, including that of the vice-consul and his wife.[19]

The most publicized of the anti-American incidents occurred on February 19 when mutinous Royal Indian Navy sailors tore down and burned a flag at the USIS office in Bombay.[20] Nehru condemned the act as childish, and an official in the External Affairs Department told Donovan that the government regretted the incident "even more deeply" than he did and stood ready to make amends. The Royal Indian Navy presented a new flag to the American consul general, and the incident was formally closed.[21] But at the end of March Donovan received a brief letter from the chief of the Political and Services Department of the Government of Bombay that contained no expression of regret and ignored Donovan's demands that the guilty parties be punished. "Moreover," Donovan continued, "five weeks were required for the Political and Services Department to formulate this masterpiece, which has a prose style reminiscent of Wallace Irwin's 'Letters of a Japanese Schoolboy,' while at the same time it bears some resemblance to Mrs. Malaprop's conversational efforts."[22]

A major concern for the United States was the fear that American soldiers in India might be forced to defend themselves and thus might end up, even if inadvertently, joining with the British to suppress a disturbance. The unhappy prospect of the Americans firing on Indians led J. J. Singh to warn the secretary of war that such an eventuality would be "dangerous and may have world-wide repercussions."[23] In the House of Representatives Congressman Celler demanded that American troops be brought home from India at once, while Representative Jerry Voorhis (D.-California) addressed a similar demand to Truman directly.[24]

The anti-American incidents were actually a very small part of widespread and at times violent demonstrations and riots in major cities across the country, some of which had begun as early as November 1945. Donovan described the Bombay mutiny and riot as "characterized by unexampled savagery," an "orgy of bloodshed and destruction." In Bombay alone there were more than 300 deaths.[25]

Representative Celler, an important force in the eventually successful efforts to secure an immigration quota for India and to grant Indians already living in the United States naturalization rights, reportedly suggested that certain British officials had planned the anti-American incidents to lower the reputation of the United States in the eyes of the Indian people. ("No subtlety in Mr. Celler's make-up!" commented a Government of India official.)[26] But American diplomats and consular officials in India had very different explanations of the causes. Donovan concluded that the Bombay mutiny itself resulted from the insensitive actions of the navy's "distinctly inferior" officers and that the riots which followed in its wake sprang from anger at the British government; the disturbances were "distinctly racial in character," he thought.[27]

Reports of these dramatic riots were received in February 1946, just as American policy toward the Soviet Union was turning toward resistance of Soviet demands. Stalin had delivered his harsh attack on the West, and Kennan's Long Telegram had just been received and distributed. Fear of communism reached new levels. Not surprisingly, therefore, the State Department wanted to know if there was any "communist instigation" of the riots.[28]

The most respected and experienced American officials in India downplayed communist involvement. In two reports Donovan acknowledged that the Communist party "always fishes in troubled waters" and no doubt tried to be involved in the disturbances. But he thought it most unlikely that communists caused the riots. Perhaps, Donovan suggested, the State Department had been unduly influenced by G. M. Kelly, the American Associated Press representative in Bombay who was "inclined to see Communist activity in every disturbance which breaks out in India." In sum, he concluded directly, "there is no evidence at this time to implicate the Communist Party in the mutiny."[29]

Merrell's response was similar. He wrote that communists were probably active in the Bombay riots "but did not initiate them and did not organize street fighting or looting." British military intelligence sources thought that inflammatory speeches by Congress politicians (Mrs. Asaf Ali in particular) were the principal cause, he reported. No link to Moscow was evident.[30]

In Madras, by contrast, Roy E. B. Bower saw serious communist involvement. He argued that since the Madras disturbances were marked by little violence, their causes were easier to discern. As evidence of communist involvement, he pointed to the profusion of communist flags. "The whole affair," he reported, "was organized, and was organized by experienced trouble-makers." While there was some anti-white feeling and certainly a good deal of anti-British sentiment, "the emphasis was on labor solidarity against employers of any race." In sum, Bower wrote, "the evidence points to premeditated communist exploitation of it for their special ends, that is, to promote class friction as a means of influencing the masses."[31] The American consul in Karachi also credited reports of communist organization of the disturbances there.

Significantly, the State Department singled out Bower's report for special commendation. Dean Acheson found it "very helpful" and asked for more reports regarding "all incidents in which communist policy can be identified." Berry seemed to agree. Comparing the various reports, he concluded that the reports from Karachi and Madras were possibly "more accurate" than those from Bombay and New Delhi because the riots in the latter cities were much larger and the underlying forces more difficult to identify.[32]

R. E. Murphy of the State Department's Office of European Affairs demonstrated most clearly how fear of international communism now influenced official thinking in Washington. Explicitly agreeing with Berry's analysis, he complained about Merrell's and Donovan's caution. While there might not be direct evidence of communist influence at the moment, he regretted their unwillingness to come to the logical conclusion. For the past twenty-five years, he wrote, communists had been the "world's greatest specialists" at creating naval mutinies. Further, the *Daily Worker* claimed that communists in Calcutta had increased their activities, noted the presence of communist flags in a Bombay demonstration, and reported that Indian sailors had sought assistance from the Indian Communist Party. All of this was sufficient for Murphy to blame the troubles on the communists. "Naturally the Indian Communist Party is not going to boast of having started such a mutiny," he wrote. But the communists alone had the experience needed to organize the event.[33] Increasingly, Murphy's attitudes became commonplace in the State Department, making a balanced approach to nationalism in Asia difficult.

Although the strongly anticommunist predilections of many American officials caused them to view events in India through that lens, anticommunism was not the determining factor in American policy toward India. Whether communists were involved in the disorders or not, it was difficult to deny that anti-British sentiment, and perhaps anti-white sentiment, had never been higher and that the need for a settlement had never been more apparent. Although the British denied this to be the case, it was probably the riots that produced a sense of urgency to find a solution. As Sarvepalli Gopal writes, the riots "finally convinced the British Government that the spring of the empire was broken."[34] There was now renewed movement toward a settlement.

The previous December there had been elections for the Central Legislative Assembly, in which the Congress won almost all the seats in non-Muslim areas, while the Muslim League ran equally strong in Muslim-majority districts. The provincial elections followed in January 1946. Again the Congress and the Muslim League emerged as the only parties of importance, with Congress being in the driver's seat. In the states that would make up future Pakistan, for example, the league won sufficient seats to form the government only in Bengal and Sindh. At the end of January the viceroy announced his intention to establish a new, representative Executive Council and to arrange for a constituent assembly as soon as possible to draft a new constitution. In sum, despite the collapse of the Simla conference the previous summer, the Labour government and Wavell had persevered, and progress had been made toward self-government.[35]

On February 19, 1946, the day after the Bombay mutiny, the British government announced the appointment of a Cabinet Mission to India, consisting of Lord Pethick-Lawrence, the secretary of state for India, Sir Stafford Cripps, the president of the Board of Trade, and A. V. Alexander, the first lord of the admiralty. Indians received the news with hope, as did some Americans. Several prominent American friends of the nationalists, led by Pearl Buck, urged Prime Minister Attlee to have the Cabinet Mission take incisive action, such as establishing an interim national government. Not all Americans were initially impressed, however, the *Nation* complaining that Pethick-Lawrence's "mental arteries have long since hardened."[36]

Before giving its blessing to the Cabinet Mission, the American government asked pointed questions about a policy of divide and rule. In the recent past the British had allowed Jinnah in effect to veto the formation of the new Executive Council, which could be interpreted as a divide and rule approach. The Americans were curious about whether the Cabinet Mission would allow a similar result if it could not find common ground between the two parties. Patrick responded enigmatically that "irrespective of degree to which such considerations may or may not have figured in British official thinking in past," the present British government was absolutely sincere in wishing to bring about a settlement. The British were going to make every effort to bring about a reconciliation, they claimed.[37]

Soon there was substance to support British assurances to the Americans. On March 15 Prime Minister Attlee told the House of Commons that the Cabinet Mission would not allow any minority element to veto a settlement. This was a major change in British policy, which had so often deferred to the wishes of the Muslim League.[38]

The response in the United States to Attlee's announcement was enthusiastic. One correspondent reported that the statement "came to many Americans as a gleam of sunshine from a dark wintry sky. . . . On every hand could be heard expressions of joy and hope." Even the *Christian Century* was won over. "This concession may lead to the most important change in the British empire since the American colonies won their freedom," the journal contended, while the *New Republic* thought Attlee's move "rare statesmanship."[39] American officials reacted similarly. Berry described Attlee's statement as "excellent," a reaction that seems to have been typical. "The degree of favourable comment for an act by Britain is unprecedented," Ambassador Halifax reported to his government.[40]

Attlee's pronouncement so impressed several State Department officials that they wanted the United States to grasp the moment and issue a public statement in support of the British efforts in India.[41] Loy Henderson, director the State Department's Office of Near Eastern and African Affairs (and later American ambassador to India), met with Halifax to see if the British wanted such a statement. Halifax, who thought the offer itself "a spontaneous and friendly move," was inclined to encourage American action. It would, he thought, have the advantage of putting the United States on record in support of the British.[42]

The British government was less enthusiastic, however. While there was appreciation for the American gesture, there were doubts that it would have any impact on Congress and might actually irritate the Muslim League. Moreover, the Prime Minister groused that the American proposal looked "like a pat on the back to us from a rich uncle who sees us turning over a new leaf."[43] Better, the British thought, to leave matters entirely in the hands of the Cabinet Mission. In light of the British attitude, the United States reluctantly held back.[44]

On March 24 the Cabinet delegation arrived in New Delhi, where it met with leaders of the major parties. Jinnah argued for two nations on the grounds that the cultural differences between Hindus and Muslims were insurmountable. Fearing that he could no longer prevent a British decision, the Muslim leader threatened violence if the Cabinet Mission did not agree to Pakistan. Congress, on the other hand, insisted on a unified India.[45]

While the Cabinet Mission tried to find common ground, rumors arose that the United States might become involved. Doubtless based on the earlier American explorations of issuing a public statement, the prospect of American intervention in any form was not well received in India by any of the parties. This was partly because of growing Indian anger at American policy elsewhere in the colonial world. In addition to their concern about American policy toward Southeast Asia, Muslim and Hindu nationalists alike were upset with American policy toward Palestine. A few weeks earlier Truman had advocated the immediate admittance of 100,000 displaced Jews into Palestine, which angered not only Middle East Muslims but also the British, who administered Palestine under the United Nations. Furthermore, the rumors of possible American intervention created the impression that Washington had determined that the talks, still under way, were about to fail. "It is my considered opinion," Merrell wrote, "that no useful purpose would be served if US were to intervene on its own initiative at this juncture."[46] The United States soon denied that it had any solution to offer.

Meanwhile, efforts to find solutions satisfactory to both Congress and the Muslim League bogged down. There was little reaction in the United States. According to Halifax, what comment did appear was "not very hopeful but at the same time sympathetic to the British position."[47]

With the Indian parties deadlocked the Cabinet Mission issued its own plan on May 16, 1946. It rejected the idea of an independent Pakistan as a practical impossibility. There were simply too many non-Muslims in predominantly Muslim areas and a sizable number of Muslims in areas that were predominantly non-Muslim. Instead, it called for a unified India but with the central government having powers only over defense, communications, and foreign affairs.[48] Questions involving communal issues would require concurrent majorities of the Muslim and Hindu representatives in the central legislature. The mission proposed further that the provincial legislatures, using a complicated formula to ensure proportional representation among Muslims, Hindus, and Sikhs, select delegates to a constituent assembly to draft the constitution. Finally, the plan assigned each province to one of three groups of provinces: Bengal and Assam; Punjab, Northwest Frontier, and Sind; and the rest of British India. Each group of provinces would, among other things, deal with provincial constitutions and determine whether to cede certain powers to the group. The plan, in essence, allowed the Muslims autonomy in provinces where Muslims were in a majority. As one British observer put it, the scheme was "designed to give them the advantages of Pakistan without the disadvantages inherent in the division of India."[49]

It was not a plan to please former Prime Minister Churchill, whom the American embassy in London described as gloomy. On the other hand Amery, who had been Churchill's secretary of state for India, praised the Cabinet Mission's proposal, thus lending support to the belief that he was "much more of a liberal in his thinking than he is given credit for being by his political opponents."[50]

The proposals also received favorable comment in the American press[51] and impressed friends of India in the United States. Louis Fischer, whose works the British had banned (the ban was lifted on April 5, 1946),[52] was one such person. He had supported Congress' rejection of the Cripps proposals in 1942, but now he urged Gandhi to accept the new plan. The Cabinet Mission's proposals were not perfect, Fischer conceded, but they represented a great advance and ought to be accepted. "India will have the world against it if it refuses to cooperate now," he wrote. The letter was transmitted through State Department channels, suggesting that Washington was sympathetic to Fischer's view.[53]

However, the reaction in Washington to the Cabinet Mission's plan was, in fact, initially confused. Joseph E. Davies, a Truman adviser and former ambassador to the Soviet Union, congratulated Prime Minister Attlee in extravagant terms. The plan, he wrote, was "in accord with the finest and highest traditions of British fair-play since the days of Runnymede to the Statute of Westminster." For the State Department, Dean Acheson stated that the United States viewed with favor the British proposal to establish an all-Indian Executive Council. But in a circular telegram to selected diplomatic and consular officers, Acheson predicted that neither Hindus nor Muslims would accept the Cabinet Mission's plan, and, presumably influenced by the negative response to previous suggestions of American involvement, he offered no hope that there would be any American efforts to bring about a settlement.[54]

Over the next several days enthusiasm for the plan grew, and the State Department indicated that it was taking another look at having the President or the secretary of state issue a statement along the lines of Acheson's public comment. The intent would be to encourage the Indian leaders to go along with the plan. Before the Americans acted, however, they again wanted to know whether the British favored such a step. This time the British response was positive, although not enthusiastic. Wavell and the Cabinet Mission's members agreed that an American statement would probably not have much influence on the Indians, although there was a chance it might do some good. The Prime Minister concurred, and on June 3 the British embassy informed the Americans that Britain would welcome a statement. The ambassador added that any such statement ought to come before June 5, the date on which the Muslim League would meet to consider the plan.[55]

But then the Americans decided that the statement had "lost its timeliness." To issue it now would make it appear as if the United

States was putting pressure on the Muslims, they said.[56] Almost surely American second thoughts related to larger issues involving United States relations with Muslims in the Middle East. The United
States considered the Middle East an area of vital economic and
strategic interest and feared Soviet influence in the region. It had
only recently faced down Stalin over Soviet troops in Iran, and fears
of a major confrontation in the Middle East with the communist
power were commonplace. Consequently, the United States sought
influence and stability in the Middle East. The tense situation then
existing in Palestine (the following month Jewish underground
forces would blow up the King David's Hotel in Jerusalem killing
nearly 100 persons) posed a threat to American hopes. Arabs were
angry at Truman's support for a large Jewish immigration to the area
(a decision based on domestic political considerations as well as genuine outrage at the sufferings of Jews under Hitler).

The State Department was well aware that any actions it took in
India that irritated Muslims there would complicate its already difficult political position in the Middle East. In April, for example, Merrell had warned against any American initiative to which Indian Muslims would not react favorably because it "might cause repercussions
in other Middle East countries."[57] Then at the end of April an Anglo-
American commission of inquiry, formed the previous year to inves-
tigate the plight of displaced Jews in Europe, recommended the creation of a binational state in Palestine and the admission of 100,000
Jews. The reaction in India was immediate and extremely negative.
Jinnah denounced the commission's recommendations as the "gross-
est betrayal of the promises made to the Arabs," while his newspaper,
Dawn, contended that if the proposals were adopted the "names of
Truman and Attlee will stink more in the nostrils of all just men than
those of Hitler and Mussolini."[58]

Given the importance attached to stability in the Middle East,
therefore, it is not surprising that the State Department backed away
from a public comment supporting the Cabinet Mission's plan. However, the American decision confused and disheartened the British.
It had, after all, taken them only about one week to respond to the
American inquiry, despite their having had to consult with their officials in India. "There is nothing that we can do about this," wrote one

Foreign Office official, "but when the State Dept. change their minds in this way, it does not help us in trying to convince I[ndia] O[ffice] (and others) that they are anxious to be of assistance to us."[59]

Meanwhile, reaction in India was generally favorable to the Cabinet Mission's recommendations. Gandhi praised them, and both Congress and the Muslim League accepted them (though with reservations), causing momentary jubilation in the American press.[60] The Indian parties were, however, unable to agree on the makeup of an interim government. On June 16, 1946, the Cabinet Mission then made its own proposal for an interim government of fourteen persons. If one or both of the major parties found the plan unacceptable, the proposal read, the viceroy would form a government as representative as possible. The Muslim League accepted the Cabinet Mission's proposal, but Congress rejected it because of what it considered to be Wavell's caving in to Jinnah on procedural matters and on his instruction that Congress could not include a Muslim among those it nominated to serve in the government. The Cabinet Mission then returned to London on June 29.

In India, American officials were divided over who was most responsible for the failure to form an interim government. Donovan sympathized with the Congress view and accused the British of being afraid of the Muslims. Merrell, on the other hand, tended to blame Gandhi and Congress for the impasse.[61] The reaction in the American press was harsh, with considerable criticism emerging of Nehru, Gandhi, and the Congress generally. The American reaction injured American relations with the nationalists. One important Congress Socialist leader, for example, told an American consular official that he "could not comprehend the anti-Indian bias of the American press," and that the press reaction, along with official American policy, was pushing India into the arms of the Russians.[62]

If the nationalists complained about American opinion, the British were pleased. "The Government Mission may fairly be said to have had a thoroughly satisfactory press from start to finish," reported Puckle. The change in the American attitude was even evident in isolationist, Anglophobic Chicago, reported the British Information Service. "There is no doubt that the turning point has come," the

information service representative stated. "No longer are we tempted to slink out to the men's room when the conversation turns to
India. The unanimity of the praise is embarrassing."[63]

Despite the failure of the Cabinet Mission to achieve an agreement on an interim government, it had made important gains. While
Congress had rejected the interim government, both parties had
accepted the Cabinet Mission's statement of May 16 (which called for
provincial groupings and a constituent assembly). Furthermore, it
seemed that all parties were now convinced that the Labour government really did want to bring a British departure from India. Consequently in the long run relations between the British and the Congress improved.

Throughout July elections for the constituent assembly took place,
but in other respects the situation deteriorated. Nehru made statements which indicated that Congress interpreted portions of the May
16 plan differently than the Muslim League (and perhaps the British
as well), and Jinnah responded by withdrawing his own acceptance
of the Cabinet Mission's plan, coupled with harsh threats of civil war.
Because the Muslim League had so seldom agreed to any plan,
Nehru's comments have often been considered, even by Congress
members, as unnecessarily provocative.[64]

Wavell, meanwhile, tried to continue to negotiate with Jinnah and
Nehru to form an interim government. This time Jinnah refused
Wavell's proposals, and on August 6 the viceroy invited Nehru to
attempt to form an interim government. Nehru offered the Muslim
League five of fourteen seats (similar to what the Cabinet Mission
had proposed), but Jinnah insisted that Congress name no Muslim
member of its own. Nehru refused, and the negotiations ended.

Jinnah then made good on his threat to cause trouble. He
declared August 16 to be Direct Action Day, which the Muslim
League government in Bengal conveniently declared a public holi-
day. This set the stage for unbelievably savage riots across Bengal,
with the worst violence taking place in Calcutta. The American consul-general reported the events in chilling language:

> The restraints of civilization were discarded, and atrocious mur-
> ders took place. Bodies were hung, burnt alive, dismembered and
> disembowelled, and even dogs and goats were without purpose

slaughtered. Primitive blood lust of the most sordid nature prevailed. . . . Houses were broken into, women were raped, whole
families were slaughtered, and arson was prevalent throughout the
city.[65]

The Muslim League government in Calcutta "took a direct part in
organizing the Muslim attack against the Hindus" who were
"butchered like sheep." British efforts to quell the violence were slow
in coming; only after Hindus and Sikhs "took the law into their own
hands and indulged in savage reprisals" did the army move in, and
even then without assistance from the local government.[66] Somewhere between 5,000 and 6,000 people died in Calcutta alone, more
than in any other riot during the long years of British rule in India.

Although the riots threatened to delay or even prevent the
appointment of the interim government, London insisted that
Wavell proceed. By August 24 the King had agreed to appoint a fourteen member government, including Nehru and five other prominent Congress leaders, as well as representatives of other communities. Three were Muslims, and two more unfilled places were allotted
to Muslims who would be appointed later. The Muslim League itself
was not represented, but the door was kept open for it to join. The
United States was pleased. It officially welcomed the appointment of
"a representative Executive Council" and commended the viceroy
and all of the parties involved. Washington also officially regretted
that the Muslim League had chosen not to participate but hoped it
would later on.[67] The State Department was now willing to take a
position against the Muslim League, probably because it supported
British efforts to end the crisis and because it had always thought its
own interests best served by a united India. In addition, the Americans may well have been angry at the league's responsibility for some
of the atrocities that had just occurred.

Dawn, Jinnah's newspaper, did not mention the State Department's announcement but a few weeks later expressed fears of a new
imperialism from across the Atlantic.[68] Shortly thereafter *Dawn* again
lambasted Truman's policy toward Palestine. Jinnah himself characterized the President's policy as "most unjust and against every canon
of morality." When representatives of the Muslim League visited the
United States in November, they found they could not get an

appointment with the President. They had to settle for a visit with the undersecretary of state, who was on record as favoring a united India.[69]

On September 2 the new government was sworn in. In addition to serving as vice president of the Executive Council, Nehru held the portfolios of defense and commonwealth relations. Soon, Merrell reported, Congress Party members, who had boycotted the viceroy's residence for years were accepting his dinner invitations.[70]

Four days after the new government took office, the United States indicated its strong support by informing Bajpai that it was now ready to upgrade its diplomatic representation with India and exchange ambassadors, though it wanted the initiative to come from the Indian government.[71] In making its views known, the United States had ignored the British Foreign Office, which assumed that the Americans were testing the degree of real independence India enjoyed. The British were not pleased with the American approach, nor did they like the idea of upgrading relations immediately to the ambassadorial level. "Mr Truman rushes about, & not always like an angel," commented the undersecretary of state for India. Wavell concluded that the Americans "were quick off the mark" to upgrade relations because they saw India as an important market.[72]

But these reservations were not matters of fundamental concern; Pethick-Lawrence even came to like the idea of an exchange of ambassadors and reminded Wavell that, given "the Russophile tendencies of some of your colleagues," they had better cultivate the Americans. The King soon gave his approval. It took another month to negotiate the modalities of the formal announcement, but on October 23, 1946, the announcement was made that ambassadors would be exchanged between the United States and the Government of India. The announcement received favorable comment in the United States.[73]

American support for the new government did not, however, prevent Indian criticism of the United States. One factor in American society that was subject to Indian criticism was the deplorable treatment of African Americans. Late in September 1946, American historian Merle Curti delivered two speeches in Bombay about race relations in the United States, in which he stated that most white Americans considered blacks to be inferior beings. Curti's remarks were reported in the Bombay press, which had recently focused attention on some lynchings in the South. It was probably not coincidental that two days after Curti's speech, Gandhi stated that neither Britain nor the United States were truly democratic countries, for both "live on the coloured races by exploiting them." The United States was sensitive to attacks on its race relations, and American anticolonial rhetoric, as well as efforts to dismantle segregation, were in part responses to criticism from the newly emerging nations.[74]

Indian nationalists, especially those devoted to nonviolence, also condemned the American use of the atomic bomb. Gandhi confessed that he was horrified when he learned of its use on Japan. "I did not move a muscle when I first heard that the atom bomb had wiped out Hiroshima," he said. The bomb was "the most diabolical use of science." The following year Nehru bitterly denounced the American atomic tests at Bikini Island and more particularly the publicity which attended them. "It was a challenge and a threat," he said in an angry editorial. " . . . We have heard much of the Four Freedoms and of the brave new world to come, and yet the only freedom that the mass of humanity is likely to possess is the freedom to die and to be blown to bits; of course, to preserve democracy and liberty and the Four Freedoms."[75]

In addition, Indians of all political stripes continued to criticize strongly Truman's support of Jewish immigration to Palestine, a point that American diplomats in India thought was particularly harmful to Indo-American relations. The American decision in November to back Syria instead of India for a seat on the United Nations Security Council no doubt reflected American concern with Arab opinion. Perhaps it also reflected the less than warm state of American relations with Indian nationalists, although the United States denied it.[76]

Evincing a certain level of tension between the United States and India's nationalist leadership was the American reaction to India's choice for its first ambassador to the United States, Nehru's sister, Vijayalakshmi Pandit. Her name had already been proposed to the King for his approval when Acheson let it be known that the United States wanted instead "a man of tact, great dignity, broad knowledge, and realistic outlook."[77] The United States suggested a number of possibilities, none of whom Nehru selected. Instead, he reluctantly chose Asaf Ali. Privately, Nehru considered Ali a less than ideal choice and had, in fact, originally rejected the idea of appointing him. Ali was "a somewhat ineffective person," Nehru feared. But he was also a man of some distinction. A barrister at Lincoln's Inn and prominent member of the Congress Party who had been imprisoned on eight occasions, he was minister of transport and railways in the interim government. He was said to be internationally minded although he had not been outside of India since 1915. The British did not think Asaf Ali would impress the Americans, and a State Department official made "invidious comparisons" with Bajpai, whom the American considered "urbane, intelligent and hardworking." Furthermore, as a Muslim Ali's appointment might be seen as a challenge to the Muslim League.[78] (The Muslim League was in fact upset with Ali's appointment. When he arrived in Washington in 1947, league members refused to attend a reception in his honor.) There were even rumors that Ali was going to America to escape from his wife, whom a British official in India described as "one of the wilder members of the Congress Party." But the reality was that he was being rewarded for his long service to the independence struggle. Acheson, while clearly considering Ali better than Pandit, told President Truman that the ambassador-designate was only "satisfactory."[79]

Meanwhile, Wavell attempted once again to bring the Muslim League into the interim government, and on October 13 Jinnah, fearing the growing prestige and power of Congress and perhaps chastened by the violence, agreed and gave Wavell vague assurances that the league would renounce its policy of direct action and cooperate in the government. Americans were pleased.[80] But Jinnah did not play fair with the viceroy, and once in the government league representatives refused to accept Nehru's leadership or assume a collective responsibility. It may well be, as Gopal believes, that Jinnah's only aim was "to disrupt the interim government." If so, Wavell's anxiety to get the league into the government may have been, as Gopal put it, "among the most serious of Wavell's many disservices to India." B.

R. Nanda offers a fairer judgment, however. "The sins of Linlithgow," he writes, "were visited on Wavell and Mountbatten."[81] Jinnah also urged Wavell to postpone the constituent assembly scheduled for December 9, but the London authorities refused to give in to the Muslim leader's demands, and the invitations went out in November.

T. Eliot Weil, the American chargé d'affaires in New Delhi, was pessimistic about the future of the interim government, since Jinnah and Gandhi were both intransigent. A few factors, however, might work toward moderation, he thought. For one thing, both parties contained large conservative, propertied groups who stood to lose substantial income if there was civil war. These groups also feared the revolutionary forces that would be unleashed if social control broke down completely. Finally, in the communal violence, which had already "reached an almost unprecedented degree of savagery," the Hindus had shown themselves to be fully as ferocious as the Muslims, a fact which surprised many observers since it flew in the face of the stereotype of the passive Hindu. In light of the violent Hindu response, Jinnah might pause before leading the country to civil war, Weil thought.[82]

Further complicating the situation, Jinnah had placed Congress in a difficult, perhaps untenable position, thought Weil. If the league pulled out of the government there could be total chaos. Furthermore, a constituent assembly without league participation would be meaningless.[83] If these concerns occurred to the Congress leaders, however, they did not prevent them from demanding that the league withdraw from the government.

With civil war in the wings, Attlee invited Muslim, Sikh, and Congress leaders to join him and Wavell in London for a last ditch attempt to forge a compromise. Congress leaders were at first unwilling to go, but eventually Nehru agreed to attend. They arrived in the British capital on December 2, 1946.

The London meeting resulted in a more aggressive demonstration of American interest in the Indian situation. The United States, while following events closely, had generally remained aloof, in part because neither the Indians nor the British wanted any American intervention. But the situation was now so critical that the State Department decided that it had to play a more active role. Further delay would work against American political, economic, and strategic interests in the subcontinent. The growing interest in containing Soviet expansion required stability. Civil war might threaten world peace and could result in unwanted outside (presumably communist) intervention. It would certainly disrupt India's economy, thereby setting back American hopes for the "mutually advantageous economic relations" that a stable situation would promote. Therefore, the department proposed to inform the two Indian parties of its alarm at the dangerous situation. Among other things, the United States would urge Congress to accept the British/Muslim League interpretation of the Cabinet Mission's plan of May 16, 1946. To the Muslim League, the United States would emphasize that the organization's interests were now protected within a larger Indian union. Separation would not be necessary.[84]

The British response to the proposed American intervention was positive but cautious. They felt that an American intervention might be useful but only after the London talks ended on December 6. To intervene during the talks ran the risk of appearing to the Indians to be a coordinated move with the British that would only be resented.[85]

This time, however, the State Department decided to take unilateral action. The day after the Indian leaders arrived in England, Dean Acheson publicly expressed his "deep concern" about the outcome of the talks. Noting correctly that the major issue involved disputed interpretations about the grouping of provinces called for in the Cabinet Mission's plan of May 16, Acheson urged the principals to show magnanimity in their efforts to establish a "stable and peaceful India." To make clear how important the United States regarded the situation, Acheson asked the American embassy verbally to convey his statement to the Indian leaders who had gathered in London and to take the opportunity to present an informal elaboration of the State Department's views.[86]

Although the British were apparently taken off guard by Acheson's actions, Prime Minister Attlee praised his intervention, as did the British newspapers.[87] Privately there were some reservations. Nevile Butler, for example, thought it would have been more useful for the Americans to have focused their comments on some specific issue that was of direct concern to the United States. But even in private there was general agreement that the statement was meant to be helpful, that it might actually have some impact on the Indians, and that at least it would show the American public that if the talks collapsed it was not the fault of the British.[88]

The outcome of the London talks favored Jinnah, for the British government made it clear that Jinnah's interpretation of the disputed portion of the Cabinet Mission's plan was the correct one, and it called on Congress to give way so that the Muslim League might feel free to take part in the constituent assembly. Nehru said that the Congress would have to review the entire situation.[89]

As Nehru was flying back to New Delhi, Pethick-Lawrence proposed that the United States approach Congress leaders and urge them to accept the British interpretation of the disputed clauses. The United States "acceded without hesitation,"[90] and the very day the constituent assembly opened (without the Muslim League in attendance) on December 9, Merrell called on Nehru and delivered a verbal message from his government. (Merrell had previously delivered the same message to Vallabhbhai Patel, home and information minister in the interim government.) The United States wanted Congress to accept the British/Muslim League interpretation of the disputed section of the plan relating to provincial groupings. Acknowledging that to do so would be to Congress's disadvantage in the short run, the American government thought the move would bring the league into the constituent assembly and might make it possible for Jinnah "to cooperate loyally within the framework of the Indian Union." Nehru asked that the message be put in writing.[91]

Acheson wanted to know immediately the results of Merrell's overtures. Patel's response was not encouraging. Congress, he stated, could never accept the British interpretation of the Cabinet Mission's plan. The nationalists "had been tricked." As for the United States, Patel stated passionately that the Americans were supporting the British. Nehru, however, did not give an immediate response. His reaction upon hearing the message had been "gracious but he made no comment." Doubtless he would discuss the American position with the Working Committee. He invited Merrell to dinner a few days hence, at which time the American expected to get some response.[92]

The State Department considered Merrell's forthcoming dinner

with Nehru crucial and sent an urgent telegram to New Delhi directing Merrell to emphasize that the United States was acting on its own
in the interest of international peace. Acheson acknowledged that
some aspects of the Cabinet Mission's plan were open to criticism,
but he wanted Nehru to understand that the Americans felt that the
plan "presents a fair basis for constitution-making in a difficult situation where current political realities cannot be ignored." In particular, the State Department hoped that Nehru would accept the British
interpretation of the "groupings" question. If Congress agreed,
Acheson thought the Muslim League could be persuaded to accept
a federal union and cooperate in running the government.[93]

Merrell put the administration's case to Nehru over dinner on
December 13. Contrary to Patel, Nehru accepted the American contention that the United States was not acting at the behest of the
British (although in fact it was, at least in part). Furthermore, while
he attacked Jinnah and complained that the recent London meetings had been counterproductive in the sense that the Muslim
League now had even less incentive to enter the constituent assembly, he made a vital concession: Congress would probably submit the
question of grouping to the courts, which he knew would almost certainly rule against Congress.[94]

Although Nehru had made an important concession, in private he
resented American interference, which he regarded as patronizing.
Acheson's advice, he wrote to India's new ambassador to the United
States, was "entirely gratuitous"; he resolutely refused to be subservient to anyone.[95]

Encouraged by Nehru's concession, the State Department
attempted a similar approach to Jinnah, initially through Liaquat Ali
Khan, general secretary of the Muslim League, and then, when Ali
proved reluctant to convey the American message, through the
American consulate general in Bombay.[96] The Americans tried to
convince the Muslim League to cooperate with the Congress, in
exchange for Congress agreeing to accept the British interpretation
of the groupings question. Liaquat Ali Khan reluctantly agreed that
an unconditional acceptance by Congress might be a first step
toward reconciliation, but in the end the American approach proved
to be fruitless. There was virtually no hope that the Muslim League

would make any concessions. "In other words," as Pethick-Lawrence wrote to Attlee, the American "démarche had failed." The Indians, thought Attlee, were "very willing to get support from America, but have very little inclination to take advice from them."[97]

In spite of such setbacks, the American approach was now dramatically different than it had been in the Churchill-Linlithgow era. By late 1946, the United States was working, often hand in glove with the British government, to bring about a settlement of the dangerously volatile Indian situation. The United States informed the British of all its contacts with Nehru and Jinnah (it even seems to have provided them with Merrell's dispatches from New Delhi).[98] Wavell was pleased. The American intervention with Nehru gratified the viceroy, and he felt it would give the Congress Working Committee "pause for thought." No one, commented Sir Paul Patrick, questioned the disinterested character of the American intervention.[99]

The change in the American approach resulted from a variety of factors and changed conditions, but the work of the irrepressible Anglophile, Cornelius Van H. Engert, contributed to the new relationship. Despite his earlier indiscretions (presumably not known to the State Department), Engert had advanced in his career and was in 1946 deputed to work with the Acting Secretary Acheson on Anglo-American relations. In January 1947, Acheson assigned him to review the whole field of Anglo-American relations. As was his wont, he approached the British in confidence for information.[100] Although some British officials considered Engert so extremely Anglophilic that he did "himself a disservice" and reduced "the value which we might otherwise expect to obtain from such a friendly colleague," they supplied him with considerable material, knowing that he would use it with discretion. Among the position papers the British provided to the American was one that emphasized that any decline in the prestige of the British Commonwealth would "damage our common cause." It was a point that Engert took to heart, telling the British that the point about the Commonwealth "was the core of his own attitude to Anglo-American relations."[101] It was also the view of many Americans who felt that the Commonwealth was an important part of their efforts to contain communist expansion. In January 1947, Lewis Douglas, the new ambassador to Great Britain, told an audience that in view of the tyrannical menace loose in the world, the United States needed the Commonwealth at least as much as the Commonwealth needed the United States.[102]

Meanwhile, the constituent assembly had opened as scheduled on December 9 but soon adjourned to January 20, 1947, to await possible participation by the Muslim League and the quasi-independent Indian states. Patrick predicted the chances of anything constructive emerging from the assembly as only one in ten. In some cities violent riots continued to occur, adding to the sense of urgency. On December 23 the American consul in Bombay reported that the rioting there had eased somewhat after 450 people had died. Earlier a depressed Nehru had written, "murder stalks the streets and the most amazing cruelties are indulged in by both the individual and the mob. It is extraordinary how our peaceful population has become militant and bloodthirsty. Riot is not the word for it—it is just a sadistic desire to kill."[103]

On January 5, 1947, the All India Congress Committee met in emergency session to consider the British government's interpretation of the disputed portions of the Cabinet Mission's plan. No doubt the American position was also before it. While the committee regretted Britain's position, it decided to accept the interpretation under protest and subject to the reservation that no province nor part of a province could be forced into a settlement.[104]

Congress's conditional acceptance of the British interpretation was not enough to draw the Muslim League back into the process. Jinnah told an American diplomat that Congress's action was nothing more than propaganda.[105] When the constituent assembly reconvened on January 20 the league was not in attendance. At the end of the month the Mulsim League's Working Committee met in Karachi to determine its future course. The Americans were most interested in the deliberations, and the new secretary of state, George C. Marshall, instructed the American consulate in Karachi to keep him informed.[106] The league concluded that the Cabinet Mission had failed because, in its view, Congress had not accepted the statement of May 16. Therefore, the elections for the constituent assembly and the body itself were "invalid, and illegal." Thereupon the Congress demanded that the Muslim League representatives withdraw from the interim government. The league responded that Congress had no more complied with the Cabinet Mission's plan than the league and that therefore it had just as much right to remain in the government as Congress. Wavell sympathized with the league's position, but the secretary of state for India did not.[107] For the moment the stand-off continued, as neither Congress nor the Muslim League was willing to withdraw from the government, and the British government was not willing to insist.

Whether a different response from Congress to the Cabinet Mission's plan would have made a difference at this point—specifically, if on January 5 Congress had agreed to support the plan without condition, would the Muslim League have agreed to enter the constituent assembly and cooperate with the Congress toward a united India—is a matter of heated debate. Some historians are convinced that the conditions Congress put on its acceptance of the plan rendered that acceptance virtually meaningless and led Jinnah finally to reject cooperation. Others consider Congress's action a minor factor or even an insignificant one. Jinnah, they feel, was intent on separation, and Congress's action was nothing more than a convenient excuse to push ahead with his plans for a separate Muslim state.[108]

As for the Americans, in urging Congress to accept the plan they held out the expectation that Jinnah would go along. After the Muslim League rejected Congress's qualified acceptance of the plan, Jinnah told American diplomats that the Muslim League would have entered the constituent assembly if Congress had accepted the British/Muslim League interpretation of the plan. The Americans tended to believe him. Merrell in particular complained with considerable bitterness about Congress's ineptitude. Had it shown some magnanimity and accepted the Cabinet Mission's plans without condition, Merrell came to believe, the Muslim League would have entered the constituent assembly and a united India would probably have emerged. He was convinced that Jinnah's demands for an independent Pakistan represented nothing more than a bargaining position.[109]

The Americans were probably influenced in part by Jinnah's "complete agreement" with Acheson's statement of December 3, which had called for Indian concord on the basis of the Cabinet Mission's plan. However, Jinnah's "complete agreement" was conveniently expressed only after Congress refused to accept the Cabinet Mission's plan unconditionally, and Merrell underestimated the Muslim leader's commitment by this point to divide India. It was left to the viceroy to put equal responsibility on both India parties. In a conversation with Merrell he blamed the continuing impasse on "those 2 stubborn old men Jinnah and Gandhi."[110]

With the failure of the Cabinet Mission, it ultimately became clear that Britain had two choices. It could remain in India indefinitely and hope that it could eventually forge a settlement satisfactory to the major parties. Or it could leave India unconditionally. To take the latter road would represent a failure of its hope to keep India closely tied to Britain, and for months the government had tried desperately to find a third alternative. By February 1947, none was apparent. The option of remaining indefinitely was impossible for several reasons. For one thing the situation in India was deteriorating too rapidly. Furthermore, Britain's ability to control events had diminished as the number of British civilian and military officials in the country had declined. In addition, to remain would have invited criticism from the United States. But the fundamental consideration involved Britain's grave domestic and financial problems. Britain simply could no longer afford to bear the burden of far flung commitments. Stafford Cripps summed up the British difficulties succinctly when he told the House of Commons that it "was quite obviously impossible . . . to decide to continue our responsibility indefinitely . . . into a period when we had not the power to carry it out."[111]

Among those to conclude that the British must leave quickly was Lord Louis Mountbatten, former supreme commander of Allied forces in Southeast Asia, whom the Labour Government had chosen to replace Wavell as viceroy of India. Mountbatten made it a condition of his acceptance that a specific date be set for a British withdrawal.[112] Therefore, on February 13 the cabinet made a tentative decision to leave India no later than June 1948. It confirmed the decision on February 18, and on February 20 Attlee dramatically announced his government's intention to transfer power. If there was no agreement among the Indians by June 1948, the British would turn over responsibility to those Indian authorities that seemed most likely to further the interests of the Indian people. Attlee also announced that Mountbatten would take over as viceroy and governor general of India in March. Mountbatten's orders were to prepare for the transfer of power in such a way to as ensure the happiness of the Indian people, although he was to try to keep India in the Commonwealth and arrange for mutual defense agreements, if possible. The very next day London informed the United States that it was also pulling out of Greece and Turkey in six weeks, thus setting the stage for the Truman doctrine. Britain could no longer compete as a world power.

Attlee's announcement about India unleashed a furious debate in Britain, where many Conservatives, including former Prime Minister Churchill, opposed the plan because it did not require prior agreement among the Indian parties and because the transition period was much too short. But Halifax supported it after a great deal of anguished thought because he could suggest nothing better. Efforts to censure His Majesty's Government were soundly defeated.[113]

The American reaction was a mixed one. The *Los Angeles Times* was "appalled" that the British were pulling out so abruptly, and *Newsweek* feared that civil war would result. The *New York Times* and the *Christian Science Monitor* considered the announcement a bold move, a virtual ultimatum much as the United States had set a specific date to leave the Philippines. The *Nation* thought that the announcement was final proof that the British really meant to leave India.[114]

In the State Department, Loy Henderson agreed with the *Nation*'s perspective and added that it was now up to the Indians to agree on a plan for independence or face the prospect of a devastating civil war. They could no longer blame the British. Henderson was "thoroughly convinced of the sincerity of the British Government in its efforts to grant complete self-government to India."[115] Secretary Marshall agreed. When the British ambassador called on him, he emphasized his confidence in British policy toward India, complimented Mountbatten with unusual warmth, and offered to issue a statement of support if it would be helpful.[116] Five days later, on February 25, 1947, Marshall publicly praised the British government for its "persistent and sincere efforts" to bring about a settlement.[117]

The British welcomed Marshall's statement, as well as the direct American approaches to Indian leaders. But American policy evoked little interest in India itself. Of the twelve leading dailies, only the *Times of India* deemed Marshall's statement worthy of comment. In Bombay two newspapers ran editorials, with the *National Standard* praising the statement because, unlike previous American statements, it was not patronizing. "From warning and advice the emphasis has shifted to appreciation and hope," the editor wrote. But the newspapers were much more interested in troubles in the Punjab and the price of cloth and sugar than in the American position paper. "More space was even given to reports of the tour of the Royal family in South Africa," the American consul general in Bombay reported. Indicative of the lack of sustained interest in the American view was that two weeks after the statement had been released, Jinnah himself was unaware of it. The American consulate in Bombay was ordered informally to apprise the Muslim leader of the American position.[118]

The British action was consistent with one American goal, having the British leave India; but it threatened other objectives. It was not certain, for example, that the end result would be a stable, contented India. The burden was now on the Indians, the American statement suggested. Failure to agree, the United States held, might result in India becoming "the source of new international tensions in a world only now beginning to grope its way back to peace."[119] But even as the State Department was releasing its public statement, George Merrell reported from the Indian capital that there was no assurance that the British "shock treatment" would drive Congress and the Muslim League together. Indeed, the opposite might result, with the consequence that yet another American objective, maintaining the unity of India, would be endangered. Jinnah, Merrell felt, would now "hold out for pakistan [*sic*]."[120]

As for the Indian National Congress, Merrell found its attitude toward the British announcement to be childish, even depressing. J. J. Singh, then in India, echoed Merrell's views about Congress (indeed, he supplied the embassy with inside information about the party leaders' private deliberations). Singh thought the British announcement "wonderful" and criticized those Indians who clung to their traditional distrust of the British.[121]

Such criticism was not entirely fair. Congress's Working Committee had officially welcomed Attlee's statement and had invited the Muslim League to discuss the new situation. The league, by contrast, was unhappy and never issued any official resolution concerning the British announcement. It refused to meet with Congress and was still committed to direct action, which often translated into atrocities against Hindus and other non-Muslims. As Merrell had feared, the league was, if anything, more intransigent than ever about the need for Pakistan.[122]

The Cold War further complicated the American view of Indian developments. Because the Americans increasingly believed that international communism was conspiring to bring the entire world, and especially the newly emerging nations, under its menacing control, they could hardly avoid the issue when they looked at India. Some did not like what they saw. The previous year some officials in Washington and India saw communist involvement in the riots. Now there were suspicions that Nehru's interim government, which sometimes took positions at variance with those of the United States, was doing the Soviet Union's bidding. On January 17, 1947, John Foster Dulles, who represented the United States in the United Nations General Assembly, charged that in "India Soviet Communism exercises a strong influence through the interim Hindu government."[123]

As might be expected, Dulles's statement caused a strong and bitter response from Indian leaders. Nehru, who had denounced Indian communists during the war and who had once described the Indian Communist Party as "the stupidest of the Communist parties of the world,"[124] reacted with "surprise and regret" and said he could hardly believe that Dulles had made such a statement. Vijayalakshmi Pandit, who having failed to obtain the ambassadorship to the United States was instead given the job of representing India at the United Nations, conjectured, probably correctly, that Dulles was disturbed at India-Soviet cooperation in the Trusteeship Council. India and the Soviet Union had also worked together to try to prevent South Africa from annexing the former German Southwest Africa (today Namibia). But these instances of cooperation hardly meant that India was under communist domination, Pandit said. "Mr.

Dulles should know this," she stated. As for Dulles's foolish characterization of the interim administration in India as a "Hindu government," Pandit rightly considered it an "altogether gratuitous"
comment.[125]

Merrell also took strong exception to Dulles's comments, writing
that Congress had tried strenuously "to counteract Communist activities" in India. The State Department, which had not seen Dulles's
remarks prior to their delivery, distanced itself from them and
assured Nehru that the United States had confidence in his government. Secretary Marshall also let Dulles know of the department's
unhappiness with his comments.[126]

Dulles's observation was not eccentric, however. Azim Husain, secretary general to the Indian delegation to the United Nations General Assembly, informed Nehru of the growing criticism in the United States of the Indian delegation, while M. C. Chagla, judge of the
Bombay High Court and later ambassador to the United States, told
Nehru that responsible opinion in the United States felt that India
was virtually an ally of the Soviet Union.[127] The distinguished journalist and committed nationalist, B. Shiva Rao, agreed with Chagla.
There was "a great deal of hostile opinion against us in the United
States," he wrote.[128]

Although Nehru fumed about Dulles's remarks and defended the
Indian delegation, he did admit that some changes needed to be
made. "We shall have to do something about it," he wrote to
Chagla.[129] But he continued fiercely to defend India's right to take
whatever positions served its own interests and the cause of anti-colonialism, and he refused to back away from criticism of American
racial practices.

Although Marshall did not accept Dulles's characterization of the
Indian government, the communist issue was not one to be ignored.
About the same time that Dulles was charging that there was communist influence in the Indian government, the State Department
learned that the Indian Council of World Affairs (a private organization but one that had close ties to Nehru and the Indian government) intended to issue invitations to Asian countries to attend a
conference to discuss issues of common interest. The United States
asked twenty-five American embassies and consulates across Asia to

find out whether the governments to which they were accredited planned to send delegates and expressed particular interest in how "Communists or Communist-controlled groups" in those countries felt about the proposed conference. There was also concern that the Asian republics in the Soviet Union would be invited. "If such delegations appear in Delhi they may be expected to do their utmost to develop a pro-Soviet orientation among other Asiatic delegations," warned the American embassy in Moscow.[130]

As plans for the conference matured, the United States watched carefully. The British, who generally favored the conference, provided the Americans with much helpful information about the nature of the conference, the topics to be discussed, and the delegations that would attend.[131] By March, when the conference was scheduled to open, Merrell had come to fear that it would degenerate into a forum to attack the West. Although the conference was supposed to discuss nonpolitical topics, such questions as "National Movements for Freedom in Asia" and "Racial Problems with Special Reference to Racial Conflicts" were on the agenda. The Vietnamese and Indonesian delegations, among others, were expected to air their grievances against imperialism. In sum, Merrell believed that despite the disclaimers, "the motivation and tendency of the forthcoming conference will be in the direction of developing a solidarity among Asiatic countries to combat 'western imperialism.'"[132] The conference might not involve direct communist sponsorship or influence, but it surely threatened to attack the West, thus undermining American hopes to keep Asia on its side in the Cold War.

The United States, therefore, took actions to influence the conference. It briefed the Philippine delegation, spent several thousand dollars to pay the expenses of the Korean representatives, sent American observers to the conference, set up a special shelf of books at United States Information Service about Asian problems for the use of the delegates, and arranged to have American documentary films shown at the conference's discussions of social and educational problems.[133]

When the conference opened on March 25, Merrell reported that, as he feared, it was focusing on the need for Asian cooperation to oppose Western imperialism.[134] But by the time it ended early in

April, he was much less worried. The theme of Asian unity was balanced by support for cooperation with the rest of the world. The delegations from the Philippines, Korea, and China had supported American policy in Asia, while the Soviet system had received no support. In general, thought Merrell, the conference organizers had succeeded in avoiding divisive issues.[135]

Although the United States was relieved with the outcome of the Pan-Asian conference, Asian nationalism still posed a major challenge for the United States, both generally and specifically in its relationship with Nehru and the interim government of India. At its heart, the problem involved different kinds of anticolonialism. The Indian government championed the cause of anticolonialism without conditions as one of the polestars of its foreign policy. The United States also professed devotion to anticolonialism, but its position was hedged and encumbered with other considerations. Often it boiled down to whether support of anticolonialism in a particular situation enhanced its larger strategic objectives, such as containing the Soviet Union.[136]

Further complicating the situation was the fact that the United States needed its European allies, such as the French and the Dutch, to build a successful policy of containment in Europe. Yet these allies were desperately trying to hang onto their Asian empires which, they argued, were essential to their ability to contribute to the prosperity and security of Europe. Such arguments did not impress nationalist Indians who had no hesitation about strongly attacking America's Cold War allies. India's attitude about developments in Indochina, for example, displeased the French, who were at least as nervous about the New Delhi conference as were the Americans. They were doubtless not pleased when Ho Chi Minh himself congratulated Nehru on the meeting's opening.[137] Similarly Nehru proved to be an outspoken advocate of the Indonesian Republican cause, which led to criticism of the British and United States for their equivocal attitudes about Indonesian independence.[138]

Despite Cold War nervousness and the complications of Asian nationalism, American objectives in India remained essentially unchanged. Among other things this meant continued endorsement of the Indian interim government. An important sign of continuing

United States support was the appointment in March 1947, of Henry W. Grady as the first American ambassador. The British were pleased. Grady received high marks from Lewis Jones of the British embassy in Washington, who stated that Grady "combines prestige and ability with reliability." The British ambassador described him as "fundamentally Anglophile . . . an able and friendly man." He especially admired Grady's wife, who had studied at the London School of Economics.[139] The Foreign Office regarded the American as "entirely reliable, . . . well disposed to us, and businesslike. His prestige and ability are undoubtedly high and it is thought that he is likely to make a conspicuous success of his Mission."[140]

Despite the British endorsement, the Grady appointment caused initial embarrassment as the ambassador found himself in hot water with both Congress and the Muslim League. On April 10, 1947, before he left for India Grady stated that the report of the Technical Mission, which he had headed in 1942, could provide a suitable basis for India's current developmental needs. He also spoke of the need for a united India. Though these were doubtless well-intentioned comments, to both major communities in India they seemed to foreshadow an effort to force the United States on India, politically and economically. Jinnah's newspaper, *Dawn*, referred explicitly to Grady's "greed." The Muslim League also feared that American trade would involve business deals primarily with Hindu interests, something it feared. Grady's attempts to clarify his comments perhaps assuaged some Muslim fears but, as the British high commissioner to India expressed it, the clarification only "put the Hindu press on its guard."[141] V. K. Krishna Menon told Mountbatten that Grady's remarks convinced him that the Americans wanted "to capture all the markets, to step in an [*sic*] take the place of the British." They might even want military bases for use against the Soviet Union, Menon thought.[142] In sum, Grady had "put his foot in the hornet's nest," as one India Office official put it.[143] Despite Grady's gaffe, the Americans intended the appointment to demonstrate its support for the interim government and the transfer of power.

The continuity of American policy was also evident in the country's support for a united India. As Secretary Marshall put it on April 4, 1947, "the continued integrity of India" would best serve "our political and economic interest in that part of the world." The Americans (as well as the Labour government) continued to believe that a united India would be better positioned to resist Soviet expansion. Two weeks after Marshall's dispatch, William Phillips delivered an address at a banquet for the new Indian ambassador to the United States, in which he pointed out the advantages of union. Hinting that Cold War considerations lay in part behind his hope for unity, Phillips observed that "with conditions throughout the world as they are," it would be a "tragedy" if India emerged "a broken country." Jinnah, Phillips was certain, would take strong exception to his remarks.[144]

It looked increasingly as if American (and British) hopes for a smooth transition to an independent and unified India would not be realized, however. Ten days after Marshall's dispatch the prominent Indian Congress leader, K. M. Munshi, predicted to an American diplomat that the Muslim League would not enter the constituent assembly nor would Jinnah agree to any compromises. Munshi and others (including some British officials) compared Jinnah's control over the Muslims to Hitler's domination of the Germans. There would not be a united India, Munshi stated unequivocally.[145] Despite numerous reports from American diplomats in India that partition was increasingly likely, the United States was not yet prepared to concede this. The new viceroy was, however. Mountbatten, who had initially considered the idea of an separate Muslim state "sheer madness," had now become reconciled to India's division, although he still thought Jinnah "a psychopathic case."[146]

By mid April, then, United States policy remained unchanged in its essentials. It supported the interim government and British efforts to transfer power to Indian hands, although there were some private doubts about the speed of the proposed transfer and worries about whether a stable and united India would result. There was also nervousness about communist influence in India, but it was insufficient to affect the general direction of American policy.

The British welcomed American support but, based on past experience, feared that it was soft and could quickly evaporate. There also continued to be occasional expressions of concern about American economic designs on India. For these reasons they decided that it was worthwhile extending the assignment of the India Office's chief propagandist in the United States, Sir Frederick Puckle, into 1948. He would help keep American opinion "on the right lines."[147]

On June 8, 1947, on his way to New Delhi, Ambassador Grady stopped off in Singapore, where he reportedly stated that the United States wanted to assist India "in her fight for independence." Despite his early difficulties, he had not yet learned the value of diplomatic caution. The British found Grady's comment not only tactless but pointless as well. "Some people take time to grow up," a prominent Congress official stated to Mountbatten. Grady's remark particularly rankled Nehru, who was always suspicious of American economic intentions, and he planned to "speedily disabuse the new ambassador of any ideas he may have of embarking upon a policy of dollar diplomacy."[148] (Mountbatten himself encouraged this kind of anti-American thinking.)[149]

What made Grady's purported Singapore remarks seem especially foolish was that on June 3 the British government had announced that it would turn over most responsibility to the Indians, not in June 1948, but in mid-August 1947, scarcely two months away. The plan, based in part on the ideas of V. P. Menon, the reforms commissioner of the interim government of India, would grant India dominion status, and while a British governor general would remain for the time being the Indians would be in charge of all of their affairs and could choose to leave the dominion if they wished. Though the British would try once more for a united India, they believed that acceptance would be unlikely. They therefore planned to present a procedure for dividing India. Special provisions would apply to the Punjab and Bengal, which had the options of joining Pakistan or "Hindustan," remaining an independent dominion, or being split between Pakistan and Hindustan.[150]

The decision had evolved from Mountbatten's discussions with Indian leaders, which had convinced him that partition was the only solution. Gradually, Nehru and most other Congress leaders were convinced as well. Late in April Nehru remarked bluntly that "the Muslim League can have Pakistan if they want it."[151] Their experience of attempting to work with the Muslim League in the interim government had led them to believe that cooperation was well nigh impossible. Mountbatten was able to persuade Congress that, under the circumstances, even if a united India could somehow be agreed upon, the resulting central government would be so weak that it would be unable to retain control of the country. Gandhi considered partition morally unacceptable but pledged not to hinder implementation of the decision.[152] Finally, bloody, unreasoning communal violence continued. If, as historian R. C. Majumdar writes, the failure to suppress the violence "will forever remain a blot on the otherwise remarkable career of Lord Mountbatten in India," it was also the reason why the viceroy decided that the British had to leave almost immediately. If they delayed much longer, there might not be any competent authorities left to which power could be transferred. The Labour government's hopes for a united India were gone, but Mountbatten had performed yeoman service for Britain by keeping India in the Commonwealth, at least for the moment.[153]

The American response to the new British timetable was initially unenthusiastic, with the *Washington Post* and *Newsweek*, for example, expressing fear of civil war if the British hand were removed so suddenly. The British, well aware of the trepidations that some Americans had expressed at their previous decision to leave in 1948, feared that the American government might respond negatively to this dramatically shortened transition period. For its part, the State Department, shortly before the British announcement was made, was receiving conflicting advice about Indian conditions. J. J. Singh, now back in Washington, told Acheson that the need for improved social and economic conditions would keep India together—this at a time when the major parties had virtually agreed to partition.[154] But other reports poured in to Washington indicating that a peaceful solution was unlikely. Jinnah told Merrell that he was going to have Pakistan, "no question about it."[155] The American embassy in New Delhi predicted that Gandhi would sabotage the Congress-Muslim League talks scheduled for June 2 with Mountbatten. The Americans theorized that Gandhi wanted a deadlock that would force the British to transfer power immediately to an interim government which in turn would crush Muslim resistance. All in all, "provocative statements" from both sides provided an "ominous prelude" to the conference.[156]

The American predictions that the conference would collapse proved to be wrong. Mountbatten had worked closely with the parties, and all had agreed to the plan to expedite British departure from India. Consequently, the talks succeeded immediately. On June 3 Prime Minister Attlee announced to the House of Commons that the British plan of extending dominion status to one or two Indian authorities had been well received by the Indian parties. The Commons cheered, and Churchill himself surprised many by expressing his support for the new plan. Even the India Office was pleased, noting that the Commons "had not displayed much [such?] unanimity on any single question since the declaration of war." Joyce singled out Mountbatten for particular praise in bringing about the agreement.[157]

The British announcement, followed by public acceptance of the plan by Nehru, Jinnah, and Baldev Singh (for the Sikhs) had an immediate salutary effect in India. Jinnah appealed for calm, and though sporadic violence continued in some places, communal relations improved significantly.[158] It was now clear that India would be partitioned. On June 10 the Muslim League formally accepted the British plan for partition, and the All-India Congress Committee followed suit a few days later.

As for the Americans, the press reaction this time was very favorable to the British. The *Christian Century*, the most consistently pro-nationalist American publication, praised British statesmanship, as did influential columnist Walter Lippmann who characterized the settlement as a "work of political genius."[159] And Mountbatten himself wrote that, "generally speaking," the United States was "more alive than most to the magnitude and complexity of the Indian problem."[160] (The contrast with Linlithgow's assessment of the shallowness of American opinion is striking.) The new American ambassador shared the public's enthusiasm. Writing personally to President Truman, Grady stated with surprising nonchalance that the decision to partition of India "was inevitable" and had avoided much civil strife, though it would set back the subcontinent's economic development. Mountbatten, Grady thought, deserved great praise.[161]

The State Department, however, which was on record as believing that Indian and American interests would be best served by a united

India, was less elated, and it took a full week to react publicly to Attlee's announcement.[162] But when the official reaction came, the United States government welcomed the agreement. Praising the British and Indian governments, as well as the major parties in India, Secretary Marshall characterized the agreement as a "source of much encouragement to India's friends." The cooperation among Indian leaders, the State Department thought, "augurs well for the future of India" and could serve as a model for the resolution of similar disputes elsewhere. The statement did not mention a unified India, noting only that future constitutional developments would be decided by the Indians themselves.[163]

The India Office thought the American statement "most helpful." Joyce thought its phrasing "particularly felicitous" and, with a certain strained logic, even found reason to compliment the United States on its delay of one week in issuing the statement. Had the United States made its opinion known earlier, he said, it would have been lost in all the others. As it was, the American statement stood alone.[164]

In the few weeks before independence arrived, a myriad of matters of surpassing importance had to be addressed. The provinces had to vote for or against partition, and when partition was decided upon there were enormous problems to resolve, including the precise boundary between India and Pakistan, the division of the armed forces, the functioning of the interim government, the status of the quasi-independent Indian states, and the selection of governors-general.[165] Only on the issue of the Indian states was the United States involved. The states were theoretically free to remain out of either India or Pakistan, and a few, such as Hyderabad, were determined to try. The United States, which had only reluctantly come to accept the division of India into two states, opposed the further "Balkanization" of the subcontinent as likely to increase instability and thus threaten American interests in the region. As historian Robert McMahon concludes, the Americans felt that India, with its "vast size and population, was destined to play a major role on the world stage." Therefore, despite its concern to keep on good terms with the Middle Eastern states, the United States attempted to prevent Arab governments from extending recognition to some of the Indian states that were flirting with retaining an independent existence. The British were pleased.[166]

As India moved toward independence with almost breathtaking speed, the Cold War was developing at an equally fast pace. The United States moved toward a formal policy of containment of the Soviet Union and international communism. In June Secretary Marshall put forward a plan for Europe's economic recovery which, it was hoped, would hinder communist subversion. George Kennan's famous "X" article, which provided a philosophical justification for adopting the policy, appeared in July. As before, Cold War considerations affected American relations with Nehru's interim government. This was most evident in the continuing disagreements over colonialism in Southeast Asia. Nehru continued to criticize the Europeans for trying to hold on to their empires and the United States for its apparent support of the Europeans. "Feeling is very high in India re Dutch action," reported Ambassador Grady in July, following the first Dutch "Police Action" against Sukarno's Republic of Indonesia, "and repercussions here cannot be anything but unfavorable to US and Britain." From Bombay Howard Donovan reported similar sentiments and urged his government to use its good offices to end the hostilities and thereby defuse Indian critics.[167]

The force of Asian nationalism, something that William Phillips had glimpsed perceptively in 1943, struck Ambassador Grady as so important that he emphasized the phenomenon in his first letter from India to President Truman. "There is a growing sense of nationalism in India which takes the form of criticizing the Western Powers, particularly Great Britain and the United States," he wrote.

> This is due to India's new found independence in the first instance, and in the second, to the general attitude of all Asia toward western countries. One encounters it everywhere. The West as a whole has a job of winning back the confidence of Asia. One even sees reference to Japan as the courageous little country which had the nerve to challenge the arrogance of the Western Powers even though in doing so she destroyed herself.[168]

Truman's response did not indicate a great deal of worry. The Asian attitude toward the West was "one that is to be expected and all we can do is to try and live it down," he wrote. He did not suggest any specific actions that the United States might do to alleviate Asian concerns.[169] However, the United States took Donovan's advice about Indonesia. In August it began to pressure the Dutch to be more conciliatory.[170]

Fear of communism was, of course, increasingly central to the American response to revolutionary nationalism in Asia. In Indochina Ho Chi Minh, leader of the nationalist resistance movement to the French, was a communist, and as the Cold War developed it became almost unthinkable to support him against the French, even though the State Department knew that Ho had much more support among the populace than did the French. In Indonesia, the United States waffled until it became clear, after the Madiun Revolt in 1948, that the nationalists were anticommunists. It then supported the nationalists, concluding that their victory would be more likely to contain the spread of communism in Asia than would continued Dutch rule.[171]

Nehru's government unequivocally supported the nationalist revolutions in Southeast Asia, with the result that there were serious tensions with the United States.[172] But they were insufficient to derail American support for the interim government and for British plans to turn over responsibility to the Indian successor states in August.

By mid-August, most of the problems involved in dividing the subcontinent between India and Pakistan appeared to have been resolved, and on August 14, 1947, Mountbatten addressed the new constituent assembly in Karachi, the new capital of Pakistan. The day before the assembly had elected Jinnah President of the new country. On August 15 Jinnah was also elected governor general, and Pakistan became a British Dominion.

At midnight separating August 14 and 15, Nehru addressed the older constituent assembly in Delhi. With the uncommon eloquence that marked many of his writings and speeches, Nehru told the delegates:

> Long years ago we made a tryst with destiny, and now the time comes when we shall redeem our pledge. . . . At the stroke of the midnight hour, when the world sleeps, India will awake to life and freedom. A moment comes, which comes but rarely in history,

when we step out from the old to the new, when an age ends, and when the soul of a nation, long suppressed, finds utterance.[173]

The next morning Mountbatten became governor general of India and swore in Nehru as the country's first Prime Minister.

As India moved quickly, almost frenetically, toward independence, the United States watched with considerable interest and concern. American anticolonial sentiments, which had not disappeared, favored an early withdrawal of the British. The United States supported Nehru's interim government. At the same time it wanted India to be stable, peaceful, contented, and united. Aside from the benefits this would bring to the newly independent nation, such an India would serve American political, economic, and strategic interests. A peaceful transfer of power, followed by the installation of a moderate nationalist government, could serve as a model for the rest of colonial Asia. The Cold War provided an important context (though not the only one). The United States sought "defense in depth" and saw India as providing an important base from which to contain potential Soviet moves into the Middle East and South Asia. If India were politically weak, wracked by internal discord or even civil war, and ultimately divided, Washington officials feared that it would not be able to serve American objectives.

To achieve these ends, the United States urged Congress and the Muslim League to find a way to bring about a united India. When that failed, it supported the British initiatives and kept its lines of communication open to the Indian leaders, whom it encouraged to work with the British. It kept a close eye out for possible communist influence in India and in the interim government but never let that concern overwhelm other considerations. Although the United States favored a united India throughout, when independence with partition appeared inevitable, the United States accepted the result gracefully and began to readjust its strategic thinking to accommodate the inevitable. As independence neared, the United States often spoke with both Nehru and Jinnah about its hope for fruitful relationships in the future, and both Indian leaders distanced themselves from previous remarks about American economic imperialism. When challenged on *Dawn's* frequent charges of American economic imperialism, Jinnah replied jokingly that the editors "had to make a living."[174] Serious difference with Indian nationalists continued to exist over the communist issue, Palestine, and especially the colonial revolutions in Southeast Asia. But these differences were not sufficiently fundamental to disrupt American support for the transfer of power to Jinnah and Nehru.

When independence came, Truman sent congratulatory messages to Mountbatten, Nehru, and Jinnah, in which he welcomed each state's "new and enhanced status in the world community of sovereign nations." The President reaffirmed American confidence that India would take "its place at the forefront of the nations of the world in the struggle to fashion a society founded in mutual trust and respect."[175] But whether the staunchly anticommunist United States could work easily with Nehru's India, strongly committed to the cause of nonalignment, remained to be seen.

Conclusion

Although it has been stated that prior to 1947 the United States had no policy toward India,[1] it did, in fact, have one, at least from 1939 to 1947. That policy, while not always well defined, consistent, or wise, essentially sought a peaceful resolution of the dispute between the British and the Indians that would be acceptable to the latter. Although the Americans seldom offered advice on the specific form an Anglo-Indian agreement might take, their frequent references to their own policy toward the Philippines implied support for independence in the fairly near future. In any event as the war progressed it became increasingly apparent that nothing less than independence would satisfy nationalist Indians. The United States also believed that its own interests, as well as those of India, would best be served by keeping the subcontinent unified. Finally, from the beginning, American policy allowed for American intervention, if necessary, to bring about a settlement.

The immediate need to define a policy resulted from the outbreak of World War II. Well before the United States became a belligerent, American diplomats recognized that India could be an important source of personnel and war supplies, should the United States eventually find itself at war. India's human and material resources continued to be an important basis of American policy throughout the war. If Indians and Britons were at each other's throats, if the country was torn by revolutionary turmoil, perhaps even civil war, India's contribution to the war would be seriously lessened. Even sullen noncooperation could have serious consequences.

Once Japan declared war on the United States and Britain and in the early months of 1942 and swept almost unhindered through Southeast Asia to the very gates of India, concern about the subcontinent escalated. There was genuine fear that the Japanese would drive on through India to meet Nazi forces either in India itself or in the Middle East. This would prolong the war by depriving the Allies of the potential material and human resources of India and instead make them available to the enemy. The fall of India would also make it almost impossible to supply China, which the United States wanted to keep in the war at all costs. Now it seemed even more important than ever to have the cooperation of the Indians.

The British could have had the cooperation of India's nationalists but at a price Prime Minister Winston Churchill and the viceroy, Lord Linlithgow, were unwilling to pay: internal autonomy during the war and a guarantee of independence after the conflict. President Roosevelt thought the British shortsighted, and despite Churchill's adamant insistence that India was none of America's business he pressured the British government to make a serious effort to settle the matter. Churchill resented Roosevelt's interference but shortly after American entry into the war decided to send Sir Stafford Cripps to India to negotiate. Roosevelt sent Louis Johnson. The talks failed because Churchill was not willing to allow the Indians real power during the war, and Roosevelt accused the Prime Minister of sabotaging the talks. The President probably made a mistake by not intervening more forcefully while the talks were in progress, something Johnson had urged him to do.

While war needs were central, they were not the only determinants of American policy. The Indian freedom struggle appealed to the American anticolonial tradition, and influential Americans outside the government pressed the administration to intervene not only because it might improve Allied prospects in the war but also because it was ideologically and morally right. The United States was supposedly fighting for democracy and freedom, and they did not want the

United States to appear to be helping Britain hold on to its empire. They were joined by Indian pressure groups, such as the newly reorganized India League of America, and the Chinese leader Chiang Kai-shek who wrote a number of eloquent anticolonialist appeals to the President.

The advocates of Indian freedom were fortunate that Roosevelt in general shared their views. Although he wanted to maintain good Anglo-American relations and win the war, at heart he was a thoroughgoing anti-imperialist who disliked colonial rule and wanted to see it ended. He insisted that the Atlantic Charter applied to the entire world, not just to Axis colonies. Also, much more than Churchill and more than many Americans as well, Roosevelt had some understanding of the nationalist forces that had been let loose in Asia. Neither Roosevelt nor anyone else could foresee the future with precision, but the President, who understood that the future lay with the nationalists and not the imperialists, wanted to deal with nationalism in constructive ways. Thus, during the war he devoted much attention to establishing a trusteeship system that he hoped would provide for a smooth and peaceful transition from colonial rule to independence. He insisted that Indochina must ultimately be made independent and to the very end of his life pressed Churchill's government to return Hong Kong to China. Even Dutch colonialism could attract Roosevelt's critical eye. In June 1942, for example, he told Henry Grady that the Dutch could not remain permanently in control of the Dutch East Indies. "I am afraid," Grady quoted the President as saying, "I am going to be very unpopular before this thing is through."[2]

India was different since it was not occupied by Japanese troops, but there too Roosevelt ultimately wanted the British to depart. Still, he could not forget the necessities of war nor simply ignore the strongly held views of Churchill and Linlithgow. Sometimes he took actions that angered the nationalists, such as in the months following the collapse of the Cripps Mission. The mission's failure resulted in a serious deterioration in relationships between the British and the nationalists. In August the Indian National Congress demanded that Britain leave India and prepared to mount a campaign of massive civil disobedience. Linlithgow, insisting that this was the most serious challenge to British rule since the Indian Mutiny of 1857, arrested tens of thousands of Indians and incarcerated them.

Despite Roosevelt's belief that the British were mostly responsible for the collapse of the Cripps Mission, he did not interfere with the British arrests of nationalist demonstrators. This was primarily because the British were suffering a series of defeats in the war. There had already been serious tensions with the British over the second front issue, and he was not willing to strain further the Anglo-American alliance, which he considered essential to victory. Gandhi's occasional criticisms of the United States and American society at this time and statements that some interpreted to mean that he would not resist a Japanese takeover of India also seem to have irritated the President, particularly since they came at a time when the war was going badly for the Allies and a Japanese invasion of India was considered probable.

Nevertheless, many of those Americans who felt that British action against the nationalists was necessary also believed that the British were partly responsible for their own problems, and once the immediate emergency was over most wanted the British to resume negotiations. Churchill had no intention of doing so and in the weeks following the arrests made his most extreme statements about holding on to the empire. The result was a startling change in American public opinion against the British and in favor of American mediation.

In December 1942, Roosevelt sent William Phillips to represent him in India. The British wanted the appointment made but put great efforts into securing an American pledge that would tie Phillips's hands by not permitting mediation. They did not get the pledge, and to the surprise of many Phillips turned out to be a compelling advocate for the oppressed. He quickly concluded that Linlithgow wanted no change and was quite willing to have Gandhi die from a hunger strike. Even more than Roosevelt, Phillips saw the importance of aligning the United States with the emerging forces of nationalism in Asia, and he called on his government to pressure the British. Roosevelt would not go as far as Phillips wanted, but privately he agreed with his personal representative's analysis. When the next year Indian nationalists succeeded in leaking to Drew Pearson one of Phillips's strong reports to the President, Roosevelt refused to disavow Phillips's sentiments, despite considerable British pressure to do so.

The British, and even some Indian nationalists, were convinced that the Americans wanted the British to leave so that they could replace them economically and politically. They were especially fearful of Secretary of State Cordell Hull's calls over the years for a system of free trade which, if implemented, would mean an end to the imperial preference system. Linlithgow, virtually paranoid on this score, was convinced that all of the American wartime agencies in India were part of a conspiracy to prepare the way for an American takeover. He did what he could to inhibit their operations. The Americans were not above collecting economic information and, when the time came, driving hard bargains. But the British exaggerated the nefarious designs of American policy and ascribed to it a clearsightedness and consistency that it did not have.

By 1945 India was no longer important militarily. The Japanese were on the brink of defeat in Burma, and the road to victory would be through the Pacific, not the Asian mainland. Nationalists and their supporters could no longer claim that a political settlement was needed so that the war would be fought more effectively. But the war had never been the only reason the United States had supported Indian freedom, and the Roosevelt administration continued to let the British know of its interest in a satisfactory settlement. Roosevelt's anticolonial views continued to influence policy, and there is reason to think that had he lived the British would have felt renewed American pressure over India once the war had been won. In August 1944, Harry Hopkins told Ronald Campbell, the British minister in Washington, that Roosevelt had "very definite views" about colonies and that he "felt very strongly that a number of these colonies should not revert to their former status." At the very least, the President was determined to see living conditions improved. "He was sick and tired of being told that the natives would not know what to do with goods supplied to them, or with a higher standard of life, that they were happier poor, etc.," wrote Campbell. All of this indicated, he thought, that Roosevelt would "be tough."[3]

Furthermore, the British sensed that Roosevelt's concern went well beyond uplift. As one Foreign Office official wrote after reading

Campbell's report, "the important thing . . . is to get him off the independence track."[4] Roosevelt never did get off the "independence track," although he accepted some compromises. He agreed to allow the French back into Indochina, though only on the stipulation that they accept independence as the goal. The incorporation of Roosevelt's trusteeship system into the United Nations Charter specifically exempted the British empire from its provisions, yet the President knew that the new system would serve as a basis for attacks on colonialism in general.

Roosevelt's successor, Harry S. Truman, did not share Roosevelt's commitment to anticolonialism, at least not with the same intensity. Shortly after coming to office, for example, Truman made decisions that made it easier for the French and Dutch to regain their Southeast Asian colonies. But with respect to South Asia, Truman continued Roosevelt's policy in its essentials. This was easier after the Labour Party victory in July 1945, which brought to power people more inclined to meet Indian demands. But until 1947 even Labour leaders moved more slowly than the Indian nationalists wanted. While willing to negotiate, they hoped to retain Britain's influence in India and to keep India as a dominion. The United States stood ready to offer its assistance in bringing about a transfer of power.

In the final months of the war, serious strains in the Grand Alliance appeared. American relations with Great Britain were worse than is commonly understood, but ultimately more serious were the growing suspicions between the Soviet Union and the western allies. The year 1946 marked the beginning of the Cold War. The United States moved more and more toward a policy of containing the Soviet Union. New strategic ideas found favor in high-level American military and political circles, and attempts were begun to acquire a world wide system of bases and air rights.

As Americans looked at India, the Cold War affected their view. If during World War II India had been viewed as important because it could serve as a reserve of personnel and resources and a base from which to supply China and reconquer Southeast Asia, in the postwar era its large population, its influence in Asia, and its vital location near the strategically important Middle East were not ignored. Secret American attempts were made to keep British bases in India and to acquire bases of their own. Air rights were negotiated. There were fears that communists had inspired an Indian naval mutiny and the riots that were plaguing Indian cities. The Americans supported the new Interim Government of India when it was established in 1946, but some thought that Jawaharlal Nehru's government was susceptible to communist influence. Early in 1947 John Foster Dulles even charged that the Nehru government was subservient to the Soviet Union.

It is, however, possible to exaggerate the importance of the Cold War and the new strategic thinking as they affected American policy toward India. Most of the elements of that policy existed well before the Cold War emerged and continued to be important. A political solution satisfactory to the Indians, the desire for a peaceful transfer of power to a unified India, and an insistence that the United States not be too closely identified with British policy in India, for example, all were in place by 1939 and continued until the transfer of power.

The United States was slow to accept the necessity of Indian partition. It failed to grasp how strongly Jinnah and the Muslim League were now insisting on a separate Pakistan. The United States accepted division only because by mid 1947 there were no alternatives. Even the Indian National Congress, which had for so long pledged itself to a united India, had come to feel that separation was the only way. Once the United States accepted partition, it threw its weight behind efforts to prevent any further "Balkanization" of India by discouraging Indian states from opting for independence—one of the few ways in which the United States was in the summer of 1947 directly involved in shaping India's future.

One potential hindrance to American support of Indian nationalism was the persistence of racist and ethnocentric perceptions in the United States. By some accounts, in the years just before World War II the United States was second only to Germany "as a market for race theories."[5] Segregation remained firmly entrenched, and the number of Americans expressing sympathy with anti-Semitic ideas reached astounding proportions. During the war the forced relocation of Japanese Americans from the West Coast had a racist base. Racist perceptions of Indians were also common. Indians had suffered considerable discrimination, particularly on the West Coast, and like other Asians were barred from American citizenship. The fact that most Indians were Caucasians did not prevent the ban from applying to them. Efforts during the war to bestow citizenship on Indians living in the United States and to create a quota for Indian immigrants were frustrated.

Mother India had been published only a decade before the war, and Katherine Mayo's stereotypical and negative views of Indian culture were still very much in evidence in the 1940s. Not a few Americans were convinced that Indians were not yet ready, if they ever would be, for self-government. The American government was not immune from the general climate of opinion in the United States, and the views of Roy Bower and Cornelius Van H. Engert demonstrate the persistence of negative attitudes toward Indian culture in the State Department. Nehru, in his more pessimistic moments, felt that even well intentioned Americans considered Indians inferior.

But what stands out over the years is that most American policy-makers concluded that the nationalists were not only capable but ultimately reasonable people. To be sure, the Americans sometimes found the nationalists trying. Gandhi at times completely mystified Americans, even angered them when he urged the Americans to pull their troops out, while seeming to put no barriers in the way of a Japanese takeover of India. He also openly criticized American materialism and racial practices. Nehru, too, was willing to criticize the United States, particularly once the Cold War began. In the strongest language he berated the Americans for their ambivalent approach to the nationalist struggles in Southeast Asia. He also spoke out bitterly against American atomic testing in the Pacific. Jinnah joined Nehru in attacking American policy toward the colonial world, as well as for its policy toward Palestine. But the perception of nationalist capability, moderation, and reasonableness persisted nonetheless.

Indian nationalists in the United States and their American supporters played an important role in promoting this image of the nationalists. At least equally important was Nehru himself. With his English education, attractive personality, and expressive use of the English language, Nehru charmed those he met and made good copy for American publications. Furthermore, most of the official Americans who had dealings with both the British government of

India and the nationalists concluded that the British were unreasonable, even reactionary, whereas the nationalists, Nehru in particular, were people one could understand and work with. It took Louis Johnson less than a week to arrive at this conclusion. Within two weeks of his arrival in New Delhi, William Phillips had concluded that it was the viceroy, not the nationalists, who wanted no settlement. In the postwar period, too, the United States welcomed the interim government because it would be controlled by people who were responsible and moderate, even if they could be aggravating. Fears of communist and Soviet influence in the Indian government were real enough, but they did not control thinking at the highest level nor set policy.

The United States did not bring about India's independence. Mohandas K. Gandhi, Jawaharlal Nehru, Mohammed Ali Jinnah, and a host of other patriots associated with the Indian National Congress, the Muslim League, and other nationalist groups, in the end forced the British to give way. Also, many Britons had never shared Churchill's intransigence about India and favored a more generous policy toward the subcontinent. World War II itself was vital in that it weakened the British so severely that by 1947 they really had no choice but to get out on the best terms possible. But the United States was not without influence. It criticized British intransigence and applied pressure on them with some consistency to grant concessions to the Indians. Roosevelt even offered specific proposals on how the deadlock might be broken. The Americans freed the Philippines ("America buried imperialism here today," remarked General MacArthur on that occasion to the Philippine statesman, Carlos Romulo)[6] and constantly suggested to the British that they should follow suit. The British understandably felt that the Americans were insufferably self-righteous and even hypocritical about this, but the continual American harping had its impact nonetheless. As Ambassador M. Asaf Ali graciously stated in a ceremony in Washington marking Indian independence, "the U.S.A. undoubtedly led the way by voluntarily withdrawing its rule from the Philippines last year, and recognizing the sovereignty of the people of the Philippine Republic."[7]

When Prime Minister Nehru first visited the United States in 1949, he spoke warmly of the support the Indian nationalist movement had received from ordinary people in the United States. He was effusive in references to "that great man, President Roosevelt," whom he had so much wanted to meet. "Not only I but innumerable countrymen of mine loved and admired him," he said. He arranged to lay a wreath at Roosevelt's grave and spent time with Eleanor Roosevelt. To a large audience, speaking extemporaneously, he said, "all of us in India know very well, although it might not be so known in public, what great interest President Roosevelt had in our country's freedom and how he exercised his great influence to that end."[8]

Notes

Preface

1. Thorne, *Allies of a Kind*, pp. 6, 8–9, 158–59, 167n.28.

2. Louis, *Imperialism at Bay*, p. 5. See also Dulles and Ridinger, "The Anti-Colonial Policies of Franklin D. Roosevelt," and Sbrega, "The Anticolonial Policies of Franklin D. Roosevelt."

3. Venkataramani and Shrivastava, *Roosevelt, Gandhi, Churchill*, pp. 319–26. Although this book is co-authored, Venkataramani was the sole author of the chapter from which these quotations are taken.

4. Roosevelt, *As He Saw It*, p. 115.

5. Charles Taussig, Memorandum of Conversation with President Roosevelt, March 15, 1945, FRUS 1945, 1:124.

6. Hess, *America Encounters India, 1941–1947*, p. 185. In a later article Hess gives Roosevelt more credit for leaving "an enduring legacy" in the cause of anticolonialism. "Franklin D. Roosevelt and Anti-Colonialism."

7. Ryan, *The Vision of Anglo-America*.

8. Lord Listowel, "The Whitehall Dimensions of the Transfer of Power," *Indo-British Review* [Madras], 7 (Nos. 3 & 4):25. Listowel observed that because of his "passionate" feelings about India, even the British cabinet always deferred to Churchill on Indian questions.

9. Leopold S. Amery to Winston Churchill, February 19, 1943, FO 371 A 1865/93/45, FOR.

10. For example, Dallek, *Franklin D. Roosevelt and American Foreign Policy*, part 4.

11. Leffler, *A Preponderance of Power*.

12. I find myself agreeing with Robert Hathaway and Robert McMahon who warn against attempting to fit all aspects of American foreign policy in this period into the single mold of the Cold War or of a consistent, world-wide pattern of strategic thought. Hathaway, *Ambiguous Partnership*, and McMahon, "United States Strategy in South Asia."

13. Hess, *America Encounters India*, p. 183. See also Jauhri, *American Diplomacy and Independence for India*, a competent account based on published sources. Another important recent work is Malik, *U.S.-South Asian Relations* which focuses on the Pakistan issue. For additional references, see Hess, "Global Expansion and Regional Balances."

14. But see Jauhri, "The American Effort to Avert the Impending Partition of Pakistan," and Malik, *U.S.-South Asian Relations*, pp. 204–21.

15. Thorne, *Allies of a Kind*, and Louis, *Imperialism at Bay*, make extensive use of British archival sources. Venkataramani and Shrivastava had access to some important records in India, including the Tej Bahadur Sapru and the J. J. Singh Papers. They were also able to conduct interviews with some of the principals.

Prologue

1. Bradford Perkins, *The Great Rapprochement: England and the United States, 1895–1914* (New York: Athenaeum, 1968), p. 4.

2. George F. Kennan, *Memoirs, 1925–1950* (Boston: Little, Brown, 1967), p. 310. See also George F. Kennan, *American Diplomacy 1900–1950* (London: Seeker & Warburg, 1952), p. 19.

3. Peter W. Stanley, *A Nation in the Making: The Philippines and the United States, 1899–1921* (Cambridge: Harvard University Press, 1974), pp. 179–225.

4. Bhagat, *Americans in India*, p. [vi].

5. Jackson, *The Oriental Religions and American Thought*, pp. 3–4.

6. Gupta, *The Great Encounter*, p. 38.

7. For a discussion of Swami Vivekanada's influence, see ibid., pp. 116–23.

8. Ibid., p. 135.

9. Ibid., pp. 19–23. Jackson, *Oriental Religions*, p. 93.

10. Isaacs, *Images of Asia*, pp. 266–67. Isaacs' book was originally published as *Scratches on Our Minds* in 1958.

11. Andrew J. Rotter, "Race Matters: The United States and India, 1947–1964," Paper read at the Society for Historians of American Foreign Relations, Poughkeepsie, NY, August, 1992.

12. Jawaharlal Nehru, statement to the press, December 19, 1927, SWJN 3:1. See also Nehru, book review of Mayo, *Slaves of the Gods*, April 25, 1929, ibid., pp. 395–400.

13. Isaacs, *Images of Asia*, pp. 268–71.

14. A. M. Rosenthal, "'Mother India' Thirty Years After," *Foreign Affairs*, 35 (July 1957): 621.

15. On the assistance the British provided to Mayo, see Jha, *Katherine Mayo and India*, pp. 26–65.

16. Quoted in Jha, *Civil Disobedience and After*, p. 9.

17. Hope, *America and Swaraj*, p. 14; Hess, *America Encounters India*, pp. 8–12.

18. Gupta, "The Mahatma's American Apostle." Holmes first met Gandhi in 1931, when he traveled to London where Gandhi was attending the Round Table Conference. The American found him to be a "saint and seer."

19. Lamson, *Roger Baldwin*, p. 1.

20. Clymer, "Jawaharlal Nehru and the United States," pp. 147–50.

21. Clymer, "Samuel Evans Stokes, Mahatma Gandhi, and Indian Nationalism."

22. Bhagat, *Americans in India*, pp. 85–98. Quotation on p. 97.

23. On the Khilafat Movement, see Minault, *The Khilafat Movement*.

24. Jha, *Civil Disobedience and After*, pp. 19–23.

25. Brown, *Modern India*, p. 260.

26. Jha, *Civil Disobedience and After*, pp. 60–93.

27. Quoted in Nanda, "Nehru, the Indian National Congress and the Partition of India, 1935–47," p. 149.

28. Lumby, *The Transfer of Power in India*, pp. 19–20.

29. Quoted in Jha, *Civil Disobedience and After*, p. 184.

30. Ibid., p. 281.

1 | The United States, Great Britain, and India at the Beginning of World War II

1. Wallace Murray, "United States Policy Towards India March 1933 to December 7, 1944," December 6, 1944. Record Group 84, New Delhi Post Records, file 800-political (1943) confidential, box 1426, NRC. Hereafter cited as New Delhi Post Records, with appropriate file and box number.

2. Memorandum, Murray, "United States Policy Towards India March 1933 to December 7, 1944," December 6, 1944, ibid. Thomas M. Wilson to Murray, April 8, 1941, 845.00/1241, Record Group 59, General Records of the Department of State, National Archives, Washington, D.C. (Hereafter cited with the dispatch number only.)

3. Hess, *The United States' Emergence as a Southeast Asian Power*, pp. 9–16, 26–27. McMahon, *Colonialism and Cold War*, p. 51.

4. Hart, *History of the Second World War*, pp. 18, 208–9.

5. John Campbell White to Cordell Hull, October 11, 1938, 845.00/1031.

6. Murray to White, March 7, 1939, 845.00 N/1. Unknown author to

Henry C. McLean, March 15, 1939, 845.00/1083. McLean was a Lieutenant Colonel in G-2, the Military Intelligence Division, in the Philippines. A copy of the report was transmitted to the state department on April 25, 1939.

7. White to Murray, April 3, 1939, 845.00 N/2. Handwritten comments by Stanley Hornbeck and Joseph W. Ballantine on White to Hull, November 2, 1938, 845.00/1035.

8. White to Hull, August 22, 1939, 845.00/1105. Edward M. Groth to Hull, September 15, 1939, 845.00/1121.

9. G. P. Merriam, untitled memorandum, [October 25 (?), 1939], enclosed in Murray to Adolf A. Berle, Jr., October 30, 1939, 845.00/1113 A.

10. Majumdar, *Struggle for Freedom*, pp. 624–26. Groth to Hull, October 6, 1939, 845.00/1123.

11. Groth to Hull, October 6, 1939, 845.00/1123; Groth to Hull, October 26, 1939, 845.00/1124; White to Hull, November 9, 1939, 845.00/1127.

12. Murray to Berle, October 30, 1939, 845.00/1113A; Murray to Berle, George S. Messersmith, Sumner Welles, and Hull, November 30, 1939, 845.00/1130.

13. White to Hull, January 15, 1940, 845.00/1148.

14. Jawaharlal Nehru, statement to the press, March 8, 1940, *Hindustan Times*, March 9, 1940, in SWJN 10:347. White to Hull, March 28, 1940, 845.00/1169. White to Hull, June 10, 1940, 845.00/1185.

15. Groth to Hull, July 25, 1940, 845.00/1182.

16. Groth to Hull, August 17, 1940, 845.00/1190. For Churchill's role in the August offer, see Hill, "L. S. Amery, India and the Commonwealth," p. 329.

17. Groth to Hull, August 31, 1940, 845.00/1194. Groth to Hull, August 17, 1940, 845.00/1190. Thomas M. Wilson to Hull, November 25, 1940, 845.00/1192.

18. Groth to Hull, September 14, 1940, 845.00/1192.

19. Wilson to Hull, November 25, 1940, 845.00/1204.

20. Ibid.; Calvin Hawley Oakes to Hull, November 1, 1940, 845.00/1202. Wilson to Hull, November 26, 1940, 845.00/1213.

21. G. P. Merriam, untitled memorandum, [October 25 (?), 1939]; Murray to Berle, October 30, 1939; telegram, Hull to Groth, November 1, 1939, 845.00/1113A. White to Hull, November 2, 1939, 845.00/1114. Murray to Messersmith, Welles, and Hull, November 14, 1939, FW 845.00/1114.

22. For a partially contrary view, see Hess, *America Encounters India*, p. 21, which asserts that Wilson's dispatches were characterized by "a bystander approach."

23. Wilson to Hull, November 25, 1940, 845.00/1204. Wilson to Hull, November 27, 1940, 845.00/1211. For Wilson's views of Linlithgow, see Wilson to Hull, April 2, 1941, 845.00/1228.

24. Wilson to Hull, May 8, 1941, 845.00/1232.

25. Berle, Draft Aide-Mémoire, enclosed in Berle to Hull and Welles,

May 5, 1941, FRUS 1941, 3:177. Berle to Hull and Welles, May 5, 1941, ibid. p. 176.

26. Wilson to Hull, June 16, 1941, 845.00/1237. Other American diplomats in India shared Wilson's views. See, for example, Donovan to Hull, June 10, 1941, 845.00/1244.

27. Wilson to Hull, July 28, 1941, 845.00/1243. Wilson to Hull, August 4, 1941, 845.00/1250.

28. John G. Winant to Hull, August 1, 1941, FRUS 1941, 3:178–79. Draft telegram (not sent), Berle to Winant, August 5, 1941, ibid., pp. 180–81. Welles to Hull, August 6, 1941, ibid., p. 181.

29. John Gunther, "Incredible Mr. Gandhi," *Reader's Digest*, December 1938, pp. 111–26. (This piece was taken from Gunther's book, *Inside Asia*.) Hess, *America Encounters India*, p. 15.

30. *Time*, October 30, 1939, p. 28. "India: Britain's Acid Test," *The New Republic*, November 1, 1939, pp. 355–56. See also Henry Noel Brailsford, "India in the War," *The New Republic*, November 22, 1939, pp. 133–35.

31. Choudury, ed., *Dr. Rajendra Prasad: Correspondence and Selected Documents*, 4:262. Shiva Rao to [Rao Bahadur ?] Srinivasan, January 15, 1940, B. Shiva Rao Papers.

32. B. Shiva Rao, "Indefatigable Gandhi," *New York Times*, September 15, 1940, p. 20.

33. Hess, *America Encounters India*, p. 20. *New York Times*, August 9, 1940, p. 14.

34. Interview with J. J. Singh by Amit Kumar Gupta and S. R. Bakshi, 1970, p. 40, Oral History Project, Manuscript Division, Nehru Library.

35. Government of India, Home Department, Political (Internal) Section, 1942, "Notes on the American League for India's Freedom and the India League of America," File 9/9/41, NAI. My account of the India League of America draws primarily on the above report, the J. J. Singh interview at the Nehru Library, and Robert Shaplen, "One-Man Lobby," *New Yorker*, March 24, 1951, pp. 35–55.

36. Shaplen, "One-Man Lobby," p. 41. On *India Today*, see Government of India, "Notes on the . . . India League of America."

37. Shaplen, "One-Man Lobby," p. 38. Nehru's opinion of Singh only worsened after the war ended. In 1949 he wrote that reports from Indians who had visited the United States during the previous two or three years were "uniformly unfavourable" to Singh, whose "conceit and egotism were colossal." In 1948 Nehru was particularly upset to receive from Singh "a very long letter about himself. I have never had the misfortune to receive a letter which was so full of conceit and vulgarity," he wrote. He vowed never to communicate with Singh again and advised Richard Walsh, a member of the India League, that he might be forced to disassociate himself publicly from Singh. Nehru to Richard J. Walsh, June 27, 1949, SWJN, second series, 12:399–401.

38. As early as 1938 Singh had attempted to arrange a Nehru visit. Government of India, "Notes on the American League for India's Freedom and the India League of America."

39. Nehru to Carl Marzani, March 23, 1940, SWJN 11:12. See also Nehru to Gobind Behari Lal, March 27, 1940, Nehru Papers, vol. 29.

40. Jawaharlal Nehru, "The Unity of India," *Foreign Affairs* 16 (January 1938): 231–243. Quotation on p. 241.

41. Jawaharlal Nehru, "India's Demand and England's Answer," January 6, 1940, published in the *Atlantic Monthly*, April 1940, in SWJN 10:273–82.

42. Jawaharlal Nehru, "The Parting of the Ways," *Asia*, November 1940, reprinted in SWJN 11:101–14. Quotation on p. 105. When he was arrested later in the year, Nehru wrote an article from jail that first appeared in J. J. Singh's *India Today* but was widely reprinted. Hess, *America Encounters India*, p. 21.

43. Nehru, prison diary, February 21, 1941, SWJN 11:553. Nehru was also delighted and "quite puffed up" at the excellent review of his book, *Unity of India*, published in England, received in the *New York Times*. Nehru, prison diary, July 14, 1941, ibid., pp. 653–54.

44. Charles Fleischer, "Jawaharlal Nehru and the Cause of Indian Nationalism," *New York Times Book Reviews*, February 23, 1941, pp. 5, 27. Equally high praise came from Robert Morss Lovett, "A Prince of India," *New Republic*, April 2, 1941, pp. 538–539. Less effusive was Clifton Fadiman's note in the *New Yorker*, February 22, 1941, p. 82.

45. Hess, *America Encounters India*, pp. 19–21.

46. Lamson, *Roger Baldwin*, p. 145.

47. Frances Gunther to Nehru, December 1, 1945, Nehru Papers, vol. 29.

48. John and Frances Gunther, "Nehru of India," *Life*, December 11, 1939, pp. 93–101. *Reader's Digest*, February 1940, pp. 79–83. See also John Gunther's portrait of Nehru in *Inside Asia*, pp. 429–46.

Nehru corresponded with the Gunthers whenever he could, particularly with Frances. Beginning in February 1938, she wrote Nehru very long, highly opinionated, literate, and intelligent letters detailing her travels, commenting on current developments all over the world, giving advice on how to handle American correspondents, and revealing details of her private life. It is hard to escape the opinion that she was in love with Nehru. Nehru's responses were more circumspect, but he did not discourage Frances' attention and wrote to her whenever he could. Nehru was a widower, and the Gunthers' marriage was not a happy one. They divorced in 1944.

49. Nehru also corresponded with missionaries J. Holmes Smith and Gordon B. Halstead, both of whom had been forced out of India by the British for their pro-nationalist views, and expressed the view that greater American knowledge of conditions in India would strengthen nationalist sympathies in America. The "missionary pledge," whereby missionaries in India had to agree to avoid political involvement, first came to public atten-

tion in the United States in 1940. The ouster of four American missionaries that year was yet another cause of anti-British sentiment. Hess, *America Encounters India,* pp. 18–19.

50. Government of India, Home Department, Political (Internal) Section, 1941, "Question of the return to India of undesirable Indians abroad. Half-yearly review of the cases of." File 1/2/41, NAI. For an example of how the British scrutinized students returning to India in the 1920s, see Hauswirth, *A Marriage to India,* pp. 10, 17–19, 80.

51. Government of India, Home Department, Political (Internal) Section, 1941, "Anti-British activities of Mrs. Kamaladevi Chattopadhyaya in the U.S.A. and Japan. Question of the action to be taken against her on her return to India." File 1/3/41, NAI. Chattopadhyaya recounts her experiences in *Inner Recesses, Outer Spaces,* pp. 218–83.

52. Unless otherwise indicated, information on the Patel case is drawn from Government of India, Home Department, Political (Internal) Section, 1942, "The review committee's recommendation in regard to security prisoner Rajni Patel," appendix, NAI. Hereafter cited at Patel Report.

53. Jawaharlal Nehru, "Home-Coming," *National Herald,* September 29, 1940, SWJN, 11:434. Rajnikant M. Patel to Nehru, November 18, 1939, Nehru Papers, vol. 80. The Patel Report states that Patel did not pass the bar examination until October 1940. But it appears to be in error.

54. Chattopadhyaya, intelligence sources reported, came to dislike Patel later because he developed a "swelled head" and did "not altogether represent the Congress viewpoint." Patel Report, p. 3.

55. The Robesons, Patel wrote to Nehru, "impressed me immensely." Patel to Nehru, November 18, 1939, Nehru Papers, vol. 80. Patel's meetings with the Robesons are detailed in letters to Nehru dated May 6, July 14, and August 19, 1939, ibid. See also Eslanda Robeson to Nehru, April 10, 1940, ibid.

56. Cecil G. Hope Gill, February 1, 1940, Patel Report. Patel to Nehru, July 25, 1940, Nehru Papers, vol. 80. See also his letters to Nehru of November 18, 1939, December 13, 1939, and June 29, [1940], ibid.

57. Nehru, "Home-coming," p. 436. Patel was detained for "subversive and anti-British activities" in which he had engaged in the United States. He was not informed of the charges against him until January 23, 1942, and he responded that he had been denied a fair trial. By the time he learned of the charges, however, he had changed his views of the war, perhaps because of his communist sympathies. He now supported it, and on May 11, 1942, he was released.

58. Government of India, Home Department, Political (Internal) Section, 1941, "The India League. Efforts made by Krishna Menon to influence the American journalists in England on the question of India," File 1/5/41, NAI.

59. Government of India, Home Department, Political (Internal) Sec-

tion, 1941, "Prohibition of entry into India, under the Sea Customs Act, of certain objectionable overseas publications," file 41/20/41, NAI.

60. Government of India, Home Department, Political (Internal) Section, 1941, "Question of prohibiting the entry into India of the publications issued by the United Lutheran Publications House of the U.S.A. under the Sea Customs Act," file 41/21/1941, NAI. The quotation about "general suspicion" is contained in a minute on Government of India, Home Department, Political (Internal) Section, 1941, "Interception of the correspondence addressed to Mr. N. Jehart Hanson and Mrs. Martha Hanson of the American Mission under section 26 of the Indian Post Office Act 1898," file 32/11/41, NAI. On the expulsion of the missionaries, see Hess, *America Encounters India*, pp. 18–19.

It should be noted that government officials did not invariably ban objectionable materials. See, for example, Government of India, Home Department, Political (Internal) Section, 1941, "Question of prohibiting the entry of the American edition of Jawaharlal Nehru's autobiography entitled 'Toward Freedom,' " file 41/10/1941, NAI.

61. Government of India, Home Department, Political (Internal) Section, 1942, "Notes on the American League for India's Freedom and the India League of America," file 138/1942, NAI. Interview of J. J. Singh, pp. 2–3.

62. Stafford Cripps to Nehru, October 11, 1939, Nehru Papers, vol. 14. Moore, *Churchill, Cripps, and India*, pp. 31–37.

63. Amery to Edward Halifax, October 22, 1940, L/P&S/12/2636, IOR.

64. Ernest Bevin to Amery, June 11, 1941, in Moore, *Churchill, Cripps, and India*, p. 41.

65. Linlithgow to Amery, September 5, 1940, Linlithgow Papers, vol. 9.

66. "Extract from private letter from Mr. Amery to Lord Linlithgow," September 30, 1940, L/P&S/12/2636, IOR. Amery to Halifax, September 30, 1940, ibid. Halifax to Amery, October 1, 1940, ibid.

67. Amery to Winston S. Churchill, October 25, 1940, ibid. Churchill, Personal Minute to Amery, October 26, 1940, ibid.

68. Halifax to Foreign Office, February 7, 1941, ibid.

69. Linlithgow to Amery, February 27, 1941, Linlithgow Papers, 20:41.

70. Halifax to Foreign Office, April 24, 1941, L/P&S/12/2636, IOR.

71. Halifax to Foreign Office, April 27, 1941, ibid.; Halifax to Foreign Office, May 9, 1941, Linlithgow Papers, 20:80.

72. Hull to Halifax, May 28, 1941, L/P&S/12/2636, IOR; Halifax to Foreign Office, May 31, 1941, ibid.

73. Amery to Linlithgow, June 14, 1941, Linlithgow Papers, 20:105–6; Government of India, External Affairs Department, to Amery, June 20, 1941, L/P&S/2636, IOR; Linlithgow to Amery, June 20, 1941, Linlithgow Papers, 20:184.

74. Note by L. A. Chey (?) in Government of India, External Affairs

Department, General Branch, 1943, "Discussion of the point that the Govt. of India have not committed themselves for U. S. consular representation in Delhi," file 4(11)-G/43, NAI. The *New York Times* also referred to Wilson's "quasi diplomatic status." Mackett, "Some Aspects," p. 292.

The British wanted the American representative to have title of "Agent General" rather than "Commissioner" or "Diplomatic Agent," but Halifax successfully countered that this would require Congressional approval and might open the appointment to the vagaries of the spoils system, something everyone wanted to avoid. Foreign Office to Halifax, June 25, 1941, and Halifax to Foreign Office, July 3, 1941, L/P&S/12/2636, IOR.

75. Wilson to Hull, September 8, 1941, 845.00/1257.

76. Louis, *Imperialism at Bay*, pp. 124–25. Perhaps the most famous account of the meeting, by Roosevelt's son, Elliott Roosevelt, contends that Roosevelt confronted Churchill directly on the colonial issue. In fact, the matter was not explicitly discussed. Elliott Roosevelt is probably correct on the general point, however, that his father was genuinely anti-colonialist in his feelings. Roosevelt, *As He Saw It*, pp. 35–42.

77. Hess, *America Encounters India*, pp. 28–29. Wilson to Hull, October 30, 1941, 845.00/1261.

78. Berle to Hull and Welles, May 5, 1941, FRUS 1941, 3:177.

2 | American Entry into World War II

1. Churchill to Clement Attlee, January 7, 1942, in Mansergh, ed., *Transfer of Power*, 1:14. Churchill, *Hinge of Fate*, p. 209. Moore, *Churchill, Cripps, and India*, pp. 73–74.

2. Kirby, *The War Against Japan*, 1:xix.

3. Thorne, *Allies of a Kind*, p. 202.

4. Kirby, *The War Against Japan*, 2:54–55.

5. *Time*, March 16, 1942, p. 26. Kirby, *The War Against Japan*, 2:119–22. *New York Times*, April 11, 1942, p. 12.

6. Thorne, *Allies of a Kind*, p. 207.

7. Swing's statement is referred to in Pearl Buck to Eleanor Roosevelt, March 7, 1942, PSF, Roosevelt Papers, box 55, India folder.

8. Hess, *The United States' Emergence as a Southeast Asian Power*, p. 52. For a good discussion of self determination as a factor in twentieth century American foreign policy, see Louis, *Imperialism at Bay*, especially pp. 3–4, 121–33.

9. Roosevelt, *As He Saw It*, pp. 115–16.

10. Department of State *Bulletin*, May 30, 1942, p. 488.

11. Thorne, *Allies of a Kind*, p. 160.

12. Mackett, "Some Aspects," p. 1. Mackett claims there were at least 258 periodical articles and editorials about India in 1942, and countless newspaper articles as well. The *New York Times* ran thirty-nine editorials about India. Ibid., p. 300.

13. Churchill to Attlee, January 7, 1942, Mansergh, ed., *Transfer of Power* 1:14. The *New York Times* suggested that Gandhi had "lost touch with reality." January 1, 1942, p. 24.

14. *New York Times* February 19, 1942, p. 18.

15. Hess, *America Encounters India*, pp. 35, 38–39. Ralph Bates, "Freedom for India," *New Republic*, March 2, 1945, pp. 290–292. See also *Christian Science Monitor*, February 25, 1943, p. [22], which stated that the United States had "a very great interest in India" and could serve as a mediator.

16. *Newsweek*, March 9, 1943, pp. 33–34. *Time* was predictably critical of the British. *Time*, March 16, 1942, pp. 26–28.

17. John Haynes Holmes, J. Holmes Smith, and Roger N. Baldwin to the editor, *New York Times*, March 8, 1942. The letter was published in the *Times* on March 11, 1942, p. 18.

18. Venkataramani and Shrivastava, *Quit India*, p. 70. *Congressional Record*, 77th Congress, 2d Sess., pp. A1395–96.

19. Frank C. Laubach to Hull, January 20, 1942, 845.01/118. Frances Gunther to Harry Hopkins, February 21, 1942, Hopkins Papers, box 313, Sherwood Collection, book 5, India Folder.

20. Pearl Buck to Eleanor Roosevelt, March 7, 1942, Roosevelt Papers, PSF: container 55. "Memorandum for Mrs. Roosevelt," ibid. J. J. Singh stated that it was he who first interested Buck in the Indian question. Interview of J. J. Singh, pp. 72–73.

21. *New York Times*, February 27, 1942, p. 5. Venkataramani and Shrivastava, *Quit India*, pp. 68–69. Breckinridge Long to Welles, February 25, 1942, FRUS 1942, 1:606–7. Apparently a record of the hearing was never printed.

22. Berle to Welles, February 17, 1942, FRUS 1942, 1:603.

23. Venkataramani and Shrivastava, *Quit India*, pp. 70–71.

24. Thorne, *Allies of a Kind*, pp. 215–16.

25. Murray to Berle and Welles, December 30, 1941, file 845.00/1288–1/8.

26. Unless otherwise indicated, quotations in the following paragraphs from the OCOI reports are from the following documents: Office of Strategic Services, British Empire Section, "America and Indian's War Morale," special memorandum #24, January 7, 1942; and "Conflict in India," special memorandum #25, January 15, 1942; Office of Strategic Services/State Department Intelligence and Research Reports, Part II: China and India, microfilm, University Publications of America, Inc.

27. The OCOI arrived at a similar conclusion about Vietnam, when it reported in March 1942, that "the Annamites have proven themselves capable of self-government." Thorne, *Allies of a Kind*, p. 217.

28. William J. Donovan to Roosevelt, February 10, 1942, Roosevelt Papers, PSF: 164, OSS: Donovan Reports. The conversation with Bajpai took place on December 22, 1941, and it is significant that Donovan waited until

February to pass it along. By then he had received the OCOI reports about India, and its importance was increasingly clear.

29. Krishnalal Shridharani to Conyers Read, January 21, 1942, in Donovan to Roosevelt, February 11, 1942, ibid.

30. Draft telegram, Roosevelt to Churchill, February 25, 1942, Kimball, ed., *Churchill and Roosevelt*, 1:400–1.

31. Roosevelt to Winant, February 25, 1942, FRUS 1942, 1:604. Venkataramani and Shrivastava suggest that Roosevelt's telegram was a direct response to the Senate Foreign Relations Committee hearings (*Quit India*, p. 72), while Gary Hess suggests that it was a direct response to Berle's memorandum of February 17 arguing again that the United States should pressure the British to raise India's status (*America Encounters India*, p. 36.) Perhaps Roosevelt's telegram should be seen reflecting the pessimistic military situation, the growing feeling that the United States ought to intervene to obtain India as a secure base, and the long view accepted in part by the President that the age of imperialism was over and the United States should align itself with the future.

32. W. Averell Harriman and Elie Abel, *Special Envoy to Churchill and Stalin 1941–1946* (New York: Random House, 1975), p. 130.

33. Eden to Amery, June 29, 1942, L/P&S/12/2636, IOR; Linlithgow to Amery, March 17, 1942, Linlithgow Papers, 11:45–46; Halifax to Foreign Office, March 9, 1942, L/P&S/12/2636, IOR; Amery to External Affairs Department, Government of India, March 23, 1942, L/P&S/12/2636, IOR. The portion of Amery's letter about possible problems with a less discreet representative was omitted from the version transmitted to India.

34. P. Kodandra Rao to Sir Girja Shankar Bajpai, July 24, 1941, P. Kodandra Rao Papers, Manuscript Division, Nehru Library. Bajpai's reply suggested agreement with Rao, for he noted that his new position offered more possibilities of "doing good to India" than his current post as the viceroy's minister for education, health, and lands. Bajpai to Rao, July 30, 1941, ibid.

35. Berle to Hull, December 20, 1941, FRUS 1942, 1:593–95.

36. Donovan to Roosevelt, February 10, 1942, Roosevelt Papers PSF: 164, OSS: Donovan Reports. Though dated February 10, Donovan was reporting a conversation that had occurred on December 22, 1941.

Bajpai's efforts at this point to involve the United States in Indian affairs for reasons that differed from those of the government he represented are not discussed at length in the previous accounts by Hess, Hope, Thorne, or Venkataramani. Venkataramani and Shrivastava do note Bajpai's interest in getting an American Technical Mission sent to India and that, in doing so, he was "apparently presenting his personal views." (Venkataramani and Shrivastava, *Quit India*, pp. 51–55). Their analysis, however, does not suggest, as the present account does, that Bajpai was seriously at odds with his own government. Thorne states, perceptively, that "Bajpai privately encouraged the idea of intervention by Roosevelt in Anglo-Indian affairs," but does not elaborate. (Thorne, *Allies of a Kind*, p. 238.) Hope also provides an accurate general account of Bajpai's frustrations as agent general. (Hope, *America and Swaraj*, pp. 66–68.)

37. Paul Alling, Memorandum of Conversation, January 23, 1942, FRUS 1942, 1:595–97.

38. Berle, Memorandum of Conversation, January 28, 1942, ibid., pp. 597–98.

39. W. Leonard Parker, Memorandum of Conversation, February 3, 1942, ibid., pp. 599–601. Mackett, "Some Aspects," p. 310.

40. Berle to Welles, February 17, 1942, FRUS 1942, 1:602–4. Welles to Berle, February 18, 1942, 845.00/1288–2/8.

41. Minutes on Minister of Information, American Division, to Foreign Office, February 13, 1942, F0 371 A 1716/122/45, FOR.

42. Halifax to India Office, February 17, 1942, FO 371 A 1687/122/45, FOR. Government of India to India Office, February 21, 1942, FO 371 A 1892/122/45, ibid.

43. Minute by Nevile Butler on Ministry of Information, American Division, to Foreign Office, February 13, 1942, FO 371 A 1716/122/45, FOR. Minutes by other officials expressed similar views.

44. Linlithgow to Amery, February 9, 1942, Linlithgow Papers, 11:25. In this passage the viceroy was actually commenting disparagingly on the views of Chiang Kai-shek, who had just visited India, and was comparing his allegedly ignorant views to those of equally ignorant American liberals.

45. Amery to Linlithgow, January 25, 1941, Linlithgow Papers, 10:17–18. The quotations are from a postscript dated January 31,.

46. Amery, "A Note on Post-War Reconstruction," December 10, 1941, enclosure #2 in Amery to Linlithgow, January 5, 1942, in "Letters: From the Secretary of State for India," p. 12, ibid. Amery described American policy as a blend of "idealism and economic imperialism." Hull's economic views dated "back to somewhere around 1860," he thought, and the lend lease mechanism was a means of compelling Great Britain to abandon imperial preferences.

47. Attlee, "The Indian Political Situation," February 2, 1942, War Cabinet Paper W. P. (42) 59, in Mansergh, ed., *Transfer of Power*, 1:110–12.

48. Ibid.

49. Minute on Ministry of Information, American Division, to Foreign Office, February 13, 1942, FO 371 A 1716/133/45, FOR.

50. Amery to Linlithgow, February 13, 1942, Mansergh, ed., *Transfer of Power*, 1:159–61; Churchill to Linlithgow, February 13, 1942, ibid., p. 161. R. J. Moore contends that Churchill's support of the Defence of India Council was a tactical move to forestall sending an emissary to negotiate with the Indians. Moore, *Churchill, Cripps, and India*, p. 57.

51. Linlithgow to Churchill, February 14, 1942, in Mansergh, ed., *Transfer of Power*, 1:170. Linlithgow to M. Hallett, February 24, 1942, ibid., pp. 236–37.

52. Amery, "Memorandum by the Secretary of State for India Covering Draft Declaration," February 27, 1942, War Cabinet, Committee on India, Paper I (42) 4, ibid., pp. 256–57. Amery to Linlithgow, March 2, 1942, ibid., p. 295.

53. Churchill to Roosevelt, March 4, [1942], L/PO/6/106b, IOR; Amery to Alexander Hardinge, March 2, 1942, Mansergh, ed., *Transfer of Power*, 1:282–83; Hardinge to Amery, March 3, 1942, L/PO/423 (ii), IOR; minute by "D," an India Office official, to Amery, March 3, 1942, L/PO/4523 (ii), IOR. Indicative of the rising level of American interest in India, Halifax commented on the "greatly increased . . . number of political questions arising between the Government of India and the United States Government." Halifax to Foreign Office, March 9, 1942, L/P&S/12/2636, IOR.

Churchill drafted a longer note in response to Roosevelt, explaining in some detail why it would be unwise to promise India independence, and he thanked the President for "not pressing me unduly at this time." The much shorter telegram that was actually sent indicated that the government was giving serious thought to issuing a declaration providing for dominion status and gave only a brief summary of the possible negative consequences. See draft telegram, Churchill to Roosevelt, March 2, 1942, Kimball, ed., *Churchill and Roosevelt*, 1:373–74.

54. Amery to Linlithgow, March 10, 1942, Mansergh, ed., *Transfer of Power*, 1:401–4. Quotation on p. 404. For a contrary view, that Cripps's mission did not result from American pressure, see Venkataramani and Shrivastava, *Roosevelt, Gandhi, Churchill*, p. 22.

3 | The Johnson Mission

1. Roosevelt to Churchill, March 10, 1942, FRUS 1942, 1:615–16.
2. Bajpai to Linlithgow, March 11, 1942, FO 371/30659/044740, FOR.
3. Minutes by Foreign Office officials, attached to ibid.
4. Moran, *Churchill*, p. 34.
5. Linlithgow to Amery, March 17, 1942, Linlithgow Papers, 11:45–46. See also Amery to Linlithgow, March 18, 1942, ibid., p. 58, which includes the text of a telegram from Bajpai to the foreign office in which Bajpai, without revealing that he knew of Wilson's critical report, asked Wallace Murray if Wilson had had anything to say about Chiang's visit.
6. Information about Johnson's background and career is from clippings in the Johnson Papers and from McFarland, *Harry H. Woodring*, pp. 143–54.
7. Blum, ed., *The Price of Vision*, p. 90 (entry for June 15, 1942). Davies, *Dragon by the Tail*, p. 236.
8. Press release issued by the Department of State, March 9, 1942, FRUS 1942, 1:613.
9. "American Mission to India Headed by Louis Johnson," [March 1942], Johnson Papers, box 100. This typescript was reprinted, in slightly modified

form, as a special supplement to the *American News Letter,* a mimeographed publication of the Office of Coordinator of Information, April 2, 1942. A copy is in Hopkins Papers, box 308, Book 5: Hopkins in London. On the nonpolitical nature of the mission, see also Berle, Memorandum of Conversation, February 28, 1942, FRUS 1942, 1:609–10, and Welles to Wilson, March 11, 1942, FRUS 1942, 1:617.

10. Telegram, Linlithgow to Amery, March 14, 1942, in Government of India, External Affairs Department, General Branch, "Appointment of Mr. Louis Johnson as Personal Representative of the President of the United States of America to India," file 106-G, 1942, NAI. See also Halifax to Foreign Office, March 16, 1942, FO 371 30659/044740, FOR.

11. Roosevelt to Linlithgow, March 19, 1942, Roosevelt Papers, OF 40–69, Bajpai (through Halifax) to Foreign Office, March 21, 1942, FO 371 A 2824/122/45, FOR. See also "American Mission to India Headed by Louis Johnson."

12. Minutes by Foreign Office officials on Halifax to Foreign Office, March 16, 1942, FO 371/30659/0044740, FOR. Government of India, "Appointment of Louis Johnson." In his response to the President, Linlithgow emphasized Johnson's technical expertise, noting that his experience in military supply problems would be valuable. By the time he wrote this letter on May 1, however, the Cripps mission had failed, and his polite words about Johnson to the President could not have been sincere. Linlithgow to Roosevelt, May 1, 1942, Roosevelt Papers, PSF box 55: India.

13. "Memorandum by Assistant Secretary of State [G. Howland] (Shaw) of a Conversation with Colonel Louis A. Johnson," March 11, 1942, FRUS 1942, 1:617. Roosevelt to Johnson, March 19, 1942, Johnson Papers. Johnson carried with him to India the personal rank of minister. The British always assumed that Johnson had not actually replaced Wilson and that the commissionership remained vacant.

14. Johnson to Berle, March 22, 1942, Berle Papers, box 38.

15. Averell Harriman to Hopkins, March 7, 1942, Hopkins Papers, file 308. Gopal, *Nehru,* 1:279. Wilson to Hull, March 17, 1942, FRUS 1942, 1:620.

16. Interview of Horace Alexander by B. R. Nanda, August 9, 1967, p. 14, Oral History Project, Jawaharlal Nehru Memorial Museum and Library, New Delhi.

17. B. Shiva Rao to Sir Tej Bahadur Sapru, March 24, 1942, B. Shiva Rao Papers.

18. Moore, *Churchill, Cripps, and India,* p. 74.

19. War Cabinet Paper, Annex to No. 265, March 7, 1942, in Mansergh, ed., *Transfer of Power,* 1:357–58. War Cabinet, Committee on India, March 9, 1942, ibid., pp. 379–80.

20. "Press Statement by Sir S. Cripps," March 23, 1942, in ibid., pp. 463–64. "Broadcast by Sir S. Cripps," ibid, pp. 566–71. Amery to Linlithgow,

March 24, 1942, ibid., p. 468. Cripps to Churchill, April 1, 1942, ibid., pp. 600–602.

21. Cripps to Churchill, April 2, 1942, Mansergh, ed., *Transfer of Power*, 1:616–18.

22. Amery to Linlithgow, April 3, 1942, Linlithgow Papers, 11:86. Churchill to Cripps, April 2, 1942, in Mansergh, ed. *Transfer of Power*, 1:607.

23. Cripps to Churchill, April 4, 1942, in Mansergh, ed. *Transfer of Power*, 1:638.

24. Ibid.

25. Cripps to Churchill, April 4, 1942, in Mansergh, ed. *Transfer of Power*, 1:636–39. Johnson to State Department, April 4, 1942, Johnson Papers. Versions of cables in the Johnson Papers are sometimes more complete than those printed in the *Foreign Relations* series.

26. Moore, *Churchill, Cripps, and India*, p. 131.

27. Division of Current Information, memorandum, April 3, 1942, 845.01/181. Paul H. Alling, memorandum, April 6, 1942, ibid.

28. "Extract from a record of an interview on April 6, [1942], between Mr. O. K. Caroe . . . and Colonel Johnson, President Roosevelt's Personal Representative in India," "Cripps Mission" folder, Linlithgow Papers, vol. 141. Linlithgow to Amery, April 7, 1942, in Mansergh, ed., *Transfer of Power*, 1:691.

29. Linlithgow to Amery and Churchill, April 6, 1942, in Mansergh, ed. *Transfer of Power*, 1:653–55; Wavell to Churchill, April 6, 1942, ibid., p. 655; War Cabinet Committee on India, 11th meeting, ibid., pp. 658–59; Amery to Cripps, April 6, 1942, ibid., p. 663; Cripps to Maulana Abul Kalam Azad, April 7, 1942, ibid., pp. 683–84; Churchill to Cripps, April 7, 1942, ibid., p. 685.

30. Nehru to Johnson, April 7, 1942, Johnson Papers, box 97.

31. Nehru to Johnson, April 8, 1942, ibid.

32. Cripps to Azad, April 7, 1942, Nehru Papers, vol. 15; [Nehru], "Rough Notes as a basis of discussion," n.d. [April 1942], ibid. Sapru to Rao, April 9, 1942, Sir Tej Bahadur Sapru Papers.

33. "Note by the Marquess of Linlithgow," April 8, 1942, in Mansergh, ed. *Transfer of Power*, 1:694.

34. Cripps to Churchill, April 9, 1942, ibid., 1:697.

35. Churchill to Cripps, April 9, 1942, ibid., p. 704. Linlithgow to Amery, April 10, 1942, ibid., pp. 725–26.

36. Nehru, "Note," enclosed with Nehru to Johnson, May 11, 1942, Johnson Papers, box 97.

37. Venkataramani and Shrivastava, *Quit India*, p. 99.

38. Amery to Linlithgow, April 9, 1942, in Mansergh, ed. *Transfer of Power*, 1:711; War Cabinet, W. M. (42) 45th Conclusions, Confidential Annex, April 9, 1942, ibid., pp. 705–7; War Cabinet to Cripps, April 9, 1942, ibid., pp. 707–8; Churchill to Cripps, April 10, 1942, ibid., pp. 721–22; Moore, *Churchill, Cripps, and India*, p. 122.

39. Louis Fischer, *Imperialism Unmasked* (Revised ed.; Bombay: Hamara Hindostan Publications, 1943), p. 27, in Government of India, Home Department, Political (I) Section, 1943, "Precensorship Order on the writings of Louis Fisher, an American journalist," K. W. file No. 33/19/43-Part I, NAI.

40. Ibid., p. 37. Nehru to Johnson, April 9, 1942, Johnson Papers, box 97.

41. Azad to Cripps, April 10, 1942, Johnson Papers, box 97.

42. Nehru to Johnson, April 10, 1942, ibid.

43. Johnson to Roosevelt and Welles, April 11, 1942, ibid.

44. Ibid.

45. Hopkins, memorandum, April 9, 1942, Hopkins Papers, file 308.

46. Ibid.

47. Churchill to Cripps, April 9, 1942, in Mansergh, ed., *Transfer of Power*, 1:704. The editor of the *Transfer of Power* volumes states simply that the Roosevelt message to which Churchill referred "has not been traced in the Prime Minister's office."

48. Quoted in McJimsey, *Harry Hopkins*, p. 141.

49. One scholar contends that Hopkins knew that his disclaimer about Johnson not representing the President was untrue. Tuttle, *Harry L. Hopkins and Anglo-American-Soviet Relations*, p. 148. But I am unaware of evidence to support this claim.

50. Hopkins to Roosevelt, April 9, 1942, FRUS 1942, 1:629. Hopkins to Roosevelt, April 11, 1942, Hopkins Papers, book 5, box 308. Johnson to Department of State, April 11, 1942, Johnson Papers, box 97.

51. Roosevelt to Churchill, April 11, 1942, FRUS 1942, 1:633–34. Historians have disagreed on this question. A. Guy Hope and, more cautiously, Gary Hess, agree that Johnson represented Roosevelt's views. See Hope, *America and Swaraj*, pp. 60–61; and Gary Hess, *America Encounters India*, pp. 41–42. Christopher Thorne and M. S. Venkataramani and B. K. Shrivastava suggest that Hopkins more accurately represented the President's true views of the situation. See Thorne, *Allies of a Kind*, p. 244; and Venkataramani and Shrivastava, *Quit India*, p. 136.

52. Quoted in Kimball, *Churchill and Roosevelt*, p. 447.

53. Churchill, handwritten note, April 12, 1942, Hopkins Papers, file 308. Moore, *Churchill, Cripps, and India*, pp. 130–31.

54. Nehru, interview to the press, New Delhi, April 12, 1942, SWJN 12:226. Nehru, interview to the press, Lahore, May 22, 1942, ibid., pp. 328–29. Telegram, Churchill to Hopkins, May 31, 1942, in Choudhury, ed., *Dr. Rajendra Prasad*, 5:339.

55. Johnson to Nehru, April 23, 1942, Nehru Papers, Part I, vol. 37. "Script for Radio Broadcast by Colonel Johnson," April 23, 1942, Johnson Papers, box 100.

56. Paul Alling's handwritten comment on Calvin H. Oakes to Paul

Alling, April 23, 1942, file 123 Johnson, Louis A./25. Maurice Garner Hallett to Linlithgow, April 25, 1942, in Mansergh, ed., *Transfer of Power*, 1:855–56.

57. B. Shiva Rao's dispatch to the *Baltimore Sun*, April 13, 1942, Johnson Papers, box 100.

58. "Press Statement Issued by Jawaharlal Nehru," April 13, 1942, ibid., box 97; Nehru to Johnson, April 20, 1942, ibid.

59. Johnson to Hull, May 9, 1942, FRUS 1942, 1:651. Nehru, "Note," enclosed with Nehru to Johnson, May 11, 1942, Johnson Papers, box 97. For Johnson's notes on Nehru's "Note," see "Two Outlines," May 11, 1942, Johnson Papers, box 100.

60. Johnson to G. D. Birla, May 12, 1942, Johnson Papers, box 97.

61. Graham Spry to Stafford Cripps, "Interview with Mr. Justice Felix Frankfurter," May 13, 1942, L/PO/6/105f, IOR. When Johnson returned, he and Colonel Herrington told state department officials that the British government had deliberately sabotaged the Cripps mission. While conceding that Churchill, Linlithgow, and Wavell may well have been pleased that the mission had failed, officials in the Division of Near Eastern Affairs were not fully convinced. See Calvin H. Oakes, Memorandum of Conversation," May 26, 1942, FRUS 1942, 1:660–62.

62. Linlithgow to Amery, May 18, 1942, Mansergh, ed., *Transfer of Power*, 2:102–3. Tel. 26-U, May 27, 1942, ibid., pp. 133–34. Linlithgow to Amery, May 28, 1942, ibid., p. 144.

63. Amery to Anthony Eden, May 28, 1942, ibid., p. 144. Amery to Churchill, May 29, 1942, L/PO/42 (V), IOR.

64. Churchill to Hopkins, May 28, 1942, Mansergh, ed., *Transfer of Power*, 2:145; Churchill to Hopkins, May 31, 1942, ibid., p. 156. Hopkins replied immediately that Johnson was ill and had no plans to return to India. Hopkins to Churchill, June 1, 1942, ibid., p. 164.

Churchill's request no doubt was a major reason why Johnson did not return to India. But Johnson's return to the United States was not the result of British pressure. Roosevelt, in fact, wanted Johnson to remain in India and relented only when Johnson produced medical testimony that his condition might prove fatal if he remained there. In addition, his failure to secure a political settlement was probably a factor. On this point see Hess, *America Encounters India*, pp. 58–59.

65. Johnson to Nehru, May 12, 1942, Johnson Papers, box 97. Johnson to Nehru, quoted in Lampton Berry to Nehru, June 20, 1942, Nehru Papers, vol. 7. The Nehru Papers also contain the personal letters and memoranda, including drafts, that Nehru sent to Johnson during these weeks.

66. Correspondence about Nehru's visit to Johnson is in the Johnson Papers.

4 | From the Cripps Mission to the "Quit India" Crisis

1. Kirby, *The War Against Japan*, 2:199–220; Thorne, *Allies of a Kind*, p. 154. Kirby comments that by the end of May, "the outlook was grave" for India. (p. 197.)

2. Thorne, *Allies of a Kind*, pp. 154, 224, 156.

3. Ibid., pp. 157, 163.

4. "Cripps Must Not Fail," *New Republic*, April 13, 1942, pp. 478–79. Mackett, "Some Aspects," p. 313.

5. *New York Times*, March 31, 1942, p. 20; ibid., April 3, 1942, p. 20; ibid., April 10, 1942, p. 16. "Cripps Must Not Fail," *New Republic*, April 13, 1942, pp. 478–79.

6. "Cripps Must Not Fail."

7. Freda Kirchwey, "India's Zero Hour," *Nation*, April 11, 1942, pp. 414–15. See also *New York Times*, March 31, 1942, p. 20, and April 3, 1942, p. 20, and *San Francisco News*, April 11, 1942, p. 10, in Mackett, "Some Aspects," p. 236.

8. Amery to Linlithgow, May 6, 1942, Linlithgow Papers, vol. 11. See also Amery to Linlithgow, June 10, 1942, in Mansergh, ed., *Transfer of Power*, 2:198.

9. Ronald T. Campbell (for Jossleyn Hennessy) to Puckle, July 8, 1942, FO 371/30660 44795, FOR. Graham Spry, the able British propagandist, had a similar assessment: "India as a Factor in Anglo-American Relations," War Cabinet Document, W. P. (42) 318, July 27, 1942, L/PO/6/1054, IOR.

10. *Nation*, April 18, 1942, pp. 447–48. For critical assessments of the nationalists, see *Time*, April 20, 1942, p. 28, *Newsweek*, April 20, 1942, pp. 41–42, *New Republic*, April 20, 1942, p. 524, and *New York Times*, April 24, 1942, p. 16 and April 13, 1942, p. 14. *Newsweek* observed that "wooing Russia away from the Axis was a sinecure compared with reconciling all the conflicting Indian interests."

11. *Christian Century*, April 8, 1942, pp. 454–454; ibid., April 21, 1942, pp. 519–21. *New York Times*, April 13, 1942, p. 14.

12. Graham Spry to Cripps, "Luncheon with Mr. Lauchlin Currie . . . .," May 9, 1942, L/PO/6/105f, IOR. Spry to Cripps, "Conversation with Mr. A. A. Berle . . . , " May 11, 1942, ibid. Spry to Cripps, "Interviews at the State Department with Dr. Stanley Hornbeck and Mr. Paul Alling," May 13, 1942, ibid., IOR. In contrast to the usual British assessment of American officials, Spry found state department officials "very well-informed."

13. Bajpai to Government of India, External Affairs Department, July 17, 1942, Mansergh, ed., *Transfer of Power*, 2:401.

14. Spry to Cripps, "Interview with Mr. Justice Felix Frankfurter . . . , " May 13, 1942, ibid. "Mr. Graham Spry: Interview with the President, May 15, 1942," ibid.

15. "Mr. Graham Spry's Interview with the President, May 15, 1942."

16. Campbell to David Scott, July 17, 1942, FO 371/30660 44795, FOR.

17. Churchill to Linlithgow, May 31, 1942, in Mansergh, ed., *Transfer of Power*, 2:156.

18. Linlithgow to Amery, May 18, 1942, ibid., p. 103. Linlithgow to Amery, May 31, 1942, ibid., p. 155.

19. Halifax (for Bajpai) to Foreign Office (for Linlithgow), May 26, 1942, L/P&S/12/2637, IOR. Halifax to Linlithgow, June 22, 1942, Mansergh, ed., *Transfer of Power*, 2:249.

20. Minute by King on Campbell to Scott, July 17, 1942, FO 371 30660 44795, FOR.

21. Stafford Cripps, "Broadcast to the United States of America on India," July 27, 1942, Stafford Cripps Papers.

22. Copy, [Department of State] to Henry F. Grady, March 25, 1942, Johnson Papers, box 97.

23. W. Leonard Parker, memorandum of conversation, February 3, 1942, FRUS 1:599–601. Berle, memorandum of conversation with Bajpai, February 28, 1942, ibid., pp. 609–10.

24. Wilson to Department of State, March 18, 1942, New Delhi Post Records, box 1424, NRC.

25. Johnson to Department of State, April 4, 1942, Johnson Papers, box 97. Johnson to Department of State, April 25, 1942, ibid. Johnson claimed that he had the support of the two American industrialists on the Technical Mission.

26. Linlithgow to Amery, May 18, 1942, Mansergh, ed. *Transfer of Power*, 2:103. Halifax reported that Grady confided to him that he "deplored" Johnson's activities in India. Halifax to Foreign Office, August 2, 1942, FO 371 A 7821/122/45, FOR.

27. Extract, Sir R. Lumley to Linlithgow, May 25, 1942, in Mansergh, ed., *Transfer of Power*, 2:116–17. Gandhi's opinion of the Technical Mission was that, because it was not in the subcontinent at the invitation of India, it was suspect. Gandhi, "Interview to American Journalists," [June 6, 1942], CWMG, 76:194–95.

28. Henry F. Grady to Roosevelt, August 5, 1942, Roosevelt Papers, OF:4069. Arthur W. Herrington to Nehru, May 14, 1942, Nehru Papers, vol. 32.

29. W. A. Harriman, "Memorandum," June 12, 1942, Hopkins Papers, file 159-India. Harriman, it should be noted, was critical of the way in which the Technical Mission originated. It was, he thought, a "sad commentary on the coordination of our own effort."

30. Linlithgow to Amery, June 8, 1942, in Mansergh, ed., *Transfer of Power*, 2:191. Amery to Linlithgow, June 17, 1942, ibid., p. 225. Linlithgow commented on Amery's dispatch, "I agree—very thin—but well intentioned." The Roger Reports were produced by Sir Alexander Roger, chair-

man of the Ministry of Supply Mission. The Roger Mission produced twenty-five reports on problems in India.

When in July Grady delivered a speech in California that was mildly critical of the Indian war effort, his reputation sank further in British eyes. See Campbell to Foreign Office, July 6, 1942, FO 371/30660 44795, FOR.

31. Press release, "India to Back American Recommendations," June 10, 1942, Johnson Papers, box 100. Presumably Johnson shared the view of Gaganvihari L. Mehta, president of the Federation of Indian Chambers of Commerce and Industry, who urged a larger role for Indian industrialists and the establishment of a war production board on which Indians and American advisers would sit. Gaganvihari L. Mehta, "The American Technical Mission," *Science and Culture*, 8 (September 1942):99–103. Copy in Vai Kunth Lallubhai Mehta Papers.

32. Frank A. Waring, "Summary of the Report of the American Technical Mission to India," Hopkins Papers, file 159-India. Waring's cover letter is dated August 11, 1942.

33. Grady to Hopkins, August 14, 1942, ibid.

34. Berle, memorandum of conversation, August 18, 1942, FRUS 1942, 1:723. K. C. Mahindra to Frank A. Waring, August 19, 1942, and Waring to Hopkins, August 20, 1942, Hopkins Papers, box 313, Book 5: India. Hopkins replied cordially that he had read Mahindra's letter with "great interest" and had also read the Technical Mission's report "very carefully." But in view of his actions in the Cripps negotiations, it seems unlikely that he would have been sympathetic to another intervention by the President. Hopkins to Waring, August 22, 1942, Hopkins Papers, box 313, Book 5: India

35. Press release issued by the Department of State, September 11, 1942, FRUS 1942, 1:732–33.

36. William D. Leahy to Henry A. Wallace, September 17, 1942, Hopkins Papers, box 313, Book 5: India.

37. Norris S. Haselton to Hull, October 23, 1942, FRUS 1942, 1:742–43; Hull to Haselton, October 29, 1942, ibid., pp. 743–44. The department did hope that limited aspects of the report could still be supported.

38. Halifax to Eden, August 24, 1942, in Mansergh, ed., *Transfer of Power* 2:799.

39. Bajpai to the External Affairs Department, New Delhi, October 5, 1942, FO 371 A 9301/122/45, FOR.

40. Majumdar, *Struggle for Freedom*, p. 643. Gandhi, "Foreign Soldiers in India," April 19, 1942, CWMG 76:49.

41. Majumdar, *Struggle for Freedom*, p. 644. Gopal, *Nehru*, 1:289–90. For various draft resolutions, as well as the final resolutions of the Working Committee, see SWJN 12:276–85.

42. Gandhi, Interview to the press, May 18, 1942, CWMG 76:115. Gandhi, "Interview to American Journalists," [June 6, 1942], ibid., pp. 194–97. Gandhi, "Interview with Preston Grover," [June 10, 1942], ibid., p. 212.

43. Gandhi, "Interview with Preston Grover," [June 10, 1942], CWMG 76:207–8.

44. Gandhi to Chiang Kai-shek, June 14, 1942, enclosed in Nehru to Berry, June 14, 1942, New Delhi Post Records, box 1424, NRC. Gandhi to Roosevelt, July 1, 1942, FRUS 1942, 1:677–78. Gandhi to American friends, August 3, 1942, CWMG, 76:357–59.

45. Nehru, draft message, Nehru to Johnson, enclosed in Nehru to Lampton Berry, June 3, 1942, Nehru Papers, Vol. 7.

46. Berry to Nehru, June 20, 1942, and Nehru to Berry, June 23, 1942, ibid.

47. Cripps, "Broadcast to the United States of America on India," July 27, 1942. "Statement to the Press by Jawaharlal Nehru," July 27, 1942, Nehru Papers, Part II, S. No. 324.

48. Nehru, Interview to the press, Lahore, May 22, 1942, SWJN 12:328. Nehru, prison diary, April 2, [1943], SWJN 13:91.

49. *Newsweek*, August 3, 1942, pp. 37–38, and July 27, 1942, p. 43.

50. *New York Times*, May 5, 1942, p. 20. See also ibid., July 16, 1942, p. 18; August 3, 1942, p. 14; August 5, 1942, p. 18. For other comment that was strongly critical of the nationalists at this time, see Hanson W. Baldwin, "Japanese Naval Bases," ibid., July 18, 1942, p. 4, and *Washington Post*, quoted in *Time*, July 29, 1942, pp. 29–30.

51. *Time*, July 29, 1942, pp. 29–30.

52. Hennessy to Alec H. Joyce, July 8, 1942, FO 371 A 7429/122/45, FOR. Walter Mackett, citing certain pieces in *Time* and the *New Republic*, contends that the tide of American opinion in June was turning back toward the Indians. "Some Aspects," p. 333.

53. J. J. Singh to Nehru, August 4, 1942, Nehru Papers, vol. 94. Berry to Nehru, August 4, 1942, ibid., vol. 7.

54. Nehru, "Speech at the A.I.C.C. Meeting," Bombay, August 7, 1942, SWJN 12:454–57. For a discussion of Nehru's developing views of the United States see Clymer, "Jawaharlal Nehru and the United States."

55. Gandhi, "Interview with Preston Grover," [June 10, 1942], CWMG 76:209. Nehru agreed, noting that "our publicity is rotten." Nehru to Evelyn Wood, June 5, 1942, Nehru Papers, vol. 103.

56. Graham Spry, "India as a Factor in Anglo-American Relations," July 27, 1942, War Cabinet Paper W. P. (42) 318, in Mansergh, ed., *Transfer of Power*, 2:472. Government of India, Home Department, Political (Internal), "Indian Censorship Report on American Opinion on the Indian Political Situation as Revealed by Correspondence and Publications during the Period May 42 to Feby 43," file 20/2/43-fall, NAI.

57. Government of India, External Affairs Department, External Branch, 1942, "Proposal to Start a Propaganda Section in India for Publicizing India in America," File 78-XP/42, NAI.

58. Government of India, Home Department, Political (Internal), "Indi-

an Censorship Report on American Opinion on the Indian Political Situation as Revealed by Correspondence and Publications during the Period May 42 to Feby 43," file 20/2/43-fall, NAI.

59. India Office to Foreign Office, "Activities of American Pacifists in India," June 10, 1942, FO 371/30660 44795, FOR.

60. Merrell to Hull, May 21, 1942, FRUS 1942, 1:663. Berry to Johnson, May 26, 1942, Johnson Papers. Merrell to Hull, May 26, 1942, FRUS 1942, 1:664.

61. Calvin H. Oakes, Memorandum, "Changed Indian Situation," May 26, 1942, 845.01/228. Hull, Memorandum of Conversation, June 15, 1942, FRUS 1942, 1:670–72.

62. Oakes, Memorandum of Conversation, May 26, 1942, FRUS 1942, 1:657–59. Division of Near Eastern Affairs, Department of State, Memorandum of Conversation, May 22, 1942, enclosed in Murray to Berle, Welles and Hull, May 27, 1942, 845.00/1343.

63. Diary entry June 15, 1942, in Blum, ed., *The Price of Vision*, p. 91.

64. Hull to Merrell, June 16, 1942, FRUS 1942, 1:673. Paul Alling, covering note recommending against a preliminary decision to allow American officials in India to interview Gandhi, June 11, [1942], on a canceled telegram from the Department of State to the American mission in New Delhi, June 9, 1942, 845.00/196.

65. Amery to Linlithgow, May 27–28, 1942, Linlithgow Papers, 11:118. Two days after the raid Amery gave Linlithgow permission to arrest Gandhi at will.

66. Halifax to Eden, June 29, 1942, in Mansergh, ed., *Transfer of Power*, 2:288–89. Hennessy to Puckle, July 8, 1942, FO 371 A 7429/122/45, FOR. Bajpai to Government of India, External Affairs Department, July 17, 1942, in Mansergh, ed., *Transfer of Power*, 2:401–2.

67. Amery to Churchill, July 13, 1942, in Mansergh, ed., *Transfer of Power*, 2:376–77. Amery to Linlithgow, July 13, 1942, Linlithgow Papers, 11:149. It is not clear why Amery sought permission to have Gandhi arrested since he had already authorized Linlithgow to arrest him at will.

68. Amery to Linlithgow, July 24, 1942, in Mansergh, ed., *Transfer of Power*, 2:454–55. Bajpai to Foreign Office, July 22, 1942, FO 371 A 6881/122/45, FOR.

69. Merrell to Hull, July 17, 1942, FRUS 1942, 1:685–88. Merrell to Hull, July 21, 1942, ibid., p. 690. Merrell to Hull, July 21, 1942, ibid., pp. 690–94. Nehru commented that a Presidential guarantee would be helpful but not sufficient.

70. Merrell to Hull, July 21, 1942, ibid., pp. 690–94.

71. Interview of J. B. Kripalani by Har Dev Sharma and K. P. Rungachary, November 15, 1966, p. 186, Oral History Project, Nehru Memorial Museum and Library. Chiang Kai-shek to Roosevelt, July 25, 1942, FRUS 1942, 1:695–98. Welles, Memorandum of Conversation, July 28, 1942, FRUS 1942, 1:698–99.

72. Welles to Roosevelt, July 29, 1942, FRUS 1942, 1:699–700. Roosevelt's draft telegram to Churchill is in ibid., p. 700.

73. Churchill to Roosevelt, July 31, 1942, in Mansergh, ed., *Transfer of Power*, 2:533.

74. Robert Sherwood to Roosevelt, August 5, 1942, Roosevelt Papers, PSF:55—India. Henry Grady also urged Roosevelt to make no significant changes in the Indian government during the war. Grady to Roosevelt, August 5, 1942, ibid., OF:4069.

75. Eleanor Roosevelt to J. J. Singh, quoted in Singh to Nehru, June 26, 1942, Nehru Papers, vol. 94.

76. Beitzell, *The Uneasy Alliance*, pp. 49–50. Louis, *Imperialism at Bay*, p. 158.

77. Roosevelt to Gandhi, August 1, 1942, FRUS 1942, 1:703. Because of the subsequent arrest of Gandhi, Roosevelt's letter was not delivered to him. Rather than entrust it to the British or a Congress leader, such as Rajagopalachari, who had not been arrested, Roosevelt decided to keep it in the files of the American mission in New Delhi. See Hull to Roosevelt, September 9, 1942, Roosevelt Papers, PSF: Diplomatic, India, box 55. Hull's speech, "The War and Human Freedom," is in the Department of State *Bulletin*, July 25, 1942, pp. 639–47.

78. Roosevelt to Chiang Kai-shek, [August 8, 1942], FRUS 1942, 1:705–6.

79. Thorne, *Allies of a Kind*, pp. 134, 136.

80. Amery to Linlithgow, August 3, 1942, Linlithgow Papers, 11:159. Campbell to Eden, August 4, 1942, in Mansergh, ed., *Transfer of Power*, 2:561–62. The Foreign Office's concurrence is found in a minute on Campbell's telegram by Nevile Butler dated August 6, not published in the *Transfer of Power* volume. The minute is found on the minute sheet attached to the original telegram, FO 371 A 7216/122/45, FOR. For strongly critical comments in the American press about Gandhi based on the released documents, see Mackett, "Some Aspects," pp. 339–42.

81. Eden to Campbell, August 7, 1942, in Mansergh, ed., *Transfer of Power*, 2:608–9.

82. Merrell to Hull, August 5, 1942, FRUS 1942, 1:702. Venkataramani and Shrivastava, *Roosevelt, Gandhi, Churchill*, p. 58.

83. Merrell to Hull, August 8, 1942, FRUS 1942, 1:707.

5 | "Quit India" Arrests to the Appointment of William Phillips

1. *Christian Science Monitor*, August 11, 1942, p. [18]. *New York Times*, August 11, 1942, p. 18. *Newsweek*, August 17, 1942, p. 42. *San Francisco News*, August 11, 1942, p. 12, in Mackett, "Some Aspects," p. 346. *Saturday Evening Post*, September 5, 1942, p. 100.

2. *Congressional Record*, 77th Cong., 2nd Session, pp. 6891–95.

3. *Christian Century*, September 2, 1942, p. 1043 and August 19, 1942, p.

995. *Time*, August 17, 1942, p. 25–27 and August 24, 1942, pp. 18–21. Raleigh *News and Observer*, August 18, 1942, in *Congressional Record*, 77th Cong., 2nd Session, p. A3266–77. *Congressional Record*, 77th Cong., 2nd Session, p. 6887. See also Louis Fischer, "What Gandhi Wants," *The Nation*, August 15, 1942, pp. 121–22.

4. *Saturday Evening Post*, September 5, 1942, p. 100.

5. *New York Times*, August 11, 1942, p. 18; August 13, 1942, p. 18; September 5, 1942, p. 12.

6. *Parliamentary Debates*, 5th series, House of Commons, vol. 383, cols. 302–5. Venkataramani and Shrivastava, *Quit India*, p. 281.

7. *New York Times*, September 15, 1942, p. 22. *Saturday Evening Post*, October 31, 1942, p. 100. *San Francisco News*, September 12, 1942, p. 10, in Mackett, "Some Aspects," p. 354.

8. American Division, Ministry of Information, "Radio: The American Weekly Summary" (mimeographed), September 17, 1942, FO 371/30662 044835, FOR. Halifax to Foreign Office, September 19, 1942, FO 371 A 8720/122/45, FOR. Walter Mackett's survey of American press opinion at this time confirms the British assessment. Churchill's speech, he writes, "was not well received in America." Mackett, "Some Aspects," p. 353.

9. Ministry of Information to Foreign Office, September 16, 1942, FO 371 A 8773/122/45, FOR.

10. Bajpai to Government of India, September 16, 1942, in Halifax to Eden, September 18, 1942, in Mansergh, ed., *Transfer of Power*, 3:985–86. Minute on the original Halifax dispatch, FO 371 A 8753/122/45, FOR.

11. Minute by Joyce, September 21, 1942, in Mansergh, ed., *Transfer of Power*, 3:10–13.

12. *Parliamentary Debates*, 5th series, House of Commons, vol. 383, cols. 1388–99. See also Venkataramani and Shrivastava, *Quit India*, p. 282.

13. Amery to Linlithgow, October 5, 1942, in Mansergh, ed., *Transfer of Power*, 3:98.

14. *New York Times*, October 1, 1942, p. 22. *Life*, October 12, 1942, p. 34. Ryan, *The Vision of Anglo-America*, p. 32.

15. Louis Fischer, "What Gandhi Wants," *The Nation*, August 15, 1942, p. 123. *The Nation*, August 15, 1942, p. 123.

16. *Congressional Record*, 77th Cong., 2nd Sess., pp. 6887–88. *New York Times*, August 10, 1942, p. 12, and August 7, 1942, p. 11. *Saturday Evening Post*, September 5, 1942, p. 100.

17. Clarence Poe to Roosevelt, August 11, 1942, cited in *Congressional Record*, 77th Cong., 2nd Sess., p. 6889. Walter White to Roosevelt, August 31, 1942, Roosevelt Papers, OF, container 481, box 12: India, 1942 folder. E. Stanley Jones to Roosevelt, August 10, 1942, in Venkataramani and Shrivastava, *Quit India*, pp. 296–97. Louis Fischer wrote to Roosevelt in a similar vein. Louis Fischer to Roosevelt, August 7, 1942, Roosevelt Papers, PSF: India, box 55.

18. American Division, Ministry of Information, "Radio: The American Weekly Summary," (mimeographed), September 17, 1942, FO 371/30662 044835, FOR.

19. Ernest K. Lindley, "Still Chance for Negotiations," *Washington Post*, September 11, 1942, p. 11. Ernest K. Lindley, "Harvest of Bitterness," ibid., September 14, 1942, p. 7. Halifax to Eden, September 16, 1942, in Mansergh, ed., *Transfer of Power*, 2:969–70.

20. *New York Times*, September 28, 1942, p. 9. The idea for the newspaper appeal originated with Clare Booth Luce and J. J. Singh. See Venkataramani and Shrivastava, *Quit India*, pp. 291–92.

21. *New York Times*, October 1, 1942, p. 22. In 1949 during his first visit to the United States, Nehru singled out the appeal as one that "was very heartening to us in those days of struggle and conflict." Nehru, Address to a meeting organized by the East and West Association, the Foreign Policy Association, the India League of America, and the Institute of Pacific Relations, New York, October 19, 1949, SWJN: second series, 13:333.

22. *New York Times*, September 30, 1942, p. 8.

23. Ibid., October 1, 1942, p. 22; October 2, 1942, p. 24; September 23, 1942, p. 24; October 1, 1942, p. 5; November 25, 1942, p. 22. *Saturday Evening Post*, October 31, 1942, p. 100. For additional public reaction in the United States to the British crackdown and Churchill's speech, see Venkataramani and Shrivastava, *Quit India*, pp. 290–301.

24. Note by Paul J. Patrick, [September 25, 1942], in Mansergh, ed., *Transfer of Power*, 3:30–31.

25. Campbell to Foreign Office, August 11, 1942, FO 371 A 7433/122/45, FOR.

26. Bajpai to Foreign Officer, August 13, 1942 FO 371 A 4550/122/45, FOR.

27. Amery to Linlithgow, September 16, 1942, Linlithgow papers, 11:199–200.

28. War Cabinet W. M. (42) 111th Conclusions, Minute 4, August 12, 1942, in Mansergh, ed., *Transfer of Power*, 2:680–81.

29. Amery to Linlithgow, August 27, 1942, Linlithgow Papers, 11:192. At least 958 persons were whipped. See Venkataramani and Shrivastava, *Roosevelt, Gandhi, Churchill*, p. 58.

30. Note by Patrick, [September 25, 1942], in Mansergh, ed., *Transfer of Power*, 3:30–31.

31. Sherwood Eddy to Hopkins, September 11, 1942, Hopkins Papers, 313, Book 5: India. A draft of Eddy's letter to the President, dated September 1942, is in the Johnson Papers, box 100, as is a copy of Eddy's plan for settlement. Eddy to Linlithgow, September 11, 1942, in Mansergh, ed., *Transfer of Power*, 2:947. Halifax to Amery, August 30, 1942, in Mansergh, ed., *Transfer of Power*, 2:849.

32. Linlithgow to Churchill, August 31, 1942, in Mansergh, ed., *Transfer*

of Power, 2:853–54. Amery to Linlithgow, September 1, 1942, ibid., 2: 877. Churchill to Linlithgow,September 5, 1942, ibid., 2:910. Linlithgow to Churchill, September 5, 1942, ibid., 2:933–34.

33. Churchill to Eden and Amery, September 12, 1942, ibid., 2:953. Halifax to Eden, September 18, 1942, ibid., 2:988. Eddy stated that Hull had refused to issue him a passport good for travel to India because of Churchill's opposition. See Eddy to J. J. Mallon, January 5, 1943, FO 371 A 1510/93/45. Eddy's letter was intercepted by British authorities.

34. Later, when Linlithgow received Eddy's plan for a settlement he acknowledged that the American was "well meaning," but he was equally certain that nothing Eddy suggested would be considered. Whether Eddy's ideas were useful ones was, of course, beside the point. That an outsider had furnished them was in itself enough to dismiss them. "We cannot possibly have these well-intentioned mediators bursting into the situation, starting innumerable hares, and expecting us to tidy up whatever complications result, and to carry the blame if their endeavors fail," the viceroy complained. Linlithgow to Amery, October 10, 1942, in Mansergh, ed., *Transfer of Power*, 3:120.

The following January the British intercepted and read a letter from Eddy to a British friend in which the American revealed that his college roommate had been none other than the publisher Henry Luce, who was anathema to the British, and that Luce's son had first suggested the mediation attempt to Eddy. Had the British known this, they might not have encouraged the viceroy to receive Eddy. Eddy to Mallon, January 5, 1943, FO 371 A 1510/93/45. It is not clear if British authorities allowed the letter to go through after they had intercepted and read it.

35. Linlithgow to Amery, July 28, 1942, in Mansergh, ed., *Transfer of Power*, 2:475.

36. Amery to Linlithgow, August 3, 1942, ibid., 2:540. Eden to Amery, August 14, 1942, ibid., p. 701.

37. Linlithgow to Amery, August 18, 1942, Linlithgow Papers 11:194.

38. Linlithgow to Churchill, August 31, 1942, in Mansergh, ed., *Transfer of Power*, 2:853–54.

39. Amery to Churchill, September 1, 1942, ibid., 2:867. Amery to Linlithgow, September 1, 1942, ibid., p. 876. War Cabinet W. M. (42) 120th Conclusions, Minute 2, September 2, 1942, ibid., pp. 880–81. Churchill to Linlithgow, September 5, 1942, ibid., p. 910.

40. Venkataramani and Shrivastava, *Quit India*, pp. 318, 321–23.

41. The sections of Willkie's speech that dealt with India are quoted in the minutes to "American Opinion on India," October 16, 1942, FO 371 A 9625/2421/G, FOR. For the American response to the speech see Venkataramani and Shrivastava, *Quit India*, pp. 323–28.

42. William Phillips diary, October 28, 1942, p. 89, and December 11, 1942, Phillips Papers.

43. Minutes by Nevile Butler, October 28, 1942, on "American Opinion on India," October 16, 1942, FO 371 A 9625/2421/G, FOR.

44. Churchill to Dominion Prime Ministers, enclosed in Amery to Linlithgow, December 13, 1942, in Mansergh, ed., *Transfer of Power,* 3:362–63. Phillips to Roosevelt, December 17, 1942, PSF, Roosevelt Papers container 53.

45. Amery to Linlithgow, May 12, 1943, in Mansergh, ed., *Transfer of Power,* 3:964. Linlithgow to Amery, June 1, 1943, ibid., p. 1036.

46. John B. Ketcham to Chakravarti Rajagopalachari, October 30, 1942, Chakravarti Rajagopalachari Papers. Ketcham was the American consul at Madras. Nehru, Prison Diary, December 28, [1943], SWJN 13:322–23. Nehru to Indira Gandhi, February 29, 1944, SWJN 13:364.

47. Nehru, Prison Diary, October 8, [1944], SWJN 13:488–89. See also Nehru to Clare Booth Luce, May 4, 1946, ibid., 15:597. That Willkie made a deep and lasting impression on Nehru is evident from the fact that Nehru continued to refer to Willkie in later years. In 1947, for example, he wrote that there was "no way ultimately but the way of *One World* of which Wendell Willkie spoke." Nehru to E. C. Stucke, March 12, 1947, in SWJN, Second Series, 2:433.

48. Government of India, External Affairs Department, Far Eastern Branch, 1944, "Disallowance of the Question in the Council of States by the Honourable Raja Yuveraj Dutta Singh asking whether the Government of India in any way was responsible for suggesting directly or indirectly to President Roosevelt that it would be undesirable for Mr. Willkie to visit India," file 741 (2)/44, NAI.

49. Paul Hollander and Mark Mensh, "Louis Fischer," *Dictionary of American Biography,* Supplement 8, eds. John A. Garraty and Mark C. Carnes (New York: Charles Scribner's Sons, 1988), pp. 171–73.

50. Fischer to Roosevelt, August 5, 1942, Roosevelt Papers, PSF: 55—India. Fischer to Roosevelt, August 7, 1942, ibid.

51. Minute, August 28, 1942, on Bajpai to Foreign Office, August 24, 1942, FO 371 A 7936/122/45, FOR. "Note of a Conversation with Mr. Louis Fischer," August 26, 1942, FO 371/370661/44795, FOR. Halifax to Amery, August 30, 1942, in Mansergh, ed., *Transfer of Power,* 2:849.

52. Government of India, Home Department, Political (I) Section, 1943, "Booklet entitled 'Imperialism Unmasked!' by Louis Fischer, a 'Hamara Hindustan' publication. Decision not to take action against it." File 49/3/43, NAI. Government of India, Home Department, Political (I) Section, 1943. "Question of Withholding in Censorship of Louis Fischer's book, 'A Week with Gandhi,' " file 20/17/43, NAI. Government of India, Home Department, Political (I) Section, 1943. "Passing of a order of pre-censorship in respect of the writings and speeches of the American journalist Louis Fischer . . . ," file 22/19/43, NAI. Government of India, Home Department, Political (I) Section, 1944, "Prohibition under the Sea Customs's Act of the

entry into India of the book 'Empire' by Louis Fischer . . . ," file 41/4/44, NAI.

53. Linlithgow to Amery, January 30, 1943, in Mansergh, ed., *Transfer of Power*, 3:566.

54. Government of India, Home Department, Political (I) Section, 1943, "Passing of a order of pre-censorship in respect of the writings and speeches of the American journalist Louis Fischer . . . ," file 33/19/43, NAI.

55. Government of India, Home Department, to Amery, June 1, 1943, FO 371 A 5428/93/45, FOR. A little later a Government of India intelligence agent in the United States observed Fischer at a rally called by the India League of America and concluded that he was "a violent and bigoted individual, completely lacking in stability and one whose every utterance should be viewed with distrust." Government of India, Home Department, Political (I) Section, 1944, "Activities of the India League of America . . . ," file 48/2/44, NAI.

56. Amery to Government of India, Home Department, June 5, 1943, FO 371 A 5428/93/45, FOR. Government of India, "Passing an order of pre-censorship in respect of . . . Louis Fischer." Halifax to Foreign Office, June 11, 1943, FO 371 A 5550/93/45, FOR.

57. Linlithgow to Amery, August 13, 1942, in Mansergh, ed., *Transfer of Power*, 2:681. Linlithgow to Churchill, September 10, 1942, ibid., p. 933. Eden to Amery, August 22, 1942, ibid., pp. 785–86. Minute, Nevile Butler, August 29, [1942], on Amery to Eden, August 26, 1942, FO 371 A 4869/122/45, FOR. Linlithgow to Amery, October 10, 1942, in Mansergh, ed., *Transfer of Power*, 3:122.

Linlithgow later defended his approach with Currie on the grounds that Currie had declined his hospitality on two occasions, and when they did meet the American said he knew nothing of Indian politics and did not want to discuss them. Linlithgow to Churchill, September 10, 1942, in Mansergh, ed., *Transfer of Power*, 2:933. When Currie later allegedly claimed that, while in India, he had not discussed the political situation, Linlithgow was convinced he was lying. Linlithgow to Amery, October 10, 1942, in Mansergh, ed., *Transfer of Power*, 3:122.

58. Kirby, *The War Against Japan*, 2:127, 131, 307–8. The relatively easy advance through Southeast Asia did tempt the Japanese to invade Assam in northeastern India. A tentative plan was developed (Plan 21) for an advance late in 1942. However, problems of transport and communication, followed by military defeats in the Pacific, caused the Japanese to suspend the plan. Their position in Burma remained defensive.

59. A good contemporary account of India's strategic significance is in *Time*, September 21, 1942, pp. 28–29.

60. Hull, Memorandum of Conversation, August 8, 1942, FRUS 1942, 1:706–7. Hull, Memorandum of Conversation, August 15, 1952, ibid., pp. 721–22. Hull, Memorandum of Conversation, August 24, 1942, ibid., pp.

726–27. Hull, Memorandum of Conversation, September 17, 1942, ibid., pp. 733–34.

61. Roosevelt to George Norris, September 23, 1942, in Venkataramani and Shrivastava, *Quit India*, p. 303. For other examples of Roosevelt's determination to side with the British at this time, see Roosevelt to Harold L. Ickes, August 12, 1942, Roosevelt Papers, PPF, container 3650, Ickes folder; Roosevelt to Walter White, September 12, 1942, Roosevelt Papers, OF, container 481, box 12, India 1942 folder; and Berle, Memorandum of Conversation, August 18, 1942, FRUS 1942, 1:724.

62. *Newsweek*, September 21, 1942, p. 38.

63. Ickes to Roosevelt, August 10, 1942, Roosevelt Papers, PPF, container 3650, Ickes folder. Currie to Roosevelt (Merrell to Hull), August 11, 1942, FRUS 1942, 1:712–14. Department of State, Press Release, August 12, 1942, FRUS 1942, 1:720–21.

64. Merrell to Hull, August 8, 1942, FRUS 1942, 1:708. Merrell to Hull, August 10, 1942, ibid., p. 712.

65. Haselton to Hull, September 5, 1942, ibid., pp. 729–30.

66. Welles, Memorandum of Conversation, August 12, 1942, ibid., pp. 717–18.

67. Mahindra to Waring, August 19, 1942, Hopkins Papers, 313: Book 5, India. Waring forwarded Mahindra's letter to Hopkins with his strong personal endorsement. Waring to Hopkins, August 20, 1942, ibid.

68. Mahindra to Johnson, August 20, 1942, Johnson Papers, box 97.

69. Berle, Memorandum of Conversation, August 12, 1942, FRUS 1942, 1:719–20.

70. Berle, Memorandum of Conversation, August 22, 1942, ibid., p. 726. Paul Alling, Memorandum of Conversation, September 4, 1942, ibid., p. 729. Berle, Memorandum of Conversation, October 2, 1942, ibid., pp. 735–36.

71. Berle, Memorandum of Conversation, October 8, 1942, ibid., pp. 737–38. Murray, Memorandum of Conversation, October 13, 1942, ibid., pp. 740–42.

72. Halifax to Eden, September 16, 1942, in Mansergh, ed., *Transfer of Power*, 2:969–70. American reports are accurately summarized in Campbell to Foreign Office, August 13, 1942, FO 371 A 7549/122/45, FOR. Halifax to Eden, August 28, 1942, in Mansergh, ed., *Transfer of Power*, 2:839. Halifax to Foreign Office, September 15, 1942, FO 371 A 8627/122/45, FOR.

73. Apparently Halifax did not inform his superiors who the source was, but Nevile Butler speculated that the information came from either the Navy Department or Colonel Donovan of the Office of Strategic Services. Minute, Nevile Butler, September 29, [1942] on FO 371 A 9009/122/45, FOR.

74. Unsigned memorandum, "Relations between United States Officials in India and the Population," in unsigned report, "Summary of Indian Cen-

sorship Report (dated 15.3.43) on American Activities in India, or in relation to India," March 15, 1943, L/PS/12/4624, IOR. Neither Merrell or Haselton is mentioned by name in this memorandum, but the references seem clear.

75. Halifax to Eden, September 15, 1942, FO 371 A 8666/122/45, FOR; Bajpai to New Delhi, September 16, 1942, in Halifax to Eden, September 18, 1942, in Mansergh, ed., *Transfer of Power,* 2:985–86.

76. Hull, "The War and Human Freedom," July 23, 1942, Department of State *Bulletin,* July 25, 1942, pp. 639–47. Quotation on p. 640. Amery to Linlithgow, August 16, 1942, in Mansergh, ed., *Transfer of Power,* 2:717.

77. Churchill to Roosevelt, August 13, 1942, in Mansergh, ed., *Transfer of Power,* 2:687–88.

78. Churchill to Chiang Kai-shek, August 27, 1942, ibid., pp. 830–32. Linlithgow, of course, was grateful for the strong responses. Churchill's message to Chiang was "first class stuff." Linlithgow to Amery, August 18, 1942, Linlithgow Papers, 11:194. Linlithgow to Amery, August 29, 1942, in Mansergh, ed., *Transfer of Power,* 2:842.

79. Bajpai to Foreign Office, August 13, 1942, FO 371 A 4550/122/45, FOR. Bajpai to Foreign Office, August 23, 1942, FO 371 A 7819/122/45, FOR. Berle's comment is in the second telegram cited.

80. Campbell to Alexander Cadogan, August 12, 1942, FO 371 A 7651/122/45, FOR.

81. Minute, F. E. Evans, August 16, [1942], on Bajpai to Foreign Office, August 13, 1942, FO 371 A 4550/122/45, FOR. Campbell to Foreign Office, August 13, 1942, FO 371 A 4557/122/45, FOR.

82. Halifax told Linlithgow that he specifically emphasized these two points in his meetings with American officials and journalists. Halifax to Linlithgow, September 25, 1942, in Mansergh, ed., *Transfer of Power,* 3:41–42.

83. Minute by Basil Newton, September 25, 1942, FO 371 A 9511/122/45, FOR. David Scotty to C. J. Radcliffe, October 16, 1942, ibid. The Ministry of Information responded that the same point had already been made in a recent book by Guy Wint and Sir George Schuster, *India and Democracy,* which the ministry was pushing in the American market. A. E. Morley to Scotty, October 23, 1942, FO 371 A 9799/122/45, FOR.

84. Basil Newton, "Enlightenment of the United States Regarding the Evolution of the British Empire, Particularly India," August 20, 1942, FO 371 A 7709/122/45, FOR.

85. Attlee, paraphrased in ibid. Draft, Alexander Cadogan to Radcliffe, September 9, 1942, FO 371 A 7709/122/45, FOR.

86. Halifax to Eden, September 18, 1942, in Mansergh, ed., *Transfer of Power* 2:988–89.

87. Amery, "India as a Factor in Anglo-American Relations," August 13, 1942," War Cabinet Paper W. P. (42) 358, ibid., pp. 690–92. Amery to Linlithgow, September 18, 1942, Linlithgow Papers, vol. 11.

88. Draft, Cadogan to Radcliffe, September 9, 1942, FO 371 A 7709/122/45, FOR. Newton, "Enlightenment of the United States Regarding the Evolution of the British Empire, Particularly India."

89. War Cabinet W. M. (42) 129th Conclusions, Minutes 1–4, September 24, 1942, in Mansergh, ed., *Transfer of Power* 3:33. Amery to Linlithgow, October 1 [?], 1942, ibid., pp. 80–81. Linlithgow to Amery, October 7, 1942, ibid., p. 106. Eden made the suggestion for the broadcast. He was worried about Halifax's reports on the state of American opinion. Halifax's telegram of September 15, 1942 about the state of American opinion was especially important in shaping the British response. Nevile Butler characterized it as "clearly an important telegram." Halifax to Foreign Office September 15, 1942, FO 371, A 8666/122/45, FOR. This telegram is also printed in Mansergh, ed., *Transfer of Power*, 2:969–70, where it is dated September 16.

90. The mimeographed text of Amery's interview is contained in a Foreign Office document dated October 20, 1942, FO 371 A 10406/122/45, FOR.

91. G. M. Barker to Joyce, October 28, 1942, FO 371, A 10190/122/45, FOR. Minute by Nevile Butler on ibid.

92. Technically Johnson retained his position as the President's personal representative to India.

93. Halifax to Amery, June 4, 1942, in Mansergh, ed., *Transfer of Power*, 2:177–178. Hull, Memorandum of Conversation, June 3, 1942, FRUS 1942, 1:667. Hull, Memorandum of Conversation, June 18, 1942, FRUS 1942, 1:673. Without great enthusiasm, Linlithgow had agreed that one or more American professors would be welcome in India. Interestingly, the idea of using American professors resurfaced in October and November, when Amery suggested various ways in which their services could be used. By then Linlithgow was adamantly opposed. Next to one such idea he commented, "Save us!" Comment on Amery to Linlithgow, November 3, 1942, Linlithgow Papers, vol. 11.

94. Gary Hess argues that the British wanted the post to remain vacant. (Hess, *America Encounters India*, p. 96.) A. Guy Hope contends that the British wanted the post filled. (Hope, *America and Swaraj*, p. 76–77.) The evidence supports Hope. Venkataramani and Shrivastava acknowledge that the British wanted the post filled but contend, incorrectly, that the process of filling it was begun only in October and then as an effort to deflect possible American mediation attempts. (Venkataramani and Shrivastava, *Quit India*, p. 304.)

95. Berle, Memorandum of Conversation, August 12, 1942, FRUS 1942, 1:719.

96. Minute by Nevile Butler, August 18, 1942, on Campbell to Foreign Office, August 13, 1942, FO 371 A 7549/122/45, FOR. Eden supported the idea. See Eden to Amery August 22, 1942, in Mansergh, ed., *Transfer of Power* 2:785–86.

97. Amery to Linlithgow, September 13, 1942, in Mansergh, ed., *Transfer of Power*, 2:955.

98. Linlithgow to Amery, September 18, 1942, ibid., pp. 983–84.

99. Halifax to Eden, September 15, 1942, FO 371, A 8666/122/45, FOR; Bajpai to New Delhi, September 16, 1942, in Halifax to Eden, September 18, 1942, in Mansergh, ed., *Transfer of Power*, 2:985–86.

100. Linlithgow to Amery, September 21, 1942, in Mansergh, ed., *Transfer of Power*, 2:984–85. Linlithgow to Amery, September 18, 1942, ibid., pp. 1003–5.

101. Murray, Memorandum of Conversation, October 13, 1942, FRUS 1942, 1:740–42.

102. Eden to Halifax, September 28, 1942, in Mansergh, ed., *Transfer of Power*, 3:53–54. Welles, Memorandum of Conversation, October 2, 1942, FRUS 1942, 1:736. Halifax to Foreign Office, October 2, 1942, FO 371 A 9197/122/45, FOR.

103. Linlithgow to Amery, October 3, 1942, L/P&S/12/2636, IOR. Linlithgow to Amery, October 10, 1942, in Mansergh, ed., *Transfer of Power*, 3:121.

104. Amery to Linlithgow, October 7, 1942, in Mansergh, ed., *Transfer of Power*, 3:107–8. Eden to Halifax, October 10, 1942, ibid., pp. 118–19. Linlithgow to Amery, October 12, 1942, ibid., pp. 125–26. One confidential Government of India assessment of Engert concluded that Anglo-American solidarity was "almost a religion" with him. His insistence on close relations with the British at times went "beyond that of his own Government" to such an extent that he tried to conceal his activities from his own staff which, in turn, led to tense relationships within the American mission. The analyst also had to conclude that regretfully Engert "lacks personality" and was unable to "command the respect which he should otherwise enjoy." Government of India, External Affairs Department, Frontier Branch, 1944, "Report on the Heads of Foreign Missions in Kabul & thumbnail sketches of foreign diplomats in Kabul," July 1, 1944, file 490-F/1944 (secret), IOR.

105. Minutes on Halifax to Foreign Office, October 2, 1942, FO 371 A 9197/122/45, FOR. Campbell's view is reflected in a minute by Nevile Butler.

106. Eden to Halifax, October 10, 1942, in Mansergh, ed., *Transfer of Power*, 3:118. Eden to Halifax, October 19, 1942, ibid., pp. 138–39. Halifax to Foreign Office, October 21, 1942, FO 371 A 9837/122/45, FOR. Halifax to Eden, November 14, 1942, in Mansergh, ed., *Transfer of Power*, 3: 260–61.

107. Minute by Malcolm, November 24, 1942, on FO 371 A 11042/122/45, FOR. Nevile Butler to the Earl of Perth, November 26, 1942, ibid.

108. Earl of Perth to Butler, November 29, 1942, FO 371/30664 044835. Halifax to Linlithgow, December 3, 1942, FO 371 A 11302/122/45. Linlith-

gow to Amery, December 22, 1942, in Mansergh, ed., *Transfer of Power*, 3:407–11.

109. William Phillips Diary, October 31, 1942, p. 92. Donovan informed Phillips that Roosevelt had chosen him.

110. On this point see Hess, *America Encounters India*, pp. 94–95.

111. *New York Times*, October 28, 1942, p. 4. Louis, *Imperialism at Bay*, p. 158.

112. Welles to Hull, November 7, 1942, 123 P 54/525´. There is ample evidence in Phillips's diary that he attempted to keep abreast of Indian developments well before he was selected to go to India. Final quotation from Phillips Diary, October 31, 1942, p. 92.

113. Technically Phillips was minister to Canada at a time when the United States did not appoint ambassadors to that country.

114. Martin Weil, *A Pretty Good Club: The Founding Fathers of the U. S. Foreign Service* (New York: Norton, 1978), pp. 19–20; Robert D. Schulzinger, *The Making of the Diplomatic Mind: The Training, Outlook, and Style of United States Foreign Service Officers, 1908–1931* (Middletown, CT: Wesleyan University Press, 1975), pp. 54–56; Richard Hume Werking, *The Master Architects: Building the Foreign Service 1890–1913* (Lexington, KY: University Press of Kentucky, 1977), pp. 141, 163.

115. Weil, *A Pretty Good Club*, pp. 71–74; Schulzinger, *Making of the Diplomatic Mind*, pp. 58–59.

116. Phillips, *Ventures in Diplomacy*, pp. 184, 68–69.

117. Merrell to Hull, July 22, 1942, 845.00/1384. Hope, *America and Swaraj*, pp. 77–78. Hess, *America Encounters India*, pp. 95–96. Banerjee, "American Interest in Indian Independence," p. 325.

118. Weil, *A Pretty Good Club*, p. 37.

119. Ibid., p. 95.

120. Weil, *A Pretty Good Club*, pp. 37, 95. Venkataramani and Shrivastava, *Roosevelt, Gandhi, Churchill*, p. 61. See also Schulzinger, *Making of the Diplomatic Mind*, p. 34.

121. Weil, *A Pretty Good Club*, pp. 90, 22, 70.

122. Ibid., pp. 90, 125. Eddy to the Dean of Canterbury, December 23, 1942, FO 371 A 1510/93/45, FOR.

123. Phillips Diary, November 24, 1942, p. 120. "The Reminiscences of William Phillips," Columbia University Oral History Project, July 1951, pp. 138–39.

124. Eddy to the Dean of Canterbury, December 23, 1942, FO 371 A 1510/93/45, FOR. Kirchwey, quoted in American Division, Ministry of Information, "India: American Survey" (mimeographed), December 30, 1942, FO 371/30664 044835. Mackett, "Some Aspects," p. 398. Louis Wehle to Roosevelt, December 16, 1942, Roosevelt Papers, PPF, File 693.

125. Linlithgow to Amery, November 25, 1942, in Mansergh, ed., *Transfer of Power*, 3:299.

126. Halifax to Eden, November 25, 1942, ibid., 3:300. Halifax to Foreign Office, December 2, 1942, FO 371 A 11285/122/45, FOR. Halifax to Foreign Office, December 3, 1942, FO 371 A 11286/122/45, FOR.

127. Halifax to Foreign Office, December 3, 1942, FO 371 A 11286/122/45, FOR. In his letter to the viceroy, Roosevelt appointed Phillips "to serve near the Government of India as my Personal Representative with the rank of Ambassador." Whether the omission of the word "personal" was deliberate is not clear, but the public announcement of Phillips's appointment, not made until December 11, and worked out in negotiations with the British, referred to the personal rank of ambassador. Roosevelt to Linlithgow, December 3, 1942, in Mansergh, ed., *Transfer of Power*, 3:305.

6 | William Phillips's Mission to India

1. Kirby, *The War Against Japan*, 2:373.
2. Ibid., pp. 253–68, 331–59, 309–29.
3. *Newsweek*, February 22, 1943, pp. 45–46.
4. *New York Times*, February 28, 1943, 4:6.
5. Gardner, *Approaching Vietnam*, pp. 34–40. Hopkins, Memorandum of Conversation, March 27, 43, FRUS 1943, 3:39. Louis, *Imperialism at Bay*, pp. 225–27. Hess, *The United States' Emergence as a Colonial Power*, pp. 77–81.
6. Louis, *Imperialism at Bay*, p. 259. Mark A. Stoler, "From Continentalism to Globalism," pp. 308–9.
7. Thorne, *Allies of a Kind*, pp. 291–93, 358.
8. This is the view of Mackett, "Some Aspects," p. 365.
9. Murray to Welles, November 7, 1942, 123 P 54/525´. Phillips Diary, November 4, and November 10, 1942. Phillips, *Ventures in Diplomacy*, p. 347.
10. Halifax to Foreign Office, November 18, 1942, FO 371 A 10794/122/45.
11. Phillips Diary, October 31, 1942.
12. Hull to Winant (for Phillips), November 3, 1942, FRUS 1942, 1:744. Winant (for Phillips) to Hull, November 4, 1942, ibid., p. 745. Phillips Diary, November 4, 1942. Phillips to Roosevelt, November 4, 1942, Roosevelt Papers, PSF: 53, Great Britain: OSS.
13. Phillips Diary, November 10, 1942.
14. Hull to Winant (for Phillips), November 20, 1942, FRUS 1942, 1:746–48.
15. "The Atlantic Charter and National Independence," November 13, 1942, enclosed in [Hull], "Memorandum for the President," November 17, 1942, Phillips Papers. Hull's memorandum is of interest because the editors of the *Foreign Relations* series were unable to locate and publish it. FRUS 1942, 1:748 n. 63. The document itself did not call for immediate independence and was, by Hull's admission, the most conservative approach possible to implementing the Atlantic Charter. It applied the principle of trustee-

ship only to former League of Nations mandates and to territories taken from the Axis powers. In December the President approved the plan. Louis, *Imperialism at Bay*, pp. 185–86.

16. Murray to Welles, November 30, 1942, 123 P 54/525´. Minute by Nevile Butler, November 20, 1942, FO 371 A 10846/122/45, FOR. Halifax to Foreign Office, November 19, 1942, in Mansergh, ed., *Transfer of Power*, 3:308 n.2.

17. Eden to Halifax, November 25, 1942, in Amery to External Affairs Department, Government of India, November 27, 1942, in Mansergh, ed., *Transfer of Power*, 3:308. Murray to Welles, November 30, 1942, 123 P 54/525´. M. J. McDermott to Stephen Early, December 10, 1942, Roosevelt Papers, OF: 2314. Halifax to Government of India, December 11, 1942, in Mansergh, ed., *Transfer of Power*, 3:359.

18. Foreign Office to Halifax, December 20, 1942, FO 371 A 11559/122/45, FOR.

19. Phillips to Berle, December 4, 1942, Berle Papers, box 45.

20. Phillips Diary, December 11, and December 22, 1942.

21. Phillips to Hull, December 1, 1942, 123 P 54/535.

22. War Cabinet, "Reports for the Month of November 1942 for the Dominions, India, Burma, and the Colonies and Mandated Territories. Report by the Secretary of State for India," December 28, 1942, W. P. (R) (42) 49, p. 10. Copy in Nehru Library. Amery, "Note of a Talk with Mr. Phillips at the India Office on Tuesday, 24th November 1942," FO 371 A 11254/122/45, FOR.

23. Phillips Diary, November 24, 1942, pp. 120–21. Phillips to Roosevelt, December 17, 1942, Roosevelt Papers, PSF: container 53.

24. Phillips Diary, December 21, 1942.

25. Ibid., December 3, 1942.

26. Ibid., December 21, December 3, and December 1, 1942. Lady Willingdon also spoke unenthusiastically about Gilbert Laithwaite, the viceroy's private secretary, because he "was very much like the Viceroy in many ways." (Ibid., December 3, 1942.)

27. Ibid., November 23, 1942.

28. H. V. Hodson to F. F. Turnbull, December 17, 1942, L/P&S/12/2754, IOR. Phillips Diary, December 16, 1942. India Office fears of what Hodson might say are indicated in a note by Turnbull, an official in the Indian Office, in which he complained that Hodson had approached Phillips without first consulting with the India Office. The viceroy would not approve, Turnbull noted, adding that Hodson "might have difficulty in avoiding being drawn onto ground where he would have to express views with which the viceroy is not in agreement." See Turnbull's note on Hodson to Turnbull, December 15, 1942, L/P&S/12/2754, IOR.

29. Phillips Diary, November 27, and December 1, 1942.

30. Ibid., November 11, 1942.

31. Phillips's interview with William Paton, ibid., December 19, 1942. Ibid., December 14, 1942.

32. Ibid., December 17, 1942. British intelligence kept track of Phillips's moves and soon knew of his meeting with Menon. "I don't suppose he could have refused to see him, as Menon seems to be, unfortunately, on rather close terms with Winant," Amery reported to Linlithgow. But, he added optimistically, "I dare say Phillips was able to size him up." Amery to Linlithgow, December 23, 1942, in Mansergh, ed., *Transfer of Power*, 3:412.

33. Phillips to Hull, December 19, 1942, FRUS, 1943, 3:179. Phillips to Berle, December 4, 1942, Berle Papers, box 45.

34. "Memorandum of Conversation with Miss Cornelia Sorabji," Phillips Diary, December 9, 1942. Phillips to Hull, December 19, 1942, FRUS 1943, 3:178–79.

35. Phillips to Hull, December 19, 1943, FRUS 1943, 3:178–79. Hodson to Turnbull, December 17, 1942, L/P&S/12/2754, IOR.

36. Phillips Diary, January 5, 1943.

37. Ibid., January 11, 1943 and January 8, 1943. See also Phillips to Roosevelt, January 22, 1943, FRUS 1943, 4:181.

38. Phillips to Hull, January 22, 1943, 845.00/1785.

39. Foreign Office minute dated January 17, 1943, on a clipping from the London *Times*, January 9, 1943, reporting Phillips's remarks in New Delhi, FO 371 A 784/93/45, FOR. Linlithgow to Amery, January 11, 1943, in Mansergh, ed., *Transfer of Power*, 3:487.

40. Phillips Diary, January 26, 1943.

41. Linlithgow to Amery January 28, 1943, in Mansergh, ed., *Transfer of Power*, 3:554–55. See also Linlithgow to B. Glancy, January 27, 1943, ibid., pp. 551–52.

42. Linlithgow to Amery, January 28, 1943, ibid., pp. 554–55.

43. Phillips Diary, November 24, 1942. Phillips to Hull, November 30, 1942, Phillips Papers. Phillips to Roosevelt, December 17, 1942, Roosevelt Papers PSF: container 53. Amery, "Note of a Talk with Mr. Phillips at the India Office on Tuesday, 24th November 1942," FO 371 A 11254/122/45, FOR.

44. Amery to Linlithgow, January 29, 1943, in Mansergh, ed., *Transfer of Power*, 3:560–61. See also Amery to Linlithgow, February 1, 1943, ibid., pp. 569–70.

45. Phillips Diary, January 15, 1943.

46. Phillips to Hull, January 9, 1943, 845.00/1764. Government of India, Home Department, Political (I) Section, 1943, "Letter from Mr. William D. Tenbroeck to 'Fellow Americans' regarding Chimur Affair and Prof. Bhansali's fast and his other Anti-British activities. Warning given to him by American authorities and Bombay Police Commissioner," file 3/5/43, NAI.

47. Phillips to Hull, January 13, 1943, 845.00/1765. Phillips Diary, January 14, 1943. A little later Phillips forwarded to the State Department a book-

let entitled, *India Ravaged*, which he said provided an accurate description of the atrocities committed at Chimur. There is no clear evidence that Phillips's mention of the Bhansali matter was a factor in its solution. Linlithgow does not mention anything about Phillips in this connection. See Linlithgow to Amery, January 13, 1943, in Mansergh, ed., *Transfer of Power*, 3:501–2.

48. Phillips to Hull, January 19, 1943, 123 P 54/578.

49. Phillips to Roosevelt, January 22, 1943, FRUS 1943, 4:180–83. Phillips to Hull, January 25, 1943, ibid., p. 184.

50. Phillips to Hull, January 25, 1943, 845.00/1771.

51. Phillips Diary, January 15, 1943. "Memorandum of a Conversation I had with Devadas Gandhi," January 20, 1943, Phillips Papers. Phillips Diary, January 23, 1949.

52. Phillips to Hull, January 26, 1943, 845.00/1736. Phillips's analysis required fourteen single-spaced pages.

53. Ibid.

54. Phillips to Hull, February 8, 1943, 845.00/1821.

55. Phillips to John P. Davies, February 15, 1943, New Delhi Post Records, box 1426, File 800 (political [1943], confidential), NRC. Davies' memorandum covered much the same grounds as Phillips's dispatch of January 26. Davies, "Memorandum for General Stilwell: The Indian Problem in the Fall and Winter 1942–1943," January 23, 1943, ibid. By contrast, when Phillips transmitted to Washington a British memorandum, provided by Engert, about the present deadlock, he was openly critical of the analysis. "The Mission does not know one representative Indian, Hindu or Muslim, moderate or extremist, who is not, to say the least, skeptical of Britain's post-war intentions toward this country," he wrote. Phillips to Hull, February 1, 1943, 845.00/1825.

56. Government of India, Home Department, Political (I) Section, 1943, "Intercepted letter from Shambas P. Gidwani to Mr. Punniah, Editor, the 'Sind Observer,' Karachi, regarding the subjects discussed by the former in an interview with Mr. Phillips, the American envoy," File 20/5/43, NAI.

57. Phillips Diary, January 31, and February 5, 1943. Newspaper clippings, *Dawn*, February 6, 1943, and *Hindustan Times*, February 6, 1943, Phillips Papers.

58. Phillips Diary, February 8, 1943. Dunichand to Rajendra Prasad, August 17, 1945, Rajendra Prasad Papers, file 4-G/45–46, coll. no. 1.

59. Amery to Linlithgow, February 1, 1943, in Mansergh, ed., *Transfer of Power*, 3:570. Minutes on Amery to Eden, February 2, 1943, FO 371 A 1298/93/G45, FOR.

60. Amery to Linlithgow, February 1, 1943, in Mansergh, ed., *Transfer of Power*, 3:569–70.

61. Phillips Diary, February 8, 1943.

62. Ibid. Phillips to Hull, February 8, 1943, FRUS 1943, 4:185. Linlithgow to Amery, February 8, 1943, in Mansergh, ed., *Transfer of Power*, 3:640–41.

63. Linlithgow's several letters to Phillips about the fast are contained in New Delhi Post Records, box 1426, file 1800 (political [1943], confidential), NRC. For Phillips's appreciation of Linlithgow's action, see Phillips to Linlithgow, February 10, 1943, in Mansergh, ed., *Transfer of Power*, 3:651.

64. Phillips to Hull, February 11, 1943, 845.00/1623. Phillips Diary, February 11, 1943. In another cable Phillips commented, "reluctantly I am coming to the conclusion that the Viceroy, presumably responsive to Churchill, is not in sympathy with any change in Britain's relationship to India." Phillips to Hull, February 10, 1943, FRUS 1943, 4:187.

65. Phillips to Hull, February 11, 1943, 845.00/1623. Phillips to Hull, February 10, 1943, FRUS 1943, 4:187. Phillips Diary, February 11, 1943.

66. For example, Phillips to Hull, February 12, 1943, FRUS 1943, 4:191–92. [Phillips], "Memorandum of a Conversation I had with Sir Srinivasa Sarma, K. C. I. E.," February 15, 1943, New Delhi Post Records, box 1426, File 800 (political [1943], confidential), NRC.

67. Phillips Diary, February 12, 1943.

68. Ibid., February 17, 1943. Murray to Welles, February 16, 1943, and Welles to Murray, February 16, 1943, 845.00/1904.

69. *New Republic*, March 1, 1943, in Mackett, "Some Aspects," p. 381. Government of India, Home Department, Political (I) Section, 1943, "Mr. Gandhi's Fast of February '43—Control of Publicity," File 33/4/43, NAI. *Newsweek*, February 22, 1943, p. 45. On censorship see Foreign Office to Halifax, February 10, 1943, FO 371 A 1575/93/45. FOR.

70. Minute by Malcolm on Bajpai to Linlithgow, February 11, 1943, FO 371 A 1663/93/45, FOR.

71. Hull, Memorandum of Conversation, February 16, 1943, FRUS 1943, 4:194–95.

72. Halifax to Foreign Office, February 16, 1943, FO 371 A 1798/93/45, FOR. Although dated February 16, the telegram was not sent until February 18.

73. Thorne, *Allies of a Kind*, p. 360.

74. Hull, Memorandum of conversation with Eden and Halifax, March 22, 1943, FRUS 1943, 3:31.

75. Phillips to Hull, February 16, 1943, ibid., pp. 193–94.

76. Hull to Phillips, February 17, 1943, ibid., p. 195.

77. Phillips, "Memorandum of a conversation I had with Viceroy," February 18, 1943, New Delhi Post Records, box 1426, file 800-political (1943), NRC. Phillips to Hull, February 18, 1943, FRUS 1943, 4:196.

78. Linlithgow to Amery, February 19, 1945, in Mansergh, ed., *Transfer of Power*, 3:690. R. Lumley to Linlithgow, March 4, 1943, ibid., pp. 754–55. Phillips, "Memorandum of a conversation I had with Viceroy." Phillips to Hull, February 18, 1943, FRUS 1943, 4:195–96.

79. Phillips, "Memorandum of a conversation I had with Viceroy." Phillips to Hull, February 19, 1943, FRUS 1943, 4:197.

80. Phillips to Hull, February 19, 1943, FRUS 1943, 4:196–97.

81. Linlithgow to Amery, February 19, 1943, in Mansergh, ed., *Transfer of Power*, 3:690. Amery to Linlithgow, February 19, 1943, ibid., p. 699. Privately, Linlithgow was not convinced. Amery, he wrote, overlooked the impact of Phillips's appointment on "the Indian mind. . . . No Indian knew or cared what Wilson did or said." Linlithgow, note on ibid.

82. Amery to Eden, February 19, 1943, L/P&S/12/2754, IOR.

83. Amery to Churchill, February 19, 1943, FO 371 A 1865/93/45, FOR.

84. Halifax to Foreign Office, February 20, 1943, L/P&S/12/2754, IOR. Hull, Memorandum of Conversation, February 20, 1943, FRUS 1943, 4:199. In his memorandum, Hull does not indicate that the President had telephoned during his conversation with Halifax.

85. Hess, *America Encounters India*, pp. 102–3. Minute by Nevile Butler, February 22, 1943, on FO 371 A 2166/93/45, FOR.

86. Amery to Linlithgow, February 19, 1943, in Mansergh, ed., *Transfer of Power*, 3:698. Amery to Linlithgow, February 19, 1943, ibid., p. 695. Amery to Eden, February 19, 1943, L/P&S/12/3754, IOR.

87. Foreign Office to Halifax, February 19, 1943, FO 371 A 1864/93/45, FOR.

88. Halifax to Foreign Office, February 20, 1943, L/P&S/12/2754, IOR. Hull, Memorandum of Conversation, February 20, 1943, FRUS 1943, 4:199–200.

89. Halifax to Eden, February 21, 1943, L/P&S/12/2754, IOR.

90. Davies, "The Indian Problem, Fall and Winter 1942–43," pp. 1–2, enclosed in Davies to Phillips, January 24, 1943, 845.00/1821. The report is also found in New Delhi Post Records, box 1426, file 800-political (1943) confidential, NRC. Phillips to Hull, February 19, 1943, FRUS 1943, 4:197.

91. Phillips to Welles, February 17, 1943, Phillips Diary.

92. Phillips to Hull, February 19, 1943, FRUS 1943, 4:196–97. Phillips to Hull, February 20, 1943, ibid., p. 197. Phillips to Hull, February 21, 1943, 845.00/1811. Rajagopalachari's impassioned pleas to Phillips suggests that Linlithgow's information about the Madras nationalist was incorrect. On February 22, he wrote to Amery, "Rajagopalachari is, I hear, advising the leaders not to try to stir up too much sympathy in America over this business fearing that if the Americans take a hand, that will only harden opinion at home." Linlithgow to Amery, February 22, 1943, in Mansergh, ed., *Transfer of Power*, 3:714.

93. Phillips to Roosevelt, February 23, 1943, FRUS 1943, 4:201–3.

94. Linlithgow to Amery, February 25, 1943, in Mansergh, ed., *Transfer of Power*, 3:729. Churchill to Jan Smuts, February 26, 1943, ibid., p. 738. Linlithgow to Bajpai and Agency-General, Chunking, February 26, 1943, ibid., p. 735.

95. Phillips Diary, February 26, 1943. Phillips to Roosevelt, March 3, 1943, FRUS 1943, 4:205–7.

96. Phillips Diary, entries from March 5 to April 6, 1943. Phillips to Roosevelt, April 7, 1943, Roosevelt Papers, PSF: box 55, India Folder.

97. Howard Donovan (for Phillips) to Hull, March 11, 1943, FRUS 1943, 4:208. Murray to Welles, March 12, 1943, 845.00/1875. Phillips to Hull, April 2, 1943, FRUS 1943, 4:210. Ten days later Phillips reaffirmed his views. See Phillips to Hull, April 12, 1943, 845.00/1933.

98. Phillips to Hull, April 2, 1943, FRUS 1943, 4:211.

99. Murray to Welles and Hull, March 31, 1943, 845.00/1916. Murray also circulated John Davies' report on Indian conditions to Hull, Welles, Berle, and others, and called their attention to Phillips's enthusiastic approval of the report. Murray to Hull, Welles, Berle, and Atherton, March 19, 1943, 845.00/1914.

100. Welles to Ralph Barton Perry, April 2, 1943, 845.00/1864–. When Welles' letter appeared in the *New York Times*, it evoked much negative comment among the Indian nationalist press. See Phillips to Hull, April 16, 1943, FRUS 1943, 4:216, and Phillips to Hull, April 20, 1943, 840.50/1888.

101. Roosevelt, Memorandum for Harry Hopkins, March 19, 1943, Roosevelt Papers, PSF: Diplomatic Collection, box 55, India Folder.

102. Phillips Diary, April 14, 1943.

103. Murray to Welles, April 6, 1943, 845.00/1933. Welles to Hull, April 6, 1943, 845.00/1933. Hull penciled "Hold" on Welles' note, indicating that the telegram should be held up.

104. Hull, Memorandum of Conversation, March 22, 1943, FRUS 1943, 3:31–32. Hull, Memorandum of Conversation, March 29, 1943, ibid., p. 41. Unsigned draft cables, April 5, and April 9, 1943, 845.00/1900. Hull to Phillips, April 14, 1943, FRUS 1943, 4:215. For Murray's strong memorandum urging support of Phillips, see Murray to Welles, April 6, 1943, 845.00/1933.

105. Phillips Diary, April 8, 1943. Donovan to Phillips, April 8, 1942, New Delhi Post Records, box 1426, file 800-Political (1943) Confidential, NRC.

106. Newspaper clipping, *Dawn*, April 8, 1943, Phillips Papers.

107. Phillips Diary, April 17, and April 18, 1943.

108. Ibid., April 19, 1943. Phillips to Roosevelt, April 19, 1943, FRUS 1943, 4:217–20.

109. Linlithgow to Amery, April 26, 1943, in Mansergh, ed., *Transfer of Power*, 3:908.

110. Caroe revealed this in August, 1945. See Caroe to Dennis Macrow Cleary, August 15, 1945, L/P&S/12/2754, IOR. Retrospectively, Caroe disagreed with Engert's contention that the mission influenced Phillips. "One rather doubts whether Phillips had sufficient penetration in any case to grasp the essentials of the situation," he wrote. "He was a most difficult man to get down to business with and always struck us as very much of a facade."

111. Cornelius Van H. Engert to Phillips, January 21, 1943, Phillips Papers.

112. Government of India, External Affairs Department, Frontier

Branch, 1943, "Visit of Mr. C. V. Engert, American Minister at Kabul to India," File 217-F/43, NAI. Linlithgow to Amery, March 8, 1943, L/P&S/13/2754, IOR.

113. Just before Engert left Kabul in August, 1945, he told his British counterpart in Afghanistan, G. C. L. Crichton, about what he had seen in the American files in New Delhi in 1942. According to his story, the State Department chastised the American mission for biased reporting, but there is no evidence that this was the case. When Crichton reported Engert's comments, Caroe responded that Engert had told him in the same story two years before. See Crichton to C. W. Baxter, August 11, 1945,. L/P&S/12/2754, IOR.

114. Linlithgow to Amery, March 8, 1943, L/P&S/12/2754, IOR. Amery to Eden, March 9, 1943, L/P&S/12/2753, IOR. Prime Minister's Personal Minute to Amery, March 10, 1943, L/P&S/12/2754, IOR. Amery to Linlithgow, March 11, 1943, in Mansergh, ed., *Transfer of Power*, 3:792.

115. Minute by Cleary, September 14, [1945], L/P&S/12/2754, IOR.

116. Phillips Diary, April 24, 1943. Linlithgow to Amery, April 26, 1943, in Mansergh, ed., *Transfer of Power*, 3:908–11.

117. Linlithgow to Amery, April 26, 1943, in Mansergh, ed., *Transfer of Power*, 3:908–11. Linlithgow to Amery, 2–May 4, 1943, ibid., pp. 937–938. Minute by J. J. Tahourdin (?), May 5, 1943, IOR, on Linlithgow to Amery, April 26, 1943. The Linlithgow telegram is printed in Mansergh, ed., *Transfer of Power*, 3:908–11.

118. Phillips Diary, April 24, 1943. Phillips thought the viceroy's approval was reluctant. Linlithgow, in his account, said that Phillips "could put all the blame on me" if he wished. Linlithgow to Amery, April 26, 1943, in Mansergh, ed., *Transfer of Power*, 3:909.

119. Phillips Diary, April 25 and 26, 1943. Ministry of Information, British Information Services, "Survey Special: India" (mimeographed), May 7, 1943, FO 371/34147 044835, FOR. In spite of the criticism, Halifax thought the British got off quite lightly. Halifax to Linlithgow, May 13, 1943, FO 371 A 4653/93/45, FOR.

120. Howard Donovan to Hull, May 8, 1943, 845.00/1958.

121. For example, Government of India, Home Department, Political (Internal) Section, 1943, "Notices from Sardar Sant Singh . . . to permit Mr. Phillips, American envoy, to see Mr. Gandhi. . . ," file 24/7/43, NAI.

122. Linlithgow to Amery, April 29, 1943, in Mansergh, ed., *Transfer of Power*, 3:930. Government of India officials were pleased with Linlithgow's measured reaction to Phillips's statement. Interestingly, however, they were critical of him for not complaining that Phillips had seen too many nationalists during his recent tour. Note on Linlithgow to Amery, April 29, 1943, L/P&S/12/2754, IOR.

123. Linlithgow to Amery, March 16, 1943, in Mansergh, ed., *Transfer of Power*, 3:819.

124. Halifax to Amery, May 5, 1943, in Mansergh, ed., *Transfer of Power*, 3:945–46. Minute by Nevile Butler, May 18, on Halifax to Linlithgow, May 13, 1943, FO 371 A 4853/93/45, FOR.

125. Note by Eden, April 12, 1943, on FO 371 A 3268/93/45, FOR.

126. Philip Swinton to Amery, May 5, 1943, L/P&S/12/2754, IOR.

127. Amery to Swinton, May 15, 1943, ibid. Amery to Linlithgow, May 25, 1943, ibid.

128. Phillips Diary, April 29, 1943. Phillips to Roosevelt, May 14, 1943, FRUS 1943, 4:220–22.

129. Phillips Diary, May 21, 1943.

130. Ibid., June 9, 1943. "Reminiscences of William Phillips," p. 150.

131. Churchill to Attlee and Amery, May 23, 1945, in Mansergh, ed., *Transfer of Power*, 3:1003. Halifax to Amery, May 17, 1943, ibid., p. 992. Phillips Diary, May 22, 1943. The meeting with Phillips took place on May 14.

132. Phillips Diary, May 22, 1943.

133. Ibid. Churchill to Attlee and Amery, May 23, 1943, in Mansergh, ed., *Transfer of Power*, 3:1003–4.

134. Phillips Diary, May 22, 1943. Hess, *America Encounters India*, pp. 110–11.

135. Churchill to Attlee and Amery, May 23, 1943, in Mansergh, ed., *Transfer of Power*, 3:1004. Linlithgow to Amery, June 2, 1943, ibid., p. 1037. Minute by Horace A. F. Rumbold, June 1, 1943, L/P&S/12/2634, IOR. (Rumbold was the Joint Head of the Economic and Overseas Department.) Halifax to Amery, May 29, 1943, in Mansergh, ed., *Transfer of Power*, 3:1025. Minute on "India: Mr. Phillips," FO 371 A 5014/93/45, IOR. Minute by Roland T. Peel, June 2, 1943, L/P&S/12/2634, IOR.

136. Minute by Nevile Butler, June 18, 1943, FO 371 A 5095/93/45, FOR.

137. Phillips to Roosevelt, May 31, 1943, Phillips Diary.

138. Phillips Diary, May 22, 1943. Stimson admitted that he did not have time to think much about India, although he eventually took notes on what Phillips told him.

139. Murray, Memorandum, "United States Policy Towards India, March 1933 to December 7, 1944," December 6, 1944, New Delhi Post Records, File 800-Political (1943) confidential, NRC.

140. Phillips Diary, December 31, 1943.

141. Murray to Stettinius, October 25, 1943, 845.00/9–943. Phillips himself wrote that his views were "completely at variance with those of the British Government." Phillips Diary, September 29, 1943.

142. "Reminiscences of William Phillips," p. 165.

7 | American Disillusionment Grows

1. The following summary of the war draws on Kirby, *The War Against Japan*, vols. 2 and 3.

2. Thorne, *Allies of a Kind*, p. 337. "Report of the Agent General for India in the U.S.A. for the Months of April, May and June, 1944," L/P&S/12/4627, coll. 47, file 4, IOR.

3. In July, 1943, an important Government of India official confided to Merrell that British promises to India might not be kept. Merrell to Hull, July 15, 1943, FRUS 1943, 4:225.

4. Lampton Berry, quoted in Murray, Memorandum, October 4, 1943, ibid., pp. 229–30. Merrell to Hull, October 8, 1943, ibid., pp. 230–31.

5. Clymer, "Samuel Evans Stokes, Mahatma Gandhi, and Indian Nationalism."

6. Roosevelt, "United States Objectives in India and the Far East," *Department of State Bulletin*, February 5, 1944, p. 145.

7. Murray to Edward Stettinius, February 28, 1944, 845.00/2228.

8. Campbell to Foreign Office, August 12, 1943, FO 371 A 7565/93/45, FOR. Minute by Malcolm, August 18, 1942, on Campbell letter. See also Kykie [?Kythié] Hendy to T. A. Raman, n.d. [August 1943], in Mansergh, ed., *Transfer of Power*, 4:170–71. Linlithgow thought Phillips's speech indicated that he was "still somewhat woolly-minded" about Indian realities. Linlithgow to Amery, September 20, 1943, in Mansergh, ed., *Transfer of Power*, 4:400.

9. For example, Phillips Diary, October 9, 1943, in which Phillips recounts a luncheon discussion with the American diplomat Stanley Hornbeck who, he said, shared his view that "India's attitude is very much a part of our whole far Eastern problem and that should India turn away from the white races and join up with China and Burma, there is no telling what might be in store for the future—certainly trouble."

10. Ibid., October 21, and November 30, 1943.

11. Moon, ed., *Wavell: The Viceroy's Journal*, p. 13. Entry for September 30, 1943. Phillips to Roosevelt, September 30, 1943, FRUS 1943, 4:228–29. Phillips, quoted in Murray to Stettinius, February 28, 1944, 845.00/2227.

12. Phillips Diary, April 25, 1944.

13. Amery to Linlithgow, July 23, 1943, Linlithgow Papers, 25:197. Linlithgow to Amery, July 29, 1943, ibid., p. 346.

14. Minute by J. C. Donnelly, November 3, 1943, on American Mission in New Delhi to the Government of India, August 5, 1943, FO 371 A 9789/93/45, FOR.

15. Halifax to Foreign Office, November 5, 1943, L/P&S/12/2634, IOR.

16. Nevile Butler to Rumbold, July 14, 1943, ibid.

17. Phillips to Roosevelt, September 30, 1943, FRUS 1943, 4:228–29. Phillips Diary, September 30, 1944. On Johnson, see Venkataramani and Shrivastava, *Roosevelt, Gandhi, Churchill*, p. 27.

18. Merrell to Hull, February 19, 1944, FRUS 1944, 5:232–33.

19. War Cabinet W. M. (43) 136th Conclusions, October 7, 1943, in Mansergh, ed., *Transfer of Power*, 4:381–84. Directive to the Viceroy Desig-

nate, War Cabinet Paper W.P. (43) 450 (Revise), October 8, 1943, in ibid., pp. 387–88.

20. Moon, ed., *Wavell: The Viceroy's Journal*, p. 33. Entry for October 19, 1943.

21. "Memorandum by the Prime Minister and the Minister of Defence," War Cabinet Papers W. P. (43) 445, October 6, 1944, in Mansergh, ed., *Transfer of Power*, 4:379.

22. "Report of the Agent General for India in the U.S.A. for the month of December, 1943," L/P&S/12/4626, coll. 47, file 4, IOR.

23. American Mission in New Delhi to the Government of India, August 5, 1943, in FO 371 A 9789/93/45, FOR. Minute by J. C. Donnelly, November 3, 1943, on ibid.

24. Phillips to Roosevelt, September 30, 1943, FRUS 1943, 4:228–29.

25. Linlithgow to Amery, March 5, 1943, FO 371 A 2453/93/45, FOR. Nevile Butler to Peel, March 17, 1943, ibid.

26. Phillips to William Donovan, January 23, 1943, 103.918/924. Phillips to Donovan, February 17, 1943, 103.918/100g. Linlithgow to Amery, April 8, 1943, in Mansergh, ed., *Transfer of Power*, 3:879.

27. For example, Amery to Linlithgow, January 25, 1941, Linlithgow Papers, 10:17–18.

28. Memorandum, "Relations between United States Officials in India and the population," attached to "Summary of Indian Censorship Report (date 15.3.43) on American Activities in India, or in relation to India," March 15, 1943, L/P&S/12/4624, IOR.

29. Amery to Linlithgow, January 5, 1942, in Mansergh, ed., *Transfer of Power*, 1:7.

30. F. W. Ecker, press release, enclosed in Phillips to Hull, April 15, 1943, 845.24/409.

31. Linlithgow to Amery, July 22, 1943, L/P&S/12/2634, IOR. Minute, Patrick, July 27, 1943, ibid. Beecroft, a professor at the University of Southern California, had in fact written a series of articles in 1940 for *Amerasia* which were critical of Britain's refusal to respond constructively to nationalist desires. See Mackett, "Some Aspects," pp. 273–74.

32. "Memorandum on United States Office of War Information in India," attached to "Summary of Indian Censorship Report (date 15.3.43) on American Activities in India, or in relation to India," March 15, 1943, L/P&S/12/4624, IOR.

33. Ibid.

34. "Summary of Indian Censorship Report (date 15.3.43) on American Activities in India, or in relation to India," March 15, 1943, ibid.

35. Memorandum, "Relations between United States Officials in India and the population," attached to "Summary of Indian Censorship Report (date 15.3.43) on American Activities in India, or in relation to India," March 15, 1943, ibid.

36. Phillips to Welles, February 17, 1943, Phillips Diary.

37. Phillips to Roosevelt, February 23, 1943, FRUS 1943, 4:203. Phillips to Hull, April 10, 1943, 103.9166/4071. "Memorandum on United States Office of War Information in India," attached to "Summary of Indian Censorship Report (date 15.3.43) on American Activities in India, or in relation to India," March 15, 1943, L/P&S/12/4624, IOR.

38. Linlithgow to Amery, May 17, 1943, Linlithgow Papers, 12:130. A. F. Morley to Patrick, July 23, 1943, L/P&S/12/2634, IOR. Minute, David T. Monteath (?) to Amery, July 29, 1943, L/P&S/12/2634, IOR.

39. Elmer Davis to William D. Leahy, June 11, 1943, Ralph Block Papers, box 1. Although Smith left under something of a cloud insofar as the British were concerned, they later came to like him. In a lengthy analysis of American opinion about India in 1945–46, Puckle noted that he had come to expect friendly writing from Smith, who was now in charge of Indian matters for the *New York Times*. Recent articles in the *Times* about riots in India were, Puckle stated, "thoughtful and sympathetic." Puckle to Patrick, May 31, 1946, FO 371 AN 1839/63/45, FOR.

40. Ralph Block to Ferdie Kuhn, August 14, 1943, Block Papers, box 1.

41. "Memorandum for the Director," January 17, 1944, ibid. Graham Spry, "American Relations with the British Empire," (printed but classified secret), May 1, 1944, L/P&S/12/4624, coll. 47, file 1, IOR.

42. Block to P. N. Thapar, October 4, 1944, in Government of India, Home Department, Political (I) Section, 1944, "Decision to withhold in censorship all copies of the issue of August 1944 of the American magazine 'Asia and the Americas' . . . ," file 20/11/44, NAI.

43. Government of India, Home Department, Political (I) Section, 1945, "Question of censoring books and publications received in the library of the Bombay branch of the United States Office of War Information," file 49/2/45, NAI.

44. Government of India, Home Department, Political (I) Section, "Publication in *The People's War* of Extracts from an Alleged Letter from Marshall Chiang Kai-shek to President Roosevelt and Question of Tracing its Source," file 81/44, NAI.

45. Government of India, Home Department, Political (I) Section, 1945, "Question of censoring books and publications received in the library of the Bombay branch of the United States Office of War Information," file 49/2/45, NAI. Government of India, External Affairs Department, General Branch, "Secret Report on the Library in Bombay of the U.S. Office of War Information," December 8, 1944, file 50(16)-G/45, NAI.

46. Government of India, Home Department, Political (I) Section, "Publication in *The People's War* of Extracts from an Alleged Letter from Marshall Chiang Kai-shek to President Roosevelt and Question of Tracing its Source," file 81/44, NAI.

47. Government of India, External Affairs Department, General Branch,

"Secret Report on the Library in Bombay of the U.S. Office of War Information," December 8, 1944, file 50(16)-G/45, NAI.

48. For example, "Copy of a record of the discussion in the Congress Working Committee on the War Resolution," enclosed in M. Hallett to Linlithgow, May 31, 1942, in Choudhury, ed., *Dr. Rajendra Prasad*, 5:217–23; and Gandhi, "Interview to American Journalists," [June 6, 1942], CWMG, 76:194–95.

49. Evelyn Wood to Nehru, May 5, 1942, Nehru Papers, Part I, vol. 103.

50. Government of India, External Affairs Department, Far East Branch, 1945, "Firing on an Anglo-India Boy by Certain American Soldiers in Calcutta," file 244-F.E./45, and "Prevention of Accidents caused by careless use of firearms by American Troops in the Gurgaon district," 269-F.E./45, NAI.

51. Herbert Matthews, "Yanks in Wonderland," *New York Times Magazine*, December 13, 1942, p. 34. Murray to Berle and Stettinius, January 10, 1944, 845.00/2242.

52. Nehru, *The Discovery of India*, p. 362.

53. William Fisher, "Yanks Make a Hit in India," *Life*, January 18, 1943, pp. 11–16. Matthews, "Yanks in Wonderland," pp. 5, 34.

54. Government of India, External Affairs Department, War Branch, 1943, "Censorship Interceptions . . . 1) Americas and Americans 2) United States of America," File 42 (16)-W (secret), NAI.

55. India Office Minute, June 17, 1943, L/P&S/12/2634, IOR. Rumbold to Nevile Butler, June 17, 1943, ibid. Most reports the British received about Davies were favorable, including one by Olaf Caroe. But British authorities remained suspicious of him. Favorable assessments of Davies include Halifax to Foreign Office, July 8, 1943, FO 371 A 6422/93/45, FOR, and note by Caroe, September 17, 1943, L/P&S/12/2634, IOR. Continuing suspicious of Davies are evident in a minute by J. G. Tahourdin, September 8, 1943, on H. Seymour to Foreign Office, September 7, 1943, FO 371 A 8280/93/45.

56. K. Cornwallis to Foreign Office, January 22, 1944, FO 371 A 333/181/G45, FOR.

57. Minutes by Alan Dudley and P. Mason, January 25, 1944, on ibid. The British thought the situation serious enough to bring to the attention of President Roosevelt with a view to working on the problem jointly.

58. Minute, February 18, 1944, on A. I. Morley to Nevile Butler, February 7, 1944, FO 371 AN 532/181/45, FOR.

59. "Report of the Agent General for India in the U.S.A. for the Months of April, May and June, 1944," L/P&S/12/4627, coll. 47, file 4, FOR.

60. Adding to the Allied successes in the area, Stilwell's Chinese forces seized the important airfield at Myitkyina in May and took the town itself in August. By the summer of 1944, then, the Japanese were retreating everywhere except in China itself.

61. Phillips Diary, August 12, 1944.

62. Wavell to Amery, August 23, 1944, in Mansergh, ed., *Transfer of Power*, 4:1217.

63. Amery to Wavell, November 9, 1944, Wavell Papers, L/PO/473.

64. Wavell to Amery, December 12, 1944, in Mansergh, ed., *Transfer of Power*, 5:302. Mountbatten had some success, as Generals Mark Clark, Raymond Wheeler, and Dwight Eisenhower all eventually said some kind words about the contributions of Indian troops, which the Government of India's Information Service tried to get published in the newspapers. Government of India, External Affairs Department, External Publication Branch, 1945, "Press Releases Received from Mr. Hennessy," file 322-E.P./45, NAI.

65. Minute by Peel, September 11, 1944, on Halifax to Foreign Office, September 8, 1944, FO 371 AN 3411/181/45, FOR.

66. Minute by Peel, November 16, 1944, on Halifax to Foreign Office, November 9, 1944, L/P&S/12/4624, coll. 47, file 1, IOR. Government of India, Home Department, Political (Internal) Section, 1944, "Notes on Outward Press messages of Political Interest seen in censorship from August–December 1944," file 103/44, NAI.

67. Government of India, Home Department, Political (Internal) Section, 1943, "Entertainments proposed by Sir Evelyn Wrench . . . with the idea of getting prominent Indians of different kinds to meet American officials and others to make them realise the complication of the Indian situation," file 103/43, NAI. Government of India, Home Department, Political (I) Section, 1944, "Informal parties arranged by Sir Evelyn Wrench . . . ," file 48/10/44, NAI.

68. Mackett, "Some Aspects," pp. 391–93. *New York Times*, August 10, 1943, p. 7. See also Kate Mitchell, "An Indian Government is Possible," *New Republic*, August 30, 1943, p. 275, and I. F. Stone, "The Indian Skeleton at Atlantic City," *Nation*, December 11, 1943, p. 686. Stone's article contained well-informed comments about American policy in India.

69. Mitchell, "An Indian Government is Possible," p. 275.

70. Figures are taken from the listings under "India: Home Rule" in the *Readers Guide to Periodical Literature*.

71. "Report of the Agent General for India in the U.S.A. for the Month of February, 1944," L/P&S/12/4627, coll. 47, file 4, IOR. See also Bajpai's reports for August, September, and October 1943, ibid.

72. Amery to Linlithgow, August 5, 1943, Linlithgow Papers, 25: 213. Amery overruled Linlithgow on this matter.

73. Puckle to Wright, March 6, 1944, enclosed in Wright to North American Department, Foreign Office, March 16, 1944, FO 371, AN 1254/181/45, FOR.

74. The figure of three million comes from A. Ramaswami Mudaliar. See Venkataramani, *The Bengal Famine of 1943*, p. 10 n. 11. In 1944 Churchill admitted to Roosevelt that "at least 700,000 people" had perished. See

Churchill to Roosevelt, April 29, 1944, in Kimball, ed., *Churchill and Roosevelt*, 3:117.

75. *New York Times*, January 12, 1943, p. 6; March 30, 1943, p. 4; May 25, 1943, p. 4; August 22, 1943, p. 3.

76. *Newsweek*, October 4, 1943, p. 39. Walter Mackett concludes that "by October concern over the famine was very great." "Some Aspects," p. 397.

77. Venkataramani, *Bengal Famine*, pp. 1–39.

78. Phillips to Roosevelt, September 9, 1943, enclosed in Murray to Hull, September 10, 1943, 845.00/9–943.

79. Phillips Diary, October 20, 1943. Berle to Johnson, October 16, 1943, Berle Papers, box 38.

80. *Time*, October 18, 1943, pp. 32–33. Harold E. Fey, "Is India's Famine Political?" *Christian Century*, November 3, 1943, pp. 1261–62.

81. *The Nation*, November 6, 1943, p. 517. "Famine in India," *Life*, December 20, 1943, 38, 40–41.

82. *New Republic*, May 22, 1944, p. 698. See also Sydney D. Bailey, "Firpo's and Famine," *Christian Century*, May 10, 1944, p. 588–590; William Fisher, "The Bengal Famine," *Life*, November 22, 1943, pp. 16, 20, 28–29; *New York Times*, November 6, 1943, p. 12; Alzada Comstock, "Famine in Bengal," *Current History*, January 1944, pp. 42–46.

83. "Report of the Agent General for India for the Month of September, 1943"; "Report of the Agent General for India for the Month of October, 1943"; "Report of the Agent General for India for the Month of November, 1943"; "Report of the Agent General for India for the Month of December, 1943"; L/P&S/12/4627, coll. 47, file 4. Puckle to Michael Wright, March 6, 1944, in Wright to North American Department, Foreign Office, March 16, 1944, FO 371 AN 1254/181/45.

84. *Christian Century*, March 15, 1944, p. 325.

85. Fisher, "The Bengal Famine," p. 28. Sydney D. Bailey, "Firpo's and Famine," *Christian Century*, May 10, 1944, p. 590.

86. Wavell to Amery, February 9, 1944, Wavell Papers, Eur. D., 977/2, p. 12. Nehru, Prison Diary, December 17, [1943], SWJN 13:313.

87. Wavell to Amery, February 26, 1944, in Mansergh, ed., *Transfer of Power*, 4:762–63. Wavell to Amery, March 4, 1944, ibid., pp. 776–77.

88. Amery to Wavell, April 27, 1944, in ibid., pp. 933–34. Amery to Wavell, April 29, 1944, ibid., pp. 938–39. Moon, ed., *Wavell: The Viceroy's Journal*, p. 69. Entry for April 30, 1944.

89. Churchill to Roosevelt, April 29, 1944, in Kimball, ed., *Churchill and Roosevelt*, 3:117. Roosevelt to Churchill, June 1, 1944, ibid., p. 155. Venkataramani, *Bengal Famine*, pp. 67–68.

90. Amery to Wavell, June 2, 1944, in Mansergh, ed., *Transfer of Power*, 4:997. Amery to Wavell, June 8, 1944, in ibid., pp. 1012–13.

91. Bailey, "Firpo and Famine," p. 590.

92. H. F. C. Walsh to Campbell, June 6, 1944, FO 371 AN 2334/181/45, FOR.

93. Halifax to Foreign Office, September 1, 1942, L/P&S/12/2636, IOR. Telegram 400-SC, Linlithgow to Amery, October 3, 1942, ibid. Linlithgow to Amery, October 3, 1942, in Mansergh, ed., *Transfer of Power*, 3:82–83.

94. Moon, ed., *Wavell: The Viceroy's Journal*, pp. 13–15. Entries for July 31, and August 20, 1943. Amery to Wavell, October 21, 1943, Wavell Papers, p. 18, L/PO/472. Wavell to Amery, November 1, 1943, L/P&S/12/2636, IOR.

95. Caroe to Weightman, November 17, 1943, L/P&S/12/2636, IOR.

96. Minute by Peel, November 4, [1943], ibid. Minute by Monteath, November 8, 1943, ibid. Monteath felt that Halifax was yielding to pressure from an overly ambitious Bajpai.

97. Agatha Harrison to Horace Alexander, November 7, 1944, Alexander Papers. F. F. Turnbull and Monteath to Amery, November 13, 1943, L/P&S/12/2636, IOR. Amery, "Note by the Secretary of State," November 15, 1943, L/P&S/12/2636, IOR.

98. Wavell to Amery, November 8, 1943, L/P&S/12/2636, IOR. The references to Bajpai were omitted in the version of this letter printed in Mansergh, ed., *Transfer of Power*. Caroe to Amery, November 22, 1943, L/P&S/12/2636, IOR.

99. V. G. Lawford to Turnbull, February 24, 1944, and Turnbull to Lawford, February 28, 1944, L/P&S/12/2636, IOR. Opposition still remained entrenched (for example, minute by Patrick, March 1, 1944, ibid.), but on April 24, 1944, Eden and Amery placed a formal request before the War Cabinet to make Bajpai the Indian minister in Washington.

100. War Cabinet W. M. (44) 74th Conclusions, Minute 2, June 9, 1944, in Mansergh, ed., *Transfer of Power*, 4:1016–17.

101. Moon, ed., *Wavell: The Viceroy's Journal*, p. 76. Entry for June 23, 1944.

102. War Cabinet W. M. (44) 100th Conclusions, Minute 2, August 3, 1944, in Mansergh, ed., *Transfer of Power*, 4:1154–55. Halifax to Foreign Office, August 19, 1944, L/P&S/12/2636, IOR. Wavell to Amery, August 23, 1944, in Mansergh, ed., *Transfer of Power*, 4:1215.

103. "Christian Views on the Indian Deadlock," *Christian Century*, May 24, 1944, p. 638.

104. For example, *New Republic*, July 24, 1944, p. 93, and H. N. Brailsford, "What Hope for India?" *New Republic*, August 14, 1944, pp. 181–83.

105. Phillips Diary, May 5, 1942. Phillips to Murray, May 17, 1944, 845.00/5–1744.

106. Gandhi to Wavell, June 17, 1944, in Mansergh, ed., *Transfer of Power*, 4:1032. Churchill to Wavell, July 5, 1944, ibid., p. 1070.

107. Phillips Diary, July 22, 1944. Winant (for Phillips) to Hull, July 22, 1942, FRUS 1944, 5:237–38.

108. Drew Pearson, "Washington Merry-Go-Round," *Washington Post,* July 25, 1944, p. 6.

109. Stettinius to Winant (for Phillips), July 28, 1944, FRUS 1944, 5:240–41. Phillips Diary, July 30–31, 1944.

110. War Cabinet W. M. (44), 90th Conclusions, Minute 3, [August 1944], in Mansergh, ed., *Transfer of Power,* 4:1155.

111. Wavell to Gandhi, August 15, 1944, in Mansergh, ed., *Transfer of Power,* 4:1197–99. Wavell wanted to take the issue to the point of a collision with the home government, presumably involving his resignation. But Amery, who agreed that Churchill was bullheaded about India (he said privately that the Prime Minister hoped to avoid carrying out even those pledges already made to India), argued that he ought to take such drastic action only on a major policy issue. It might come to that in the future, he implied, but he implored the viceroy to accede to the War Cabinet's view. Amery to Wavell, August 16, 1944, Wavell Papers, L/PO/472. Amery to Wavell, August 14, 1944, in Mansergh, ed., *Transfer of Power,* 4:1196–97.

112. Wavell to Gandhi, August 15, 1944, in Mansergh, ed., *Transfer of Power,* 4:1197–99.

113. Wavell to Amery, August 23, 1944, in ibid., pp. 1213–14.

114. Extract of a letter from Puckle, August 16, 1944, FO 371 AN 3272/181/45, FOR. Roosevelt made very similar comments about the need to keep India, and Asia in general, loyal to the West. His comments almost echoed those of William Phillips on this point. See, for example, Roosevelt's comments to Stanley Hornbeck in November, 1944, in Louis, *Imperialism at Bay,* p. 425.

115. Murray to Phillips, August 17, 1944, 845.00/8–444.

116. Minute by J. C. Donnelly, August 18, [1944], FO 371 AN 3159/181/45, FOR.

117. Campbell to Eden, July 26, 1944, in Mansergh, ed., *Transfer of Power,* 4:1120. Hull, Memorandum of Conversation, July 25, 1944, 845.00/7–2544.

118. Campbell to Foreign Office, July 28, 1944, FO 371/38611 XC/A 04019, FOR.

119. Foreign Office to British Embassy, Washington, August 1, 1944, FO 371 AN 2894/181/45, FOR.

120. Stettinius, Memorandum of Conversation, August 8, 1944, FRUS 1944, 5:241. Campbell to Stettinius, August 8, 1944, ibid., pp. 241–42.

121. Stettinius to Hull, August 15, 1944, Roosevelt Papers, PSF: Departmental, box 94. Hull to Roosevelt, August 15, 1944, FRUS 1944, 5:242.

122. Campbell to Richard Law, August 14, 1944, FO 115, G 131/1 (piece 3637), FOR. Law to Campbell, August 24, 1944, ibid. Louis, *Imperialism at Bay,* pp. 225–28.

123. Halifax to Stettinius, August 25, 1944, FRUS 1944, 5:242–43.

124. Hull, Memorandum of Conversation, September 16, 1944, 845.00/9–1644. "Reminiscences of William Phillips," p. 157.

125. Halifax to Foreign Office, September 11, 1944, FO 371 AN 3487/181/45, FOR. Minute by Malcolm, September 13, 1944 on ibid.

126. Minute by Malcolm, September 8, 1944, FO 371 AN 3569/181/45, FOR.

127. Both the *New Republic* and the *Christian Century*, for example, felt that Phillips was being forced to resign. Mackett, "Some Aspects," p. 413.

128. Phillips Diary, August 11, 1944.

129. Drew Pearson, "Washington Merry-Go-Round," *Washington Post,* August 28, 1942, p. 2. What Eden had stated in a telegram to Halifax on August 1, 1944 was, "we have no wish to lose or embarrass Mr. Phillips but India is much more important." FO 371 AN 2894/181/45, FOR.

130. *Congressional Record,* Senate, August 28, 1944, vol. 90, pt. 6, p. 7336.

131. Eden to Halifax, August 30, 1944, in Mansergh, ed., *Transfer of Power,* 4:1231–32. Foreign Office to Halifax, August 30, 1944, L/P&S/12/4629, coll. 47, file 6, IOR. Halifax to Foreign Office, August 31, 1944, tel. 4698, FO 371/38612 45091, FOR. Halifax to Foreign Office, August 31, 1944, FO 371 AN 3345/181/45, FOR.

132. Halifax to Foreign Office, August 31, 1944, tel. 4698, FO 371/38612 45091, FOR.

133. Breckinridge Long, Memorandum, "Ambassador Phillips and the Pearson Leak," September 2, 1944, 845.00/9–244. On Bloom, see *New York Times,* September 2, 1944, p. 5.

134. Merrell to Hull, September 4, 1944, FRUS 1944, 5:247.

135. Halifax to Foreign Office, September 2, 1944, FO 371 AN 3362/181/45, FOR.

136. *New York Times,* September 6, 1944, p. 3. *Times* (London), September 6, 1944, p. 3. Minute by Butler, September 6, 1944, on Halifax to Foreign Office, September 4, 1944, FO 371 AN 3393/181/45, FOR.

137. Foreign Office to Halifax, September 5, 1944, FO 371 AN 3345/181/45, FOR.

138. Foreign Office to Halifax, September 7, 1944, L/P&S/12/4629, coll. 47, file 7, IOR. Untitled memorandum, n.d. [but probably September 7, 1944], FO 371 AN 3362/181/45, FOR.

139. Churchill to Halifax, September 15, 1944, L/P&S/12/4629, coll. 47, file 6, IOR. Minute by Peel (?), September 18, [1944] on ibid. See also Ryan, *Vision of Anglo-America,* pp. 35–36. The first suggestion that Churchill become involved came from Roland Peel, who minuted that if Halifax could get no satisfaction, it then became a matter for the Prime Minister. Peel, minute on Halifax to Foreign Office, September 8, 1944, (tel. 4878) FO 371 AN 3411/181/45, FOR.

140. A few days later Halifax did succeed in getting the *Washington Post* to publish an article, based on information that the ambassador supplied, that by implication refuted Phillips. In addition, the British Information Service claimed that it inspired a number of pro-British stories that appeared in

several important newspapers. Halifax to Foreign Office, September 22, 1944, Tel. 273, L/P&S/12/4629, IOR. Halifax to Foreign Office, September 22, 1944, Tel. 274, ibid. R. J. Cruikshank to Butler, September 22, 1944, FO 371 AN 3770/181/45, FOR.

141. On American cooperation, which involved George Merrell and General Sultan, see minute by R. R. Burnett, Jr., August 11, 1944, on Government of India, Home Department, Political (I) Section, 1944, "Decision to withhold in censorship all copies of the issue of August 1944 of the American magazine 'Asia and the Americas' . . . ," file 20/11/44, NAI.

142. Wavell to Amery, September 12, 1944, in Mansergh, ed., *Transfer of Power*, 5:31.

143. Newspaper clipping, "Cant about India Unmasked," *Statesman*, September 7, 1944, enclosed in Merrell to Hull, September 8, 1944, 845.00/9–844. The *Statesman* quoted the *Hindustan Standard*. The *Amrita Bazar Patrika* had a similar reaction to Phillips, as did the *Hindustan Times*. See ibid. and Merrell to Hull, September 11, 1944, 845.00/9–1144.

144. Bhola N. Pande to Sapru, December 6, 1944, Sapru Papers, microfilm reel S1/4.

145. Howard Donovan to Hull, September 11, 1944, 845.00/9–1144.

146. Wavell to Amery, August 23, 1944, in Mansergh, ed., *Transfer of Power*, 4:1217.

147. For example, *The Legislative Assembly Debates. Official Report. Vol. IV, 1944 (1st to 13th November 1944). Twenty-First Session of the Fifth Legislative Assembly 1944*, p. 63.

148. Wavell to Amery, October 1, 1944, L/P&S/12/4629, coll. 47, file 6, IOR. Wavell to Amery, October 3, 1944, in Mansergh, ed., *Transfer of Power*, 5:76. Wavell to Amery, October 8, 1944, L/P&S/4629, coll. 47, file 6, IOR.

149. Butler to Patrick, October 13, 1944, FO 371/38613, FOR. Somewhat contradictorily, Butler suggested that if the Government of India had to respond to questions in the assembly, it should give the briefest of answers, admit the authenticity of the telegram, and even circulate it if necessary. "Admitting that an old cat did get out the official bag is of much less news value than a litter of new kittens," Butler wrote. But it is clear from subsequent correspondence that neither the Foreign Office or the India Office wanted the authenticity of the Caroe telegram confirmed.

150. Amery to Wavell, October 19, 1944, FO 371/38613, FOR. Halifax to Foreign Office, October 22, 1944, FO 371 AN 4021/181/45, FOR. Wavell to Amery, October 24, 1944, FO 371 AN 4097/181/45, FOR.

151. Wavell to Amery, November 15, 1944, L/P&S/12/4629, coll. 47, file 6, IOR. Mansergh, ed., *Transfer of Power*, 4:1203–4.

152. Merrell to Hull, May 19, 1944, FRUS 1944, 5:234–35. Hull to Roosevelt, June 2, 1944, ibid., p. 235. Hull to Merrell, June 16, 1944, ibid., p. 236.

153. Merrell to Hull, July 10, 1944, 845.00/7–1044.

154. Donovan to Merrell, July 10, 1944, in Murray to Hull and Stettinius, August 15, 1944, 845.00/7–1044.

155. Venkataramani and Shrivastava, *Roosevelt, Gandhi, Churchill,* p. 186.

156. Louis, *Imperialism at Bay,* p. 356.

8 | Renewed American Interest in India

1. A detailed investigation of the leakages is Clymer, "Indian Nationalism and Anglo-American Relations in the Second World War."

2. Amery to Richard Law, November 1, 1944, and Law to Amery, November 21, 1944, Wavell Papers, L/PO/472.

3. For military developments in this and the following paragraphs I have relied primarily on Kirby, *The War Against Japan,* vols. 4 and 5.

4. Puckle to Patrick, April 25, 1945, FO 371/44561, FOR.

5. Hathaway, *Ambiguous Partnership,* pp. 70–101. Anderson, *The United States, Great Britain, and the Cold War,* pp. 1–51.

6. Anderson, *The United States, Great Britain, and the Cold War,* p. 1. Hathaway, *Ambiguous Partnership,* pp. 101–7.

7. Hess, *The United States Emergence as a Southeast Asian Power,* pp. 90–91.

8. Ibid., pp. 80–81; Louis, *Imperialism at Bay,* pp. 425, 437, 446. Macmillan quoted in Anderson, *The United States, Great Britain, and the Cold War,* p. 5.

9. Donovan to Stettinius, January 3, 1945, 845.00/1–345.

10. Ray L. Thurston, Memorandum for the Files, February 19, 1945, enclosed in Donovan to Stettinius, February 24, 1945, 845.00/2–2445.

11. For example, Clayton Lane to Stettinius, January 10, 1945, 845.00/1–1045. Lane to Stettinius, January 13, 1943, 845.00/1–1345. Howard Donovan stated, "I personally do not see how any solution can be arrived at so long as Gandhi and Jinnah are alive, especially Jinnah." Donovan to Stettinius, February 11, 1945, 845.00/2–1145.

12. Joseph Grew, statement to press conference, January 29, 1945, FRUS 1945, 6:29.

13. Merrell to Stettinius, February 26, 1945, 845.00/2–2645.

14. Roosevelt to Samuel Dickstein, March 5, 1945, Harry S. Truman Papers, PSF: India. Congressman Dickstein chaired the Committee on Immigration and Naturalization.

15. Clipping, "A Welcome Gesture," *Hindustan Times,* February 1, 1945, enclosed in Merrell to Stettinius, February 3, 1945, 845.00/2–345.

16. Amery, "Visit of Nehru's Sister and Nieces to U.S.A.," January 3, 1945, War Cabinet, India Committee, Paper I (45) 3, in Mansergh, ed., *Transfer of Power,* 5:356–57. In her memoirs, Pandit wrote that it was because of intervention by American authorities, including the President, that she was allowed to come to the United States. She traveled on an American Air Force airplane. See Pandit, *The Scope of Happiness,* pp. 186–90. British records do not mention any intervention, however.

17. *India Today*, 5 (February, 1945).

18. Clipping, *Hindustan Times*, February 1, 1945, in Merrell to Stettinius, February 3, 1945, 845.00/2–345.

19. Hathaway, *Ambiguous Partnership*, pp. 117–26.

20. Ibid., pp. 124–25.

21. See, for example, Gardner, *Approaching Vietnam*, p. 50.

22. Louis, *Imperialism at Bay*, pp. 448, 459–64.

23. Samuel I. Rosenman, *Working with Roosevelt* (London: Rupert Hart-Davis, 1952), pp. 478–80.

24. Office Memorandum (from NEA), March 6, 1945, 845.00/3–645. Merrell to Stettinius, March 21, 1945, New Delhi Post Records, file 800-Political 1945, NRC.

25. Amery to Wavell, January 4, 1945, Wavell Papers, Weekly letters, L/PO/473. Amery, "The Indian Problem," January 5, 1945, War Cabinet, India Committee. I (45) 4, in Mansergh, ed., *Transfer of Power*, 5:365–76.

26. Amery's comments to the War Cabinet, India Committee, I (45) 8th Meeting, February 28, 1945, in Mansergh, ed., *Transfer of Power*, 5:620. Amery, "The Indian Problem," ibid., pp. 365–76.

27. The War Cabinet's India Committee discussed Amery's proposal at considerable length on February 28, at which time the majority opposed Amery's ideas. At the end of the meeting, Amery "said that he recognized that the sense of the Committee was against him, though he remained of the opinion that his scheme was right and practicable and would bide his time." War Cabinet, India Committee, I (45) 8th Meeting, February 28, 1945, ibid., p. 627.

28. Merrell to Stettinius, March 22, 1945, 845.00/3–2245; Merrell to Stettinius, March 24, 1945, 845.00/3–2445. Winant to Stettinius, March 28, 1945, 845.00/3–2845.

29. Wavell to Amery, March 15, 1945, in Mansergh, ed., *Transfer of Power*, 5:696.

30. Acheson to Merrell, April 4, 1945, 845.00/4–445. Merrell to Stettinius, April 7, 1945, 845.00/4–745.

31. Donovan to Stettinius, April 11, 1945, 845.00/4–1145. There are two telegrams of the same date on the same topic. Puckle to Patrick, May 31, 1946, FO 371 AN 1839/63/45.

32. Bernard M. Baruch, *Baruch: The Public Years* (New York: Holt, Rinehart and Winston, 1960), p. 343. When Baruch brought up the President's concern about Hong Kong, he received no response. "His silence was more eloquent than anything he might have said," thought Baruch, who actually agreed with Churchill on this point.

33. Charles Taussig, Memorandum of Conversation, March 15, 1945, FRUS 1945, 1:124.

34. Patrick Hurley to Truman, May 29, 1945, Truman Papers, Top Secret File, 1945, April-May. Hurley's cable caused much discussion in the state

department. See Archibald MacLeish's comments, June 4, 1945, Confidential U.S. State Department Central Files, Indochina: Internal Affairs, 1941–1945, 851G.01/6–445.

35. *India Today*, 5 (January 1945). *India Today* was the India League of America's publication. Copies are found in the Government of India, Home Department, Political (I) Section, 1945, "Issue by the India League of America of a monthly entitled 'India Today' and question of countering the propaganda contained therein," file 48/1/45, NAI.

36. Government of India, External Affairs Department, Far Eastern Branch, 1945, "Round up of American Press Comment on India in Washington," file 249-E.P./45, NAI. Government of India, External Affairs Department, External Publicity Branch, "American Opinion on International Issues," file 343-E.P./45, NAI. Foreign Office Document, [ca. February 28, 1945], FO 371 AN 708/24/45, FOR.

37. Eleanor Roosevelt to Stettinius, April 4, 1945, 845.00/4–445.

38. LaFeber, "Roosevelt, Churchill, and Indochina."

39. Anderson, *The United States, Great Britain, and the Cold War*, pp. 40–51.

40. Thorne, *Allies of a Kind*, p. 642.

41. Stettinius to Eleanor Roosevelt, April 7, 1945, 845.00/4–445.

42. Amery to Wavell, February 7, 1945, Wavell Papers, Weekly Letters, L/PO/473. Mackett, "Some Aspects," p. 426. Puckle to Patrick, May 31, 1946, FO 371 AN 1839/63/45, FOR. Government of India, External Affairs Department, Far Eastern Branch, 1954, "Round up of American Press Comment on India in Washington," file 249-E.P./45, NAI.

43. Harrison to Alexander, July 19, 1945, Alexander Papers.

44. "Report of the Agent General for India in the United States of America for the quarter Ending 31st March, 1945," FO 371 AN 1372/24/45, FOR.

45. "Report of the Agent General for India in the U.S.A. for the Quarter Ending 30th June, 1945," FO 371 AN 2448/24/45, FOR.

46. Nehru to Pandit, July 26, 1945, SWJN, 14:62. Mehta to Pandit Goving Ballabh Pant, July 30, 1945, Nehru Papers, vol. 47.

47. Government of India, External Affairs Department, Far Eastern Branch, 1945, "Question in the L/A by Sardar Mangal Singh regarding press interview given by Mr. G. L. Mehta . . . concerning money spent on propaganda in U.S.A. against Indian National Movement. . . ," file 720 (20)-F.E./45, NAI.

48. See, for example, Government of India, Home Department, Political (I) Section, 1945, "Issue by the India League of America of a monthly entitled, 'India Today' and question of countering the propaganda contained therein" (dropped), file 48/1/45, NAI.

49. Government of India, External Affairs Department, External Publicity Branch, 1945, "Report on Col. Himatsinhji's Publicity work in the U.S.A.," file 352-E.P./45, NAI. Note by D. M. Ormerod, n.d., ibid.

50. Mackett, "Some Aspects," pp. 422–25.

51. Hathaway, *Ambiguous Partnership*, pp. 133, 151.

52. Ibid., pp. 167, 224.

53. Quoted in Ryan, *The Vision of Anglo-America*, p. 36. See also Thorne, *Allies of a Kind*, p. 595.

54. Hathaway, *Ambiguous Partnership*, pp. 202–3.

55. See, for example, Herring, "The Truman Administration and the Restoration of French Sovereignty in Indochina;" Hess, *The United States' Emergence as a Southeast Asian Power*, pp. 151–53; Thorne, *Allies of a Kind*, pp. 631–32; Herring, *America's Longest War*, p. 8.

56. McMahon, *Colonialism and Cold War*, p. 73.

57. "Report of the Agent General for India in the U.S.A. for the Quarter Ending 31st March, 1945," FO 371 AN 1372/24/45, FOR.

58. Merrell to Stettinius, May 15, 1945, New Delhi Post Records, 800-Political-1945, NRC. Joseph E. Davies to Truman, June 12, 1943, FRUS: The Conference of Berlin (The Potsdam Conference) 1945, 1:69.

59. "Report of the Agent General for India in the U.S.A. for the Quarter Ending 30th September, 1945," FO 371 AN 770/63/45, FOR.

60. Donovan to Stettinius, April 11, 1945, 845.00/4–1145. There are two telegrams of the same date on the same topic.

61. Phillips, Memorandum, April 19, 1945, FRUS 1945, 6:249–50.

62. Grew to Stettinius, April 24, 1945, ibid., pp. 250–51. Stettinius to Grew, April 28, 1944, ibid., p. 251. Grew to Winant, May 17, 1945, ibid., pp. 251–52.

63. Merrell to Stettinius, April 30, 1945, 845.00/4–3045. Raymond A. Hare to Stettinius, May 19, 1945, 845.00/5–1945.

64. Grew to Merrell, June 8, 1945, New Delhi Post Records, 800-political-1945, box 1431, NRC.

65. *India: Statement of the Policy of His Majesty's Government made by the Secretary of State for India on June 14th, 1945* (London: His Majesty's Stationery Office, 1945). Hess, *America Encounters India*, pp. 160–61.

66. Berry to Loy Henderson, June 19, 1945, 845.00/6–1945.

67. "Another Chance in India," *Nation*, June 23, 1945, p. 683. Mackett, "Some Aspects," pp. 428–29.

68. "Report of the Agent General for India in the U.S.A. for the Quarter ending 30th June, 1945," L/P&S/12/4627, coll. 47, file 4, IOR. Government of India, External Affairs Department, External Publicity Branch, "American Opinion on International Issues," 16–July 30, 1945, file 343-E.P./45, NAI.

69. Nehru to Pandit, June 26, 1945, Nehru Papers, part 1, vol. 78. Donovan to Stettinius, June 16, 1945, 845.00/6–1645. (Three telegrams, same date.)

70. Grew to Merrell, June 16, 1945, 845.00/6–1645. Merrell to Stettinius, June 23, 1945 and June 19, 1945, 800-Political-1945, New Delhi Post Records, box 1431, NRC.

71. Berry to Henderson, June 27, 1945, 845.00/6–2745.

72. Merrell to Stettinius, July 13, 1945, 845.00/7–1345.

73. Grew to Merrell, June 27, 1945, 845.00/6–2645. Byrnes to Merrell, July 4, 1945, 845.00/7–445.

74. In an early and important study of the transfer of power, E. W. R. Lumby observed that, although the Congress was still officially banned and its leaders had only recently been released from long prison stays, the Congress' "attitude was nevertheless moderate and free from bitterness." Lumby, *Transfer of Power*, p. 53. The moderation of Congress was a significant factor in ultimate American support for the nationalists.

75. Berry to Henderson and George V. Allen, July 10, 1945, 845.00/7–1045.

76. Winant to Stettinius, July 13, 1945, 845.00/7–1345. Foreign Office to British Embassy, Washington, July 13, 1945, FO 371 AN 2211/24/45, FOR.

77. Hare to Stettinius, July 14, 1945, 845.00/7–1445.

78. Merrell to Stettinius, July 15, 1945, 845.00/7–1545.

79. Berry to Henderson and Allen, January 8, 1946, 845.00/1–846.

80. Merrell to Stettinius, July 27, 1945, 845.00/7–2745. Merrell to Stettinius, August 8, 1945, 845.00/8–845.

81. Mackett, "Some Aspects," p. 431.

82. Government of India, External Affairs Department, External Publicity Branch, "American Opinion on International Issues," 1–July 15, 1945, file 343-E.P./45, NAI. "Report of the Agent General for India in the U.S.A. for the quarter ending 30th September, 1945," FO 371 AN 770/63/45, FOR. Several months later in a thoughtful review of American opinion Puckle concluded that the collapse of the Simla conference made Americans more aware of Indian complexities. Puckle to Patrick, May 31, 1946, FO 371 AN 1839/63/45, FOR.

83. Roy E. B. Bower to Stettinius, April 28, 1945, 845.00/4–2845. Bower to Stettinius, September 22, 1945, 845.00/9–2245. Bower to Byrnes, November 14, 1945, 845.00/11–1445. Bower to Stettinius, April 28, 1945, 845.00/4–2845. Bower to Stettinius, September 22, 1945, 845.00/9–2245.

84. Bower to Stettinius, April 28, 1945, 845.00/4–2845. Bower to Stettinius, July 5, 1945, 845.00/7–545. Bower to Stettinius, September 22, 1945, 845.00/9–2245.

85. Bower to Stettinius, September 22, 1945, 845.00/9–2245.

86. George D. LaMont to Stettinius, September 22, 1945, 845.00/7–2645. LaMont's interview with Kripalani, included in Donovan to Stettinius, August 11, 1945, 845.00/8–1145.

87. Donovan to Stettinius, February 11, 1945, 845.00/2–1145.

88. Donovan to Stettinius, April 12, 1945, 845.00/4–1245.

89. Donovan to Stettinius, June 16, 1945, 845.00/6–1645. Donovan to Stettinius, August 30, 1945, 845.00/8–3045.

90. Donovan to Byrnes, August 29, 1945, 845.00/8–2945. Donovan to

Byrnes, September 9, 1945, 845.00/9–945. Donovan to Byrnes, October 1, 1945, 845.00/10–145.

91. Government of India, External Affairs Department, General Branch, 1945, "Appointment of the Honourable George R. Merrel [*sic*] as Commissioner of the U.S.A. to India," file 50-G/45 (secret), NAI.

92. Merrell to Stettinius, July 13, 1945, 845.00/7–1345.

93. Grew to Merrell, January 31, 1945, FRUS 1945, 6:256–57. Wavell to Amery, January 23, 1945, Wavell Papers, Weekly Letters, L/PO/473. Minute by Sir Cecil Kisch, February 14, [1945] on "Extract from Private and Secret Letter from Lord Wavell to Mr. Amery, Dated 23rd January, 1945," L/P&S/12/2639, IOR.

94. Minute by Monteath, February 15, [1945] on "Extract from Private and Secret Letter from Lord Wavell to Mr. Amery, Date 23rd January, 1945," L/P&S/12/2639, IOR. Merrell to Stettinius, February 8, 1945, FRUS 1945, 6:258.

95. Government of India, External Affairs Department, to Amery, May 15, 1945, FO 371 AN 1601/24/45, FOR. Government of India, External Affairs Department, to Amery, June 4, 1945, FO 371 AN 1773/24/45, FOR.

96. Fieldhouse, "The Labour Government and the Empire-Commonwealth, 1945–1951," pp. 85–86.

97. Moon, ed. *Wavell: The Viceroy's Journal*, pp. 165, 167–68 (entries for August 26 and 31, 1945). Government of India, Home Department, Political (I) Section, 1945, "Supply of Newspaper Cutting," file 100/45, NAI.

98. "Extract from Note of Discussion Between Lord Wavell, the Secretary of State and Mr. Arthur Henderson on 27th August [1945]," L/P&S/12/2639, IOR. Arthur Henderson to Pethick-Lawrence, September 3, 1945, ibid. For the objections of India Office bureaucrats, see Notes by Monteath and others, September 1, 1945, ibid.

99. Wavell to Pethick-Lawrence, September 23, 1945, in Mansergh, ed., *Transfer of Power*, 6:295–96. Pethick-Lawrence, "Indian Diplomatic Representation in Washington," Cabinet Paper C.P. (45) 147, ibid., pp. 215–17.

100. Halifax to Bevin, October 29, 1945, L/P&S/12/2639, IOR. Byrnes to Halifax, November 7, 1945, FRUS 1945, 6:263.

101. Green H. Hackworth to Henderson, November 13, 1945, FRUS 1945, 6:265–67.

102. Halifax to Bevin, November 17, 1945, FO 371 AN 3518/24/45.

103. Halifax to Bevin, December 5, 1945, FO 371 AN 3709/24/45. Acheson to Merrell, January 14, 1946, FRUS 1946, 5:78.

104. Henderson, Memorandum of Conversation with Bajpai, Henderson, and Berry, November 8, 1945, FRUS 1945, 6:263–65.

105. Bevin to Halifax, December 31, 1945, FO 371 AN 3709/24/45, FOR. Halifax to Bevin, January 12, 1946, FO 371 AN 127/63/G45, FOR.

106. Government of India, External Affairs Department, to Pethick-

Lawrence, January 25, 1946, L/P&S/12/2639, IOR. Eion Pelley Donaldson to Berkeley Gage, January 29, 1946, ibid.

107. Aide Memoire, Government of India, External Affairs Department, March 14, 1946, ibid. Actually, the India Office and the Foreign Office thought the Americans had made a good case for opening a consular section in New Delhi and suspected that the Americans' refusal to upgrade Bajpai's status was in retaliation for the Government of India's refusal to allow the Americans to open a consular section. See Donaldson to Hugh Weightman, April 12, 1946, in Government of India, External Affairs Department, General Branch, 1946, "Aide Memoire from the United States Mission regarding the establishment of a consular section in the Mission at New Delhi," file 1(6)-G/46, NAI.

108. Clipping, "Annexationist Policy?" *Hindustan Times*, April 12, 1945, in Merrell to Stettinius, April 12, 1945, 845.00/4–1245. Clipping, "Salesmen of Life and Liberty!" *Blitz* [Bombay], April 28, 1945, in LaMont to Stettinius, May 2, 1945, 845.00/5–245.

109. Merrell to Stettinius, August 21, 1945, 845.00//8–2145.

110. Jinnah, quoted in Donovan to Byrnes, October 13, 1945, 845.00/10–1345. Clipping, "Nehru Warns Against New Crisis in India," *Hindustan Times*, October 29, 1945, enclosed in Block to Ferdinand Kuhn, Jr., October 29, 1945, 845.00/10–2945.

111. James F. Byrnes to Matthew J. Connelly, October 10, 1945, 845.00//10/1545. Connelly was a Presidential secretary.

112. Clipping, "Truman Deplores Inter-Allied Differences," *Hindustan Times*, October 29, 1945, in Block to Kuhn, Jr., October 29, 1945, 845.00/10–2945.

113. Donovan to Byrnes, January 18, 1946, 845.00/1–1846. Clipping, "Nehru Warns Against New Crisis in India," *Hindustan Times*, October 29, 1945, enclosed in Block to Kuhn, 845.00/10–2945.

114. Clipping, "Nehru Warns Against New Crisis in India." For a discussion of Nehru's complicated views of the United States, see Clymer, "Jawaharlal Nehru and the United States."

115. Nehru, Presidential address to the All India States People's Conference, Udaipur, December 30, 1945, SWJN, 14:407–8. Donovan to Byrnes, January 2, 1946, 845.00/1–246. Donovan to Byrnes, January 4, 1946, 845.00/1–446.

116. Nehru, interview given to Alice Thorner in Delhi, January 18, 1946, published in *The Nation*, March 2, 1946, in SWJN, 15:652.

9 | To Independence

1. Gaddis, *Strategies of Containment*, pp. 55–88.
2. Yergin, *Shattered Peace*, p. 220.

3. Leffler, "The American Conception of National Security and the Beginnings of the Cold War, 1945–48," pp. 349–52. Stoler, "From Continentalism to Globalism," pp. 303–21 (quotation on p. 303).

4. Hathaway, *Ambiguous Partnership*, p. 273. McMahon, "United States Cold War Strategy in South Asia," p. 815.

5. Anderson, *The United States, Great Britain, and the Cold War*, p. 131. Hathaway, *Ambiguous Partnership*, pp. 244–46. Leffler, "The American Conception of National Security," p. 353.

6. Hathaway, *Ambiguous Partnership*, pp. 307, 380n39. Regarding Henderson, the words quoted are Hathaway's summarizing his personal conversation with Henderson.

7. Pethick-Lawrence to Wavell, December 14, 1945, in Mansergh, ed., *Transfer of Power*, 6:644. In April, 1946, in a meeting of the Cabinet Mission to India, Secretary of State for India Pethick-Lawrence "referred to the question of the American desire to secure air bases in India. It was felt that this was a request which must be turned down unless it could be arranged under U.N.O. regional security arrangements." Record of Meeting of Cabinet Delegation and Field Marshall Viscount Wavell on Monday, April 15, 1946, in Mansergh, ed., *Transfer of Power*, 7:266. Leffler, "The American Conception of National Security," p. 353. See also Leffler, *A Preponderance of Power*, pp. 55–59.

8. Lampton Berry, "India" (manuscript), March 27, 1946, 845.00/5–2746. Although dated March 27, 1946, this document is filed as May 27.

9. Fieldhouse, "The Labour Governments and the Empire-Commonwealth," pp. 89–95. Pethick-Lawrence to Wavell, December 14, 1945, in Mansergh, ed., *Transfer of Power*, 6:644.

10. Hathaway, *Ambiguous Partnership*, p. 255.

11. Ibid., pp. 235, 241. Anderson, *The United States, Great Britain, and the Cold War*, pp. 114, 154. Secretary of Commerce Henry A. Wallace also criticized British imperialism.

12. Iftikar H. Malik, for example, seems to me to overemphasize the "fear of communist expansion in Asia" in explaining American interest in Indian developments in 1946. *US-South Asian Relations, 1940–47*, p. 205.

13. The document itself was burned in October 1946, but some of its content can be discerned from George Merrell's lengthy analysis of it. See Byrnes to Merrell, February 27, 1946, and Merrell to Byrnes, March 26, 1946, New Delhi Post Records, 800-Policy Statement re India, box 1432, NRC.

14. Berry, "India."

15. Unterberger, "American Views of Mohammed Ali Jinnah and the Pakistan Liberation Movement," pp. 313–36.

16. Berry, "India."

17. Donovan to Byrnes, January 6, 1946, 845.00/1–646. Donovan to Byrnes, January 9, 1946, 845.00/1–946. For example, the *Bombay Chronicle*

thought that a recent treaty between Thailand and Britain indicated that Thailand was now a British protectorate "with America a nominal partner." In fact, the United States and the British were seriously at odds over Thailand. The Thai-British treaty of January 1, 1946, was significantly more moderate as a result of American actions. See Hess, *The United States' Emergence as a Southeast Asian Power*, pp. 252–56.

18. Donovan to Byrnes, January 18, 1946, 845.00/1–1846. Donovan to Byrnes, February 3, 1946, 846.00/2–346.

19. Donovan to Byrnes, February 14, 1946, 845.00/2–1446. Donovan to Byrnes, February 22, 1946, 845.00/2–2246. Donovan to Byrnes, February 24, 1946, 845.00/2–2446. Dispatch 2632, Donovan to Byrnes, February 27, 1946, 845.00/2–2746.

20. Donovan to Byrnes, February 23, 1946, 845.00/2–2346.

21. American consulate general to Byrnes, February 27, 1946, 845.00/2–2746. Note by R. R. Burnett, February 21, 1946, in Government of India, External Affairs Department, Far Eastern Branch, 1946, "Burning of U. S. Flag and attack on American Sergeant by R. I. N. Ratings in Bombay," file 22-F.E./46, NAI. Donovan to Byrnes, February 27, 1946, 845.00/2–2746. Merrell to Byrnes, March 6, 1946, 845.00/3–646.

22. Dispatch 2701, Donovan to Byrnes, April 9, 1946, 845.00/4–946. About the time this incident was closed, another flag incident occurred. An intoxicated British soldier attempted to lower the flag at the USIS office. He was stopped and British authorities notified. Donovan received prompt apologies from the army but only an acknowledgement from the Political and Services Department. "I have no hesitancy in stating that the stupidity, incompetence, and rudeness of the Political and Services Department are by-words among all consuls in Bombay," he reported. Dispatch 2698, Donovan to Byrnes, April 9, 1946, 845.00/4–946.

23. J. J. Singh to Robert P. Patterson, January 7, 1946, All India Congress Committee Papers, file O.S. 3, 1946.

24. Puckle to Patrick, May 31, 1946, FO 371 AN 1839/63/45. Jerry Voorhis to Truman, February 20, 1946, Truman Papers, file OF 48H. Truman replied to Voorhis that he could not bring the troops home because there were billions of dollars in American property in India that could not be abandoned.

25. Dispatch 2632, Donovan to Byrnes, February 27, 1946, 845.00/2–2746. Dispatch 2631, Donovan to Byrnes, February 27, 1946, 845.00/2–2746.

26. Celler's comment appeared in the *Indian Express* [Madras], February 23, 1946; the official was R. R. Burnett; both in Government of India, External Affairs Department, Far Eastern Branch, 1946, "Burning of U.S. Flag and attack on American Sergeant by R. I. N. Ratings in Bombay," file 22-F.E./46, NAI.

27. Donovan to Byrnes, February 26, 1946, 845.00/2–2646. Donovan to

Byrnes, February 27, 1946, 845.00/2–2746. He also thought some of the more extreme Congress politicians were culpable but acknowledged that several important Congress leaders, including Gandhi and Nehru, strongly condemned the violence.

28. Byrnes to Merrell, February 26, 1946, New Delhi Post Records, 800-C Mission Political Telegrams (1946) Confidential, NRC.

29. Dispatch 2631, Donovan to Byrnes, February 27, 1946, 845.00/2–2746. Donovan to Byrnes, February 28, 1946, 845.00/2–2846.

30. Merrell to Byrnes, March 1, 1946, 845.00/3–146. Merrell to Byrnes, March 1, 1946, New Delhi Post Records, 800-C Mission Political Telegrams (1946) Confidential, NRC. See also Merrell to Byrnes, February 28, 1946, ibid.

31. Bower to Byrnes, February 27, 1946, 845.00/2–2746.

32. Acheson to Bower, March 29, 1946, 845.00/32–2746. Berry to Henderson, April 4, 1946, 845.00/4–446.

33. R. E. M. Murphy to Henderson, April 8, 1946, 845.00/4–846.

34. Gopal, *Nehru*, 1:312. For a British denial that the riots had moved the political process forward, see Winant to Byrnes, February 21, 1946, FRUS 1946, 5:79.

35. Majumdar, *Struggle for Freedom*, pp. 721–26.

36. Pearl Buck et. al. to Clement Attlee, n.d., All India Congress Committee Papers, file 46, 1946. Mackett, "Some Aspects," p. 446.

37. Winant to Byrnes, February 21, 1946, FRUS 1946, 5:80. Waldemar J. Gallman to Byrnes, February 28, 1946, ibid., 5:83–84.

38. Majumdar, *Struggle for Freedom*, pp. 727–28.

39. Emma Wold, "American Interest in India," *Bombay Chronicle*, May 1, 1946, in Donovan to Byrnes, May 1, 1946, 845.00/5–146. "Labor Offers Freedom to Peoples of India," *Christian Century*, March 27, 1946, p. 388; "Attlee Makes a Promise," *New Republic*, March 25, 1946, pp. 398–99. For other press reaction to Attlee's speech, see Mackett, "Some Aspects," pp. 447–48.

40. Berry, "India." Halifax to Bevin, March 23, 1946, L/P&S/12/1111, IOR.

41. See, for example, Berry, "India."

42. Halifax to Bevin, March 22, 1946, FO 371 AN 846/63/45, FOR. Halifax to Bevin, March 24, 1946, ibid.

43. Attlee, Prime Minister's Personal Minute, March 25, 1946, FO 371 AN 847/63/G45, FOR.

44. Halifax to Bevin, April 5, 1946, FO 371 AN 1066/63/G45, FOR.

45. My account of the Cabinet Mission and its aftermath relies primarily on Majumdar, *Struggle for Freedom*, pp. 728–50.

46. Merrell to Byrnes, April 15, 1946, New Delhi Post Records, 800—Cabinet Mission, NRC.

47. Halifax to Bevin, May 10, 1946, L/P&S/12/1112, IOR.

48. Some historians see a Cold War connection here. They note that the

British military leaders were pleased with the Cabinet Mission plan because it provided for "a large group of provinces in the north-west which would be logistically defensible in a war with the Soviet Union, could be a base for attack on Siberia if necessary and yet would be linked with the industrial and economic heartland of the rest of India." Gupta, "Imperialism and the Labour Government of 1945–51," p. 103.

49. Lumby, *Transfer of Power*, p. 81.

50. Hare to Byrnes, May 23, 1946, 845.00/5–2346.

51. Mackett, "Some Aspects," pp. 449–50.

52. Government of India, Home Department, Political (I) Section, 1946, "Inquiry by the Secretary of State for India about the ban on Louis Fischer's book *Empire*," file 41/3/46. NAI. Only six books in all remained on the blacklist as of April 5, including Katherine Mayo's *The Face of Mother India*.

53. Fischer to Gandhi, June 8, 1946, enclosed in Merrell to Gandhi, June 8, 1946, New Delhi Post Records, 800—Gandhi, Mahatma; Fischer, Louis; NRC.

54. Joseph E. Davies to Attlee, May 17, 1946, FO 371 AN 1860/63/45, FOR. Halifax to Bevin, May 18, 1946, FO 371 AN 1570/63/45, FOR. Circular telegram, Acheson to certain American diplomatic and consular officers, May 17, 1946, 845.00/5–1756.

55. Balfour to Bevin, May 26, 1946, FO 371 AN 1635/63/45, FOR. Cabinet Mission to India Office, June 2, 1946, FO 371 AN 1797/63/45, FOR.

56. Lord Inverchapel to Bevin, June 3, 1946, FO 371 AN 1738/63/45, FOR. Minute, P. Mason, June 4, 1946, on ibid. Inverchapel had replaced Halifax as British ambassador to the United States.

57. Merrell to Byrnes, April 15, 1946, New Delhi Post Records, 800—Cabinet Mission, NRC.

58. Merrell to Byrnes, May 2, 1946, New Delhi Post Records, 800—Press Comment re Palestine Question, NRC. Congress spokespersons and newspapers were also highly critical of the Anglo-American Commission's recommendations, as were pro-British newspapers. The commission's recommendations were not carried out, although Truman continued publicly to urge the admission of 100,000 Jews to Palestine. See Hathaway, *Ambiguous Partnership*, pp. 277–80.

59. Inverchapel to Bevin, June 3, 1946, FO 371 AN 1738/63/45, FOR. Minute, P. Mason, June 4, 1946, on ibid.

60. Mackett, "Some Aspects," pp. 451–52.

61. Donovan to Byrnes, June 25, 1946, and Merrell to Byrnes, June 17, 1946, New Delhi Post Records, 800—Cabinet Mission (1946), box 1431, NRC.

62. Mackett, "Some Aspects," p. 453. Dispatch 2911, Donovan to Byrnes, July 5, 1946, 845.00/7–546.

63. Puckle to Joyce, July 29, 1946, in Mansergh, ed., *Transfer of Power*, 8:142–43.

64. Majumdar, *Struggle for Freedom*, pp. 742–44. Gopal also cites important critics, including Maulana Azad and Vallabhbhai Patel, but defends Nehru's actions. Gopal, *Nehru*, 1:327–28. A. G. Noorani contends that the argument that the Muslim League later withdrew its acceptance of the Cabinet Mission's plan because of Nehru's remarks is a "legend." "The Cabinet Mission and its Aftermath," p. 109. B. R. Nanda insists that Nehru's comments have been taken out of context and badly misunderstood. Nehru, he argues, "had no intention to repudiate the framework of the cabinet mission plan." "Nehru, the Indian National Congress and the Partition of India 1935–1947," pp. 178–80.

65. Samuel J. Fletcher to Byrnes, August 22, 1946, 845.00/8–2246.

66. Majumdar, *Struggle for Freedom*, pp. 749–50. Gopal, *Nehru*, 1:330. In an early account, E. W. R. Lumby argues that Jinnah did not intend to provoke violence. Lumby, *Transfer of Power*, p. 111.

67. State Department press release, August 27, 1946, 845.00/8–2746. Technically the new "government" was still the viceroy's Executive Council. However, popularly it was referred to as the Cabinet, with Nehru, technically Vice-President of the Council, being the Prime Minister. The Muslim League, however, objected to these informal designations.

68. Merrell to Byrnes, August 28, 1946, 845.00/8–2846. Merrell to Byrnes, September 18, 1946, New Delhi Post Records, 800-C Mission Political Telegrams (1946), NRC. Other newspapers did carry the State Department's announcement.

69. Merrell to Byrnes, October 8, 1946, New Delhi Post Records, 800—Palestine, box 1432, NRC. Merrell to Byrnes, October 17, 1946, ibid. Henderson, Memorandum of Conversation, November 14, 1946, 845.00/11–1446.

70. Merrell to Byrnes, September 11, 1946, 845.00/9–1146.

71. Pethick-Lawrence to Government of India, External Affairs Department, September 7, 1946, L/P&S/12/2639, IOR. On September 3, 1946, Truman had approved Acheson's recommendation of August 30 to exchange ambassadors with India if India wanted the exchange. Truman's notation on Acheson to Truman, August 30, 1946, FRUS 1946, 5:92–93.

72. Inverchapel to Bevin, September 8, 1946, L/P&S/12/2639, IOR. Note on ibid. by Patrick, September 10, 1946. Monteath, minute, September 14, 1946, on Inverchapel to Bevin, September 10, 1946, ibid. Wavell to Pethick-Lawrence, September 17, 1946, in Mansergh, ed., *Transfer of Power*, 8:536.

73. Pethick-Lawrence to Wavell, September 20, 1946, in Mansergh, ed., *Transfer of Power*, 8:559–60. Bajpai to Government of India, External Affairs Department, October 22, 1946, L/P&S/12/2639, IOR. Inverchapel to Bevin, October 26, 1946, L/P&S/12/1112, IOR.

74. LaMont to Byrnes, October 2, 1946, 845.00/10–246. Gandhi, in *Harijan*, September 29, 1946, in Donovan to Byrnes, September 30, 1946,

845.00/9–3046. Fraser, "Understanding American Policy Towards the Decolonization of European Empires," pp. 110–11.

75. Gandhi, in *Harijan*, September 29, 1946, in Donovan to Byrnes, September 30, 1946, 845.00/9–3046. Nehru, editorial in *National Herald*, July 2, 1946, in SWJN 15:543–44.

76. Merrell to Byrnes, October 10, 1946, New Delhi Post Records, 800—Palestine, box 1432, NRC. T. Eliot Weil to Byrnes, November 21, 1946, ibid., 800—India Policy Statement Comment. Acheson to Merrell, November 5, 1946, ibid., box 1431.

77. Acheson to Merrell, November 25, 1946, 845.00/11–2346.

78. Owen Jones of the India Office, cited in a Minute by B. E. F. Gage of the Foreign Office, December 6, 1946, FO 371 AN 3673/63/45, FOR. Inverchapel to Bevin, December 7, 1946, in Mansergh, ed., *Transfer of Power*, 9:311.

79. Reuters dispatch 1522, January 17, 1947, L/P&S/12/2639, IOR. Reuters dispatch 0619, February 27, 1947, ibid. Acheson to Truman, December 3, 1946, Truman Papers, OF 48H. Background information on Asaf Ali comes from Information Department, Indian Office, "Biographical Notes of Members of the New Government," August 24, 1946, IOR, and "Extract from Despatch No. 4. dated 14th December 1946. From the Office of the High Commissioner for the United Kingdom, 6 Albuquerque Road, New Delhi," L/P&S/12/2639, IOR.

80. Mackett, "Some Aspects," pp. 455–56.

81. Gopal, *Nehru*, 1:335. Nanda, "Nehru and the Partition of India," p. 185.

82. T. Eliot Weil, "Memorandum for General Brownell," November 15, 1946, New Delhi Post Records, box 1432, NRC.

83. Ibid.

84. The American plan is summarized in Bevin to Attlee and Pethick-Lawrence, November 29, 1946, in Mansergh, ed., *Transfer of Power*, 9:213–15. The quotation is from Acheson to Gallman, November 30, 1946, FRUS 1946, 5:97.

85. Pethick-Lawrence to Bevin, November 30, 1946, in Mansergh, ed., *Transfer of Power*, 9:232.

86. Acheson, statement to press conference, December 3, 1946, in Acheson to American Embassy, London, December 3, 1946, 845.00/12–246. Gallman to Byrnes, December 4, 1946, 845.00/12–446.

87. Gallman to Byrnes, December 4, 1946, 845.00/12–446. Gallman to Byrnes, December 5, 1946, New Delhi Post Records, 800-C Mission Political Telegrams, 1946, NRC.

88. Minutes on Inverchapel to Bevin, December 3, 1946, FO 371 AN 3673/63/45.

89. Majumdar, *Struggle for Freedom*, pp. 753–54. Gopal, *Nehru*, 1:338.

90. Pethick-Lawrence to Bevin, December 6, 1946, in Mansergh, ed.,

Transfer of Power, 9:303. Inverchapel to Bevin, December 7, 1946, ibid., p. 311.

91. Merrell to Nehru, December 9, 1946, New Delhi Post Records, box 1431, NRC.

92. Merrell to Acheson, December 11, 1946, FRUS 1946, 5:101–3. Acheson to Merrell, December 10, 1946, 845.00/12–1046. Merrell to Byrnes, December 10, 1946, 845.00/12–1046.

93. Acheson to Merrell, December 11, 1946, FRUS 1946, 5:103–4.

94. Merrell to Byrnes, December 14, 1946, ibid., p. 105.

95. Nehru to Asaf Ali, December 21, 1946, SWJN, second series, 1:556–57.

96. Acheson to Merrell, December 26, 1946, 845.00/12–2546. Acheson to Merrell, December 31, 1946, 845.00/12–2946. The American chargé d'affaires in London had talked with Jinnah on December 12, at which time the Muslim leader was pessimistic about a solution. "He did not seem disturbed by this but seemed to view future developments coldly, calmly and in a very detached way," the chargé reported. Gallman to Byrnes, December 12, 1946, FRUS 1946, 5:104.

97. Merrell to Byrnes, December 27, 1946, FRUS 1946, 5:106–9. Pethick-Lawrence to Attlee, January 1, 1947, in Mansergh, ed., *Transfer of Power*, 9:440. Attlee to Bevin, January 2, 1947, in Mansergh, ed., *Transfer of Power*, 9:446.

98. John Colville to Pethick-Lawrence, December 10, 1946, in Mansergh, ed., *Transfer of Power*, 9:321. Inverchapel to Bevin, December 13, 1946, ibid., pp. 345–46.

99. Acheson to Merrell, December 10, 1946, 845.00/12–1046. Merrell to Byrnes, December 10, 1946, 845.00/12–1046. Gallman to Byrnes, January 2, 1947, 845.00/1–247.

100. In the fall of 1946 Engert had prepared a position paper on Britain and the Middle East, for which he drew generously on material supplied by the British government. When he had finished the top secret paper, which was approved by the department and shown to the White House, he allowed the British ambassador to see it. Inverchapel to Bevin, January 20, 1947, FO 371 AN 252/1/45, FOR.

101. Inverchapel to Bevin, January 20, 1947, FO 371 AN 252/1/45, and accompanying minutes, FOR.

102. John Duncan Miller to W. P. N. Edwards, January 24, 1947, FO 371, AN 1138/1/45.

103. Gallman to Byrnes, January 2, 1947, 845.00/1–247. LaMont to Byrnes, December 23, 1946, 845.00/12–2346. Nehru to Krishna Menon, November 17, 1946, in Gopal, *Nehru*, 1:337.

104. For a text of the resolution, see Menon, *Transfer of Power in India*, pp. 332–33. Despite Nehru's mentioning to Merrell that Congress would probably submit the dispute to the courts, on December 22 the Congress Working

Committee rejected the idea on the grounds that the Muslim League did not recognize the courts' jurisdiction. Ibid., p. 331.

105. Joseph F. Sparks to Byrnes, January 6, 1947, FRUS 1947, 3:137–38.

106. George Marshall to American Consul, Karachi, January 30, 1947, 845.00/1–3047.

107. Majumdar, *Struggle for Freedom*, p. 755.

108. Ibid., pp. 754–55. Gopal considers the reservation minor. Gopal, *Nehru*, p. 338. Lumby speculates that Muslim League intransigence resulted from a renewed determination to seek an independent Pakistan. Lumby, *Transfer of Power*, p. 135. Anita Inder Singh in her recent book, *The Origins of the Partition of India, 1936–1947*, makes no mention of the reservation at all and blames Muslim League intransigence for India's problems at this point (pp. 207–9).

109. Sparks to Byrnes, January 6, 1947, FRUS 1947, 3:137–38. Merrell to Marshall, April 22, 1947, ibid., pp. 152–54.

110. Sparks to Byrnes, January 6, 1947, ibid., p. 137. Merrell to Marshall, February 15, 1947, 800.00/2–1547. Some scholars place primary blame for the ultimate failure of the Cabinet mission on Congress's "persistent refusal unequivocally to accept the groupings provisions." (Noorani, "The Cabinet Mission and its Aftermath," p. 114.) Others blame the Muslim League, contending that it never intended that the interim government should function because, if it were successful, the case for an independent Pakistan would be negated. (Singh, *The Origins of the Partition of India*, p. 203.)

111. Quoted in Lumby, *Transfer of Power*, p. 138.

112. Singh, *The Origins of the Partition of India*, p. 212.

113. For good discussions of the debate, see Majumdar, ed., *Struggle for Freedom*, pp. 758–60, and Lumby, *Transfer of Power*, pp. 142–44.

114. Mackett, "Some Aspects," pp. 471–73.

115. Henderson to Marshall, February 20, 1947, 845.00/2–2047.

116. Inverchapel to Bevin, February 20, 1947, FO 371 F 2306/905/61, FOR.

117. Department of State, press release no. 142, February 25, 1947, 845.00/2–2547.

118. Lewis Douglas to Marshall, March 18, 1947, 845.00/3–1847. Merrell to Marshall, February 27, 1947, 845.00/2–2747. John J. Macdonald to Marshall, April 1, 1947, 845.00/4–147. Acheson to Macdonald, March 18, 1947, 845.00/3–847.

119. Department of State, press release no. 142, February 25, 1947, 845.00/2–2547.

120. Merrell to Marshall, February 25, 1947, 845.00/2–2547.

121. Ibid. Macdonald to Marshall February 27, 1947, 845.00/2–2747.

122. Majumdar, *Struggle for Freedom*, p. 758.

123. Merrell to Marshall, January 21, 1947, FRUS 1947, 3:138.

124. Quoted in Harrison, *The Widening Gulf*, p. 48.

125. Merrell to Marshall, January 21, 1947, FRUS 1947, 3:138–39. Terence Shone to the Secretary of the Cabinet, February 1, 1947, FO 371/63529 80941, FOR.

126. Merrell to Marshall, January 21, 1947, FRUS 1947, 3:139. Marshall to Merrell, January 22, 1947, ibid., pp. 139–40. In the House of Representatives, Congressman Celler attempted to refute Dulles, arguing that India's religious and cultural traditions were antithetical to communism. Mackett, "Some Aspects," p. 469.

127. Nehru, Note, January 18, 1947, SWJN, second series, 1:477. On Chagla, see ibid., p. 477n.

128. Rao to Sapru, January 9, 1947, B. Shiva Rao Papers. Rao put much blame on V. K. Krishna Menon for disregarding Nehru's advice to avoid appearing subservient to anyone.

129. Nehru to M. C. Chagla, January 20, 1947, SWJN, second series, 1:477.

130. Circular telegram, Byrnes to twenty-five American embassies and consulates, January 9, 1947, 845.00/1–947. Department of State Office Memorandum, MEI to NEA, January 13, 1947, 845.00/1–1347. Smith to Byrnes, January 15, 1947, 845.00/1–1547.

131. See, for example, the lengthy report by Terence Shone, the United Kingdom's high commissioner in India, to his government on January 30, 1947, which he made available to the American embassy. G. Lewis Jones to Marshall, February 14, 1947, 845.00/2–1447.

132. Merrell to Marshall, March 15, 1947, 845.00/3–1547.

133. Smith to Byrnes, January 15, 1947, 845.00/1–1547. Acheson to AMPOLAD, Seoul, Korea, March 14, 1947, 845.00/3–1447. Merrell to Marshall, March 15, 1947, 845.00/3–1547.

134. Merrell to Marshall, March 25, 1947, 845.00/3–2547.

135. Merrell to Marshall, April 3, 1947, 845.00/4–347. Nehru considered the conference "a very great success." Nehru to Eslanda Robeson, June 26, 1947, SWJN, second series, 3:390. The State Department was quick to praise the Philippine delegation in particular for its outspoken defense of American policy at the conference. Department of State, Office Memorandum, Mr. Ogburn (SEA) to Mr. Ely (PI), April 30, 1947, 845.00/4–2947.

136. This point is made nicely in Fraser, "Understanding American Policy Towards the Decolonization of European Empires," pp. 105–25.

137. Charles S. Reed II (in Saigon) to Marshall, received February 25, 1947, 845.00/2–2447. J. L. O'Sullivan (in Hanoi) to Marshall, March 27, 1947, 845.00/3–2747.

138. Clymer, "Jawaharlal Nehru and the United States," p. 160.

139. Patrick to E. P. Donaldson, March 28, [1947], L/P&S/12/2643, IOR. Inverchapel to Bevin, June 4, 1947, FO 371 AN 2012/8/45, FOR.

140. Draft paragraph for inclusion in a proposed letter from Pethick-Lawrence to Mountbatten, enclosed in Donaldson to H. Beeley, March 31,

1947, FO 371 F 4890/905/61/G. The draft paragraph was later incorporated into Pethick-Lawrence's letter to Mountbatten, April 3, 1947, in Mansergh, ed., *Transfer of Power*, 10:106.

141. Shone to the Secretary of the Cabinet, April 25, 1947, L/P&S/12/2643, IOR.

142. Record of Viceroy's Interview No. 87 with V. K. Krishna Menon, April 22, 1947, Mountbatten Papers, file 192.

143. Donaldson to M. E. Dening, May 3, 1947, L/P&S/12/2643, IOR.

144. Acheson to Douglas, April 4, 1947, ibid., IOR. Phillips to Loy Henderson, April 16, 1947, 845.00/4–1647.

145. Singh, *Origins of Partition in India*, p. 210. But if Munshi was critical of Jinnah, he was also unsparing in his criticism of Gandhi, whose intransigence, he thought, was "weakening the Congress cause." Gandhi, he thought, had "outlived his usefulness." Macdonald to Marshall, April 14, 1947, 845.00/4–1447. By contrast, about the same time Nehru wrote of Gandhi, "the old man is still the cleverest politician of us all!" Nehru, quoted in Shone to Sir William Croft, May 30, 1947, FO 371 F 7794/905/61/G, FOR.

146. Moore, "Mountbatten, India, and the Commonwealth," p. 10. Singh, *Origins of the Partition of India*, pp. 227–29.

147. Patrick to Nevile Butler, February 14, 1947, FO 371 AN 680/1/45, FOR.

148. Reuters dispatch, "Mr. Grady at Singapore," June 8, 1947, L/P&S/12/2643, IOR. Mountbatten to Listowel, June 12, 1947, in Mansergh, ed., *Transfer of Power*, 11:300. Shone to Secretary of the Cabinet, July 3, 1947, L/P&S/12/2643, IOR. In August 1947, Grady denied categorically that he had ever said anything of the sort that Reuters had attributed to him. But the British wondered if Grady was telling the truth. In any case, they thought the incident would have a salutary effect. R. H. S. Allen to Donaldson, August 29, 1947, L/P&S/12/2643, IOR.

149. Mountbatten told Terence Shone, the British high commissioner to India, that Grady had been sent to India for only one reason, and that was to "sell the American industrialisation to the Indians at the earliest possible moment." Much later, when Grady learned of Mountbatten's attitudes he complained to the State Department that the governor general was warning Indians about the dangers of "dollar imperialism." In 1951 Churchill challenged Mountbatten on his anti-American attitudes. Mountbatten replied that individually Americans were charming people, but "taken as a corporate mass, they were immature, and if they were allowed their own way they would probably take a course which would not only destroy this country but would ultimately end in the destruction of their own system." Ziegler, *Mountbatten*, pp. 467–68, 503.

150. Menon, *The Transfer of Power*, pp. 350–86. Douglas to Marshall, June 2, 1947, FRUS 1947, 3:155–56.

151. Quoted in Lumby, *Transfer of Power*, p. 155.

152. Singh, *Origins of the Partition of India*, p. 230. In 1944 Gandhi himself seems to have accepted partition in talks with Jinnah. See Nanda, "Nehru and the Partition of India," p. 184.

153. Majumdar, *Struggle for Freedom*, p. 772. Moore, "Mountbatten, India, and the Commonwealth," p. 38.

154. Mackett, "Some Aspects," p. 482. Marshall to Merrell, May 27, 1947, 845.00/5–2747. Department of State, Memorandum of Conversation with Acheson, Singh, and C. W. Adair, June 2, 1947, 845.00/6–247.

155. Merrell to Marshall, May 29, 1947, 845.00/5–2947.

156. Samuel H. Day to Marshall, May 31, 1947, 845.00/5–3147.

157. Douglas to Marshall, June 3, 1947, 845.00/6–347. As R. C. Moore has shown, the British and Mountbatten do not deserve complete credit for the plan, which was really an amalgam of Congress and British plans. Moore, "Mountbatten, India, and the Commonwealth."

158. Menon, *Transfer of Power*, p. 380. Majumdar, *Struggle for Freedom*, p. 778.

159. "British Propose to Partition India," *Christian Century* June 18, 1947, p. 755, in Mackett, "Some Aspects," pp. 484–85. R. A. Butler to Mountbatten, June 5, 1947, in Mansergh, ed., *Transfer of Power*, 11:155. Lippmann, quoted in Menon, *Transfer of Power*, p. 383.

160. Mountbatten to R. A. Butler, June 17, 1947, in Mansergh, ed., *Transfer of Power*, 11:155.

161. Grady to Truman, July 19, 1947, Truman Papers, PSF, Subject File: India.

162. On State Department disappointment, see Inverchapel to Bevin, June 7, 1947, L/P&S/12/1228, IOR, and Mackett, "Some Aspects," p. 485. This suggests that Betty Miller Unterberger's judgment that the American government "greeted the resolution of the Indian dilemma with relief" may be an overstatement. Unterberger, "American Views of Mohammed Ali Jinnah and the Pakistan Liberation Movement," p. 335.

163. Marshall to Douglas, June 9, 1947, 845.00/6–947.

164. Gallman to Marshall, June 11, 1947, 845.00/6–1147.

165. Detailed discussions of how the many issues were resolved are discussed in several books. A convenient, well written one is Lumby, *Transfer of Power*, pp. 168–256.

166. McMahon, "United States Cold War Strategy," p. 817. Acheson to Douglas, April 4, 1947, FRUS 1947, 3:151–52. Marshall to American Consulate, Madras, July 16, 1947, FRUS 1947, 3:162–63. Listowel to Mountbatten, July 25, 1947, in Mansergh, ed., *Transfer of Power*, 12:342. Cabinet Office to Shone, August 8, 1947, in Mansergh, ed., *Transfer of Power*, 12:582.

167. Grady to Marshall, July 25, 1947, 845.00/7–2547. Donovan to Marshall, July 25, 1947, 845.00/7–2547.

168. Grady to Truman, July 19, 1947, Truman Papers, PSF, Subject File: India.

169. Truman to Grady, August 8, 1947, ibid.

170. McMahon, *Colonialism and Cold War*, pp. 130–32.

171. Ibid., pp. 243–44.

172. After independence, American policy toward Indonesia and Indochina continued to irritate Nehru. In February, 1950, he wrote presciently, "I am quite sure that the policy the U.S.A. and the U.K. are adopting in Indo-China is wrong and will lead to evil consequences. I cannot help their policy, but I see no reason to fall in line with a policy which I consider absolutely wrong." Nehru to B. N. Rau, February 14, 1950, SWJN: second series, 14:202.

173. Nehru, Speech in the Constituent Assembly, August 14–15, 1947, SWJN, Second Series, 3:135.

174. Merrell to Marshall, May 2, 1947, FRUS 1947, 3:154.

175. Clipping, "Truman Sends Best Wishes to India, Pakistan," datelined August 15, [1947], Truman Papers, OF 48-H.

Conclusion

1. Wolpert, *Roots of Confrontation in South Asia*, p. 140. "The United States had no South Asian policy prior to 1947," Wolpert writes.

2. Grady is quoted in a memorandum by T. A. Raman, June 15, 1942, enclosed in Campbell to Eden, July 6, 1942, FO 371 A 6578/122/45. It is usually argued that Roosevelt was less harsh in his criticism of Dutch imperialism, partly because of his personal regard for Queen Wilhelmina and perhaps also because of his own Dutch background. See, for example, Hess, *The United States' Emergence as a Southeast Asian Power*, pp. 54–55.

3. Campbell to Richard Law, August 14, 1944, FO 115 G 131/1 (piece 3637), FOR.

4. Richard Law, minute, August 24, 1944, on ibid.

5. Denis Brogan, quoted in Thorne, *Allies of a Kind*, p. 159n.

6. Quoted in Fifield, *Americans in Southeast Asia*, p. 72.

7. M. Asaf Ali, "Address . . . on the Occasion of Hoisting the new flag of India at the embassy of India, Washington," August 15, 1947, file 5-I/47, Rajendra Prasad Papers.

8. Nehru, Speech at the University of Wisconsin, November 4, 1949, in Nehru, *Visit to America*, pp. 172–73. Remarks after laying a wreath on the grave of Franklin D. Roosevelt, October 16, 1949, SWJN: second series, 13:312. Nehru, address to the East and West Association, the Foreign Policy Association, the India League of America, and the Institute of Pacific Relations, New York, October 19, 1949, in *Jawaharlal Nehru's Speeches*, vol.2 ([New Delhi]: Publication Division, Minister of Information and Broadcasting, Government of India, 1954), p. 203.

Bibliography

Bibliographies

Barrier, N. Gerald, ed. *India and America: American Publishing on India 1930–1985.* New Delhi: American Institute of Indian Studies, 1986.

Hess, Gary R. "Global Expansion and Regional Balances: The Emerging Scholarship on United States Relations with India and Pakistan," *Pacific Historical Review* 56 (May 1987):259–95.

Primary Sources

Manuscript Collections in India

I. National Archives of India, New Delhi. Papers of:

External Affairs Department, Government of India
Home Department, Government of India
Prasad, Rajendra

II. Jawaharlal Nehru Memorial Museum and Library, New Delhi, Manuscript Division. Papers of:

Alexander, Horace
All India Congress Committee
Gunther, Frances
Mehta, Vai Kunth Lallubhai
Nehru, Jawaharlal
Rao, B. Shiva

Rao, P. Kodandra
War Cabinet Papers (duplicates)
Oral History Interviews with:
Alexander, Horace
Kripalani, J. B.
Rajagopalachari, C.
Singh, Sardar J. J.

III. Jawaharlal Nehru Memorial Museum and Library, New Delhi, Microfilm Division. Papers of:

Rajagopalachari, Chakravarti
Sapru, Sir Tej Bahadur

IV. In possession of Mrs. Vidya Stokes, Simla, Himachal Pradesh. Papers of:

Stokes, Samuel Evans

Manuscript Collections in the United Kingdom

I. Public Record Office, Kew. Papers of

The Foreign Office, FO 371 (United States)
Cabinet Papers

II. India Office Library, London. Papers of

The India Office
Linlithgow, Lord
Mountbatten, Lord Louis
Wavell, Sir Archibald

III. Nuffield College, Oxford University. Papers of

Cripps, Sir Stafford
Mountbatten, Lord Louis

Manuscript Collections in the United States

I. National Archives, Washington, D.C. Papers of:

Department of State, Record Group 59, General Records of the Department of State

II. National Records Center, Suitland, Maryland. Papers of

Department of State, Record Group 84, New Delhi Post Records

III. Franklin D. Roosevelt Library, Hyde Park, New York. Papers of
Berle, Adolf A., Jr.
Hopkins, Harry
Roosevelt, Franklin

IV. Houghton Library, Manuscript Division, Harvard University. Papers of
Phillips, William

V. Oral History Institute, Columbia University. Interview with
Phillips, William

VI. University of Virginia Library, Manuscript Division. Papers of
Johnson, Louis A.

VII. Harry S. Truman Library. Papers of
Block, Ralph
Truman, Harry S.

VIII. University Publications of America, Inc. Papers of
Office of Strategic Services/State Department Intelligence and Research Reports, Part II: China and India. (microfilm)

Published Primary Sources (Selected)

I. Government Documents

The British Cabinet Mission to India: A Documentary Record, March-June 1946. Delhi:1962.
Chopra, P. N., ed. *Quit India Movement: British Secret Documents.* New Delhi: Interprint, 1986.
Congressional Record.
Department of State *Bulletin.*
Department of State. *Foreign Relations of the United States.* (1939–1947)
Mansergh, Nicholas, ed. *The Transfer of Power.* 12 vols. London: Her Majesty's Stationery Office, 1970–83.

II. Letters, Memoirs, Autobiographies and other participant accounts

Azad, Abul Kalam. *India Wins Freedom: An Autobiographical Narrative.* New Delhi: Orient Longman, 1959.

Bajpai, Sir Girja Shankar. *India and the United States of America.* (Pamphlet) New Delhi: Indian Institute of International Affairs, 1944.

Baruch, Bernard M. *Baruch: The Public Years.* New York: Holt, Rinehart and Winston, 1960.

Blum, John M., ed., *The Price of Vision: The Diary of Henry A. Wallace.* Boston: Houghton Mifflin, 1973.

Campbell-Johnson, Alan. *Mission with Mountbatten.* London: Hamish Hamilton, 1985.

Chattopadhyay, Kamaladevi. *Inner Recesses Outer Spaces: Memoirs.* New Delhi: Navrang, 1986.

Choudery, Valmiki, ed. *Dr. Rajendra Prasad: Correspondence and Select Documents.* 6 vols. New Delhi: Allied Publishers Private Limited, 1984–86.

Collected Works of Mahatma Gandhi. 90 vols. New Delhi: Publication Division, Ministry of Information and Broadcasting, Government of India, 1958–1984.

Davies, John Paton, Jr., *Dragon by the Tail: American, British, Japanese, and Russian Encounters with China and with One Another.* New York: W. W. Norton & Company, 1972.

Gandhi, Mohandas K. *An Autobiography or The Story of My Experiments with Truth.* Ahmedabad, India: Navajivan Publishing House, 1927.

Gopal, Sarvepalli, ed. *Selected Works of Jawaharlal Nehru.* 15 vols. New Delhi: Jawaharlal Nehru Memorial Fund, 1984–87.

Gopal, Sarvepalli, ed. *Selected Works of Jawaharlal Nehru: Second Series.* 14 vols. New Delhi: Jawaharlal Nehru Memorial Fund, 1984–1992.

Gunther, John. *Inside Asia.* New York: Harper & Brothers, 1939.

Hauswirth, Frieda. *A Marriage to India.* London: Hutchinson & Co., 1931.

Jawaharlal's Discovery of America. Delhi: East & West Publishers, 1950.

Kimball, Warren F.. ed. *Churchill & Roosevelt: The Complete Correspondence.* 3 vols. Princeton: Princeton University Press, 1984.

Lal, Chaman. *British Propaganda in America.* Allahabad, India: Kitab Mahal, 1945.

Listowel, Lord. "The Whitehall Dimension of the Transfer of Power." *Indo-British Review* [Madras]. 7 (Nos. 3 & 4):22–31.

Loewenheim, Francis L., Langley, Harold D., and Jonas, Manfred, eds. *Roosevelt and Churchill: Their Secret Wartime Correspondence.* New York: Saturday Review Press, 1975.

Mazumdar, Haridas T. *America's Contribution to India's Freedom.* Allahabad: Central Book Depot, 1962.

Menon, Vapal Pangunni. *The Transfer of Power in India.* New Delhi: Orient Longman, 1957.

Moon, Penderel, ed. *Wavell: The Viceroy's Journal.* Delhi: Oxford University Press, 1973.

Moran, Lord. *Churchill, Taken from the Diaries of Lord Moran: The Struggle for Survival 1940–1960.* Boston: Houghton Mifflin, 1966.

Nehru, Jawaharlal, ed. *A Bunch of Old Letters: Written Mostly to Jawaharlal Nehru and Some Written By Him.* Bombay: Asia Publishing House, 1958.

Nehru, Jawaharlal. *An Autobiography*. New Delhi: Jawaharlal Nehru Memorial Fund/Oxford University Press, 1980.

Nehru, Jawaharlal. *Glimpses of World History: Being Further Letters to His Daughter Written in Prison*. . . . New Delhi: Jawaharlal Nehru Memorial Fund/Oxford University Press, 1982.

Nehru, Jawaharlal. *The Discovery of India*. Garden City, NY: Doubleday & Company, 1959.

Pandey, B. N., ed. *The Indian Nationalist Movement, 1885–1947: Selected Documents*. London: Macmillan, 1979.

Pandit, Vijaya Lakshmi. *The Scope of Happiness: A Personal Narrative*. New York: Crown Publishers, 1979.

Phillips, William. *Ventures in Diplomacy*. Boston: Beacon Press, 1952.

Rao, B. Shiva. *India's Freedom Movement: Some Notable Figures*. New Delhi: Orient Longman, 1972.

Roosevelt, Elliott. *As He Saw It*. New York: Duell, Sloan and Pearce, 1946.

Rosenman, Samuel I. *Working with Roosevelt*. London: Rupert Hart-Davis, 1952.

[Stokes, Florence]. *A Sketch of the Life of Samuel Evans Stokes Written for his Children by their Mother*. Philadelphia: Biddle Press, n.d.

Stokes, Satyanand [Samuel Evans]. *National Self-Realisation and Other Essays*. New Delhi: Rubicon, 1977.

Secondary Sources

Books, Dissertations, Theses

Anderson, Terry H. *The United States, Great Britain, and the Cold War 1944–1947*. Columbia, MO: University of Missouri Press, 1981.

Apsler, Alfred. *Fighter for Independence: Jawaharlal Nehru*. New York: Julian Messner, 1963.

Beitzel, Robert. *The Uneasy Alliance: America, Britain, and Russia, 1941–1943*. New York: Alfred A. Knopf, 1972.

Betts, Raymond F. *Uncertain Dimensions: Western Overseas Empires in the Twentieth Century*. Minneapolis: University of Minnesota Press, 1985.

Bhagat, Goberdhan. *Americans in India 1784–1860*. New York: New York University Press, 1970.

Brands, H. W. *India and the United States: The Cold Peace*. Boston: Twayne, 1990.

Brands, H. W. *The Specter of Neutralism: The United States and the Emergence of the Third World, 1947–1960*. New York: Columbia University Press, 1989.

Brecher, Michael. *Nehru: A Political Biography*. London: Oxford University Press, 1959.

Brown, Judith M. *Modern India: The Origins of an Asian Democracy*. Delhi: Oxford University Press, 1984.

Brown, William Norman. *The United States and India, Pakistan, and Bangladesh*. 3rd ed. Cambridge, MA: Harvard University Press, 1972.

Callahan, Raymond A. *Churchill: Retreat From Empire.* Wilmington, DE: Scholarly Resources, 1984.

Chalapathi Rau, M. *Gandhi and Nehru.* Bombay: Allied, 1967.

Chandrasekhar, Sripati, ed. *From India to America.* LaJolla, CA: Population Review, 1982.

Cochran, Bert. *Harry Truman and the Crisis Presidency.* New York: Funk & Wagnalls, 1973.

Dallek, Robert. *Franklin D. Roosevelt and American Foreign Policy, 1932–1945.* New York: Oxford University Press, 1979.

Desai, Tripta. *Indo-American Relations between 1940–1974.* Washington, D.C.: University Press of America, 1977.

Donovan, Robert J. *Conflict and Crisis: The Presidency of Harry S Truman, 1945–1948.* New York: W. W. Norton, 1977.

Dutt, R. Palme. *India To-day.* Revised ed. Calcutta: Manisha, 1970.

Fifield, Russell. *Americans in Southeast Asia: The Roots of Commitment.* New York: Thomas Y. Crowell, 1973.

Fischer, Louis. *The Life of Mahatma Gandhi.* London: Granada, 1982.

Gaddis, John Lewis. *Strategies of Containment: A Critical Appraisal of Postwar American National Security Policy.* New York: Oxford University Press, 1982.

Gardner, Lloyd. *Approaching Vietnam: From World War II Through Dienbienphu, 1941–1954.* New York: W. W. Norton, 1988.

George, Thagil J. S. *Krishna Menon: A Biography.* New York: Taplinger, 1965.

Glendevon, John. *The Viceroy at Bay: Lord Linlithgow in India, 1936–1943.* London: Collins, 1971.

Gosnell, Harold F. *A Political Biography of Harry S. Truman.* Westport, CT: Greenwood Press, 1980.

Gopal, Sarvepalli. *Jawaharlal Nehru: A Biography.* 3 vols. Delhi: Oxford University Press, 1975–1984.

Gupta, R. K. *The Great Encounter: A Study of Indo-American Literary and Cultural Relations.* New Delhi: Abhinav Publications, 1986.

Harbutt, Fraser J. *The Iron Curtain: Churchill, America, and the Origins of the Cold War.* New York and Oxford: Oxford University Press, 1986.

Harrison, Selig S. *The Widening Gulf: Asian Nationalism and American Policy.* New York: The Free Press, 1978.

Hart, Basil H. Liddell. *History of the Second World War.* New York: G. P. Putnam's Sons, 1970.

Hathaway, Robert M. *Ambiguous Partnership: Britain and America, 1944–1947.* New York: Columbia University Press, 1981.

Herring, George. *America's Longest War: The United States and Vietnam, 1950–1975.* 2d ed. New York: Alfred A. Knopf, 1986.

Hess, Gary R. *America Encounters India, 1941–1947.* Baltimore: The Johns Hopkins Press, 1971.

Hess, Gary R. *The United States' Emergence as a Southeast Asian Power, 1940–1950.* New York: Columbia University Press, 1987.

Hodson, H. V. *The Great Divide: Britain-India-Pakistan.* London: Hutchinson, 1969.

Holmes, John Haynes. *My Gandhi*. New York: Harper, 1953.

Hope, A. Guy. *America and Swaraj: The U.S. Role in Indian Independence*. Washington, D.C.: Public Affairs Press, 1968.

Hutchins, Francis G. *India's Revolution: Gandhi and the Quit India Movement*. Cambridge, MA: Harvard University Press, 1973.

Isaacs, Harold R. *Images of Asia: American Views of China and India*. New York: Capricorn, 1962.

Jackson, Carl T. *The Oriental Religions and American Thought: Nineteenth Century Explorations*. Westport, CT: Greenwood, 1981.

Jauhri, R. C. *American Diplomacy and Independence for India*. Bombay: Vora, 1970.

Jeffrey, Robin, ed. *Asia: The Winning of Independence*. London: Macmillan, 1981.

Jha, Manoranjan. *Civil Disobedience and After: The American Reaction to Political Developments in India During 1930–1935*. Meerut and Delhi: Meenakshi Prakashan, 1973.

Jha, Manoranjan. *Katherine Mayo and India*. Delhi: People's Publishing House, 1971.

Kimpell, Lawrence L. "Katherine Mayo's India." M.A. thesis, University of Texas at El Paso, 1991.

Kirby, S. Woodburn. *The War Against Japan*. 5 vols. London: Her Majesty's Stationery Office, 1957–1969.

Krishnan, T. V. Kunhi. *The Unfriendly Friends: India and America*. New Delhi: Indian Book Company, 1974.

Lamson, Peggy. *Roger Baldwin: Founder of the American Civil Liberties Union*. Boston: Houghton Mifflin, 1976.

Leffler, Melvin P. *A Preponderance of Power: National Security, the Truman Administration, and the Cold War*. Stanford, CA: Stanford University Press, 1992.

Louis, William Roger. *Imperialism at Bay: The United States and the Decolonization of the British Empire*. New York: Oxford University Press, 1978.

Mackett, Walter Charles. "Some Aspects of the Development of American Opinion on India, 1918–1947." Ph.D dissertation, University of Southern California, 1957.

Majumdar, R. C. *Struggle for Freedom*. 2nd ed. Bombay: Bharatiya Vidya Bhavan, 1978.

Malik, Iftikhar H. *U.S.-South Asian Relations, 1940–47: American Attitudes toward the Pakistan Movement*. New York: St. Martin's, 1991.

McFarland, Keith D. *Harry H. Woodring: A Political Biography of FDR's Controversial Secretary of War*. Lawrence, KS: University Press of Kansas, 1975.

McJimsey, George. *Harry Hopkins: Ally of the Poor and Defender of Democracy*. Cambridge, MA: Harvard University Press, 1987.

McMahon, Robert J. *Colonialism and Cold War: The United States and the Struggle for Indonesian Independence, 1945–49*. Ithaca: Cornell University Press, 1981.

Merrill, Dennis. *Bread and the Ballot: The United States and India's Economic*

Development, 1947–1963. Chapel Hill, NC: University of North Carolina Press, 1990.

Minault, Gail. *The Khilafat Movement: Religious Symbolism and Political Mobilization in India.* Delhi: Oxford University Press, 1982.

Moore, Robin J. *Churchill, Cripps, and India, 1939–1945.* Oxford: Oxford University Press, 1979.

Pandey, B. N. *Nehru.* London: Macmillan, 1976.

Panigrahi, D. N. *Quit India and the Struggle for Freedom.* Delhi: Vikas, 1984.

Patil, V. T., ed. *Studies on Nehru.* New Delhi: Sterling, 1987.

Philips, C. H. and Wainwright, Mary Doreen, eds. *The Partition of India: Policies and Perspectives 1935–1947.* London: George Allen and Unwin, 1970.

Riepe, Dale. *The Philosophy of India and Its Impact on American Thought.* Springfield, IL: Charles C. Thomas, 1970.

Rao, P. Kodandra. *Foreign Friends of India's Freedom.* Bangalore and Madras: P. T. I. Book Company, 1973.

Rotter, Andrew J. *The Path to Vietnam: Origins of the American Commitment to Southeast Asia.* Ithaca: Cornell University Press, 1987.

Ryan, Henry Butterfield. *The Vision of Anglo-America: The US-UK Alliance and the Emerging Cold War, 1943–1946.* Cambridge: Cambridge University Press, 1987.

Singh, Anita Inder. *The Origins of the Partition of India, 1936–1947.* Delhi: Oxford University Press, 1987.

Singh, Harnam. *The Indian National Movement and American Opinion.* Delhi: Central Electric Press, [1962].

Talbot, Phillips, and Poplai, S. L. *India and America: A Study of Their Relations.* Westport, CT: Greenwood, 1973.

Tewari, S. C. *Indo-U.S. Relations, 1947–1976.* New Delhi: Radiant, 1977.

Thompson, Kenneth W. *Winston Churchill's World View: Statesmanship and Power.* Baton Rouge: Louisiana University Press, 1983.

Thorne, Christopher. *Allies of a Kind: The United States, Britain, and the War Against Japan.* Oxford: Oxford University Press, 1978.

Tuttle, Dwight William. *Harry L. Hopkins and Anglo-American-Soviet Relations, 1941–1945.* New York: Garland, 1983.

United States Information Service. *As America Remembers Jawaharlal Nehru.* New Delhi: William H. Weathersby for the United States Information Service, 1964.

Venkataramani, M. S. *The American Role in Pakistan. 1947–1958.* New Delhi: Radiant, 1982.

Venkataramani, M. S. *The Bengal Famine of 1943: The American Response.* New Delhi: Vikas and the Jawaharlal Nehru Memorial Museum and Library, 1973.

Venkataramani, M. S. and Shrivastava, B. K. *Quit India: The American Response to the 1942 Struggle.* Delhi: Vikas, 1979.

Venkataramani, M. S. and Shrivastava, B. K. *Roosevelt, Gandhi, Churchill: America and the Last Phase of India's Freedom Struggle.* New Delhi: Radiant, 1983.

Wolpert, Stanley. *India.* Englewood Cliffs, NJ: Prentice-Hall, 1965.

Wolpert, Stanley. *Jinnah of Pakistan.* Delhi: Oxford University Press, 1985.

Wolpert, Stanley. *Roots of Confrontation in South Asia: Afghanistan, Pakistan, India, and the Superpowers.* New York: Oxford University Press, 1982.

Yergin, Daniel. *Shattered Peace: The Origins of the Cold War and the National Security State.* Boston: Houghton Mifflin, 1977.

Ziegler, Philip. *Mountbatten: The Official Biography.* London: Collins, 1985.

Articles and Chapters in Books

Adamthwaite, Anthony. "Britain and the World, 1945–9: The View from the Foreign Office." *International Affairs.* 61 (Spring 1985):223–35.

Banerjee, Somendu K. "American Interest in Indian Independence 1930–43." *India Quarterly* (1968):311–32.

Clymer, Kenton J. "The Education of William Phillips: Self Determination and American Policy Toward India, 1942–45." *Diplomatic History.* 8 (Winter 1984):13–25.

Clymer, Kenton J. "Franklin Roosevelt, Louis Johnson, India, and Anticolonialism: Another Look." *Pacific Historical Review.* 57 (August 1988):261–84.

Clymer, Kenton J. "Indian Nationalism and Anglo-American Relations: Another Look at Some Unauthorized Disclosures," *International Studies* [Jawaharlal Nehru University, New Delhi]. 25, 4 (1988):343–62.

Clymer, Kenton J. "Jawaharlal Nehru and the United States: The Pre-independence Years." *Diplomatic History.* 14 (Spring 1990):143–61.

Clymer, Kenton J. "Samuel Evans Stokes, Mahatma Gandhi, and Indian Nationalism." *Pacific Historical Review.* 59 (February 1990):51–76.

Dulles, Foster Rhea, and Ridinger, Gerald E. "The Anti-Colonial Policies of Franklin D. Roosevelt." *Political Science Quarterly* 70 (March 1955):1–18.

Fieldhouse, D. K. "The Labour Government and the Empire-Commonwealth, 1945–1975." In *The Foreign Policy of the British Labour Governments, 1945–1951,* ed. Ritchie Ovendale, pp. 83–120. Leicester: Leicester University Press, 1984.

Fraser, Cary. "Understanding American Policy Towards the Decolonization of European Empires, 1945–64." *Diplomacy & Statecraft* 3 (March 1992):105–25.

Gupta, Partha Sarathi. "Imperialism and the Labour Government, 1945–51." In *The Working Class in Modern British History: Essays in Honor of Henry Pelling.* Cambridge: Cambridge University Press, 1983, pp. 99–124.

Gupta, Sikharam Prasanna Kumara. "The Mahatma's American Apostle." *Span* [New Delhi]. 23 (October 1982):24–28.

Habibuddin, S. M. "American Response to the Emergence of Pakistan." *Indian Journal of Politics.* 13 (April-August 1979):47–62.

Herring, George C. "The Truman Administration and the Restoration of

French Sovereignty in Indochina," *Diplomatic History.* 1 (Spring 1977):97–117.

Hess, Gary R. "Franklin D. Roosevelt and Anti-Colonialism," *Indian Journal of American Studies.* 13 (January 1983):23–37.

Hess, Gary R. "Franklin Roosevelt and Indochina." *Journal of American History.* 59 (September 1972):353–68.

Hill, Peter. "L. S. Amery, India and the Commonwealth:1940–42." *Journal of Indian History.* 57 (Nos. 2–3, 1979):315–41.

Jauhri, R. C. "The American Effort to Avert the Impending Partition of India, 1946–47." *Indian Journal of American Studies.* 8 (July 1978):1–11.

Jeffreys-Jones, Rhodri. "Turning the Big Cat Inside Out: U. S. Secret Agents in the British Empire in Two World Wars." In *Eagle Against Empire: American Opposition to European Imperialism, 1914–1982,* ed. Rhodri Jeffreys-Jones. Aix-en-Provence: Universite de Provence, 1983, pp. 77–90.

Kahin, George McT. "The United States and the Anticolonial Revolutions in Southeast Asia, 1945–50." In *The Origins of the Cold War in Asia,* eds. Yonosuke Nagai and Akira Iriye. Tokyo: University of Tokyo Press, 1977, pp. 338–61.

Kahir, M. A. "William Phillips' Mission to India 1942–1943." *Journal of the Asiatic Society of Pakistan* 9:2 (1964), 65–72.

LaFeber, Walter. "Roosevelt, Churchill, and Indochina." *American Historical Review.* 80 (December 1975):1277–95.

Leffler, Melvyn P. "The American Conception of National Security and the Beginnings of the Cold War, 1945–48." *American Historical Review* 89 (April 1984):346–81.

Louis, William Roger. "American Anti-colonialism and the Dissolution of the British Empire." *International Affairs.* 61 (Summer 1985):395–420.

McMahon, Robert J. "United States Cold War Strategy in South Asia: Making a Military Commitment to Pakistan, 1947–1954," *Journal of American History* 75 (December 1988):812–40.

Moore, R. C. "Mountbatten, India, and the Commonwealth." *Journal of Comparative & Commonwealth Politics.* 19 (March 1981):5–43.

Nanda, B. R. "Nehru, the Indian National Congress and the Partition of India, 1935–1947." In *The Partition of India: Policies and Perspectives 1935–1937,* eds. C. H. Philips and Mary Doreen Wainwright. London: George Allen and Unwin, 1970, pp. 148–87.

Noorani, A. G. "The Cabinet Mission and Its Aftermath." In *The Partition of India: Policies and Perspectives, 1935–1947,* eds. C. H. Philips and Mary Doreen Wainwright. London: George Allen and Unwin, 1970, pp. 104–16.

Rizvi, S. A. G. "Lord Linlithgow and the Reviewers." *Indo-British Review* [Madras], 7 (Nos. 1 & 2):11–17.

Sbrega, John M. "The Anticolonial Policies of Franklin D. Roosevelt: A Reappraisal." *Political Science Quarterly* 101:1 (1986), 65–84.

Shrivastava, B. K. "The United States and the Cabinet Mission to India." In

Studies in Politics National and International, ed. M. S. Rajan. Delhi: Vikas, 1970, pp. 410–30.

Shaplen, Robert. "One-Man Lobby [J. J. Singh]," *New Yorker,* 24 March 1951, pp. 35–55.

Siracusa, Joseph. "The United States, Viet-Nam, and the Cold War: A Reappraisal." *Journal of Southeast Asian Studies.* 5 (March 1974):82–101.

Smith, Raymond, and Zametica, John. "The Cold Warrior: Clement Attlee Reconsidered:1945–7." *International Affairs.* 61 (Spring 1985):237–52.

Stoler, Mark A. "From Continentalism to Globalism: General Stanley D. Embrick, the Joint Strategic Survey Committee, and the Military View of American National Policy during the Second World War." *Diplomatic History* 6 (Summer 1982):303–21.

Unterberger, Betty Miller. "American Views of Mohammed Ali Jinnah and the Pakistan Liberation Movement." *Diplomatic History* 5 (Fall 1981):313–36.

Venkataramani, M. S. and Shrivastava, B. K. "The United States and the Cripps Mission." *India Quarterly* 19 (July 1963):214–65.

Watt, D. C. "American anti-colonialist policies and the end of the European colonial empires 1941–1962." In *Contagious Conflict: The Impact of American Dissent on European Life,* ed. A. N. J. den Hollander. Leiden: E. J. Brill, 1973. pp. 93–125.

Winkler, Allan M. "American Opposition to Imperialism in World War II." In *Eagle Against Empire: American Opposition to European Imperialism, 1914–1982,* ed. Rhodri Jeffreys-Jones. Aix-en-Provence: Universite de Provence, 1983, pp. 77–90.

Index

Acheson, Dean, 244, 259–60, 263–65, 267, 358n71; on riots, 248; on London Conference (1945), 262

Afghanistan, 121

Air bases: American desire for, 241–42, 290–91, 354n7

Alexander, A. V., 249

Ali, Asaf, 260

Ali, Asaf, Mrs., 247

Alling, Paul, 88, 113; on Johnson, 69

Ambalvi, Lala Dunichand: interview with Phillips, 144

Ambedkar, B. R., 103

Amerasia, 30, 219

American Civil Liberties Union, 7

American Civil Liberties Union *News*, 30

American League for India's Freedom, 22, 42

American soldiers in India, 81–84, 164, 178–80, 246, 355n24; relations with British soldiers, 179–80

American views of Indians, 227–30

Amery, Leopold S., 20, 31, 71, 99, 110, 136, 149, 163, 171, 192, 209, 211–12, 223, 325n93, 333n81, 333n92, 344n111, 348n27; and National Defence Council, 31; on appointing an Indian representative to U.S., 32, 34; on imperial preference system, 52; on India's future, 53–54; on Congress' rejection of Cripps proposals, 61; on Johnson mission, 64; and Technical Mission, 78; and arrest of Gandhi (1942), 89, 316n65, 316n67; and Quit India movement, 92; on American opinion re: Quit India crisis, 98; and Sherwood Eddy, 103; and Willkie, 104, 106; and Fisher, 108; interview by Murrow, 117–18; and Phillips, 118–19, 122, 135, 139–40, 144, 330n2; on Churchill, 135; opposes commercial treaty with U.S., 174–75; on Stilwell, 181; and Bengal famine, 185, 187; and Cabinet Mission, 252; on Bajpai's status, 343n99

Amritsar massacre, 7

Anderson, Terry H., xvii

Aney, Madhao Shrihari: on divide and rule policy, 142

Argentina: Anglo-American differences about, 206
Armstrong, Hamilton Fish, 44
Asia: article by Nehru in, 24–25
Assam: Japanese invasion of, 181
Atlantic Charter, 34–35, 43, 96, 130,
133, 146, 151, 153, 157, 191, 194,
196, 203, 210, 235, 287, 328*n*15;
Roosevelt on, 122
Atlantic: article by Nehru in, 24
Attlee, Clement, 37, 40, 54, 93, 231,
241, 249, 250–51, 253, 265, 271,
280; on Churchill's view of India,
xiv; and Atlantic Charter, 35; on
Linlithgow, 52; on American opinion, 52–53; on British idealism,
116; on raising Bajpai's status, 232;
and London conference (1946),
261–62; and British withdrawal
from India, 268–69, 279
Auchinleck, Claude, 168, 223
Azad, Abul Kalam, 23; and Cripps
mission, 65; on possible U.S.
intervention to end Quit India
crisis, 89–90; and Cabinet mission, 358*n*64

Bajpai, Girja Shankar, 56, 76, 101,
114, 125, 153, 168, 181, 209, 217,
218; background of, 32; appointed
agent general of India to U.S., 34;
on India's future, 48–50; urges
U.S. intervention in India, 49; and
Technical Mission, 77, 80–81; and
Quit India movement, 88–89,
92–93; on American opinion
about India, 97–98, 173, 183–84;
on Gandhi, 112; disenchanted
with Government of India, 112–13;
on Churchill, 113; on Linlithgow,
113; and appointment of Phillips,
118–20; and Bengal famine, 186;
official status of, 188–90, 230–33,
258, 343*n*99, 353*n*107; and published Phillips letter, 203; and *persona non grata* telegram, 204; on

American anticolonialism, 220–21;
and Simla conference (1945), 224
Bajpai, Ramlal, 7
Baldwin, Hanson: on Indian army,
218
Baldwin, Roger: and Indian freedom,
7
Bannerman, Helen: *Little Black Sambo*,
5–6
Baruch, Bernard, 213; on Hong
Kong, 348*n*32
Bates, John: on imperialism, 41
Beaverbrook, Lord, 162
Becker, E. A., 86
Beecroft, Eric, 175–76; and colonial-
ism, 338*n*31
Bengal famine (1943–44), 184–88,
201, 341*n*74, 342*n*76
Berle, Adolf A., Jr., 15, 20, 49, 50, 59,
87, 112, 134, 185, 193, 334*n*99;
urges American pressure on
British, 21; urges intervention in
India, 43; and Technical Mission,
81; on Bajpai, 113
Berry, Lampton, 71, 84–85, 192–93,
199–200, 233, 243, 244–45; on
Indian despair, 169; on Wavell,
223–24; and Simla conference
(1945), 225–26; on riots, 248; and
Cabinet Mission, 250
Bevin, Ernest, 231; and National
Defence Council, 31–32
Bhagat, Goberdhan, 8
Bhansali, J. B.: fast of, 141; 331*n*47
Birla, G. D., 70, 200
Block, Ralph, 177–78
Bloom, Sol, 196
Board of Economic Warfare: and
Bengal famine, 185
Bolshevik revolution, 124
Bombay mutiny, 246–47
Bose, Subhas Chanda, 14, 16
Bower, Roy E. B., 230, 292; on Indian
culture and politics, 228–29; on
riots, 247–48
Bowman, Isaiah, 44

Brockingham, Leonard: on British idealism, 116

Bryan, William Jennings: on British rule in India, 6

Buck, Pearl, 25, 42–43, 183, 249

Buell, H. E., 86

Bureau of Economic Warfare, 174–75

Burma, 100, 109, 289, 322n58, 337n9; fighting in, 38, 128–29, 168, 181, 205

Burma Road, 129, 167

Butler, Nevile, 118, 197, 262, 323n73, 325n89; on Roosevelt, 56; and Willkie, 105; on Linlithgow, 108–9, 150; and Amery, 118; and Phillips mission, 133, 160; on *persona non grata* telegram, 346n149

Byrnes, James F., 235, 243; on raising Bajpai's status, 232–33; and Soviet Union, 238

Cabinet Mission (1946), 249–56, 263–64, 357n48, 361n110; American views of, 250–54

Cadogan, Alexander: on British idealism, 116

Cairo conference (1943), 130, 207

Camacho, Avila, 111

Campbell, Ronald, 93, 289; and Phillips, 121, 133; and published Phillips letter, 193–94

Capper, Arthur, 243

Caroe, Olaf K., 158, 178, 334n110, 346n149; on Johnson mission, 59; on Edward Clark Carter, 184; on raising Bajpai's status, 189; describes Phillips as *persona non grata*, 196–97, 199, 203–4

Casablanca conference (1943), 130

Celler, Emmanuel, 206, 246–47; and American soldiers in India, 246; on Dulles, 362n126

Chagla, M. C., 272

Chandler, Albert B., 171, 195–97

Chattopadhyaya, Kamaladevi: criti-

cizes India League of America, 23; visits U.S., 28–30

Checker, N. R.: founds India League of America, 22

Chennault, Claire, 167

Chiang Kai-shek, 56–57, 82, 100, 105, 130, 167, 178, 181, 205, 207, 221, 287, 324n78; on Indian nationalism, 41; urges U.S. intervention, 90, 114; and Churchill, 114–15; American efforts to supply, 129

Chiang Kai-shek, Madame, 114, 149, 151

Chimur massacre, 141, 331n47

Chindit operations, 129

Choate, Joseph, 123

Christian Century, The, 183; on Gandhi, 21; and Cripps mission, 75; on U.S. press opinion about India, 96; and Bengal famine, 186–87; on Gandhi's release (1944), 190; and Cabinet Mission, 250; and British withdrawal from India, 279; and Phillips, 345n127

Christian Science Monitor, The, 214; on Gandhi, 21; on British policy, 22; on Quit India crisis, 95; and British withdrawal from India, 269

Churchill, Winston, xiv–xv, 2, 40, 48, 49, 54–55, 58, 73, 90, 97, 99, 107, 110, 122, 125, 130–31, 135, 149, 154, 155, 158, 161, 162, 168, 169, 173, 182, 194, 201, 202, 210–13, 221, 222, 223, 265, 286–87, 324n78, 332n64, 344n111, 345n139; and Atlantic Charter, xiii, 34–35, 191; and offer of August 8, 1940, 17; opposes discussions with nationalists (1940), 31; on appointing an Indian representative to U.S., 32–33; and Roosevelt, 37–38, 44–45, 56, 122; on fall of Singapore, 38; supports Defence of India Council, 53; and Cripps mission, 61, 63–69, 311n61; tries to prevent Johnson from

Churchill, Winston (*continued*) returning to India, 71; on Johnson, 76–77; and Sherwood Eddy, 103, 320*n*33; and Willkie, 104–6; Bajpai on, 113; and Chiang Kaishek, 114–15; on Gandhi's fast (1943), 153; on Phillips, 163; and Bengal famine, 187, 341*n*74; on raising Bajpai's status, 190; on Gandhi's release from detention (1944), 191; on Gandhi, 192; and published Phillips letter, 197; on Athens, 206; Iron Curtain speech of, 238, 243; and Cabinet Mission, 252; and British withdrawal from India, 269, 279; and Johnson, 310*n*47, 311*n*64; American opinion about September 1942 speech, 318*n*8; on Hong Kong, 348*n*32; on Mountbatten, 363*n*149

Ciano, Galeazzo, 124

Clapper, Raymond: on Gandhi, 95

Clark, Mark: on Indian army, 341*n*64

Cold War: influence on U.S. policy, xii, xv, xvii–xviii, 237, 238–45, 247–49, 265–66, 271–74, 276, 281–84, 290–91, 356*n*48

Congregational Ministers Association (St. Louis), 42

Connally, Tom, 196; on Indian independence, 96

Cornwallis, K., 180

Coupland, Reginald, 218–19

Crichton, G. C. L., 335*n*113

Cripps, Stafford, 31, 37, 54, 55, 59–70, 74–77, 81, 88, 90, 93, 94, 96, 101, 117, 138, 139, 146, 153, 162, 165, 200, 223–24, 249, 252, 268, 287–88; urges Roosevelt to intervene in India, 61; on Johnson, 63; American opinion of Cripps mission, 74–77; broadcast to U.S. by (1942), 83–84; Fischer on Cripps mission, 107; on Linlithgow, 135; proposes means to end conflict in India, 136

Currie, Lauchlin, 102, 111, 322*n*57; visit to India (1942), 108–9

Curti, Merle: on American race relations, 258–59

Daily Worker, The, 248

Daniels, Josephus: on Quit India crisis, 96

Davies, John Paton, 151, 340*n*55; on Johnson, 58; report on Indian conditions, 143, 331*n*55, 334*n*99; British views of, 180, 182, 340*n*55; on Churchill, 221

Davies, Joseph E.: and Cabinet Mission, 253

Davis, Elmer, 177

Davis, Norman H., 44

Dawn, 254, 257, 283; on Grady, 275

Defence of India Council, 53

Desai, Mahadev, 224

Donovan, Howard, 198, 200, 235, 236, 245–46, 255, 355*n*22, 356*n*27; on bitter Indian feelings, 156; on Gandhi, 229–30, 347*n*11; on riots, 247–48; on Indonesia, 281–82; on Jinnah, 347*n*11

Donovan, William J., 44, 171, 323*n*73; urges Roosevelt to intervene in India, 46–47

Douglas, Lewis, 265–66

Dulles, John Foster: and communist influence in India, 271, 291; Emmanuel Celler on, 362*n*126

Dutch East Indies: *see* Indonesia

Ecker, F. W., 175

Economist, The, 206

Eddy, Sherwood, 320*n*33, 320*n*34; and Indian Nationalism, 26; proposed visit to India, 102–3; on Phillips, 124–25

Eden, Anthony, 147, 149, 155–56, 162, 164, 169, 196, 222, 325*n*89; and Sherwood Eddy, 103; and Willkie, 104; and Currie, 108; on Linlithgow, 108; and Phillips,

120–21, 133–34, 160–61, 195,
345n129; on Bajpai's status,
188–90, 343n99
Eisenhower, Dwight D., 128; on Indi-
an army, 341n64
El Alamein: battle of, 128, 130
Emerson, Herbert, 137
Emerson, Ralph Waldo: and India, 4
Engert, Cornelius Van H., 121, 265,
292, 315n111, 326n104, 334n110;
Anglophilic views of, 157–58,
360n100; and Phillips, 331n55

Fellowship of Reconciliation, 87
Fey, Harold E: on Bengal famine, 186
Fischer, Louis, 102, 318n17, 322n55;
urges U.S. intervention (1942), 98;
background of, 107; and Gandhi,
107; on Cripps mission, 107; visit
to India (1942), 107–8; British
views of, 107–9; and Cabinet Mission, 252–53
Fisher, William: on Quit India crisis,
96
Foreign Affairs, 44; article by Nehru in,
24
Fortune, 184
Frankfurter, Felix: and Johnson mission, 70–71
Frazer, Robert, 8

Gaddis, John L., 239
Gandhi, Devadas: on Britain's divide
and rule policy, 142
Gandhi, Mohandas K., 6, 7, 9, 16, 21,
22, 45–46, 89, 98, 102, 104, 110,
112, 114, 131, 136, 137–38, 141,
154, 165, 171, 189, 192–93, 222,
227, 229–30, 261, 267, 278, 292,
293, 356n27; march to make salt at
Dandi, 8; American views of, 9, 95
(during Quit India crisis); and
World War I, 14; and Nazism, 15;
resumes control of Congress, 17;
prepares to lead civil disobedience
campaign (1940), 17–18; on

Cripps mission, 60–61; urges
British to leave India, 81–82; on
American soldiers in India, 81–84,
178; on the U.S., 82–83, 259
(racism), 288; on British propaganda in U.S., 85; Roosevelt on,
90–92, 94; and Fischer, 107; Bajpai
on, 112; Henry Wallace on, 115;
Phillips's efforts to visit, 144–45,
155–60; fast of (1943), 145–53;
released (1944), 190; delivery of
letter from Roosevelt delayed,
199–201; American diplomats on,
208; and Simla conference (1945),
225; on Truman, 235; and Cabinet
Mission, 255; and atomic bomb,
259; on Technical mission,
313n27; arrest of (1942), 316n65,
316n67; undelivered letter from
Roosevelt, 317n77; Nehru and
Munshi on, 363n145; on partition,
364n152
George V. Vroman American Legion
Post No. 2, 42
Ghose, Sailendra Nath, 7
Gidwani, Shambas P., 143
Glimpses of World History (by Nehru),
30
Gopal, Sarvepalli, xviii, 361n108; on
riots, 249; on Jinnah, 260; on
Wavell, 260; on Nehru and Cabi-
net mission, 358n64
Government of India Act (1935), 9
Grady, Henry F., 277, 287, 314n30,
363n148, 363n149; and Technical
Mission, 58–59, 77–81; British
views of, 78–79; appointed first
U.S. ambassador to India, 275; on
partition of India, 279; on Indone-
sia, 281; on nationalism, 281; and
Johnson, 313n26; urges Roosevelt
not to intervene in India, 317n74
Great Britain: withdrawal from India
of, 269–70, 278, 280
Greece: Anglo-American differences
about, 206

Grew, Joseph, 100, 119–21, 123, 208–9, 222–24,

Groth, Edward M., 14

Guadalcanal: battle of, 128

Gunther, Frances: and Nehru, 25–26, 300*n*48; on imperialism, 42

Gunther, John: on Gandhi, 21; and Nehru, 25–26, 300*n*48

Gupta, R. S.: on Tagore, 5

Hackworth, Green H., 232

Halifax, Earl, 8, 50, 110, 116, 118, 125, 170–72, 182, 194, 196–97, 199, 207, 209, 219, 232–33, 244, 252, 323*n*73, 324*n*82, 325*n*89, 345*n*129, 345*n*139; on appointing an Indian representative to U.S., 33–34; on Johnson, 77; on American opinion during the Quit India crisis, 97 and Sherwood Eddy, 102–3; and Willkie, 104; and Fischer, 107–8; on Linlithgow, 108; and Currie, 108; and appointment of Phillips, 118–22, 126; and Phillips mission, 133–34, 146–47, 149–52, 160; and Phillips, 161, 345*n*140; on raising Bajpai's status, 188–90; on Truman, 220; and British withdrawal from India, 269; and Johnson mission, 313*n*26

Hamid, Abduhl, 153

Harriman, Averell, 48; on Cripps, 59; and Technical mission, 78, 313*n*29

Harriman, Henry I.: urges U.S. intervention (1942), 100

Harrison, Agatha, 216–17; on Cripps mission, 60; on F. F. Turnbull, 189

Haselton, Norris S., 158; criticizes Government of India, 111

Hathaway, Robert M., xvii, 242

Hearst press: on Technical Mission, 50

Henderson, Arthur, 232

Henderson, Loy, 233, 340–41, 250; and British withdrawal from India, 269

Heppner, Richard P., 131

Herrington, Arthur W.: and Technical Mission, 78; on Indian opinion, 87; and Cripps mission, 311*n*61

Hess, Gary R., xiv, xv; on replacement for Johnson, 325*n*94

Himatsinhji, Colonel, 218

Hindu Mahasabha, 143; on Simla conference (1945), 224, 227

Hindustan Standard: on Phillips, 198

Hindustan Times, 209; on American postwar ambitions, 234

Hitler, Adolf, 14, 21, 73, 95, 254, 276

Ho Chi Minh, 1, 39, 274, 282

Hodson, H. V., 136, 138, 329*n*28

Holmes, John Haynes: on Gandhi, 6

Hong Kong, 210, 213, 220, 287, 348*n*32

Hoover, Herbert: condemns Japanese aggression, 12

Hope, A. Guy, xv; on replacement for Johnson, 325*n*94

Hopkins, Harry, 71, 102, 112, 155, 158, 194, 289; and Johnson mission, 66–69, 310*n*49, 310*n*51; and Johnson, 311*n*64; and Cripps mission, 76; on Truman, 219; and Technical Mission, 314*n*34

Hornbeck, Stanley, 337*n*9

Hughes, John: on Quit India crisis, 97; urges U.S. intervention (1942), 100

Hull, Cordell, 87–88, 91, 93, 114, 122, 141, 147, 148, 160, 191–94, 197, 201, 289, 328*n*15, 334*n*99, 334*n*103; on international trade, 52, 175; and Technical Mission, 80; and Sherwood Eddy, 103; on British policy, 110; on British idealism, 116; and appointment of Phillips, 121, 123–24; instructions to Phillips, 132–33; on Gandhi's fast, 146; and Phillips mission, 149–51, 155–56

Hurley, Patrick, 214, 348*n*34; on American soldiers in India, 180

Husain, Azim, 272

Ickes, Harold: urges Roosevelt to Intervene, 111
India: early American views of, 3–10; U.S. concern about partition of, 275–76, 279–80, 283, 285, 291; partition of, 277–80; interim government of, U.S. attitudes toward, 283, 291
India and Democracy (by Guy Wint and George Shuster), 324n83
India Home Rule League: founding of, 6
India League (London), 30
India League of America, 22–23, 31, 42, 100, 132, 218, 287, 322n55
India Today, 23, 218
Indian army: American views of, 168–69, 181, 341n64
Indian Communist Party: Nehru on, 271
Indian Council of World Affairs: conference of Asian nations (1947), 272–73
Indian National Congress, 4, 6–7, 9, 16–17, 39, 63, 85, 129, 192, 207, 249, 251; origins of, 1; and the British war effort, 15; on British war aims (1939), 21–22; and Cripps mission, 60, 65–66; and Quit India resolutions, 89; Phillips' views of, 138; and Cabinet Mission, 255–56, 264, 266, 361n110; and London conference (1946), 262; and interim government, 266–67; and British withdrawal from India, 270–71, 279; on Grady, 275; and partition of India, 291; and Quit India campaign, 287; moderate nature of, 351n74
Indian nationalism: impact of World War II on, 2; publicity in U.S. about, 21–26
Indian Trade Commission, 32
Indochina, 40, 220–21, 235–36,
273–74, 282, 287; Roosevelt's views on, 130, 214; American policy and, 365n172
Indonesia, 38, 40, 220–21, 236, 281–82, 287; nationalism in, 1; American interests in oil in, 12–13; Indian nationalists and, 234–35; American policy and, 365n172
Institute of Pacific Relations, 136
International Labor Organization, 136
Irwin, Lord, *see* Halifax, Earl
Isaacs, Harold, 5
Ismail, Mirza M., 208

Japan: military position of, xii, 1–2, 11–13, 26, 35, 37–38, 41, 45, 73–74, 83–84, 92–93, 109, 128–29, 151, 167–68, 181, 205–6, 286, 289
Japhteth, M. D., 234
Jinnah, Mohammed Ali, 60, 142, 153, 182–83, 190, 229, 250, 256, 265, 270, 276, 278, 282–84, 291, 293, 358n66, 360n96, 364n152; American diplomats on, 208; and Simla conference (1945), 224–27; and Indonesia, 234–35; U.S. and, 244; and Cabinet Mission, 251; and Anglo-American Commission on Palestine, 254; and Direct Action Day, 256–57; and interim government, 260, 268; and London conference (1946), 263–64; on U.S. policy, 292
Johnson, Calvin D., 196
Johnson, Louis, 83, 112–13, 118, 120, 125–26, 131–32, 179, 234, 244, 286, 293, 314n31, 325n92; on reasonableness of Indian nationalists, 46; mission to India of, 55–72, 313n26; career of, 57; urges Roosevelt to intervene in India, 61; and Nehru, 71–72; on Indian nationalists, 71–72; British views of, 76–77, 79; and Technical Mission, 77–79, 81, 313n25; on Indian opinion, 87; and

Johnson, Louis (*continued*)
    Bengal famine, 185; and Linlith-
    gow, 188; and published Phillips
    letter, 203; and Cripps mission,
    311*n*61; and Roosevelt, 311*n*64
Jones, E. Stanley: urges U.S. interven-
    tion (1942), 99
Jones, Lewis: on Grady, 275
Joshi, P. C., 229
Joy, Benjamin, 8
Joyce, Alec H., 98, 279–80

Kelley, G. M., 247
Kennan, George F., 238–39, 247, 281;
    on American imperial rule, 3
Khan, Liaquat Ali, 264
King, Ernest J., 205
King David's Hotel incident, 254
Kirchwey, Freda, 75: on appointment
    of Phillips, 125
Kripalani, J. B., 229

La Guardia, Fiorello H., 214
Laithewaite, Gilbert, 329*n*26; on Fis-
    cher, 108
Lajpat Rai, Lala: and India Home
    Rule League, 6
Lal, Chaman, 178; and published
    Phillips letter, 203–4; and *persona
    non grata* telegram, 204; on British
    propaganda, 217
LaMont, George D.: on Indian lead-
    ers, 229
Landon, Alfred M.: urges U.S. inter-
    vention (1942), 100
Lattimore, Owen, 214
Laubach, Frank: and Indian national-
    ism, 26; on imperialism, 42
Laval, Pierre, 115
Leahey, William D., 240
Ledo Road, 129
Leffler, Melvyn, xv
Lend Lease program, 27, 174–75
Life, 30, 184; on Nehru, 25–26; and
    Quit India crisis, 98; and Bengal
    famine, 186

Lindley, Ernest K. 114, 119; urges
    U.S. intervention (1942), 99–100
Linlithgow, second marquis, 16, 49,
    58, 60–61, 86, 107, 112, 135–36,
    163, 169, 171–72, 174, 179, 182,
    261, 265, 286–88, 324*n*82, 329*n*26,
    330*n*32, 331*n*47, 333*n*92, 335*n*118,
    335*n*122; offer of August 8, 1940,
    17; and National Defence Coun-
    cil, 31; on appointing an Indian
    representative to U.S., 32–34; on
    Americans, 51–54, 325*n*93; oppos-
    es Defence of India Council, 53;
    on Thomas M. Wilson, 57, 120; on
    Johnson, 62, 76; and Cripps mis-
    sion, 63–64, 66, 311*n*61; and John-
    son mission, 71; and the Techni-
    cal Mission, 78, 313*n*30; on Grady,
    78; on arrest of Gandhi (1942),
    89; and Quit India movement,
    92–93; and Sherwood Eddy,
    102–3, 320*n*34; and Willkie,
    103–7; and Currie, 108, 322*n*57;
    Bajpai on, 113; and appointment
    of Phillips, 119–22, 125, 333*n*81;
    and Phillips mission, 138–61, pas-
    sim; on Phillips, 159, 337*n*8; on
    need for British to remain in
    India, 173; efforts of to restrict
    American presence in India,
    174–77; on OWI, 177; and Bengal
    famine, 187; on raising Bajpai's
    status, 188–89; on American post-
    war ambitions, 233–34, 289; and
    Chiang Kai-shek, 324*n*78; Phillips
    on, 332*n*64
Lippmann, Walter: on imperialism,
    41; and British withdrawal from
    India, 279
London conference (1946), 261–63;
    U.S. and, 261–63
Long, Breckinridge, 43, 196–97; and
    Phillips, 124
Los Angeles Examiner: on imperialism,
    40
Los Angeles Times: on British policy,

22; and British withdrawal from India, 269

Lothian, eleventh marquis, 31, 33

Louis, William Roger, xiii, xvii; on Atlantic Charter, 35; on Roosevelt and colonialism, 91, 207; on trusteeships, 211

Luce, Clare Boothe, 183, 319*n*20

Luce, Henry, 320*n*34

Lumby, E. W. R.: on moderate nature of the Indian National Congress, 351*n*74; on Jinnah, 358*n*66; and Muslim League, 361*n*108

Lumley, R., 161

Lytton, Lord: on Linlithgow, 171

MacArthur, Douglas, 205, 293

MacMillan, Harold: on Roosevelt's anti-colonialism, 207

Mahindra, K. C., 178, 314*n*34; and Technical Mission, 79–81; disenchanted with Government of India, 112–13; and *persona non grata* telegram, 204

Majumdar, R. C., xviii; on Mountbatten, 278

Malaya, 100; falls to Japanese, 38; massacres in, 38

Malcolm, Angus C. E.: on published Phillips letter, 195; on Phillips mission, 144

Malik, Iftikar H.: on fear of communism as factor in U.S. policy, 354*n*12

Marshall, George C., 239, 266, 275–76, 281; and British withdrawal from India, 269–70, 280; on Dulles, 272

Mather, Cotton: interest in India, 4

Matthews, Herbert L., 86, 130, 179–80; on American soldiers in India, 179

Mayo, Katherine, 9, 228, 292, 357*n*52; views of Indian culture, 5–6

McKinley, William, 3

McMahon, Robert J., 240, 280

Mehta, Gaganvihari L., 217, 314*n*31

Menon, V. K. Krishna, 30, 137–38, 362*n*128, 330*n*32; on Grady, 275

Menon, V. P., 277

Merrell, George, 87, 199, 208, 212, 223, 234, 263–64, 267–68, 270, 346*n*141, 360*n*104; on possible U.S. intervention to end Quit India crisis, 90; on British policy, 94; criticizes arrest of Gandhi (1942), 111; British views of, 114; and appointment of Phillips, 123–24; on Indian despair, 169; and Simla conference (1945), 224–25, 227; on Indian leaders, 230; on riots, 247; on Dulles, 272; on Pan-Asian conference, 273–74

Merriam, G. P., 15

Miéville, Eric: on Linlithgow, 135

Missionaries: and India, 5; views of Indian nationalism of, 86

Mitchell, Kate, 183

Monteath, David T., 231; on raising Bajpai's status, 189

Moore, R. C.: on partition plan, 364*n*157

Moore, Robin J.: on Cripps mission, 60

Morrison, Charles Clayton: on Gandhi, 21

Mott, John R.: and Indian Nationalism, 26

Mountbatten, Edwina, 171

Mountbatten, Louis, 168, 182, 221, 261, 275, 277–79, 282–83, 341*n*64; and British withdrawal from India, 268–69; accepts India's division, 276; on U.S. postwar ambitions, 363*n*149; and partition plan, 364*n*157

Mudaliar, A. Ramaswami, 217; on British rule, 136; on Bengal famine, 341*n*74

Mudie, Francis, 213

Munshi, K. M.: on Indian disillusionment with the U.S., 170; on Muslim League, 276; on Gandhi, 363*n*145; on Jinnah, 363*n*145

Murphy, R. E., 248
Murray, Wallace, 16, 154, 160–61,
    171, 334n99; on American inter-
    ests in India, 15; urges American
    intervention in India, 43–44; and
    Cripps mission, 76; on Indian
    opinion, 87; and appointment of
    Phillips, 123–24, 126; and Phillips
    mission, 131, 146, 154–55, 165–66;
    and Bengal famine, 185; on
    Wavell, 193
Murrow, Edward R.: interviews
    Amery, 117
Muslim League, 144, 151, 226–27,
    249, 252, 361n104, 361n108;
    rejects viceroy's proposals (1941),
    20; U.S. and, 244; and Cabinet
    Mission, 255–56, 264, 358n64,
    361n110; and Direct Action Day,
    256–57; visit of representatives of
    to U.S., 257–58; and Asaf Ali, 260;
    and London conference (1946),
    262; and constituent assembly,
    263, 266; and interim government,
    266–67, 358n67; and British with-
    drawal from India, 270, 279; on
    Grady, 275; and partition of India,
    291
Mussolini, Benito, 115, 123–24, 254
Muzumdar, Haridas T., 22
Myitkyina: fighting in, 340n60

Nanda, B. R.: on Linlithgow, Wavell,
    and Mountbatten, 261; on Nehru
    and Cabinet mission, 358n64
Narayan, Jaya Prakash: arrest of, 17
Nation, The, 107; on Indian national-
    ism, 21; and Cripps mission, 75;
    urges U.S. intervention (1942),
    98–99; Bengal famine, 186; on
    Simla conference (1945), 224; and
    British withdrawal from India, 269
National Defence Council, 31
National Standard, 270
Nawaz, Begum Shah, 108
Nájera, Francisco Castillo, 111–12

Nehru, Jawaharlal, 7, 8, 28, 30, 43, 94,
    100, 102, 136–38, 154–56, 178, 227,
    230, 260, 263–65, 272, 282–84, 291,
    293, 316n69, 356n27, 362n128; on
    Katherine Mayo, 5–6; American
    views of, 9; on Nazism, 15, 82–83;
    on Jaya Prakash Narayan, 17;
    arrested (1940), 18; on J. J. Singh,
    23; on visiting the U.S., 23–24; pub-
    licity in U.S. about, 24–26; on Rajni
    Patel, 30; and Cripps mission, 62,
    65; and Johnson, 70–72; on Ameri-
    can soldiers in India, 81–83; urges
    British to leave India, 82; on Amer-
    ican opinion about India, 82–85,
    319n21; on Cripps, 83–84; on
    Gandhi, 84, 363n145; on possible
    U.S. intervention to end Quit India
    crisis, 89–90; views of the U.S.,
    106–7; and Willkie, 106–7, 321n47;
    on Americans in India, 179; and
    Bengal famine, 187; and Simla con-
    ference (1945), 225; on U.S. for-
    eign policy, 235–36, 245, 292; and
    U.S. policy toward Indochina and
    Indonesia, 235–36, 281, 365n172;
    U.S. concern about communist
    influence on, 242; and interim gov-
    ernment, 256–58, 358n67; and
    atomic testing, 259; and London
    conference (1946), 261; on Dulles,
    271; on Grady, 277; on Pakistan,
    277; and colonialism, 281–82; rea-
    sonableness of, 292–93; views of
    Roosevelt, 294; on nationalist pub-
    licity in the U.S., 315n55; and Cabi-
    net mission, 358n64, 360n104; on
    pan-Asia conference (1947),
    362n135
Netherlands East Indies, see Indonesia
New Republic, The, 41, 184; on British
    war aims, 21; on Indian National-
    ism, 21; and Cripps mission, 74; on
    British policy, 146; and Bengal
    famine, 186; and Cabinet Mission,
    250; and Phillips, 345n127

New York Herald Tribune, 181
New York Journal and American: on imperialism, 40
New York Post, 51
New York Times, 86, 100–101, 183, 210; on British war aims, 21–22; on Nehru, 25; on possible Japanese invasion of India, 38; on imperialism, 41; and Cripps mission, 74–75; on Quit India crisis, 84, 96–98; on Gandhi, 95; on Churchill, 97; and Bengal famine, 184; ignores Pandit at San Francisco Conference, 217; on Indian army, 218; and British withdrawal from India, 269
News and Observer (Raleigh, NC): on Quit India crisis, 96
Newsweek, 110, 129, 146; on Gandhi, 21, 84, 95; on imperialism, 41; and Bengal famine, 184; and British withdrawal from India, 269, 278
Newton, Basil, 115
Nichols, Beverly, 219
Nimitz, Chester W., 205
Noorani, A. G.: and Cabinet mission, 358n64
Norris, George W., 110; on Indian independence, 95–96

Office of Coordinator of War Information (OCOI): on U.S. interest in India, 44–46
Office of Strategic Services (OSS), 174
Office of War Information (OWI), 174, 176–78; activities of in India, 46
One World (by Willkie), 105–6
Operation ARAKIM, 109

P.M., 118
Pakistan, 2, 60, 142, 252, 270–71, 277–78, 280, 282
Palestine, 219, 251, 254, 257, 259, 284, 292, 357n58

Pan-Asia conference (1947), 272–74; U.S. and, 362n135
Pande, Bhola N.: on Phillips, 198
Pandit, Vijayalaskshmi, 231, 235, 259–60, 271–72; in U.S. (1944–45), 209–17, 347n16; and San Francisco Conference, 216; on Dulles, 271–72
Parliament of Religions, 4
Patel, Rajnikant ("Rajni"): visits U.S., 28–29; arrested, 29–30
Patel, Vallabhbhai, 230, 263; and Cabinet mission, 358n64
Patrick, Paul, 175–76, 265–66; and Simla conference (1945), 226
Patterson, Robert, 57
Pearl Buck: urges U.S. intervention (1942), 100
Pearson, Drew, 200–203, 206, 209, 231, 288–89; on American diplomats, 124; and Davies report, 182; publication of Phillips letter, 191, 193–201, 218
Peel, Roland T., 163, 345n139; on raising Bajpai's status, 189
People's War, 178
Pepper, Claude, 243; on Indian independence, 96
Perth, Earl of: on appointment of Phillips, 122
Pethick-Lawrence, Lord, 231–32, 249, 258, 263, 265; and American desire for air bases in India, 354n7
Philippine Islands, 56, 213, 220, 285, 293; nationalism in, 1; American policy toward, 3
Phillips, Caroline, 123; and Soviet Union, 124
Phillips, Wendell, 165
Phillips, William, 100, 167, 170–71, 173–74, 178, 180, 192, 202, 208–9, 216, 234, 244, 276, 288, 293, 327n112, 327n113, 329n28, 333n81, 333n92, 334n97, 334n99, 334n110, 335n118, 335n122, 337n8, 337n9, 344n114, 345n127,

Phillips, William (*continued*)
345*n*129, 345*n*140; British views of,
79; and Willkie, 105; appointment
as President's representative to
India, 118–27, 328*n*127; career of,
123–24; mission to India of,
128–66; British efforts to limit
scope of Phillips mission, 133–34;
on Gandhi, 145, 190–91 (on Gandhi's release from prison); meets
with Churchill (1943), 162–63;
changed by his stay in India,
164–66; on Wavell; 172: on OWI,
176–78; and Wedemeyer, 181; and
Bengal famine, 185; letter of published by Pearson, 191, 193–201,
203–5; and *persona non grata* incident, 195–97; British views of, 198;
Indian views of, 198; urges intervention in India (1945), 211, 222;
on nationalism, 281; and Chimur
massacre, 330*n*47; and Engert,
331*n*55; and Krishna Menon,
330*n*32; on Linlithgow, 332*n*64
Poe, Clarence: urges U.S. intervention (1942), 99
Poland, 215
Potsdam conference (1945), 220,
227
Prasad, Rajendra, 16, 144; on publicity in U.S., 22
Puckle, Frederick, 192–93, 213, 255,
339*n*39, 351*n*82; on American
opinion about India, 183–84; and
Bengal famine, 186

Qadir, Altaf: and *persona non grata*
telegram, 204
Quisling, Vidkun, 115
Quit India movement (1942), 81–94,
112, 193; American attitudes
about, 87–94, 315*n*52; U.S. opinion about arrests, 95–109

Racism: in U.S., 5–6, 258–59, 291–92
Rahman, Obaidur: and published

Phillips letter, 203; and *persona non
grata* telegram, 204
Rajagopalachari, Chakravarty R., 151,
182–83, 317*n*77, 333*n*92; on Quit
India movement, 82; and Willkie,
106
Rao, B. Shiva, 22, 272; on Johnson,
70; and Currie, 108; on divide and
rule policy, 142; on Krishna
Menon, 362*n*128
Rao, P. Kodandra, 48
Reader's Digest, 219; on Gandhi, 21; on
Nehru, 26
Reuters, 51
Reynolds, Robert R.: on Indian inde-
pendence, 96; urges U.S. intervention (1942), 99
Riots, 245–49, 256–57, 261, 266;
against Americans, 245–47; U.S.
fears of communist instigation of,
247–49
Rivers, W. F.: on American soldiers in
India, 180
Roger, Alexander, 79, 313*n*30
Rommel, Erwin, 128
Romulo, Carlos, 293
Roosevelt, Eleanor, 28–29, 42–43,
149, 163, 209, 294; and Cripps mission, 91; and Phillips, 123; on Indian nationalists in U.S. (1945),
214–17
Roosevelt, Franklin D., xi, 13, 50–51,
54, 55–56, 83, 87–88, 90–92, 102,
130, 136, 138, 145–46, 157–58,
160, 167–70, 172, 191, 199–201,
209, 216, 221, 229, 231, 234–36,
244, 286–88, 293–94, 329*n*15,
340*n*57, 341*n*74, 344*n*114; racial
views of, xiii; views of colonialism
and imperialism, xiii–xv, 37–39,
46–48, 91, 109–110, 130, 194,
201–2, 206–7, 210–11, 213–15,
287–90, 365*n*2; supports British
(1939–41), 26–27; and Atlantic
Charter, 35, 122; pressures on to
intervene in India, 37–38, 41–44,

49, 61–62, 99–101, 111–14,
145–48, 151–53, 155, 157, 161–62,
169, 286, 288; and Johnson mission, 58, 67–69, 72, 311*n*64; and
Cripps mission, 76–77; and Quit
India movement, 89–94; and Chiang Kai-shek, 90–92, 114; and
Willkie, 105, 107; and Fischer, 107;
and Currie, 108; and Gandhi, 110,
150; on Churchill, 122, 211; and
appointment of Phillips, 122–23,
127, 130–31, 328*n*127; and Phillips
mission, 130–34, 151–52, 154–55,
161–63, 164–65; on Indochina,
130, 214, 287; and Bengal famine,
185, 187; and published Phillips
letter, 194–95; undelivered letter
to Gandhi, 199–201, 317*n*77; and
China, 205–6; and Indian immigration, 208–9; and Yalta conference, 210; on Hong Kong, 210,
213, 287, 348*n*32; anger of at Stalin, 215; on Indonesia, 287; and
Pandit, 347*n*16
Roosevelt, Theodore, 123
Rosenthal, A. M.: on Katherine Mayo,
6
Rowlatt bills, 7–8
Russo-Japanese War (1904–5), 52
Ryan, Henry Butterfield, xvii, 98

San Francisco Conference (1945),
214–15, 219, 222
San Francisco News: on imperialism,
41; on Churchill, 97
Sapru, Tej Bahadur, 198, 208
Saturday Evening Post, The, 99; on
Gandhi, 95; on Quit India crisis,
95–96; urges U.S. intervention
(1942), 101
Scribner's Commentary, 30
Shaplen, Robert: on J. J. Singh, 23
Sherwood, Robert: and Quit India
movement, 91
Shridharani, Krishnalal, 22, 209, 214;
on imperialism, 47

Shrivastava, B. K., xvi, 43, 105; and
delayed delivery of Roosevelt letter
to Gandhi, 200–201; on replace-
ment for Johnson, 325*n*94
Siam, *see* Thailand
Simla conference (1945), 223–27, 249
Singapore: falls to Japanese, 38
Singh, Anita Inder, xviii; on Muslim
League, 361*n*108
Singh, Anup, 22, 214, 209; and pub-
lished Phillips letter, 203–4
Singh, Baldev, 279
Singh, Jagjit ("J. J."), 22, 26, 42, 84,
132, 218, 246, 319*n*20; reorganizes
India League of America, 23;
Nehru on, 23; on Nehru, 23–24;
and British withdrawal from India,
270
Slim, William, 205
Smedley, Agnes, 7
Smith, James, 8
Smith, Robert Aura, 176–77; British
views of, 339*n*39
Soviet Union, 210, 215, 219, 238, 244,
247, 253, 290–91, 293; U.S. recog-
nition of, 124; Anglo-American dif-
ferences about, 206; views of Indi-
an nationalists of, 236
Spry, Graham, 76, 117, 312*n*12; on
American opinion, 85, 94
Stalin, Joseph, 107, 130, 207, 210,
215, 219, 247
Stalingrad: battle of, 128
Stanley, Oliver, 207
Stettinius, Edward R., Jr., 194, 216–17,
222–23
Stilwell, Joseph W., 168, 182, 143,
340*n*60; British attitudes toward,
180–81
Stimson, Henry, 57, 164
Stokes, Samuel Evans, 169; interest in
Indian nationalism, 7; and World
War I, 14
Stone, I. F., 341*n*68; on American
diplomats, 124; on appointment of
Phillips, 125

Sukarno, 40, 281
Sultan, Daniel I., 346n141
Sumatra, 168
Swerling, Simon, 175
Swing, Raymond Gram, 39; on Cripps mission, 89; on Quit India crisis, 97
Swinton, Philip: and Phillips, 161

Tagore, Rabindranath, 5; condemns Japanese aggression, 14
Taussig, Charles, 213
Technical Mission to India (1942), 49–50, 58–59, 77–81, 110, 175, 275, 313n25, 313n27, 313n29, 313n30, 314n34
Teheran conference (1943), 130, 207
TenBroeck, William M., 141
Thailand: falls to Japanese, 38; treaty with Britain, 355n17
Thomas, Elbert: on Indian independence, 96
Thomas, Lowell, 86
Thompson, Dorothy, 51
Thompson, Edward, 137
Thompson, John: on imperialism, 41
Thoreau, Henry David, 83; and India, 4
Thorne, Christopher, xvii, 38, 44; on Stilwell, 168
Time, 30, 96, 184; on Gandhi, 21; on Indian nationalism, 21; on Quit Indian movement, 84; and Bengal famine, 186
Times of India, 270
Transcendentalism, 4
Truman, Harry S., xi, 72, 235–36, 239, 241–43, 253, 257–58, 260, 279, 284, 357n58, 358n71; views of colonialism and imperialism of, xv, 219–20, 235, 281–82, 290; continues Roosevelt's policies, 219, 221; and Bajpai, 231–32, 258; on Soviet Union, 238; and Palestine, 251; policy of toward Palestine criticized, 259; on American troops in India, 355n24
Truman doctrine, 237–38, 269
Trusteeship system, 210–11, 213, 287, 290, 328n15
Turnbull, F. F., 329n28; on raising Bajpai's status, 189
Twynam, Henry, 208

United Automobile Workers, 99–101
United States: anticolonial tradition of, xi–xiv, 2–3, 6–8, 27, 39–40, 105–7, 220–21, 242–44, 274, 283, 286–87, 293
United States: intervention in Indian affairs, 20–21, 27, 35–37, 44, 46–47, 49, 54–56, 61, 89–90, 98–100, 111, 130–35, 139–40, 144–166, 208, 221–23, 232–33, 250, 257, 261–65, 269–70, 271–74, 277, 280, 285–86, 288–89, 293, 317n74
United States: postwar ambitions of, 40, 52, 174–78, 182, 233–34, 237, 262, 275, 289
United States: views of India prior to World War II, 3–10
Unity of India (by Nehru), 30
Unterberger, Betty Miller: on partition, 364n162
U.S.S.R., see Soviet Union

Vaidya, D. J., 30
Vandenberg, Arthur: and Atlantic Charter, 206
Vandivert, William: and Bengal famine, 186
Venkataramani, M. S., xiii, xv–xvi, 43, 105; and delayed delivery of Roosevelt letter to Gandhi, 200–201; on replacement for Johnson, 325n94
Vietnam, see Indochina
Vivekenanda, Swami, 4
Voorhis, Jerry, 355n24; and American soldiers in India, 246

Wallace, Henry, 87–88; on Johnson, 58; on Gandhi, 115

Walsh, Richard, 25, 184

Waring, Frank: and Technical Mission, 79

Washington Post, 181; on Indian army, 218; and British withdrawal from India, 278; on Phillips, 345*n*140

Washington Star, 214

Wavell, Archibald, 38, 64, 168–69, 174, 177, 182, 191, 199, 207, 211–13, 222–23, 249, 253, 257–58, 267–68, 344*n*11; career of, 172; American views of, 172–73; on Stilwell, 181; and Bengal famine, 186–87; on Bajpai's status, 188–90, 230–32; releases Gandhi (1944), 190; criticized by Churchill, 192; on negotiations with Congress, 192; and Simla conference (1945), 223–27; and interim government, 260–61; and Cripps mission, 311*n*61

Wavell, Lady, 225

Wedemeyer, Albert, 181

Weil, Martin, 124

Weil, T. Eliot: and interim government, 261

Welles, Sumner, 50, 87, 112, 334*n*99, 334*n*103; refuses to pressure the British, 21; on imperialism, 40; and Technical Mission, 80; and appointment of Phillips, 120, 122–23, 125; and Phillips mission, 133, 146, 155; and published Phillips letter, 203

Wheeler, Raymond: on Indian army, 341*n*64

Whipping of Indian prisoners, 96–97, 101

White, John C., 16, 34

White, Walter, 242–43; urges U.S. intervention (1942), 99

Wilhelmina, Queen, 365*n*2

Willingdon, Lady, 329*n*26; on Linlithgow, 136

Willingdon, Lord, 136

Willkie, Wendell, 50–51, 122; proposed visit to India, 102–7; on colonialism, 105–7; and Nehru, 321*n*47

Wilson, Thomas M., 56, 58, 118, 333*n*81; appointed consul general at Calcutta, 19; on Linlithgow, 19; on Government of India, 20; appointed U.S. commissioner to India, 34; on British rule in India, 44; Linlithgow on, 57, 120; and Technical Mission, 77

Wilson, Woodrow, 96; and the Philippines, 3

Winant, John G., 192; urges American pressure on British, 20–21

Wood, Evelyn: on American soldiers in India, 178

Woodring, Harry H., 57

World War II, xi–xii, 1–2, 10, 11–15, 21–22, 26–27, 35, 37–38, 41, 45, 73–74, 91–92, 109, 128–29, 167–69, 181, 205–6, 285–86, 293

Wrench, Evelyn, 86; parties for Americans, 182–83

Yalta conference (1945), 205–6, 210, 219

Yamamoto, Isoroku, 167

Yergin, Daniel, 239

Zetland, second marquis, 15

ZIPPER, Operation, 206